THE ZULU KINGDOM AND THE BOER INVASION OF 1837-40

'The engagement on Sunday 16 December 1838.' A composite image of the battle of Blood River on the left, and of the battle of Bloukrans on the right. (Adulphe Delegorgue, *Voyage dans l'Afrique Australe* (Paris: René et cie, 1847))

The Zulu Kingdom and the Boer Invasion of 1837-40

John Laband

 Helion & Company

Helion & Company Limited
Unit 8 Amherst Business Centre
Budbrooke Road
Warwick
CV34 5WE
England
Tel. 01926 499 619
Email: info@helion.co.uk
Website: www.helion.co.uk
Twitter: @helionbooks
Visit our blog at blog.helion.co.uk

Published by Helion & Company 2022
Designed and typeset by Mary Woolley (www.battlefield-design.co.uk)
Cover designed by Paul Hewitt, Battlefield Design (www.battlefield-design.co.uk)

Text © John Laband 2021
Images © as individually credited 2021
Maps drawn by George Anderson © Helion & Company 2021

Cover: 'De moord van Piet Retief en zijne mannen in Dingaan's kraal Gugunekloof', by Elia Musschenbroek, 1906. (MuseumAfrica, Johannesburg, with permission)

Every reasonable effort has been made to trace copyright holders and to obtain their permission for the use of copyright material. The author and publisher apologize for any errors or omissions in this work, and would be grateful if notified of any corrections that should be incorporated in future reprints or editions of this book.

ISBN 978-1-914059-89-6

British Library Cataloguing-in-Publication Data.
A catalogue record for this book is available from the British Library.

All rights reserved. No part of this publication may be reproduced, stored in a retrieval system, or transmitted, in any form, or by any means, electronic, mechanical, photocopying, recording or otherwise, without the express written consent of Helion & Company Limited.

For details of other military history titles published by Helion & Company Limited contact the above address or visit our website: http://www.helion.co.uk.

We always welcome receiving book proposals from prospective authors.

Contents

List of Maps		vi
Acknowledgements		vii
Preface: Monuments at War		viii
1	Breaking Down the Maize Stalks	13
2	Always Talking of War and Battles	18
3	Port Natal	30
4	Wizard Whose Liver Is Black	36
5	An Inexpedient Scheme of Colonisation	43
6	On *Kommando*	50
7	The House of Bondage	61
8	A Chosen People	67
9	Transorangia	72
10	I Had to Keep Open Veld around Me	80
11	They Came with Wagons	88
12	We Are Here to Kill You	96
13	Our God Delivered Mzilikazi into Our Hands	102
14	The Chief of Port Natal	112
15	The Place that Encloses the Elephant	120
16	Do You Hear the King?	129
17	They Desired Port Natal	137
18	You Thrust an Evil Spear into Your Own Stomach	145
19	O My God, Shall the Blood of the Sucklings Be Unavenged?	155
20	I Will Die with My Father!	163
21	The Great Elephant Will Trample You Underfoot!	172
22	The Place of the Game-Pits	180
23	At the Ncome We Turned Our Backs	189
24	They Are Surrounded, Men of the King	203
25	Building Two Countries	211
26	You Who Crossed All the Rivers on the Way to Restoring Yourself	220
27	He Has Ruined My Army	227
28	The Wild Beasts Have Killed One Another	234
29	Return to Mpande and Pay Homage to Him	240
Glossary		248
Bibliography		252
Index		261

List of Maps

Transorangia and the Great Trek to Zululand, 1836–37	89
Diagram of emGungundlovu	121
Battle of Bloukrans, 16–17 February 1838	156
Battle of eThaleni, 10 April 1838: Phase One	165
Battle of eThaleni, 10 April 1838: Phase Two	169
Battle of the Thukela or Dlokweni, 17 April 1838	174
Battle of Veglaer or emaGebeni, 13–15 August 1838: First Day of Battle	183
Battle of Blood River or Ncome, 16 December 1838: Phase One	194
Battle of Blood River or Ncome, 16 December 1838: Phase Two	198
Battle of the White Mfolozi or oPathe, 27 December 1838	207
Battle of the amaQongqo Hills, 29 January 1840	230
The Dismemberment of the Zulu Kingdom, 1838–43	241

Acknowledgements

This book was researched, written, edited and produced during the COVID-19 pandemic. Normal access to libraries, museums and archival repositories was restricted or curtailed altogether and travel periodically prohibited. In many cases, it was possible to surmount these hurdles through the resources of my personal library and the marvels of the electronic media. In others, considerable perseverance was required by my two intrepid researchers, Ameerah Moola in Johannesburg and Alice Morrison in Pietermaritzburg. Their assistance was made possible through the Faculty Research Support funding provided by Stellenbosch University. In that regard, I wish to express my thanks to Dr Anton Ehlers, the retiring Chair of the History Department, Stellenbosch University, and to Leschelle Morkel, the Administration Officer: History, for all their encouragement and cheerful assistance over the past years.

The pandemic notwithstanding, in South Africa I received liberal help for which I am most grateful from the following: Kenneth Hlungwane, Research Officer, MuseumAfrica, Johannesburg; Elrica Henning, Head of Research, uMsunduzi Museum, Pietermaritzburg; Pieter Nel, Head of the Pietermaritzburg Archives Repository and his assistant, Thabani Mdladla; Senzosenkosi Mkhize, Head of the Campbell Collections, Durban, and Mbalenhlele Zulu, the Senior Librarian there; and Pam McFadden, the Curator of the Talana Museum, Dundee.

In writing this book, I have benefited enormously from the scholarship of other historians, past and present, although all opinions expressed or conclusions reached are mine. I am particularly indebted to several international authorities in my field, especially Professor Rolf Michael Schneider and Professor Elizabeth Rankin for their open-handed assistance, and to Professor Michał Leśniewski for his expertise.

This is the third work of mine to have been published by Helion & Co Ltd. I am grateful to Duncan Rogers, the owner and Managing Director of Helion, who, on the strength of my original proposal, decided to commission the book. Once more, I am indebted to Dr Christopher Brice, the series editor of *From Musket to Maxim, 1815–1914*, for his scrupulous care, considered advice and friendly reassurance. I must also thank the members of the production team at Helion, especially George Anderson, the cartographer, who transformed my busy sketches into elegant, uncluttered maps.

As ever, this book is dedicated to Fenella whose unstinting support continues to sustain me.

Greyton
Western Cape
South Africa

Preface

Monuments at War

Not all battlefields retain their disturbing aura of long-past bloodlust and grim exaltation, of courage and fortitude, unmanning dread and panic, anguish, pain, and violent death. Nor are their sites all marked by memorials that serve as the continuing focus of emotional commemoration. Indeed, not all battles themselves remain the pivot of heated debate, their disputed significance freighted with present-day discord. One that does is the battle of Blood River—called Bloedrivier in Afrikaans and Ncome in isiZulu—that was fought on 16 December 1838 on flat, bleakly open, treeless grassland in what is now the Province of KwaZulu-Natal in the Republic of South Africa. Blood River vindicated the superiority of concentrated musket-fire from within an all-round defensive enclosure of wagons (a laager) over greatly superior numbers of warriors armed primarily with spears. It was the climacteric battle in a bitter war of betrayal, massacre, fierce resistance, and retribution that began in late 1837 when groups of Dutch-speaking pioneers (or *Voortrekkers*), who were part of a mass migration from the British-ruled Cape Colony—a movement which has gone down in history as the Great Trek—invaded the Zulu kingdom ruled by King Dingane. The intention of these Boers was to settle there and to establish their own independent republic on its soil. They fought the Zulu armies in alliance with English-speaking hunter-traders from the little enclave of Port Natal, and the war ended only in early 1840 once the Boers were able to take advantage of a civil war that broke out in the dislocated and weakened Zulu kingdom and drove Dingane from his throne.

Successive generations of Afrikaners continued to celebrate their forebears' victory over the amaZulu at the battle of Blood River as the triumph of Christianity over barbarism, and embraced it as an unmistakable sign of the favour in which God held their nation. The battle thus affirmed the God-given right of Afrikaners to rule over the Africans they had defeated, and out of this stirring foundation myth arose the ideology of apartheid. Afrikaners long held that this crucial event required commemoration. With the Union of South Africa in 1910 that brought the British colonies and Boer republics of the subcontinent together in one country, 16 December was proclaimed a public holiday. It remained one until the eventual fall of apartheid 84 years later, and during these years it was annually celebrated with increasing fervour. The battlefield itself was elevated to a sacred site that became a place of pilgrimage that celebrated the Afrikaner nation and reaffirmed its political and cultural ascendancy.

With increasing confidence in their dominance, Afrikaners required monuments to celebrate their history and its heroes. The most imposing of these is the enormous, monolithic Voortrekker Monument on its hill outside Pretoria, designed by Gerard Moerdyk and inaugurated on 16

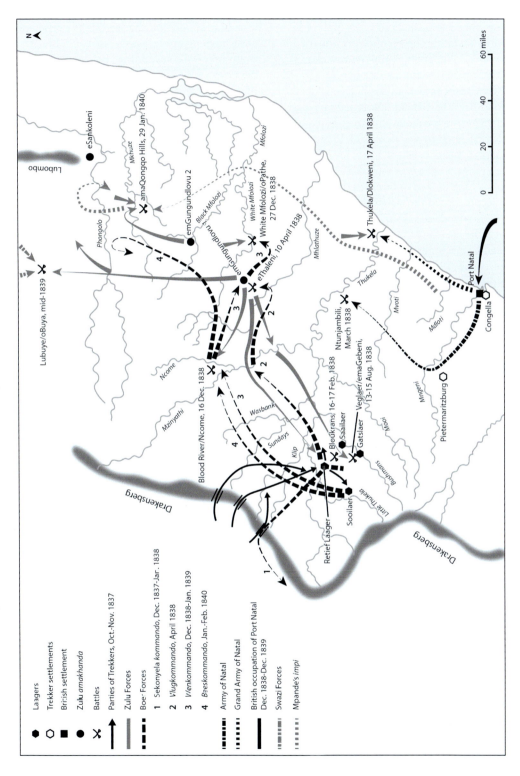

Preface ix

The War in Zululand, 1837–40

December 1949. The floor of its Hall of Heroes has a central opening that reveals the cenotaph commemorating the *Voortrekkers* who died in violently opening up the South African hinterland to white domination, while the vast chamber's surrounding walls are adorned by a marble frieze with 27 panels that illustrate heroic scenes from the Great Trek.[1]

Two years earlier, in 1947, a considerably smaller monument had been inaugurated on the Blood River battlefield. Designed by Coert Steynberg, it took the form of a massive but sombre ox-wagon sculpted out of granite and embedded into flights of steps. Over the doorway on the side dedicated to the victory of 1838 is a lunette filled by a crowded sculpture depicting three mounted Boers overwhelming four fleeing amaZulu and forcing them to the ground. In 1971 the granite wagon was moved to its present site to make way for a new monument designed by Kobus Esterhuizen to be erected closer to the river where the battle was fought. This ambitious project recreated the laager the Boers defended against the attacking amaZulu with a formation of 64 bronzed, cast-iron, life-sized, and authentically recreated ox-wagons, each weighing eight tons. The bronze wagons encircle the original stone cairn marking the site of the battle, but this metal laager is not really an accurate reconstruction of the real one because in its positioning it unaccountably ignores the logic of the topography. Even so, it makes an astonishing statement on the empty plain and incontrovertibly puts the seal of Afrikaner ownership on the battlefield. Significantly, the metal laager was paid for in part by contributions raised from among ordinary Afrikaners, and spoke to their ongoing obsession with the symbolism of the site.[2]

Yet, the battlefield was also of significance to the amaZulu whose ancestors had fought and died there. This ostentatious new memorial to the Boer victory was not only taken as an affront to smouldering Zulu nationalism, but was also spurned as yet another flaunted symbol of Afrikaner domination and apartheid policy. When the new democratic government came to power in 1994, it was very aware of the significance of Blood River for the former regime, and the extent to which it was repudiated by Africans. In 1995 it renamed the public holiday on 16 December the Day of Reconciliation, and set about making the contentious battlefield and its existing monuments more acceptable to the values of the post-colonial, democratic, all-inclusive and multi-cultural society it was then (if now no longer) sincerely promoting.

And certainly, there was no disguising that the Blood River monuments echoed the situation in 1994 where 97 per cent of all existing monuments in South Africa reflected the values and interests of the colonial and apartheid eras, and were viewed by blacks as symbols of their past alienation and disempowerment. For the new government, the challenge lay in somehow

---

1   See Elizabeth Rankin and Rolf Michael Schneider, *From Memory to Marble: The Historical Frieze of the Voortrekker Monument. Part I: The Frieze* (Berlin and Boston: Walter de Gruyter, 2019), *passim*.

2   The ensuing discussion concerning the two monuments on the Blood River/Ncome site is based on Nsizwa Dlamini, 'Monuments of Division: Apartheid and Post-apartheid Struggles over Zulu Nationalist Heritage Sites', in Benedict Carton, John Laband and Jabulani Sithole (eds), *Zulu Identities: Being Zulu, Past and Present* (Pietermaritzburg: University of KwaZulu-Natal Press, 2008), pp.388–9, 391; Pieter Labuschagne, 'A Spatial Analysis of the Ncome/Blood River Monument/Museum Complex as Hermeneutic Objects of Reconciliation and Nation Building', *South African Journal of African History*, 28: 3 (2013), pp.107–16; Elizabeth Rankin and Rolf Michael Schneider, *From Memory to Marble: The Historical Frieze of the Voortrekker Monument. Part II: The Scenes* (Berlin and Boston: Walter de Gruyter, 2020), pp.453–9; Scott M. Schönfeldt-Aultman, 'Monument(al) Meaning-Making: The Ncome Monument & Its Representation of Zulu Identify', *Journal of African Cultural Studies* 18: 2 (December 2006), pp.215, 217, 220–1, 223–4, 227, 231.

ensuring that these monuments reflected the diverse history and values of the new post-apartheid society without, at the same time, undermining its efforts to promote reconciliation and nation-building by physically removing them. As a first step in this regard, and to allay the fears of formerly dominant groups that their culture would be assailed, the government saw to it that the country's new constitution of 1996 assured persons of all cultural groups that they would not be denied their right to enjoy their own culture.³ Yet, in practice, how were contentious monuments, offensive to large segments of the population, to be both retained and, as it were, rendered neutral? It was precisely because of the heavy ideological freight they carried that the government homed in on the monuments on the Blood River site to attempt a solution that could then be adopted elsewhere.

Monuments fell under the new Department of Arts, Culture, Science and Technology, and in 1998 it appointed the Battle of Blood River Reinterpretation Committee. It comprised a panel of so-called 'diverse' academic historians consisting of one 'Afrikaner' historian, two 'English' historians (the author was one of them), and three 'Zulu' ones. The committee presented its final report on 31 October 1998 at a seminar at the University of Zululand. In retrospect, the committee's attempt to formulate an interpretation of the battle that satisfied all the 'stakeholders' (to use the parlance of the time) was not entirely successful, and it ended up largely reflecting the views of those most concerned to assert Zulu nationalist identity. More practically useful than this weighted 'correction' of past interpretations of the battle was the committee's recommendation that the government, in order to 'create a spirit of reconciliation', should erect 'a monument that would make noble the loss of Zulu life and extol Zulu bravery as much as the present monuments at the site do for the Voortrekkers.'⁴

This recommendation was carried through with the construction of a new monument across the Ncome (Blood River) from the bronzed Boer laager and opposite to it, deliberately placed to confront it as the Zulu army had on the day of battle. Maintaining the military theme, the Ncome monument is designed to reflect the classic Zulu battle formation with the central round building representing the 'chest' of the attacking bull, and the curving g extension either side of it the encircling 'horns'. The outer walls of the pinkish façade are adorned by replicas of ox-hide shields painted in different patterns and colours to represent the Zulu 'regiments' that fought in the battle. As intended, the elegant building radiates energy and is dedicated to the brave Zulu who fell in the battle defending their independence. Thousands (including the author) were present on 16 December 1998 when King Goodwill Zwelithini unveiled the monument. Representatives from all political parties and many cultural organisations were among the guests. Numerous amaZulu were in traditional dress and carried traditional weapons.⁵

The Boer laager and the Zulu monument confronting it across the river are assumed to complement each other by those who believe in the value of post-colonial monuments being

---

3   See the *Constitution of the Republic of South Africa Act 108 of 1996*, Chapter 2, Article 31 (1). Unfortunately, the Rhodes Must Fall movement of 2015 and related subsequent developments suggest an officially condoned move away from the principles of reconciliation and cultural tolerance enshrined in the constitution.
4   'Report of the Panel of Historians (Professors J.S. Maphalala, J. Laband, C.A. Hamilton and Dr J.E.H. Grobler)', in Department of Arts, Culture Science and Technology, *The Re-Interpretation of the Battle of Blood River / Ncome:* (Kwa-Dlangezwa: University of Zululand, seminar, 31 October 1998), p. 68.
5   The Ncome Museum was opened on 26 November 1999, and it and the monument comprise the Ncome-Blood River Heritage Site and Museum Complex.

positioned in the proximity of colonial ones in order that they might interact and thus define and legitimise each other. Such placement, it is suggested, allows us to acknowledge differing perspectives. And by ending one-sided representation, it helps us reconcile conflicting historical portrayals and so fosters reconciliation. That indeed was the intention at Blood River/Ncome, and the opening in 2014 of a long-deferred pedestrian bridge over the river connecting the two sites was intended (apart from any practical considerations with tourists in mind) to reconfirm symbolically the reconciliation of ancient enemies.

The problem, though, is that memorialisation cannot help but always be highly charged both politically and culturally, and simply cannot avoid leading to a contestation of the past. And a battlefield is probably the most compromised place of all to cultivate reconciliation. Monuments permanently fix the past in physical form, so when you have one that is conceived of as an attacking force and the other as a defensive formation, they belie the noble rhetoric of mutual understanding and forgiveness. The Ncome monument unashamedly celebrates traditional Zulu warrior identity and is just as grounded in ethnic nationalism as are the Afrikaner Blood River monuments opposite. The annual celebrations of the battle are still conducted separately on either side of the river by different racial groups who persist in regarding each other as the adversary, revealing ingrained antagonisms that the connecting footbridge cannot eradicate. And, as the reconciliatory spirit—so compelling when the Ncome monument was inaugurated in 1998—continues to fade in an increasingly polarised South Africa, the bronze laager symbolically keeps on defending while the Ncome monument opposite is always attacking.

In writing this book, I am deeply aware of the historic antagonisms that the war of 1837–1840 between the *Trekkers* and amaZulu set in motion. I can see that, despite efforts to encourage mutual respect and reconciliation, animosities between the descendants of the original combatants still simmer on and are expressed through the battle monuments they have raised. Nor is that surprising, because the war was a critical one in South Africa's blood-stained history of colonial conquest and African resistance, one that spawned myths that fed the conflicting ideologies that shaped the future course of the country. A war laden with as much historical baggage as this one is, presents a considerable challenge for any historian who attempts to present an acceptably balanced account of it. For my part, I did not approach the task as an advocate for either side. My aim was to describe the wider historical context of the war, to analyse the contrasting military cultures of the antagonists, to explain why the conflict broke out, to track the course of the campaign, and to elucidate the reasons for victory and defeat. In doing so, it was essential to enlarge on the part the amaZulu played in the war. All too often, the war has been approached from the perspective of the ultimately triumphant Boers, with too little effort made to explore the mainsprings of Zulu policy and action. I have attempted as best I can to remedy this imbalance through consulting recorded Zulu oral testimony alongside contemporary written accounts. By according the two sides as even a weighting as I can, I hope that even if the result does not secure a measure of ever-elusive reconciliation among readers, it will at least promote a better level of understanding.

1

Breaking Down the Maize Stalks

The *Elizabeth and Susan*, a 30-ton timber-built schooner with one mast fore and another aft, tacked on 4 May 1828 into the wide, exposed sweep of Algoa Bay on the southern coast of Africa. Four days before, the little vessel had set sail from Port Natal, a tiny, scruffy settlement of British traders and hunters established in May 1824 on the shore of the Zulu kingdom, 383 nautical miles away to the north-east. The schooner's commander was James King, a discharged midshipman of the Royal Navy who liked to pose as an ex-lieutenant.[1] He was accompanied by several other hunter-traders (some bare-footed and partially dressed in animal skins) along with a consignment of hippopotamus ivory to sell. On board there were also several Zulu dignitaries, envoys despatched by Shaka kaSenzangakhona, the Zulu king. It was primarily on their account that the *Elizabeth and Susan* was making the voyage, for King Shaka desired to establish friendly relations with the British authorities governing the Cape Colony.[2]

Shaka had entrusted his embassy with fifty tusks of elephant ivory to cover expenses and to be disbursed as gifts. The senior ambassador was Sothobe kaMpangalala, one of the king's most distinguished and trusted councillors, an extremely arrogant, deep-chested giant of a man, celebrated for regularly eating a whole goat by himself.[3] As a sign of his especial favour, Shaka had permitted Sothobe to bring along two of his many wives. Sothobe was subsequently celebrated in his *izibongo* (the praises declaimed during a person's lifetime and after his death in celebration of his deeds) for his heroism in sailing out to sea in a ship:

> Splasher of water with an oxtail,
> Great ship of the ocean,
> The uncrossable sea,
> Which is crossed only by swallows and white people ...[4]

---

1. For King's career, see Edward C. Tabler, *Pioneers of Natal and South-Eastern Africa 1552–1878* (Cape Town and Rotterdam: A.A. Balkema, 1977), pp.63–4.
2. For a full account of Sothobe's embassy to the Cape, see John Laband, *The Assassination of King Shaka* (Johannesburg and Cape Town: Jonathan Ball, 2017), pp.86, 103–6.
3. C. de B. Webb and John Wright (eds), *The James Stuart Archive of Recorded Oral Evidence Relating to the History of the Zulu and Neighbouring Peoples (JSA)*, vol. 6 (Pietermaritzburg: University of Natal Press; Durban: Killie Campbell Africana Library, 2014), p.281: Tununu ka Nonjiya, 6 June 1903.
4. Trevor Cope, *Izibongo: Zulu Praise Poems* (Oxford: Oxford University Press, 1968), p.180.

The amaZulu on board the *Elizabeth and Susan* had been anticipating unimaginable wonders in the white men's country, but they were swiftly disabused. The only contrivance that seems to have made a lasting impression was a pump that marvellously drew water 'out of a hole'.[5] Port Elizabeth, the Zulu embassy's destination, was still in an embryonic state. It had been founded in 1820 on the western shore of Algoa Bay by the acting governor of Cape Colony, Sir Rufane Donkin, who named it to commemorate his deeply mourned wife who had died in India. Until the middle of the 19th century the port had no proper jetties, no lighthouse or breakwater. From ships anchored in the bay, passengers and cargo were brought through the angry surf on lighters, and were then transferred to the shoulders of African porters who carried them to shore. Once deposited on dry land, the Zulu ambassadors would have found Port Elizabeth (in the words of English contemporaries) an 'ugly, dirty, ill-scented, ill-built hamlet, resembling some of the worst fishing villages on the English coast', a disreputable place with a well-earned reputation for disorderly 'drunkenness and immorality'.[6]

Yet, for all its undeniable drawbacks, Port Elizabeth was vital for the economic development of the eastern districts of the Cape Colony. In 1652 the Dutch East India Company, or *Vereenigde Oost-Indische Compagnie* (VOC), had established a refreshment station at the Cape of Good Hope at the southern tip of Africa, strategically situated on the sea route to its commercial empire in the East Indies.[7] It was not long before De Kaap (as the Dutch called their fortified base) developed into a colony of settlement producing beef, wheat, wine, and other foodstuffs for the passing ships. Its population steadily grew with the arrival of Dutch, French, and German settlers from Europe (all of whom took on Dutch identity) and slaves from East Africa, Madagascar, and the East Indies. Inevitably, the expansion of De Kaap was at the expense of the indigenous peoples of the Cape, the Khoikhoin and San, who already occupied the grazing lands and hunting grounds of a vast area stretching north to the Orange River 600 miles away, and 500 miles east along the coast to the Keiskamma River. In a series of skirmishes and more protracted wars over the next hundred years, the colonists pushed the boundaries of De Kaap ever further east and north. The dispossessed Khoikhoin and San were either driven away northwards over the Orange River into the interior of the sub-continent, or were subjugated as labourers or menials on the settlers' farms and in their villages.

Towards the end of the 18th century, the advancing Dutch settlers encountered another people just west of Algoa Bay. These were the amaXhosa, Nguni-speaking pastoralists closely related linguistically and culturally to other African peoples settled for 800 miles up the eastern coastal lands of southern Africa, notably (from south to north) the abaThembu, amaMpondomise, amaMpondo, amaZulu and amaSwazi. Tentative contact between the Dutch and the amaXhosa soon turned violent as both sides attempted to secure control of desirable grazing and agricultural land. During the course of nine Cape Frontier Wars of ever-increasing ferocity that began in 1779 and would only end in 1878 with the complete conquest of the amaXhosa, the colonists steadily drove them eastwards as they appropriated their territory.

---

5   *JSA* 5 (2001), p.5: Nduna ka Manqina, 24 April 1910.
6   Quoted in Alan F. Hattersley, *An Illustrated Social History of South Africa* (Cape Town: A.A. Balkema, 1973), p.80.
7   For the history of the Cape between 1642 and 1815, see John Laband, *The Land Wars: The Dispossession of the Khoisan and AmaXhosa in the Cape Colony* (Cape Town: Penguin Random House, 2020), pp.41–132.

In 1780 the Dutch East India Company fixed the eastern boundary of *Kaapkolonie* (as the Dutch now referred to their South African colonial possession) east of Algoa Bay, along the Great Fish and Baviaans Rivers. Soon thereafter the Dutch were caught up in the world-wide French Revolutionary and Napoleonic Wars which broke out in 1792 and continued until 1815. Early in the conflict, the British grasped the strategic significance of the Cape as a naval station on their own route to their empire in India, and seized it from the Dutch in 1795. As a condition of the Treaty of Amiens (a temporary truce that Britain signed with France in 1802) the Cape was restored to Dutch rule. But after the war resumed the following year, Britain once again conquered the Cape from the Dutch in 1806, and British possession of Cape Colony (as they called it) was confirmed by the Final Act of the Congress of Vienna, signed on 9 June 1815 between all the great powers.

With British rule came the assertion of English cultural supremacy at the Cape, whether it be its language, emblems, dress, architecture, food or social conventions.[8] The Governor, Lord Charles Somerset, was more than happy to do his best to 'civilise' the colony, but found the Dutch-speaking colonists determined to preserve their own language and cultural distinctiveness, especially when it came to their strict Calvinist religion. The further from the urban centres of the Western Cape, the less the Boers (literally, 'farmers' or *boere*) of the countryside were ready to accept or adopt the new British ways. For the British, who regarded the Cape as primarily a strategic naval possession, the distant but expanding, porous and unstable eastern and northern frontiers of white settlement were an annoying problem, especially since the Boers living there were acutely resentful of the new British order. So, although obliged to protect the fractious frontier farmers, the British government remained unwilling to commit sufficient troops to exercise absolute military control over the frontier zone. That meant that the amaXhosa in the east and the few still independent Khoisan in the north were not deterred from continuing to resist further settler encroachment and from trying to win back what they had lost.[9]

Following the Fourth and Fifth Cape Frontier Wars, in 1829 the British set the Colony's eastern frontier along the Keiskamma, Tyhume, and Klipplaat Rivers, thereby annexing 3,000 square miles of Xhosa territory. Meanwhile, the British government had approved an assisted emigration scheme to stabilise the frontier by creating a rural buffer of farmers against Xhosa incursions. Since the new settlers were of British extraction, the government hoped that their presence would dilute the regional influence of the chronically disaffected frontier Boers. Between December 1819 and March 1820, 21 crowded chartered emigrant ships left England and Ireland for the Cape carrying about 1,000 men and 3,000 women and children. The settlers took up their farms in what was named the Albany District between the Bushmans and Great Fish Rivers. Grahamstown, Albany's administrative and military centre, rapidly developed into a brisk commercial hub peopled with a politically aware mercantile community that erected churches and increasingly elegant houses. The Albany settlers' economic future depended on having a suitable port for trade and export, and Port Elizabeth addressed that need.

Many of the Albany settlers were officially encouraged to trade deep into the interior beyond the boundaries of the Colony, bartering goods such as cloth, iron utensils, beads, and buttons

---

8   For British rule at the Cape and the Albany Settlers, see Laband, *Land Wars*, pp.133–4, 151–7.
9   Khoisan is a useful portmanteau word for describing the intermixed Khoikhoi and San peoples.

with Africans for valuable commodities like cattle hides, ivory, and gum.[10] Earlier, Boer settlers in the Eastern Cape had sought land for their pastoralist, essentially subsistence economy, that differed little from that of the amaXhosa. Now, the Grahamstown merchants were beginning to flourish on the so-called 'Inland Kaffir Trade' up the east coast of southern Africa and north across the Orange River onto the highveld, the great inland plateau. To sustain this trade, they set about instituting the essential elements of a capitalist economy: credit and banking facilities and the formation of joint-stock trading companies. Some of these commercial interests began to take cognizance of the economic possibilities of a particular region which, in the early 1820s, had become the Zulu kingdom.

Until the late 18th century, there were no large chiefdoms in the territory of the future Zulu kingdom. Then a process of political consolidation and expansion began which, during the first decades of the 19th century, detonated turbulent migrations of peoples that violently ripped apart most of the pre-colonial societies of southern Africa north of the boundaries of Cape Colony. The causes of these upheavals remain a matter of considerable academic debate. Explanations have long concentrated on ecological and demographic pressures, and more recently on growing African competition to control trade routes in ivory and cattle (and possibly slaves) with Europeans operating primarily from Delagoa Bay on the east coast, and north across the Orange River from Cape Colony. What is certain is that widespread warfare, devastation and the formation by conquest or incorporation of newly militarized and centralized states accompanied these developments. Historians have applied the term *Mfecane* to this complex and revolutionary period in the eastern coastal lands. This is an isiXhosa word, derived from the root '*-feca*', meaning 'to crack, bruise, or break down the maize stalks', and was employed contemporaneously to describe the general turmoil. Subsequently, historians began to use the Sesotho term '*Difaqane*' with reference to the wars on the highveld of the interior in the same period. It means 'those who cut their enemies in pieces', and in the early 19th century seems already to have gained the broader meaning of 'wars waged by wandering hordes'.[11]

The increasing turmoil compelled the little chiefdoms of the territory that would become the Zulu kingdom to strengthen themselves and undertake social and political adjustments in order to compete and survive.[12] Most notably, these involved the transformation of *amabutho*, age-set units of youths originally banded together into circumcision sets, into military 'regiments' organised under the close control of their *amakhosi*, or chiefs, to act as their instruments of internal control and as armies against external enemies.

During the first decade of the 19th century the two most aggressively expanding chiefdoms between Delagoa Bay and the Thukela River to its south (the site of the future Zulu kingdom) were the abakwaNdwandwe and the abakwaMthethwa. In about 1817 the abakwaNdwandwe

---

10   Between August 1824 and March 1825 alone, more than 50,000 lbs of ivory were obtained, as well as 16,800 lbs of gum and 15,000 hides.
11   See John Wright, 'Turbulent Times: Political Transformations in the North and East, 1760s–1830s', in Carolyn Hamilton, Bernard K. Mbenga and Robert Ross (eds), *The Cambridge History of South Africa, Volume I: From Early Times to 1885* (Cambridge: Cambridge University Press, 2012), pp. 212–13, 218–19, 249–50; John Laband, 'Mfecane (1815–1840)', in Gordon Martel (ed.), *The Encyclopedia of War* (Oxford: Wiley-Blackwell, 2011), <http://onlinelibrary.wiley.com/doi/10.1002/9781444338232.wbeow400/abstract>, accessed 7 August 2020.
12   For the rise of the Zulu kingdom under Shaka, see John Laband, *The Eight Zulu Kings from Shaka to Goodwill Zwelithini* (Johannesburg and Cape Town: Jonathan Ball, 2018), pp.16–46.

crushed their rivals, and only the small Zulu chiefdom in the valley of the White Mfolozi River, ruled by Shaka kaSenzangakhona, a former Mthethwa tributary, remained in the field to oppose them. Despite heavy losses, the amaZulu held fast because their *inkosi* (chief, king) was a military commander of extraordinary abilities. He had gained his expertise in the service of the abakwaMthethwa, and set about enhancing the military capability of his small army. He did so through rigorous training, refining, and improving upon the military techniques already being practiced in the region, and by inculcating a culture of remorseless combat.

Over the course of a series of successful campaigns, Shaka combined his growing military weight with the exercise of ruthless but extremely skilful diplomacy to extend his burgeoning kingdom. By the mid-1820s he ruled over the entire region between the Phongolo River to the north, the foothills of the Drakensberg to the west, the Indian Ocean shore to the east, and the Mzimkhulu River to the south. When defeated, more powerful rivals like the abakwaNdwandwe were faced with the unpalatable options of flight or submission; while many smaller chiefdoms prudently gave in without a fight. The *amabutho* of all these incorporated chiefdoms no longer served their old *amakhosi*, but transferred their full loyalty to their new ruler, Shaka, whose army they increasingly swelled. Until the fall of the Zulu kingdom in the Anglo-Zulu War of 1879, these *amabutho* under their king's sole command constituted the central prop of royal power.

2

Always Talking of War and Battles

All the men in the Zulu kingdom—with the exception of a few individuals in specialist callings such as diviner (*isangoma*) or blacksmith—shared the common experience of being enrolled in an *ibutho*.[1] Boys between the ages of five and 12 were put to work by their elders, herding, hoeing, harvesting, threshing, keeping watch for intruders or dangerous animals. Some among them, the tougher and more mettlesome ones, would be sent off to serve as *izindibi*, baggage-carriers, for warriors quartered in an *ikhanda*.[2] These *amakhanda*, great circular assemblages of domed grass huts (*izindlu*) constructed around a central cattle enclosure and parade ground, ranged in size from several hundred *izindlu* to a thousand or more, and were situated at strategic points across Zululand where they functioned as hubs of royal authority.

At the age of 14 or a year or two younger, adolescents of the same age-grade from all around the kingdom mustered at the *ikhanda* nearest to them. There they were said to *ukukleza*, to drink milk directly from the udder, while they served as cadets for several years herding cattle, working the fields and practicing military skills. From the outset they were in strenuous competition with one another, and would select forceful, courageous individuals from among their own ranks as the junior officers of the future to command the *amaviyo*, or companies, that made up an *ibutho*. An *iviyo* was formed from recruits who came from the same district and who already knew each other, thus bonding naturally as a unit.[3] At about 17 or 18, once they had passed puberty, cadets of the same age-grade would be brought before the king for him to *ukubuthwa* them, form them into a new *ibutho* with their own *ikhanda*. Older and younger brothers would often be *buthwa'd* together in the same *ibutho*, although this meant the elder's enrolment would be delayed.[4]

An *induna* (officer) was appointed to command between one and three *amaviyo*, and each had a subordinate officer. The size of an *iviyo* or of a whole *ibutho* was never a constant, and depended on factors such as the degree of favour in which it was held by the king. Thus, *amaviyo* could be

---

1   For a detailed description of the Zulu military system, see Ian Knight, *The Anatomy of the Zulu Army from Shaka to Cetshwayo 1818–1879* (London: Greenhill Books, 1995), pp 46–90; Michał Leśniewski, *The Zulu–Boer War 1837–1840* (Leiden; Boston: Brill, 2021), pp.84–100; and John Laband and Paul Thompson, *The Illustrated Guide to the Anglo-Zulu War* (Pietermaritzburg: University of Natal Press, 2000), pp.9–19.
2   *JSA* 5, p.213: Nungu ka Matshobana, 13 September 1903.
3   *JSA* 6, p.88: Socwatsha ka Papu, 4 June 1912.
4   *JSA* 6, p.294: Tununu, 14 June 1903.

Distant view of emGungundlovu from the south in Allen Gardiner, *Narrative of a Journey to the Zooloo Country in South Africa Undertaken in 1835* (London: William Crofts, 1836). (Campbell Collections, Durban, by permission)

anything from 40 to 100 strong; while the strength of an *ibutho* could vary from a few hundred men to several thousand. New *amabutho*, or those that had become under-strength on account of casualties or natural attrition though age, were often incorporated into larger, more favoured ones.

The *amabutho* served for a few months a year in their *amakhanda*, when they looked after the royal cattle, kept the *amakhanda* in repair, collected tribute from outlying districts and acted as the king's police against malefactors. They all mustered at the king's 'great place' (the *ikhanda* where he principally resided) to celebrate the great national festivals, and also in time of war preparatory to going on campaign as the king's army, or *impi*. They had no special training in military exercises, and had learned to throw their spears while cadets by hunting buck. As youngsters they had become accustomed to combatting each other in rough-and-tumble scrimmages, and contesting as determined rivals in the stick-fighting that required considerable skill, sharp reflexes and a willingness to endure bruises, bloody scalps and broken bones. As cadets and members of an *ibutho* they were always being urged on by their *izinduna* not to be cowards and to stand up for themselves. They became inured to the frequent beating they received from their elders and officers for every little transgression, and when quartered in an *ikhanda* they scrapped over their rations, snatching food from each other and coming to blows. There was, as it was said, 'no restraining' of the warriors who, not content with treating each other aggressively, were constantly asserting their own *esprit de corps* by picking quarrels with members of younger *amabutho* who, in turn, bragged that they possessed as much prowess as their elders – and set out to prove it. Nor must it be forgotten that the unmarried, younger warriors were males in search of a mate, and when they danced for the girls who brought them their food, they shoved and pushed to be in the front rank where they could cut an eye-catching dash in all their finery of feathers and animal skins and display their vigorous young manhood before their sweethearts.[5]

Zulu girls were also formed into *amabutho*, primarily for the purpose of regulating marriage. At intervals, the king gave members of a female *ibutho* of child-bearing age leave to marry the middle-aged men of a designated male *ibutho* who then put on the distinctive *isicoco*, or headring, a circlet of animal tendons or fibres that was sewn into the hair, coated with beeswax or gum, and then greased or polished. Wearing an *isicoco* indicated that a man had attained full adulthood and so had the right to marry, set up his own family homestead as an *umnumzane*, or head of a household, and procreate. By withholding permission for a male *ibutho* to marry, the king was prolonging the period during which its members continued to be regarded as youths in Zulu society, and therefore remained more thoroughly under the control their elders.

When a Zulu king decided to go to war, messengers would shout the mobilisation order from hill to hill and word would dutifully pass from *umuzi* to *umuzi*, each the circular family homestead of huts that scattered the countryside. Over the next few days, the *amabutho* would assemble at their regional *amakhanda*. Before leaving his own home, a warrior would be presented with a tiny skin bag two inches square made of otter, weasel, leopard, bushbaby or baboon skin filled with *intelezi* (ritual medicines to counteract evil influence or sorcery) along with other charms (*amakhubalo*) to be worn on a string around the neck. Fully armed, he would then be served a ritual meal that a dog had licked to give him stamina in running should he be defeated

A typical Zulu *umuzi* constructed with the *izindlu* surrounding the *isibaya*, anonymous engraving. (Campbell Collections, Durban, with permission)

---

5   *JSA* 6, pp.74–5: Socwatsha, 17 December 1909.

and forced to flee for his life. After that, he would go into the *isibaya* (the enclosure for livestock in an *umuzi*) where the women supplicated the *amadlozi* (ancestral spirits) on his behalf.[6]

The members of the *amabutho* would arrive at the king's great place in groups, singing the *amahubo*, or solemn anthems of the nation, salute him and *ukugiya*, that is, perform the leaping, aggressive war-dance. 'They would cry, "Is it war, Nkosi?" The king replies: "I have said! I have said! I have said!"' Once the king had ascertained from his *izinduna* that the whole *impi* had assembled, he would give the order for the war preparation rituals to commence.[7]

Knowledge of the form the rituals took and the sequence in which they were performed is to be gleaned mainly from Zulu oral testimony recorded many decades later. Faulty or failing memory thus plays its part; while the experiences of witnesses naturally differed depending on when and where they participated in the ceremonies. Our most detailed information concerns the period in the late 1870s, at the time of the Anglo-Zulu War. However, the description below is based primarily on the reminiscences of elderly individuals who, in their young manhood, took part in the Zulu campaign against the amaNdebele in 1837 during the reign of Shaka's successor King Dingane. They described the rituals that took place at precisely the moment when the *Voortrekkers* were poised to invade the Zulu kingdom, and we can be reasonably confident that was how they were performed during the ensuing war.

With a small force the various rituals might take only a day to complete, but with a large *impi* several days were required.[8] Before dawn, the assembled *amabutho* went down to the river to *ukuphalaza*, or vomit the *imithi* (occult medicines) administered

Lunguza kaMpukane, was born in 1820 and was a member of the uKhokhothi *ibutho* formed in 1837–38. He was one of James Stuart's most reliable informants when the magistrate was recording Zulu oral testimony concerning their history and customs. Photographed in 1909. (Campbell Collections, Durban, with permission)

6   *JSA* 6, pp.61, 110: Socwatsha, 4 August 1908, 16 April 1916; *JSA* 5, pp. 164–5, 168: Nsuze ka Mfelafuti, 17 and 18 May 1912.
7   *JSA* 6, p 61: Socwatsha, 4 August 1908.
8   For two accounts of the order of the rituals in Dingane's time that complement each other but disagree on many details, see *JSA* 6, pp.61–2: Socwatsha, 4 August 1908; and *JSA* 6, pp. 286–7: Tununu, 7 June

to them by the *izinyanga*, or traditional healers. The purpose of this ritual was to cleanse the warriors of *umnyama*, evil occult influences and the forces of darkness such as might be induced by sorcery, as well as to cause a mystical mist to envelope their enemies so that they would be taken by surprise.[9] The warriors vomited into the open centre of the *inkatha*. This was a great, twisted grass coil full of *imithi* and other ritual objects symbolising the unity of the nation, and was the visible expression of the hope that none would ever break away from the kingdom.[10] After the *ukuphalaza* ceremony was over, Dingane gave the order for the *amabutho* to go to his father Senzangakhona's grave on the hill above the kwaNobamba *ikhanda* (the site of his original *umuzi*) to *ukukhetha*, or perform a rhythmical, showy dance in praise of the royal ancestors. When there, they symbolically whetted the blades of their spears on Senzangakhona's old sharpening stone, the ceremony rousing 'the warlike spirit to an extraordinary degree'.[11]

Next, the warriors had to be ritually strengthened against the dangers of combat and to be inspired with courage and a fighting spirit. In a hazardous exercise some sections of the older *amabutho*, several hundred men strong, would catch a number of black or reddish bulls (never, for occult reasons, particoloured) with their bare hands and kill them by breaking their necks. With a large *impi* the number of bulls despatched in this way could range between five and 10. Their carcases were carried into the great cattle enclosure at emGungundlovu, Dingane's principal *ikhanda*, where the king had been watching hidden behind his attendants. The *izinyanga* cut the dead bulls into myriad thin strips, roasted them over wood fires and smeared them with pungent and bitter *imithi* until they were quite black, and then laid them out in heaps on skins. Meanwhile, the *amabutho* had returned from the river after the *ukuphalaza* ceremony and were standing in a great *umkhumbi*, four or five ranks deep. (An *umkhumbi* was an open crescent of warriors who only formed a complete circle just before going off to engage the enemy.)[12] The *izinyanga* then threw the doctored strips to the waiting *amabutho* who were holding their shields and spears in their left hands. They caught the meat in their right ones, chewed it slightly, swallowed the doctored juice and passed it on by throwing it to others who were waiting to catch it in the air above their heads.[13]

After this ritual, the whole *impi* was treated with *intelezi*, the occult charms intended to counteract *umnyama* and render it innocuous. The *izinyanga* administered the *intelezi* by sprinkling the warriors using a grass broom (old women who were no longer menstruating might assist in this—no other women were permitted to be present during the rituals),[14] or by burning it so that the smoke enveloped the *umkhumbi*. The warriors were thereby rendered 'slippery' so that enemy spears would not stab them and their bullets would miss.[15] It was also usual to *ukuncinda* at this stage. Warriors dipped their hands into potsherds of *intelezi* dissolved in boiling water, then sucked their fingertips and squirted the liquid in the direction of the

---

    1903.
9   *JSA* 5, pp.166, 172: Nsuze, 17 and 19 May 1912.
10 For the *inkatha*, see *JSA* 5, p.77: Ngidi ka Mcikaziswa, 18 October 1905; p.373, Sivivi ka Maqungo, 10 March 1907; *JSA* 6, p.15: Socwatsha, 1 January 1902.
11 *JSA* 5, p. 3: Ngidi, 22 October 1905.
12 *JSA* 5, p.172: Nsuze, 19 May 1912.
13 *JSA* 5, pp.165, 169, 170: Nsuze, 17 and 18 May 1912.
14 *JSA* 6, p.15: Socwatsha, 1 January 1902.
15 *JSA* 5, p.173: Nsuze, 19 May 1912.

enemy, shouting: 'Fall, So and so! Fall, So and so!'[16] They might also splash the protective *intelezi*-infused water over their bodies and not wash again until hostilities were over.[17]

On account of these accumulated rituals, the *amabutho* were in a supernaturally active state and were required to *ukuzila*, to observe ritual abstinence. The *izinyanga* cautioned them against having sexual intercourse since this would subvert the powers of the *intelezi* that encompassed them. If the *impi* subsequently fared badly, this was attributed to some men having disobeying the injunction. The defaulters would, moreover, lay themselves open to being wounded or killed.[18]

The next element of war preparations was that of ritual challenges lasting a full day. The competitive *amabutho* were called before the king who declared: 'Let the *impi* discuss war: let the men challenge one another' (*ukuqomana*).[19] Then 'a bad commotion arose' and mediation would be required as the men defied each other, *giya'd* and boasted of the valiant deeds they would perform on campaign and asserted they would surpass their rivals. When they later returned from war their boasts would be remembered and they would be held account, with some braggarts humiliated and other rewarded for their prowess.[20]

After all these taxing ceremonies, the *amabutho* were sent back to their *amakhanda* for a few days to recuperate, after which they were called up again to perform the ceremony of sending off the *impi*. All the *amabutho* led by their *izinduna* formed up into a great *umkhumbi* facing the king who stood alone, arrayed in all his finery and carrying his shield and spears. He held a stick of war with which he pointed in the direction of the enemy as he strutted back and forth while the assembly yelled out, 'You will hear about us, as you will see what we do.' Then, one by one, each *ibutho* moved off in the designated order of march, accompanied in turn by the king as far as the gate to the enclosure.[21]

Even then, the rituals were not over. The army went to sleep at emaHlabaneni, the *ikhanda* presided over by Mnkabayi kaJama, the *inDlovukazi*, 'Great She-Elephant', Dingane's aunt. The next day it was drawn up in an *umkhumbi* on a hillock close to the gate to emaHlabaneni and Mnkabayi took them through a final round of *ukuthetha* ceremonies when the generals and the other great *izinduna* and men of high birth declaimed the praises of the royal ancestors.[22]

On campaign during the reigns of Shaka and Dingane, *amabutho* wore their full panoply of precious furs and feathers, a practice that fell increasingly away in subsequent times. All members of an *ibutho* wore a cowhide penis sheath for modesty (otherwise there was no shame in nudity among men) beneath a thick bunch of animal skins twisted to resemble tails. These tails might be continued all around the waist like a kilt, or be replaced over the buttocks by an oblong cowskin flap, often supplemented by further tails. In 1905 the ancient Ngidi kaMcikaziswa, who had been born in about 1818, described his attire during the Zulu campaign of 1837 against the amaNdebele. Besides the basic loin covering of tails, around his neck, sewn onto a thong,

---

16   *JSA* 5, p.171: Nsuze, 19 May 1912.
17   *JSA* 5, p.172: Nsuze, 19 May 1912. It was permissible, though, to smear legs and feet with fat to soothe them during the march.
18   *JSA* 5, p.168: Nsuze, 18 May 1912. It was also believed that if a man were wounded on campaign, he could blame it on another man who had stayed home and enjoyed sex.
19   *JSA* 6, pp.61–2: Socwatsha, 4 August 1908.
20   *JSA* 6, pp.61–2, 74–5: Socwatsha, 4 August 1908, 17 December 1909.
21   *JSA* 6, p.287: Tununu, 7 June 1903. See also, *JSA* 6, pp.61–3: Socwatsha, 4 August 1908.
22   *JSA* 5, pp.83–4: Ngidi, 22 October 1905.

Inkosi Ngoza kaLudaba photographed in *c*.1860 with young, unmarried *amabutho* in full festival attire.
(Campbell Collections, Durban, with permission)

he wore long cow-tails falling over his chest and back. As a member of the iHlaba *ibutho*, on his head he carried a very large crest of black and dun-coloured vulture feathers and the red feathers of the crested crane. These feathers were fixed into a headband of blue monkey and otter skin with flaps on either side of the face and longer ones at the back of the head reaching some way down the back. 'So covered up would a person become with this this head dress,' remembered Ngidi, 'that you would not be able to recognise him for some time'.[23]

On the army's march, the *izindibi* ported the warriors' sleeping mats, neck-rests, calabashes, cooking pots, and skin cloaks made from the hides of young steers scraped until they were soft. In Dingane's day, girls did not go out with the army carrying supplies, as they had in Shaka's time. Maize and sorghum were carried by the whole army, and firewood too if fuel was scarce in the area of operations. A herd of inferior cattle with missing teats or horns that grew crooked was driven along with the *impi* for meat if the need arose, but it was preferable to consume captured enemy cattle and drive the herd home uneaten.[24] If meat ran out, the warriors went out hunting for eland, buffalo, and buck, and it was the practice to raid the gardens of any *imizi*

---

23 *JSA* 5, pp.81, 82: Ngidi, 22 October 1905.
24 *JSA* 6, pp.63, 89: Socwatsha, 4 August 1908, 4 June 1912.

they passed without offering compensation, even if still in Zulu territory.²⁵ When the *impi* came to a halt to rest, the men would stack their shields and share out their snuff, some puffing away at cannabis in their smoking horns while declaiming the praises of the king.²⁶ Decoy fires might be made (or aloes set alight) to deceive enemy spies into believing the *impi* was encamped where it was not.²⁷

Inkosi Ngoza kaLudaba photographed in *c.*1860 with senior, married *amabutho* in war dress. (Campbell Collections, Durban, with permission)

Many warriors were unable to keep up on a long march. The sinews in their legs gave way and their bare feet cracked open and became a mass of cuts. Those who put on sandals were beaten and told to go home in disgrace. Indeed, no sympathy was accorded to the weak, and the order would be given: 'Let the maggots [because they moved with difficulty] go home'. Those who turned back were called young locust not yet able to fly, meaning people who could not walk far.²⁸

An *impi* was guided by spies who had gone deliberately to live among the people to be attacked so as to learn all about them.²⁹ As the army advanced through enemy territory, scouts were sent

25 *JSA* 5, p.174: Nsuze, 19 May 1912.
26 *JSA* 5, p.87: Ngidi, 23 October 1905.
27 *JSA* 5, p.174: Nsuze, 19 May 1912.
28 *JSA* 5, pp.86–7: Ngidi, 23 October 1905.
29 *JSA* 5, p.88: Ngidi, 23 October 1905.

forward in groups of 10, 15, or 50 men to keep a lookout for the enemy. They kept in constant touch with the *impi*, sending messengers back regularly to report, and their runners sounded the alarm when the enemy was close.[30] Ideally, the enemy remained in ignorance of the *impi* so that it could advance secretly by night and surprise the foe at dawn.[31] If the opportunity arose, the amaZulu were content to lay an ambush for the enemy, allowing their unsuspecting adversaries to pass between two waiting bodies of men and then suddenly surrounding them, taking them at a disadvantage. But, when there was a reasonable chance of success, the Zulu preference was for a pitched battle in the open, in full daylight.[32]

On the march no cattle were sacrificed to the royal ancestors,[33] but when the *impi* came in sight of the enemy, a calf being driven along with the accompanying herd was deliberately separated from its mother so that they both began to bellow and thus *ukuthetha* the *amadlozi*, firing up the warriors who began to shout: 'We will be wide awake when we die; we will be wide awake when we kill them.' The *imbongi* (praise-singer) with army then started singing out the praises of Senzangakhona and shouting out phrases such as 'Crush! Grind to powder! the dust straight into the air [as it arises when forces clash].[34] The *izinyanga* accompanying the army (a whole 'pathful' of them) carried *intelezi* with them in baskets, and sprinkled it on the *amabutho* drawn up in a circular *umkhumbi* just before combat was joined.[35]

A Zulu *impi* was made up of a combination of married and unmarried *amabutho*. The former were the dependable, biddable veterans; while the latter could be expected to exhibit dash, foolhardiness, and a relative lack of discipline.[36] In battle the tactical intention of these *amabutho* was to outflank and enclose the enemy in a flexible manoeuvre, evidently developed from the hunt, which could be readily adapted to a pitched battle in the open field or to a surprise attack. This was the famous bull's chest and horns formation. It was the married veterans, who could be depended upon not to lose their nerve and run away, who made up the chest (*isifuba*) and engaged first with the enemy, and it was the younger, less reliable warriors who manoeuvred in the two encircling horns (*izimpondo*) and who came to blows later in the battle.[37] The loins (*umuva*), a reserve usually made up of a very young *ibutho*, was sent in for support if necessary, in pursuit of the flying enemy, or to round up captured cattle.

The amaZulu did not attack in a solid body, shoulder-to-shoulder, but advanced in open skirmishing order. They only concentrated when upon the enemy, casting a shower of long-shafted throwing-spears (*izijula*)—which could find their target up to 30 yards away—to distract the foe as they rushed in behind their great, cow-hide war-shields (*izihlangu*) to engage in hand-to-hand fighting with their short-hafted, long-bladed stabbing-spears (*amaklwa*) or with their *amawisa*, skull-crushing knobbed wooden sticks. After a few vicious minutes of frenzied stabbing and clubbing they would fall back and regroup before re-engaging as many times as was necessary before the enemy broke. No quarter was given to the defeated foe, and the pursuit

---

30 *JSA* 5, p.174: Nsuze, 19 May 1912.
31 *JSA* 6, pp.63, 68: Socwatsha, 5 August 1908.
32 *JSA* 6, p.69: Socwatsha, 6 August 1908; *JSA* 5, pp.177–8: Nsuze, 20 May 1912.
33 *JSA* 5, p. 88: Ngidi, 23 October 1905.
34 *JSA* 5, pp.83–5, 88: Ngidi, 22 and 23 October 1905.
35 *JSA* 5, p.171: Nsuze, 19 May 1912.
36 For a discussion on Zulu battle tactics, see John Laband, *The Rise and Fall of the Zulu Nation* (London: Arms & Armour, 1997), pp.39–41.
37 *JSA* 5, p.88: Ngidi, 23 October 1905.

and routing-out of fugitives (often including non-combatants who had been bystanders during the battle) was prolonged and merciless. Warriors might seize surviving women and children to keep as concubines and menials, but all the highly-prized cattle were retained for the king to distribute as he thought fit. Not so the less regarded goats and sheep, said contemptuously to be like 'mouldy or rotten grain'[38]

Face-to-face, heroic combat that sorely tested a warrior's physique and endurance, tried his skill with weapons, and assessed his courage was the ultimate yardstick of manliness in Zulu society.[39] Socwatsha kaPapu, whose father was an older contemporary of Shaka's and who had himself fought spear-to-spear at close quarters in 1837, graphically described the experience when in his old age:

> The men of both sides would charge forward … their shields would clash together and their heads would strike together. When battle started you became mixed up with the enemy; your eyes were fixed on the enemy in front darting glances at your comrades either side to make sure they were still full of fight and advancing. If you saw they were running away, you too would run. But if they prevailed they would take heart and become 'harder'. They would pursue the flying enemy and 'stab a melon', that is, kill those in flight, stab them in the back, those who had already surrendered and were defenceless. Those who escaped from fighting would be caught up in an exhausted state and killed.[40]

If the amaZulu won the battle and remained in possession of the field, they 'buried' their slain comrades by covering each man with his own shield. Naturally, if they were defeated, they could not do so, and left their dead to be consumed by wild animals, by the vultures and hyenas.[41] The veterans of the campaign of 1837 did not leave an oral record of the rites performed by their *impi* on its return home. However, we know from the testimony of those who took part in later wars that these would have been extensive, for the warriors were ritually polluted through the spilling of blood and could not present themselves before the king or resume normal life until they had been purified. For several days they washed ritually in a stream, and went on to *ukuncinda* in the direction of the enemy to obtain occult ascendancy over the spirits of their vengeful victims, and to ward off *umnyama*. Finally, an *inyanga* sprinkled them with *intelezi*.[42]

Because a man's prowess in war was under the constant scrutiny of his comrades, nothing better consolidated a warrior's reputation than to be in the very forefront of the battle.[43] After the campaign the king would discuss with his officers which *ibutho* had the distinction of being the first to engage the enemy at close quarters. Men who were members of that *ibutho* and who had killed in battle were designated heroes or warriors of distinction and the king ordered them to wear a distinctive necklace made from small blocks of ritually significant willow wood

---

38 *JSA* 6, p.66: Socwatsha, 5 August 1908.
39 For Zulu military culture, see John Laband, *Zulu Warriors: The Battle for the South African Frontier* (New Haven and London: Yale University Press, 2014), pp.11–13, 210–11, 213–15; and John Laband, 'Zulu Civilians during the Rise and Fall of the Zulu Kingdom', in John Laband (ed.), *Daily Lives of Civilians in Wartime Africa from Slavery Days to Rwandan Genocide* (Westport and London: Greenwood Press, 2007), pp.51–2.
40 *JSA* 6, p.65: Socwatsha, 5 August 1908.
41 *JSA* 5, p.198: Ntshelele ka Godide, 27 February 1922.
42 *JSA* 3 (1982), pp. 303–304: Mpatshana ka Sodondo, 24 May 1912.
43 See the celebrated incident of single combat between Zulu and Ndebele champions in the campaign of 1837 described in *JSA* 5, p. 5: Nduna, 24 April 1910.

(known as an *isiqu*) which was looped around the neck or slung across the body bandolier-style.[44] However, those who failed to live up to the required ideals of heroic masculinity, and whose courage deserted them in combat, were singled out by their comrades and publicly degraded by the king.[45] By contrast, proven excellence as a warrior invariably opened the avenue to personal glory, wealth and political power in the Zulu state.

As a means of maintaining the loyalty of his *amabutho*, the king assigned them a large portion of the cattle and other commodities they seized on their raiding forays and during full-blown military campaigns. It was thus in the interests of the king, as well as of the *amabutho*, to go to war regularly. Consequently, while *amabutho* were in practice part-time soldiers—members of a militia rather than a standing army—who spent the bulk of each year at home, their culture was a highly militarized one. This militaristic outlook was crucial for the creation of Zulu self-identification as a warrior nation that has persisted to this day. As Ngidi, who had lived through the reigns of all the Zulu kings from Shaka until the destruction of the kingdom in 1879, pithily put it in 1904 when he was close to 90 years of age, 'We are always talking of war and battles, even at this day.'[46]

Zulu women, although never active combatants, had their own recognized sphere when it came to war.[47] Besides giving birth to future warriors, they played an essential role while their men in the field, performing the prescribed rituals at home to keep them safe in battle, such as turning the top rolls of their leather skirts inside out.[48] And besides summoning supernatural protection, Zulu women contributed significantly to the war effort by supplying the *amabutho* with food while they were mobilizing and assembling the supplies they carried with them on campaign. And while their men were away fighting, women kept the *umuzi* and its agriculture functioning with the help of their children and the superannuated. And, when the warriors returned home wounded or weakened by the privations of war, they tended them with their simple remedies, soothing and healing wounds with herbal poultices, tying up open gashes with grass and setting fractures with splints.[49]

Despite the ingrained bellicosity of Zulu society, distance, logistical problems, and difficult terrain imposed a natural limit on the extent of territory Shaka or his successors could effectively conquer and control. By the later 1820s Shaka's armies were generally confining their campaigns to the extraction of tribute from subordinate chiefdoms along the margins of the Zulu domain proper, as did Dingane's in the 1830s. But, on occasion, they raided more distant, powerful neighbours, such as the kingdom of the amaSwazi (or abakwaDlamini) in their easily defensible mountainous country across the Phongolo River to the north of the Zulu kingdom, the less

---

44 It sometimes happened that brave but modest men without patrons among the officers were not recognised and their gallant feats were 'eaten up and snatched away by others'. See *JSA* 6, pp. 66–7: Socwatsha, 6 August 1908. See too, *JSA* 3, p. 317: Mpatshana, 28 May 1912.
45 *JSA* 3, p.141: Mjobo ka Dumela, 26 January 1912; pp.304–5: Mpatshana, 24 May 1912; *JSA* 4 (1986), pp.147–8: Mtshayankomo ka Magolwna, 23 January 1922.
46 *JSA* 5, p.57: Ngidi ka Mcikaziswa, 6 November 1904.
47 For the role of Zulu women in warfare, see Sifiso Ndlovu, 'A Reassessment of Women's Power in the Zulu Kingdom', in Benedict Carton, John Laband, and Jabulani Sithole (eds), *Zulu Identities: Being Zulu, Past and Present* (Pietermaritzburg: University of KwaZulu-Natal Press, 2008), pp. 111–13.
48 *JSA* 5, pp.164–5: Nsuze, 17 May 1912.
49 Laband, *Zulu Nation*, p 41.

well-integrated Mpondo kingdom to the south beyond the Mzimkhulu River, and even the bellicose amaNdebele on the highveld to the west.[50]

---

50 Laband, *Zulu Nation*, pp.15–21; Wright, 'Turbulent Times', pp. 225–6.

3

Port Natal

Shaka and his kingdom did not exist in an African void, untouched by the growing colonial presence. The king was familiar with the Portuguese at Delagoa Bay where in 1787 they had established a fort and trading post called Lourenço Marques. A lucrative trade was conducted through this port, and in return for their ivory and cattle the amaZulu received those seductive, exotic wares that so gladdened the hearts of the king and his *izikhulu* (or nobles): brass and copper beads, woollen and cotton blankets, calico, and cotton salempore cloth from India, usually coloured blue. Shaka took active steps to dominate this desirable commerce by compelling all the coastal chiefs between the Zulu kingdom and Delagoa Bay to pay him tribute. But Lourenço Marques was 350 miles away from the heart of his kingdom through challenging, malaria-infested terrain, and Shaka was eager to welcome a less remote supplier of foreign goods. Yet Cape Colony, of which Shaka was gradually becoming more aware, was twice as far away by land from the Zulu heartland as was Delagoa Bay. Besides, the way southwards along the coast was barred beyond the Mzimkhulu River by the Mpondo kingdom and by the Xhosa, Thembu, and other polities. The most viable trade route to the Cape, therefore, seemed to be by sea. And that is where the Port Natal settlers provided Shaka with the means.

European sailors had long known from exploratory voyages up the east coast of southern Africa that the only good, natural harbour between Port Elizabeth and Lourenço Marques was situated about half-way between the Thukela and Mzimkhulu rivers. There, a massive, bush-covered bluff thrust out into the sea on the southern side of a great bay that enclosed several small wooded islands. Deep channels between the sandy flats allowed passage for vessels. In these pristine days the bay abounded with flamingoes, hippopotami, turtles, and fish. The one drawback for the purposes of a harbour was a sandbar that impeded entrance to the bay to all but vessels of shallow draft.

On 10 May 1824 the 21-year-old Henry Francis Fynn (known to the Zulu as Mbuyazi),[1] son of the owner of the British Hotel in Long Street, Cape Town, along with his five companions, landed in this bay from the tiny, single-masted sloop, *Julia*. They were the advance-party of a larger group of 26 prospective settlers under the command of Lieutenant Francis George

---

1   For Zulu names for the settlers, see *JSA* 1 (1976), p.110: Dinya ka Zokozwayo, 3 April 1905; *JSA* 2 (1979), p.267: Maziyana ka Mbekuzana, 21 April 1905. For Fynn's career, see Tabler, *Pioneers*, pp.42–7.

Farewell, RN (whom the Zulu called Febana).[2] Farewell had secured the support of J.R. Thompson & Co. of Cape Town for a permanent trading post at the bay. He and Fynn were to act as agents for these merchants in obtaining ivory, hides and maize from the amaZulu. They also planned to extend their operations north to capture some of the flourishing trade flowing through Lourenço Marques.

It was Fynn's and Farewell's wish that the Cape annex their settlement, which they called Port Natal,[3] and so bring them under the protection of the British flag. However, their petition to Governor Somerset was smartly rejected, and it was made clear to them that no attempt to claim Port Natal for the Crown would be sanctioned, and that the traders were on their own.[4] With no other option open to them, in August 1824 Fynn and Farewell approached Shaka. He summoned them to visit him at kwaBulawayo, his chief *ikhanda*, and on their way there, Zulu children screamed with fright at the pale apparitions 'who had come out of the water' with blonde hair 'like maize tassels'.[5] Horrified mothers gathered their offspring up in their arms and fled into the bush.[6] The *amabutho* at kwaBulawayo were equally dismayed. When Fynn arrived he was, in Zulu recollection, 'mounted on a horse [itself a strange, unfamiliar beast in Zululand] with his hat on his head, gun in hand, hair like cattle tails … All present were moved with wonder and awe, so much so that the regiments shuffled back as far as the fence.'[7] When the white men came before him, Shaka himself could not help but be 'astonished at their colour.'[8]

Yet, outlandish as they appeared, Shaka welcomed them because he immediately grasped that they could supply him with the same goods as those traded through Lourenço Marques. Moreover, the hunter-traders' proximity at the bay meant that he could control them far more effectively than he could the distant Portuguese. Shaka also saw how they might act as the conduit through which he could foster friendly relations with the British authorities at the Cape. The desirability of doing so would have been brought home to him by news reaching him of the British military success in the recent Fifth Cape Frontier War of 1818–1819, and the defeat of Hintsa, the Xhosa paramount, whom he acknowledged as being a powerful African ruler in his own league.[9] So Shaka welcomed the strangers at Port Natal—initially known among the Zulu as 'makers of wonderful things' with reference to their ships and firearms, or less approvingly as 'the little red ones' or 'the little wild beasts'[10]—and conferred on them the favoured status of 'people of our house', or kinsmen.

2   For Farewell's career, see Tabler, *Pioneers*, pp.40–2.
3   On Christmas Day, 1497, Vasco da Gama, on his epochal voyage from Portugal to India, sighted land off his port bow to which he gave the name of 'Natal' in honour of the day of Christ's birth. See Edgar H. Brookes and Colin de B. Webb, *A History of Natal* (Pietermaritzburg: University of Natal Press, 1965), p.3.
4   John Bird, *The Annals of Natal 1495 to 1845* (facsimile reprint, Cape Town: C. Struik, 1965) (*Annals*), vol. 1, pp. 71–3: Lt. Farewell to Lord Charles Somerset, 1 May 1824; P.G. Brink to Farewell, 5 May 1824.
5   *JSA* 2, p.162: Makewu, 8 October 1899.
6   James Stuart and D. McK. Malcolm (eds), *The Diary of Henry Francis Fynn* (Pietermaritzburg: Shuter & Shooter, 1969), p.63.
7   *JSA* 1, p.96: Dinya, 27 February 1905.
8   *JSA* 3, p.73: Melapi ka Magaya, 27 April 1905.
9   Dr B.J.T Leverton (ed.), *Records of Natal, Volume One 1823–August 1828* (Pretoria: The Government Printer, 1984) (*RN 1*), p.37, no. 22: F.G. Farewell to Lord Charles Somerset, 6 September 1824.
10 *JSA* 6, p.281: Tununu, 6 June 1903.

On 8 August 1824 Shaka solemnly put his mark to a document that Farewell placed before him. It granted Farewell & Co. permission to occupy the land immediately surrounding Port Natal, along with a further stretch of territory extending 50 miles inland and 25 miles along the coast. Shaka also gave the hunter-traders the right to exercise authority over this territory, as well as permission to trade.[11] Thus, with enormous implications for the future, the Zulu kingdom was brought within the Cape's commercial and political orbit, even if it was still at an unofficial level.

Most of the initially hopeful Port Natal settlers were rapidly daunted by the hardships they encountered and returned to the Cape. By December 1824 the settlement had been reduced to only six men: Farewell, Fynn, the clean-shaven John Cane (called Jana)—a London-born former labourer and carpenter who traded in buffalo hides was remembered as the 'tallest of all the Englishmen, and…very strong and industrious'[12]—Henry Ogle (known as Wohlo or Hohlo),[13] and Joseph Powell (Farewell's servant). They were reinforced by another small party whose two-masted brig, *Mary*, was driven by a gale onto the sandbar across the bay on 1 October 1825 and foundered on the beach. Their leader was James Saunders King who had been vainly trying to drum up support in England for the Port Natal project. He brought with him his 17-year-old assistant, Nathaniel Isaacs, who had spent two years in St Helena in the counting-house of his uncle, the 14-year-old Thomas Halstead and the nine-year-old Charles Maclean, known as 'John Ross'.[14]

Maclean recorded his first impressions of the rudimentary settlement at Port Natal. Farewell's 'fort' on the north side of the bay was a 'very primitive, rude looking structure' consisting of a quadrangular palisaded enclosure protecting a cluster of several barn-like wattle-and-daub structures of typical Cape Khoikhoi design. Ten years later, only one dwelling at the Port had even the semblance of a European house. As for European furniture, that was almost entirely lacking. Numerous beehive Zulu *izindlu* surrounded the 'fort'. Maclean found the white traders and their Khoisan servants to be in an indescribably tattered condition. Their attire was characteristically a picturesque combination of local Zulu costume and garments sewn from skins with European touches like Fynn's famous crownless straw hat.[15] Within a very few months of arrival the settlers had adopted local customs. They took wives and concubines (*izixebe*) from the local people, as well as from the Khoisan they had brought with them from the Cape as servants.[16] As with any Zulu man, many traders legitimised their marriages through the payment of *ilobolo*, the goods or cattle handed over to the bride's father to recompense him for the loss of her labour in the family unit. And like any Zulu notable with multiple wives, they positioned their wives' beehive huts around their residences in conformity with the typical layout of an *umuzi* (the circle of huts around the cattle byre that constituted a Zulu family homestead). Fynn and Ogle were remembered to have possessed the 'largest number of wives.'[17]

---

11 For this document, see *RN 1*, pp.38–40, no. 22, annex. 1: Chaka's [sic] grant to F.G. Farewell, 8 August 1824.
12 *JSA* 1, p.112: Dinya, 5 April 1905. For Cane's career, see Tabler, *Pioneers*, pp.16–19.
13 *JSA* 6, p.14: Socwatsha, 1 January 1902. For Ogle, see Tabler, *Pioneers*, pp.82–4.
14 For Isaacs, Halstead and Maclean, see Tabler, *Pioneers*, pp. 55–6, 59–61, 90.
15 Charles Rawdon Maclean, edited by Stephen Gray, *The Natal Papers of 'John Ross'* (Pietermaritzburg: University of Natal Press; Durban: Killie Campbell Africana Library, 1992), pp.62–3.
16 Maclean, *'John Ross'*, pp.149–50.
17 *JSA* 1, p.111: Dinya, 5 April 1905.

Shaka, deeming the Africans in the vicinity of Port Natal 'very scattered', decided it would suit him if the settlers drew them in under their control and accepted their allegiance as if they were Zulu *amakhosi*. As *amakhosi*, the settlers were in turn responsible to their overlord, the Zulu king.[18] As happened with people putting themselves under a chief's protection, some acknowledged one settler as their *inkosi*, some another. Consequently, as was typical in Zulu political life, the power and fortunes of the various settler 'chiefs' waxed and waned with the number of adherents they could attract to their banner.

The agricultural and domestic labour the settlers required from their African subjects allowed the settlers to give their full attention to trading and hunting for commercial gain. To their delight, the vicinity of Port Natal still teemed with game of every variety, although indiscriminate hunting would decimate it in remarkably short order. The settlers fanned out in hunting-parties under Fynn, Cane, and Ogle in search especially of elephant and hippopotamus ivory and of buffalo hides. Their Khoisan retainers and African adherents assisted them as hunters, carriers, and guides. The Khoisan were already familiar with muskets, and the settlers also trained some of their favoured African retainers in their use, so that they too soon became good marksmen.

Shaka was very much taken up with the settlers' firearms and their military potential.[19] Invoking his authority as their overlord, in October 1826 he called them up to serve in his final campaign against the abakwaNdwandwe. Along with their armed retainers, the Port Natal traders played some part in Shaka's decisive victory at the battle of the izinDolowane hills. This was the first occasion firearms were deployed in combat in that part of southern Africa. Appreciating the disproportionate effect a few muskets had on the battlefield, Shaka repeatedly thereafter summoned the Port Natal traders to take the field with him.[20]

Besides valuing the Port Natal settlers as traders and musketeers, Shaka made good his intention to use them to make diplomatic contact with the British at the Cape. As we have seen, he turned to King, whose workmen were constructing the *Elizabeth and Susan* at the bay, because he appreciated that the vessel would be ideal for carrying his envoys to the Cape. In February 1828 Shaka made his 'scrawling, fishbone' mark through the last few lines of a document which King put before him. It superseded the original grant Shaka had made to Farewell in 1824 and granted King 'free and full possession' of Port Natal and surrounding territories along with 'the free and exclusive trade' of all of Shaka's domains. It also placed him in charge of the embassy, led by Sothobe, which was soon to set off for the Cape, and commissioned him to 'negotiate a treaty of friendly alliance' between the Zulu kingdom and that of King George IV, known to the Zulu as 'Mjojo'.[21]

While the Cape authorities took Shaka's unexpected embassy seriously, it is not surprising that they were at something of a loss as how best to handle it. There was Sothobe, Shaka's

---

18   C. de B. Webb and J.B. Wright (eds), *A Zulu King Speaks: Statements Made by Cetshwayo kaMpande on the History and Customs of His People* (Pietermaritzburg: University of Natal Press; Durban: Killie Campbell Africana Library, 1978), p.9.
19   *JSA* 1, p.200: Jantshi ka Nongila, 16 February 1903.
20   John Laband, '"Fighting Stick of Thunder": Firearms and the Zulu Kingdom: The Cultural Ambiguities of Transferring Weapons Technology', *War & Society*, 33: 4 (October 2014), pp.233–4.
21   *RN* 1, pp.247–8, no. 235, annex. 1, enc. 1: notarial deed signed by J.A. Chaboud on 29 July 1828 verifying Shaka's mark, Jacob's mark, and Isaac's signature as witness on the document of February 1828. 'Jacob' was Jakot Msimbithi, the traders' interpreter they had brought with them from the Cape.

ambassador, who, when meeting Cape officials, always insisted on donning his full ceremonial dress of skins, on wearing his headdress with its tall crane feather, and on carrying his spear and cow-hide shield.[22] And there was the shady pseudo-lieutenant King, dubiously in charge of the embassy and determined on his own account to persuade the British to establish some sort of authority over Port Natal to safeguard the trading rights and territorial concessions Shaka had granted him in February 1828.

The halting negotiations soon foundered. The Cape government refused to deal any further with the slippery 'Lieutenant' King, while the Zulu envoys became increasingly impatient and disillusioned by their lack of progress. Nevertheless, the main reason why the negotiations failed, and the British decided to send the Zulu delegation back home, was word that in May 1828 Shaka had launched a raid-in-force against the Mpondo kingdom to his south with an army of about 3,000 men accompanied by some musketeers from Port Natal. Why Shaka had chosen that inopportune moment to attack, just when his envoys were negotiating with the British can, for lack of evidence, only be conjectured. But the damage was done. For a tense moment it seemed as if Shaka's army was approaching the eastern borders of the colony, and it was not until mid-July that the Cape authorities could be certain that Shaka's army had turned back with some 10,000 cattle as booty. Although relieved, the Cape officials remained extremely nervous of a fresh Zulu incursion. They were determined to give Shaka practical warning to stay out of Mpondo territory by mounting a counter military demonstration of their own.

On 26 July 1828, deep in Mpondo territory, a Cape force with African allies drawn from local chiefdoms that themselves felt threatened by the amaZulu, attacked a large group of warriors whom, from their dress and military style, they presumed were amaZulu. In a sense, they were, but they were not part of Shaka's army. They were in fact amaNgwane under the leadership of Matiwane kaMasumpa, and he and his people had been dislodged during the wars of the *Mfecane* from their original home near the headwaters of the White Mfolozi in what was now the heart of the Zulu kingdom. The clash on 26 July was not decisive, however. The colonial forces and their allies attacked the amaNgwane again on 27 August in the battle of Mbholompo on the banks of the Mthatha River, close to the present-day town of that name. The amaNgwane were taken by surprise, cut down and decisively broken up as a political or military entity. The Cape military authorities remained convinced, however, that they had dealt Shaka a sharp warning to stay away from the eastern borders of the Cape.[23]

Ten days before the battle of Mbholompo, the members of Shaka's unsuccessful delegation were landed at Port Natal from the British sloop-of-war, HMS *Helicon,* which had brought them home from Port Elizabeth.[24] Fynn recorded that at about this time Shaka dreamed that the vessel in which his ambassadors sailed had a broken mast. The *amadlozi* spoke through dreams, so the king deduced something had gone seriously amiss with the mission.[25] Nor was he mistaken. Instead of a treaty of friendship, all his crestfallen and apprehensive envoys brought back with them was the ambivalent statement that, while the Cape government was anxious to be on good terms with Shaka, it would oppose by force any Zulu incursion south of the Mzimkhulu River that threatened the Cape eastern frontier.

22 *JSA* 2, p.267: Mazinyana, 21 April 1905.
23 Laband, *Land Wars*, pp. 163–6.
24 For the return of Sothobe's embassy, see Laband, *Assassination*, pp. 112–13.
25 Stuart and Malcom (eds), *Fynn's Diary*, p.154.

Shaka would not have been the ruler he was had he not acted to retrieve the situation by despatching a fresh embassy to the Cape, this time by land. It was to be led by John Cane (Jana).[26] He set out on foot for the Cape in early September 1828 with a small party of amaZulu. After an arduous, 23-day journey he reached Cape territory. British officials interviewed Cane in Grahamstown on 7 October, and again in Cape Town on 10 November, and his embassy enjoying considerably more success than had King's.[27] Colonial policy had undergone a change in the previous few months following Shaka's alarming Mpondo raid and the battle of Mbholompo. The new governor, Sir Lowry Cole, who had taken up office on 8 September 1828, was committed to a more active diplomatic engagement with the African polities bordering the Cape. On 26 November Cane was informed that he was to return to Shaka with an armed escort, and that he was to convey assurances of Cole's 'friendly disposition' towards the Zulu monarch. However, like his predecessors as governor, Cole continued to abjure any British responsibility for the Port Natal traders, and reiterated the warning given to Shaka's previous embassy not to disturb the border regions within the Cape's sphere of interest.

Cane and his party had only just reached the Cape eastern border on their return to Zululand when, on 26 December 1828, they were suddenly turned back, their promising diplomatic mission aborted.[28] What had happened was that on 15 December Farewell had arrived in Port Elizabeth on board the *Elizabeth and Susan* along with all of the other residents of Port Natal with the exception of Fynn and Ogle. He brought the startling news that Shaka had been assassinated on 23 September 1828 nearly three months before, and that the Zulu kingdom was in turmoil. Although the Port Natal settlers had not been in immediate danger, they had considered it prudent to withdraw on 1 December until the disputed succession to the Zulu throne was decided.

---

26 For Cane's embassy, see Laband, *Assassination*, pp.114–16.
27 King had died soon after his return from his unsuccessful mission, a humiliated and disappointed man. Shaka endowed Isaacs with the lands he had previously granted King around Port Natal.
28 Cane and the Zulu envoys languished in Grahamstown until March 1829 when they were finally allowed to depart for Zululand

4

Wizard Whose Liver Is Black

In many African kingdoms, regicide and bloody civil war long characterised the royal succession. It was no different in the Zulu kingdom where King Cetshwayo, the fourth in the line of monarchs, had a dream in which he was visited by the *amadlozi* of two of his royal predecessors. They said to him, '[W]e shall give you only one son, for you of the Zulu [royal house] are always killing one another in disputing the kingship if there are many of you.'[1] That was almost inevitable in Zulu society where the king and all men of high status had a large number of wives and a great many children. In an attempt to secure a smooth succession, the amaZulu adopted the practise of recognising as heir the eldest son of a man's designated *inkosikazi*, or great wife (who had not necessarily been his first-married wife, but was deemed of suitably distinguished lineage to carry on the line, or who was particularly favoured). However, in the royal house this procedure was not necessarily followed. It was considered too dangerous for an ageing king to have an official heir (*inkosana*) hovering impatiently in the wings, so naming him was delayed until the last moment to reduce the possibility of usurpation. An alternative was, like Shaka, to have no acknowledged children at all. But this was no solution either, because then any male of the Zulu royal lineage was technically qualified to mount the throne, and a succession dispute would be the consequence.

Shaka himself was a usurper.[2] The *inkosana* of his father Senzangakhona kaJama was Sigujana, the son of his eighth and favourite wife, Bhibhi kaNkobe. On Senzangakhona's death in about 1816, Shaka turned to his half-brother, Ngwadi kaNgendeyana, to arrange to have Sigujana ambushed and stabbed to death when he went down to the river to bathe. In commemoration of his obliging treachery, Ngwadi would be come to be known as 'the stick of one who cuts down trees',[3] and would remain high in Shaka's favour.

Even with Sigujana out of the way, Shaka might have struggled to be accepted as *inkosi* of the Zulu chiefdom, had it not been for the support of his aunt, Mnkabayi kaJama, Senzangakhona's

---

1   *JSA* 3, p.201: Mkebeni ka Dabulamanzi, 18 September 1921.
2   For Shaka's seizure of the Zulu chieftainship, see, Laband, *Assassination*, pp. 20–6.
3   *JSA* 3, p.151: Mkando ka Dhlova, 13 July 1902.

older, unmarried sister.[4] Tall with very small breasts and described as sleek and softly fat,[5] she was celebrated as a wise facilitator, 'The opener of all the main gates so that people may enter.'[6] Zulu society was certainly patriarchal, but a king's or chief's female relations, his wives and the widows of his predecessor, exercised subtle authority from behind the scenes. Royal women thus had it in their power to manipulate the outcome of the succession, and of Mnkabayi it was said that the Zulu kings were 'placed' by her.[7]

Once firmly on the throne, Shaka ruthlessly executed all those whom he suspected of opposing his right to rule. Only then, did all of Shaka's surviving half-brothers, thoroughly cowed, tender him their allegiance, or *ukukhonza*.[8] But the more ambitious or disgruntled among these *abantwana*, or princes of the Zulu royal lineage, bided their time until the opportunity arose to strike back against the usurper. The evidence indicates that they made three attempts to assassinate Shaka, one in 1824, another in 1827 and a third in 1828 at the end of the Mpondo campaign. All three failed, but the plotters succeeded in hiding their tracks, even though Shaka's suspicions were certainly aroused.[9]

So, Shaka did what so many other rulers have done when confronted by treacherous, but highly-born conspirators. He sent them away on a dangerous military campaign to give himself a breathing space, and with the hope that they would perish.[10] Even before John Cane set off on Shaka's second embassy to the Cape, the king had despatched his fully mobilised army of some 15,000 men north on a risky and unnecessary campaign against Soshangane kaZikode of the migratory Gaza kingdom, one of the Ndwandwe fragments making their way north after Shaka's victory over them in 1819. In 1828 the Gaza kingdom was situated over 400 miles away in the hill country to the north-west of Delagoa Bay, somewhat elevated above the humid and malaria-infested bushveld south of the Olifants, or Lepelle River—known to the Zulu as the Bhalule. Shaka made sure that all his senior brothers marched north with the Bhalule *impi*, and they in turn would have understood his motives and must have feared that he would execute them if they survived the campaign and returned home. Several of the *abantwana* therefore secretly agreed to kill Shaka, but were uncertain which of them should succeed him as king. The two leading contenders were Dingane whom Shaka seemingly favoured as his likely successor and who, like him, was a member of the amaWombe *ibutho* and wore an *isicoco*. The other was his half-brother, Mhlangana. Genealogically, Mhlangana was probably Shaka's rightful *inkosana* because he was born of Mzondwase, Senzangakhona's fifth wife, whereas Dingane was

---

4   Mnkabayi had a twin sister, Mmama, but she was of lesser significance because 'among Zulus there is a great and small twin; the first born is the great one.' (*JSA* 6, p.12: Socwatsha, 28 December 1901.)
5   *JSA* 2, p.92; Magidigidi ka Nobebe, 8 May 1905; *JSA* 5, pp.40, 84: Ngidi, 14 August 1904 and 22 October 1905.
6   Deuteronomy Bhekinkosi Ntuli, '"Praises Will Remain"', in Natalie Wood (coordinator), *Zulu Treasures: Of Kings and Commoners. A Celebration of the Material Culture of the Zulu People* (Ulundi: KwaZulu Cultural Museum; Durban: The Local History Museums, 1996), p.29.
7   *JSA* 5, p.84: Ngidi, 22 October 1905. See Ndlovu, 'Women's power', pp. 114–19.
8   *Annals* I, p. 168: N. Isaacs, 'History of Chaka'; Stuart and Malcolm (eds), *Fynn's Diary*, pp.13–14; *JSA* 1, p.182: Jantshi, 14 February 1903; *JSA* 2, p.80: Magidi ka Ngomane, 7 May 1903; *JSA* 4, p. 205: Ndhlovu ka Timuni, 9 November 1902.
9   Laband, *Assassination*, pp.13–19, 99–101, 124.
10 For the Bhalule *impi*, see Laband, *Assassination*, pp.119–27.

the son of Mphikase kaMyiyeya, Senzangakhona's sixth wife.[11] Dingane and Mhlangana were known to be fond of each other, and decided to put the matter of the succession aside until after they had dealt with Shaka.[12]

Their plans made, the royal conspirators abandoned the army and made their way back towards kwaDukuza, Shaka's main *ikhanda* south of the Thukela River.[13] Once in the vicinity of the *ikhanda*, they made secret contact with Mbopha kaSitayi, Shaka's principal but ambitious *inceku* who, in his position as the king's confidential body servant, possessed the easy access to his royal master that was crucial for the planned assassination. Critically for the success of the plot, Mnkabayi, Shaka's redoubtable aunt who had secured the throne for him, gave the conspirators her active blessing. Having once been Shaka's most ardent supporter, she had come to believe—along with a great many of his subjects— that his incessant campaigns and repeated acts of violence were destroying the kingdom.

Predictably, the circumstances surrounding Shaka's assassination are difficult to reconstruct with any precision.[14] Towards sundown on 23 September 1828 the assassins approached Shaka who was seated in the open space outside his hut in kwaNyakamubi, the small *umuzi* built outside kwaDukuza where he could relax in relative privacy. Wrapped snugly against the evening chill in one of his woven blankets obtained from the Port Natal traders, he was complacently watching his immense herds of cattle being driven homewards. It is uncertain which of the three assassins killed Shaka—perhaps all three stabbed him—but the accounts closest to the moment of his death are in agreement that Shaka only had time to gasp out incredulously, 'What is the matter my father's children?'[15] Later, retrospectively prophetic last words were ascribed to him, all referring to the impending rule of the white men, frequently described as 'swallows' because they came 'up from the sea' like those migratory birds,[16] and because they also build their houses of mud (that is, bricks).

With Shaka dead, Dingane and Mhlangana agreed to wait until the Bhalule *impi* returned and made known which of the two *abantwana* it favoured as Shaka's successor.[17] Dingane, who was extremely anxious to placate the vengeful fury of his murdered brother's *idlozi* (spirit), gave him an appropriately royal burial. Meanwhile, with the Bhalule *impi* still away on campaign and their available military resources very limited, Shaka's assassins were anxious to avoid any external conflicts. Before most of the Port Natal traders—who feared being caught up in a Zulu civil war—sailed for Port Elizabeth on 1 December 1828, Dingane and Mhlangana

---

11 *JSA* 6, p.12: Socwatsha, 28 December 1901.
12 For the plot to assassinate Shaka and its implementation, see Laband, *Assassination*, pp.128–40.
13 In 1873 the village of Stanger was laid out on the site. In 2006 the name of Stanger was officially change to KwaDukuza.
14 Not even the date of the assassination is certain. Shaka Day, which was subsumed into Heritage Day in South Africa in 1995, is celebrated annually on 24 September, but contemporary evidence makes it most likely that Shaka was killed on Tuesday, 23 September 1828.
15 *RN* 2, p. 74, no. 78, annex. 1, enc. 1: H.F. Fynn to Lt. Col. Somerset, 28 November 1828. The English translation of the Zulu wording varies from one version to the next, but the meaning is the same. Essentially the same formulation can be found as an element in longer versions of Shaka's last words preserved in oral memory. See Laband, *Assassination*, p.140.
16 *JSA* 1, p.307: Lunguza ka Mpukane, 13 March 1909.
17 For Shaka's burial, the power struggle between his assassins and Dingane's accession, see Laband, *Assassination*, pp.141–53.

entrusted Farewell with a verbal message for the Cape officials that assured them that 'now Chaka was dead, they wished to live on friendly terms with every nation and by no means would do anything to displease them.'[18]

Everything would depend on how the Bhalule *impi* would take the news of Shaka's assassination. It had met with disaster on the campaign and had failed to take any of the Gaza strongholds. Mdlaka kaNcidi, its commander, was leading it home and deliberately taking his time for fear of reporting back to Shaka whom he had no reason to think was dead. Dingane was confident that the returning army would favour him, but Mhlangana insisted he had a better claim than Dingane because he had taken the most active part in killing Shaka and had jumped over his corpse, thus proclaiming that he was the murdered king's conqueror and successor. Ironically, it was this very assertion that undid him when in late November the senior members of the royal house and the *izikhulu* gathered to discuss the succession.

Mnkabayi dominated the meeting and convinced the assembled notables that a man who had killed his king was not fit to rule. It was therefore decreed that 'The one with the red assegai shall not rule.'[19] As for Dingane's undeniable part in the assassination, that was brushed aside on the grounds that he had merely caught hold of his brother while the other two stabbed him, and was therefore not guilty of shedding Shaka's blood.

The way was now clear for Dingane to be declared king, but what was to be done with Mhlangana? He had his many supporters, and to stave off a likely civil war Mnkabayi and her allies resolved that Mhlangana must be put to death. Egged on by Mnkabayi, Dingane invited Mhlangana to go bathing with him in the Mavivane, a small stream close by kwaDukuza. Mnkabayi's men were concealed at the spot, and sprang out to drown Mhlangana. Dingane's *izibongo* recalled the deed in these chilling words:

> Deep river pool at Mavivane, Dingana,
> The Pool is silent, and overpowering,
> It drowned someone intending to wash
> And he vanished, headring and all.[20]

A week or so after Mhlangana's was put to death, and some two months after Shaka's assassination, the Bhalule *impi* began at last drifting home through the coastal lands in small, exhausted groups, ill with malaria and dysentery, and on the verge of starvation, its numbers catastrophically reduced by about two-thirds. It was as Isaacs reflected, 'the most signal defeat the Zoolas had ever sustained.'[21]

The returning army found that Dingane, with the support of the *izikhulu*, had already stepped into Shaka's place. He was calling himself '*uMalamulela*' (Intervener) because he had intervened

---

18   *RN 2*, p.49, no. 49: F.G. Farewell to Lt. Col. Somerset, 15 December 1828.
19   *JSA* 4, p.346: Ndukwana ka Mbengwana, 27 December 1901.
20   D.K. Rycroft and A.B. Ngcobo (eds), *The Praises of Dingana (Izibongo zikaDingana)* (Pietermaritzburg: University of Natal Press; Durban: Killie Campbell Africana Library, 1988), p. 71.
21   Nathaniel Isaacs, edited by Louis Herman and Percival R. Kirby, *Travels and Adventures in Eastern Africa Descriptive of the Zoolus, Their Manners, Customs with a Sketch of Natal* (Cape Town: C. Struik, 1970), p. 173.

between the people and the madness of Shaka,[22] and his *izibongo* celebrate him as 'The one who acted on behalf of the people! Mediator!'[23] He summoned all those whose fathers had been killed by Shaka, saying he would 'bring them forward' (*ukuveza*). This earned him the name of '*uVezi*' for he brought forward those without father of mother.[24] Indeed, Dingane had moved very cannily and swiftly to win popular approval by decreeing that he would allow unmarried *amabutho* freely to enjoy premarital sex, and that he would immediately permit several of the older *amabutho* to assume the heading, take wives and set up as *abanumzane*. He also relaxed military discipline and ensured that warriors serving at the *amakhanda* were well supplied with meat. Consequently, as the bringer of peace to war-weary Zululand,[25] Dingane did not find it difficult to win over the dispirited remnants of the Bhalule *impi* and persuade them to accept – or, at least, not oppose—his succession.

With that assurance, the Day of Interrogation could be held. This, King Cetshwayo later explained, was the day of ceremonial questioning when 'all the great men of the country assemble and talk to one another about the heir, whom they look upon as king already.' They say to each other, continued Cetshwayo, '"You must take care of this king and not act out of an evil heart against him."' Having agreed among themselves, they would then send a deputation to the *inkosana* inviting him to leave the *ikhanda* where he had been living and to transfer to the former king's chief *ikhanda* 'as king'.[26] And so it was with Dingane, at about 30 years of age the undisputed *inkosana* selected (it must be said) by Mnkabayi and acclaimed as king by the nation. As soon as Dingane heard he had been chosen, he burst out alone from the assembly and performed an energetic war-dance (*ukugiya*) and then entered the *isihlambelo* (the sacred enclosure where the king washes). When he emerged 'he was covered in coloured patches…of different medicines used on him by the doctors, who were strengthening him'.[27]

Despite initially governing with a light hand to gain popular support, Dingane was soon ruling with as heavy a hand as had Shaka. He first set about killing almost all his brothers, and his *izibongo* crowed:

> Hornless calf of the daughter of Donda, [ancestor of Mphikase, Dingane's mother]
> That went and kicked the other calves,
> And blood flowed from their nostrils.[28]

In later days, Mpande would publicly declare that while Dingane 'used to say he had killed Tshaka for troubling the people; in fact it was he who finished off the Zulu [royal] house.'[29] And indeed, in the eyes of some amaZulu, extensive fratricide did make Dingane 'a bad king'.[30] Nevertheless, most understood that Dingane, having already had a hand in killing both Shaka

---

22 *JSA* 1, p.6: Baleka ka Mpitikazi, 16 July 1919.
23 Rycroft and Ngcobo (eds), *Praises*, p.75.
24 *JSA* 5, p. 339: Singcofela kaMtshungu, 29 March 1910.
25 *JSA* 6, p. 264: Tununu, 31 May 1903.
26 Webb and Wright (eds), *Zulu King Speaks*, pp. 97–98: Cetshwayo's evidence to the Cape Government Commission on Native Laws and Customs, 7 July 1881: Additions and Notes VII.
27 *JSA* 6, p. 97: Socwatsha, 26 October 1913.
28 Rycroft and Ncobo (eds), *Praises of Dingane*, p. 95.
29 *JSA 4*, p. 94: Mtshapi ka Noradu, 11 May 1918.
30 *JSA 1*, p.19: Baleni ka Silwana, 10 May 1914.

and Mhlangana, naturally feared that his surviving brothers 'would one day rise and kill him' in his turn, and that he had to act pre-emptively.[31] In his *izibongo* Dingane is called 'Wizard whose liver is black, even among his father's children.' An actual *umthakathi*, or wizard, was loathed and feared, but in metaphorical terms a 'wizard' denoted a person with amazing powers; while a 'black liver' meant profound courage. Dingane was therefore being lauded for his resolve in purging about 20 of his brothers.[32]

Having disposed of most of his brothers and side-lined the few survivors, Dingane next rid himself of Shaka's leading councillors and military commanders, along with their wives and children, as well as his favourites and close associates. Dingane also eliminated a number of over-powerful, independently minded *izikhulu* who might have been tempted to resist his authority.[33] Sothobe, who had led Shaka's first embassy to the Cape, had astutely thrown his hand in with the conspirators before their assassination of Shaka and was the most eminent survivor of Shaka's regime. Dingane appointed him his viceroy in the region south of the Thukela River, and honoured him by addressing him as 'father' on account of his age and status.[34] As for Mbopha, as a regicide he could not be permitted to live and prosper. Dingane cannily succeeded in presenting Mbopha as the ambitious and unscrupulous schemer principally responsible for Shaka's assassination,[35] and his execution satisfied the returning *Bhalule impi*.

The inescapable fact was that if Dingane wished to be an effective ruler, he had to maintain the fundamental character of the monarchy Shaka had established, and had to be seen to assert his overriding power and authority. Nevertheless, there was leeway to make certain adjustments of his own. He was concerned about Shaka's military overreach to the south, and decreed that the Mzimkhulu must be regarded as the southernmost boundary of the Zulu kingdom because 'the land south of the river belonged to Faku, the Pondo king.'[36] Dingane was also uneasy with Shaka's decision in 1826 to centre royal authority south of the Thukela at kwaDukuza. He was probably right to fear that such close proximity to Port Natal gave the traders an inordinate degree of influence over Zulu policy. Consequently, on becoming king he immediately moved the hub of the kingdom away from kwaDukuza and back north across the Thukela to its traditional core in the emaKhosini valley where, in 1829, he built his new 'great place', emGungundlovu.

Suspicious as he might have been of the hunter-traders, Dingane resolved to maintain relations with Port Natal. Like Shaka before him, he continued to view them as the means through which he could open diplomatic relations with the British officials at the Cape in order to reassure them of his pacific intentions and of his desire to facilitate trade. His choice fell on John Cane, 'Jana', who had led Shaka's second diplomatic mission, to convey this message. Travelling overland, Cane's embassy reached Grahamstown on 21 November 1830, but got no further. This time, the officials were non-committal in dealing with Cane and declined to accept the 'four elephant's teeth' Dingane had sent as a present.[37] Disappointed, Cane returned

---

31 *JSA* 6, p.98: Socwatsha, 26 October, 1913.
32 Rycroft and Ncobo (eds), *Praises*, pp.87, 175. See too, *JSA* 6, p.254: Tununu, 28 May 1903.
33 Webb and Wright (eds), *Zulu King Speaks*, p.10. For a list of henchmen executed, see *JSA* 2, p.272: Maziyana ka Mahlabeni, 22 April 1905; and also, those named in Dingane's praises, Rycroft and Ncobo (eds), *Praises*, pp.87, 89.
34 *JSA* 6, p.281: Tununu.
35 *JSA* 6, p.97: Socwatsha, 20 October 1913.
36 *JSA* 4, p. 7: Mqaikana ka Yenge, 10 May 1916.
37 *Annals* I, pp.196 –197: D. Campbell to Lt. Col. John Bell, 26 November 1830.

to Zululand without any specific undertaking from the Cape officials. Dingane was furious, and in April 1831 sent an *impi* to seize Cane's cattle as punishment for his failure. He and the other Port Natal settlers took to the bush, and it was several months before Dingane's temper had cooled sufficiently for them to feel it was safe enough to return.[38]

In Dingane's message Cane had relayed to the Cape authorities, the king had expressed his intention of living 'in peace and harmony' with his neighbours, but he was no more able to do that than had Shaka. He was likewise obliged to keep his *amabutho* employed and well rewarded, and his *izikhulu* content with the lavish redistribution of booty. So, raids against his African neighbours continued, although he kept his army out of the Cape's proclaimed sphere of interest. Some of the chiefdoms integrated by Shaka into the Zulu kingdom seized the opportunity presented by Dingane's initially uncertain hold on power to attempt to break away. The new king could not afford the loss of subjects and their wealth in cattle, and had no choice but to act harshly against the rebel chiefdoms to dissuade others from contemplating revolt.[39]

As a consequence, it soon appeared to the Port Natal hunter-traders and the Cape officials alike that very little had changed with Shaka's death. Under Dingane the Zulu kingdom would continue to be an unpredictable, bellicose, and destabilising element threatening all of south-eastern Africa. But the Port Natal hunter-traders hung on, despite periodic scares. The Zulu kingdom continued to present commercial prospects for merchants and opportunities for settlement that were tempting to hardy spirits among traders and would-be settlers in the Cape. For their part, the colonial officials had a separate incentive for keeping a wary eye on developments in the Zulu kingdom. The report reached Cape Town that in late 1830 an American schooner had been trading for several weeks at Port Natal, and that there were apparently designs to plant an American settlement in Zululand. The Governor of the Cape, Sir Lowry Cole, alerted the Colonial Office as to 'how embarrassing such a neighbour might eventually prove' to the Cape. He went on to report that to forestall the Americans he had decided to follow up Cane's recent but abortive diplomatic mission by sending a person he could trust to Zululand 'to ascertain the real wishes of Dingaan … as well as the nature and capabilities of his country.'[40] Perhaps, if these proved favourable, it would be in British interests to intervene actively in Zululand.

---

38 Laband, *Zulu Nation*, p.75.
39 Laband, *Zulu Kings*, pp. 108–109.
40 *Annals* 1, p.196: Sir Lowry Cole to R.W. Hay, 11 January 1831.

5

An Inexpedient Scheme of Colonisation

The individual whom Governor Cole selected for the Cape's mission to Dingane was a Scottish assistant staff surgeon on the medical staff of the Cape's British garrison, Dr Andrew Smith. He seemed the ideal choice because in 1828–1829 he had already undertaken an official mission of scientific exploration up the west coast of southern Africa.[1] In 1829 Smith had written to Cole seeking his support for further, extensive expeditions to the interior of the sub-continent that had the objectives of extending knowledge of the region, introducing its 'barbarous' inhabitants to the advantages of Western civilisation, and of opening it up under British control to the benefits of agriculture and commerce.[2]

On the Governor's apparently verbal instructions the purpose of Smith's expedition was kept under wraps, and Smith gave out that his journey to Zululand was being undertaken solely for the scientific purpose of describing the flora, fauna, and human inhabitants he encountered. As a consequence of this secrecy, the true aims of Smith's mission are to be found only in scattered contemporary references, in the private field notes that he made during his mission and after his return, and in the report he submitted in 1834. Much of the anthropological and historical material he collated about the Zulu in these sources came from two of the Port Natal traders, Henry Francis Fynn (Mbuyazi) and Francis Farewell (Febana), whom he consulted closely.[3]

When Smith set off by ox-wagon from Grahamstown on 8 January 1832 for Port Natal, only a few traders, missionaries and emissaries had gone that way before him. There was no settled route to follow and the traveller was at the mercy of unreliable local guides. That is why Smith, who foresaw the commercial potential of the greater movement of goods between the Cape and Zululand, wasted no time in publishing his detailed itinerary for the benefit of future traders and settlers journeying that way. Smith finally reached Port Natal on 27 March, 79 days after setting forth, having travelled on average only three-and a-half miles a day. Smith moved on to emGungundlovu, which he reached on 3 April, five days after leaving Port Natal.

1   Smith, the son of Scottish shepherd, served in the Cape from 1821 to 1837. He eventually rose to be Director-General of the Army and Ordinance Medical Department, and was made KCB on his retirement in 1858. See Tabler, *Pioneers*, pp.95–6.
2   Percival R. Kirby (ed.), *Andrew Smith and Natal. Documents Relating to the Early History of That Province* (Cape Town: The Van Riebeeck Society, 1955), pp.243–6: Dr Andrew Smith to Sir Lowry Cole, 26 May 1829.
3   Kirby (ed.), *Smith*, pp.1–7.

There he had several interviews with Dingane, and returned to Port Natal on 14 April.[4] The observations Smith made on his exploratory visit to Dingane were significant for being those of a scientifically trained outsider who cast a sharp, acquisitive eye over the Zulu king, his capital and his kingdom; while the conclusions he drew would go far to forming opinion in the Cape about the Zulu country.

When in late June 1832 Dr Smith returned to the Cape from Zululand, word soon spread of what he had found there, confirming for Cape merchants the desirability of the territory for colonisation. Determined to overcome longstanding official reluctance to recognise Port Natal and its environs as a British settlement, a group of Cape Town merchants held a public meeting on Monday, 20 January 1834 in order to petition the British government to sponsor a settlement in Zululand. The resulting memorial addressed to the King in Council attracted 190 signatures.[5] The petitioners invited Smith to write a detailed, accompanying report to elucidate the memorial.[6] Both the memorial and Smith's report emphasised Zululand's desirability as a future colony since the territory's geographical situation, soil and climate were eminently suitable for profitable trade and agriculture. A further motivation for forming a permanent settlement—one that was aired during the meeting held in January 1834 rather than in the subsequent memorial—reflected the prevailing spirit of the age. Increasingly, people in Britain were embracing the expansion of Christianity as central to the whole imperial venture. Protestant missionary societies had been growing out of a renewed proselytising movement in Britain, and by the end of the eighteenth century evangelical Christians and the missionaries they sponsored overseas were going confidently forth to convert the world. Consequently, missionary endeavour was becoming a significant factor in colonial policy and an inextricable element in colonial societies.[7] As Advocate Cloete expressed it at the January meeting, a colony in Zululand would 'serve as a starting point from whence Christianity and civilization would flow into the interior of Africa.'[8]

But, as Dr Smith made very clear in his report, more was in play than making a commercial profit in Zululand and evangelising Africans: strategic imperial concerns were at stake. From his personal observations while in Zululand, and from 'various conversations' with the Zulu king himself, he downplayed the assertion made in the memorial that the Cape remained 'liable to hostile incursions by the Zoolas'.[9] Nonetheless, such apprehensions were not entirely groundless. In July 1833 the traders at Port Natal had fallen out with Dingane and fled once

4   Smith's itinerary can be put together from his letter to the *Graham's Town Journal*, from his field notes, and from the diary written by one of his companions, Carl Friedrich Drège. See Kirby (ed.), *Smith*, pp.9–47.
5   Kirby (ed.), *Smith*, pp.146–51: report in *South African Commercial Advertiser*, 25 January 1834; *RN 2*, pp. 251–2, no. 199, annex. 1: Hamilton Ross et al. to His Majesty the King in Council, n.d. (Merchant's Memorial).
6   *RN 2*, pp.253–62, no. 19, annex. 2: Andrew Smith, Report on the memorial of merchants and others of the Cape of Good Hope regarding the occupation of Natal, 6 May 1834 (Smith's Report).
7   Andrew Porter, 'Religion, Missionary Enthusiasm, and Empire', in Andrew Porter and Alaine Low (eds), *The Oxford History of the British Empire*, vol. III, *The Nineteenth Century*, (Oxford: Oxford University Press, 2001), pp.222–3, 228.
8   Kirby (ed.), *Smith*, p. 147.
9   Merchants' Memorial, p. 251.

again to the Cape in fear of their lives, only for the Zulu king to lure them back with soft words and assurances.[10]

More dramatically, and at much the same time, a Zulu army several hundred strong, supported by several thousand auxiliaries from local chiefdoms, appeared before the Portuguese settlement of Lourenço Marques. Relations between Dingane and Dionisio Antonio Ribeira, who had been the governor of Lourenço Marques since 6 October 1829, had been deteriorating for some time. Dingane, who regarded the Portuguese at Lourenço Marques as his tributaries (much as he did the Port Natal settlers), expected Ribeira to pay him tribute. But Ribeira encountered economic difficulties in meeting Dingane's demands once the slave trade with Brazil became illegal in February 1830, significantly reducing the value of Lourenço Marques's export trade. To make things worse, Ribeira evidently lacked both tact and common sense, so when in 1830 Dingane demanded tribute as usual, the governor provocatively responded by handing his emissaries two cannon balls and two musket balls, declaring these were the only 'beads' the Zulu king could expect from him. To add injury to insult, in order to secure better control over the elephant ivory trade, Ribeira then set about expanding Portuguese sway in the region of Delagoa Bay, imposing titular rule over various chiefs whom Dingane regarded as his tributaries.

Thoroughly provoked, Dingane resolved to punish Ribeira as he had the Port Natal settlers when they defied him. However, when the Zulu *impi* descended on Lourenço Marques on 26 July 1833, Ribeira succeeded in buying it off with 100 large brass bangles. But Dingane was not satisfied with this outcome, and his army returned with specific instruction to punish Ribeira for his effrontery. Warned of the *impi's* approach, Ribeira took refuge on Chefina Island 10 miles offshore from Lourenço Marques. The amaZulu sacked the abandoned fort as a symbolic act to assert their king's mastery, but sensibly left untouched the surrounding buildings from which trade was conducted. As for Ribeira, their main quarry, when he tried to make for safer territory further north up the coast, his boat was driven ashore by bad weather and the waiting amaZulu captured and executed him on 12 October 1833. Having forcefully made his point and reasserted his authority in the environs of Delagoa Bay, Dingane successfully demanded tribute from Ribeira's replacement, Dario Rodrigues de Vasconcellos, who took over as governor of Lourenço Marques on 21 August 1834.[11]

Smith naturally knew of Dingane's two recent strikes against Port Natal and Lourenço Marques, but they certainly could be explained as legitimate acts to maintain his authority in his own realm, and (in his opinion) did not indicate the Dingane had any hostile intentions against the Cape. Indeed, Smith was 'firmly persuaded' that Dingane was eager to enter into an alliance with the Cape, that he valued the trade with its merchants, and that he would refrain from attacking any of the Colony's African allies.[12] Yet, if the Cape was in no imminent danger from Dingane, Smith went along with the further argument made in the memorial that a British colony centred on Port Natal would prevent Dingane from obtaining yet more firearms 'from the irregular trade with foreign vessels.'[13] Smith knew that Dingane had recently bartered 'nearly fifty stands of arms and a tolerable quantity of gunpowder' from an American ship. In

---

10 Felix N.C Okoye, 'Dingane: A Reappraisal', *Journal of African History*, 10: 2 (1969), pp. 228–9.
11 Gerhard Licsegang, 'Dingane's Attack on Lourenço Marques in 1833', *Journal of African History*, 10: 4 (1969), pp.571–8.
12 Smith's Report, p. 258.
13 Merchants' Memorial, p. 252.

conversation with Smith, Dingane had told him, moreover, that hitherto the amaZulu had employed firearms 'only in their little wars', but warned that 'should he find himself unable to overcome his enemies by the weapons most familiar to his people he would then have recourse to them.'[14]

It has commonly been assumed that the amaZulu in Dingane's time had no use for firearms, but this was not so. Indeed, in his *izibongo* Dingane was celebrated as being 'like a fighting-stick of thunder [a gun],'[15] a clear recognition of the weapon's awesome power. Smith, along with all settlers and soldiers in the Cape, was alert to the dangers posed by a large number of firearms coming into African hands, and was keen to prevent this development in Zululand. What complicated the matter was that Dingane's current suppliers were Americans who had their eyes on establishing a base of their own on the Zululand coast, both for their trading vessels and for the 'hundreds of American whalers nearby the whole year off the coast.'[16] In other words, for strategic reasons Smith was advocating the British occupation of Port Natal and environs in order to forestall a competitive American presence, as well as to prevent the amaZulu from acquiring large numbers of firearms which, in the future, they might conceivably use against the Cape.

Smith's report, based as it was on his first-hand impressions of the Zulu country, its people and its ruler, inevitably carried much weight with merchants, speculators, prospective settlers and the officials responsible for the Cape's military security. In forming popular colonial preconceptions of the Zulu kingdom, the report also played a critical part in creating the convincing – but misleading – notion that Dingane was such a cruel and unpopular king that it would easy to overthrow him and establish a secure British settlement. In making this case, Smith was not above playing the fashionable evangelical card when he suggested that it would be to the benefit of the downtrodden indigenes if Dingane were dethroned:

> All his [Dingane's] people ... would with pleasure attach themselves to any power that could ensure their protection ... If a military party were to be posted near the Bay I would engage in twelve months after its arrival to be able to dethrone Dingaan by means of the very people who are at present his support. It is impossible for men to feel attachment to such a monster and it appears to me an act of great inhumanity to permit his murdering, torturing and destroying even hundreds of his own subjects in the course of a day when only the most trifling exertion would be required effectively to restrain him.[17]

Meanwhile, on 10 January 1834 a new governor took up his post at the Cape. Major General Sir Benjamin D'Urban had distinguished himself in the Peninsular War (1807–1814) during the struggle against Napoleon, and had lately served as the Governor of Antigua. However, despite his fine military reputation, he was known to be slow and cautious, and had yet to take the full measure of the colony he had been sent to govern. Nevertheless, his sympathies lay instinctively

---

14 Smith's Report, p.262.
15 Rycroft (ed.), and Ngcobo (ed.), *Praises of Dingana*, p.75.
16 Smith's Report, p.262.
17 Smith's Report, pp.261–2.

with the settlers and their aspirations.[18] Thus, when on 17 June 1834 D'Urban finally transmitted the merchants' memorial to London together with Smith's report, his covering letter stated that he believed it would be 'found advantageous hereafter' if the government responded positively.[19] Lord Melbourne's economising Whig administration did not take the bait, however. On 10 November 1834 T. Spring Rice, the Secretary of State for War and Colonies, tersely informed D'Urban in a despatch that arrived only in March 1835 that 'in the present state of the finances of the Cape any additional expense for the establishment of a new settlement would be highly inconvenient and could not with propriety be incurred.'[20]

The Cape Town mercantile speculators might have been foiled, but the residents of Port Natal now made their own bid for the official British occupation of Port Natal. At a meeting on 23 June 1835 they resolved to lay out a town at the settlement to be called D'Urban in honour of the governor whose support they needed to forward their accompanying petition to the British government.[21] The petition urged the annexation of all the country between the Mzimkhulu River to the south and the Thukela River to the north – the entire southern half of Dingane's kingdom—as a full-blown British colony, to be known as Victoria in honour of the young princess who was heir to the British throne then occupied by her uncle, King William IV. The 30 petitioners urged D'Urban to adopt their cause 'for the sake of humanity, for the upholding of the British character in the eyes of the natives, for the well-being of this increasing community, for the cause of morality and religion.'[22] D'Urban gave the petition his earnest recommendation for, as he explained to Lord Glenelg, the new Secretary of State for War and Colonies, his growing 'personal experience of the country' had convinced him how necessary it was to annex 'Victoria' in the interests of the Cape's future security and prosperity.[23] But Glenelg was an Evangelical Christian, ill at ease with the many questionable consequences of colonial conquest and the expense it entailed. He responded unequivocally on 29 March 1836, informing D'Urban that his government were 'so deeply persuaded of the inexpediency of engaging in any scheme of colonisation or of acquiring any further enlargement of territory in Southern Africa that I feel precluded from offering any encouragement of the project.'[24]

Although these two attempts to cajole a reluctant government in London into annexing Port Natal were both rejected, details of the merchants' memorial, Smith's report and the traders' petition became widely known in colonial society through the circulation of newspapers and by word of mouth. Many farmers and speculators in the Cape continued to be excited by the possibilities of a prosperous future in the region of Port Natal or elsewhere in the subcontinent. In mid-February 1834 D'Urban learned of the rumours that 'certain individuals' who were 'discontented with their situation and prospects in the colony' were intending to move beyond

---

18 Laband, *Land Wars*, pp.171–2, 177, 182.
19 *RN 2*, p.250, no. 199: B. D'Urban to E.G. Stanley, 17 June 1834.
20 *RN 2*, pp.276–7, no. 213: T. Spring Rice to D'Urban, 10 November 1834; pp.281–2, no. 218: John Bell to members of the Commercial Exchange, 12 March 1835.
21 Dr B.J.T Leverton (ed.), *Records of Natal, Volume Three August 1835–June 1838* (Pretoria: The Government Printer, 1990) (*RN 3*), pp. 6, 18, no. 10, annex. 1, enc. 4: Resolution of Meeting, Port Natal 23 June 1835. However, the name Port Natal only fell out of common usage with the proclamation in 1854 of the Borough of Durban.
22 *RN 3*, p.16, no. 10, annex. 1, enc. 3: James Collis and 29 others, n.d. [23 June 1835].
23 *RN 3*, pp.9–10, no. 10: D'Urban to Lord Glenelg, 4 December 1835.
24 *RN 3*, pp.30–1, no. 17: Glenelg to D'Urban, 29 March 1836.

its borders, some over the Orange River onto the highveld, and others up the east coast. The latter, inspired by the 'florid descriptions' of its fertility disseminated by traders and the likes of Dr Smith, had their eyes on the so-called 'unoccupied land' between the St John's River in Mpondo territory and Port Natal, at which place they hoped to find a ready market for their agricultural produce.[25] D'Urban was singularly unimpressed by those harbouring these intentions. On 6 June 1834 he uncompromisingly laid down official policy regarding 'the farmers or other inhabitants [of the Cape] who wilfully choose to wander, with or without their cattle, beyond the frontier line, which is at once illegal and imprudent.' Such people, D'Urban made crystal clear, were entitled to no official protection if they ran themselves 'into scrapes by such unauthorized pursuits.'[26]

Undeterred by this tough line, groups of Dutch-speaking settlers who were indeed contemplating moving from the British-ruled Cape, decided to send out three exploring parties, *kommissietrekke*, to find a suitable place to settle. One, under Johannes Pretorius, went north-west over the Orange River into what is now Namibia, and brought back an unfavourable report. A second, under J. Scholtz, penetrated as far north as the Soutpansberg, a mountain range just south of the Limpopo River, and was encouraged by what it found. A third *kommissietrek*, organised by some of the farmers of the Albany and Uitenhage Districts of the Eastern Cape, had the territory around Port Natal as its objective. They chose Petrus Lafras Uys to lead the expedition.

Piet Uys, as he was commonly known, was born in 1797 at Hessequas Kloof in the Swellendam District, the second son of Jacobus Uys, a miller nicknamed 'Koos Bybel' [Bible] on account of his deep, fundamentalist Calvinist faith that he instilled in his family. In 1823 'Koos Bybel' moved east with his family to the Uitenhage District, to the farm Brakfontein at the mouth of the Kromme River. At the age of 18 Piet Uys married his 16-year-old cousin Alida, and they had three sons whom they brought up on his own farm on the Bushman's River. Piet Uys was stocky, blue-eyed and fair-haired with a long, shaggy beard. He was known for his quick temper but also esteemed for his fairness and honourable conduct, his religious convictions and kindly disposition. Although without much education, he wrote clear and concise Dutch and was well-spoken. He was, in other words, a natural leader with many friends among his Boers neighbours as well as among British settlers, officials and officers.[27]

On 19 July 1834 Piet Uys and three other farmers from the Uitenhage District gave notice of their intention to proceed beyond the limits of the colony 'for the purpose of trafficking with the bordering nations', and on 27 August 1834 received D'Urban's permission to do so.[28] Uys and his party of 14, including two of his brothers (one of whom brought his wife along) left for Port Natal on 8 September 1834. They reached the Port in December where they held discussions with the traders, went hunting in its neighbourhood, and negotiated at a distance with Dingane's envoys across the Thukela River which was in spate and unpassable. It would

---

25 *RN 2*, pp.241–2, no. 195: Acting Secretary to Government, 14 February 1834
26 *RN 2*, pp.248–9, no. 198, annex 1, enc. 1: memorandum by D'Urban, 6 June 1834.
27 Ian S. Uys, 'Her Majesty's Loyal and Devoted Trekker Leader: Petrus Lafras Uys', *Natalia*, 18 (December 1988), p. 31. Ian S. Uys, 'A Boer Family', *Military History Journal*, 3: 6 (December 1976), <www.boereafrikana.com/Mense/Groot_Trek_Leiers/Piet_Uys/Piet_Uys.htm>, accessed 18 May 2020
28 *RN 2*, pp.269–70, no. 204: Memorial by Petrus Lafras Uys and three others to D'Urban, 19 July 1834.

seem that Dingane indicated he was willing to allow Boers to settle in his territory, although nothing definite was agreed upon. At that moment, in early 1835, news reached Uys and his party that war had broken out again on the Cape Eastern Frontier. They decided they must return and reached home in March 1835.[29]

It would seem from statements gathered by the resident magistrate of Uitenhage, along with reports from Port Natal, that Uys and his companions had returned to the Cape with every intention of soon quitting the Colony with their families and friends and settling permanently in Natal as farmers, rather than as traders. When in June 1835 the resident magistrate taxed Uys with harbouring this unlawful plan, Uys equivocated. He denied the charge and declared that he had never done more than let it be known that if the British took possession of Natal he would be happy to reside there, his intention being 'solely to assist in civilizing the savages.'[30]

Be that as it may, the war in the Cape had put any plans being formulated by Uys and the other returned leaders of the *kommissietrekke* on hold. On 21 December 1834 perhaps as many as 10,000 Xhosa fighters had launched a series of raids into the Colony along a broad, 90-mile front from the Winterberg in the north to Algoa Bay in the south. The ensuing conflict – the Sixth Cape Frontier War—proved the most brutal and wide-ranging along the Cape Eastern Frontier up to that time. The unanticipated Xhosa invasion of the Colony unleashed widespread panic and confusion in the Albany, Somerset, and Uitenhage Districts and inflicted considerable destruction and loss of property. Between 22 December 1834 and 12 January 1835, 32 settlers and about 80 of their Khoikhoi servants were reported killed (their womenfolk and children were spared, usually left to go free, as was the Xhosa custom in war), 456 farmhouses were besieged, 300 were pillaged and burned—including Piet Uys's on the Bushman's River – and (according to doubtless greatly inflated estimates) some 5,700 horses, 115,000 cattle and 162,000 sheep were driven off by the exalting amaXhosa. Thousands of colonists were reduced to destitution overnight.[31]

Uys did not shirk his duty. As a young man he had served in the Fifth Cape Frontier War of 1819–1820 with the Swellendam Commando, and in May 1835 he joined Commandant Linde's Swellendam Commando as a field cornet in Colonel John Peddie's First Division. When the commando was recalled, he served as a field commandant in Colonel Henry Somerset's Second Division. In September, during the final stage of the war, he was commended for bravery during a skirmish at the Keiskamma River. Uys ended his service in late October 1835 with his credentials as a leader of men and a courageous soldier firmly established among his fellow Boers.[32]

29 Uys, 'Petrus Lafras Uys', pp.31–2; Uys, 'Boer Family'.
30 *RN 2*, p.304, no. 221, annex. 1, enc. 3: statement by P.L. Uys, June 1835. See also, *RN 2*, pp.301–3, no. 221 and annex. 1, encs 1–3: in the case of Cobus Moolman and others, 24 June 1835; and *RN 3*, p.21, no. 10, annex. 2: Allen F. Gardiner to D'Urban, 24 November 1835.
31 Laband, *Land Wars*, pp. 175–6.
32 Uys, 'Petrus Lafras Uys', p.32.

6

On *Kommando*

Piet Uys's service on commando (*kommando*) in 1835 was no more than was expected of a frontier farmer such as he, and when a few years later the Boers trekked into the interior, they carried this military system with them. There it served the same function of organised armed violence—or merely the threat of it—that it had in the past when it had made possible the white settlers' gradual but persistent encroachment onto the original inhabitants' grazing and hunting lands to the north and east of the initial Dutch settlement at De Kaap.[1]

The VOC maintained a garrison of soldiers in Cape Town to defend the port and naval station against possible sea-borne attacks by rival European powers, as did the British when the Cape became their colonial possession. In addition, both powers raised a militia of burghers (white citizens), or *burgers*, that was periodically called upon as a mobile force to help protect the colony against African raiders on land. The Dutch first formed a *burger* corps in 1659 and made it a civic obligation for every *burger* to possess a musket in good working order. By the early eighteenth century every *burger* household, with the exception of those headed by widows, was armed with muskets, sabres, and pistols. The VOC required *burgers* to attend militia practice that included drilling and shooting. In 1670 the first, small horse-based military unit was formed to undertake frontier policing actions. After 1672 the militia was organised into local *kommandos* comprised of all able-bodied *burgers* between the ages of 16 and 60. When called out, they were responsible for supplying their own horse and saddle along with enough provisions for about a week. They served without pay, but the government continued to supply the *burgers* with muskets and ammunition until the British stopped the practice in

---

[1] For the *kommando* system, see George Tylden, 'The Development of the Commando System in South Africa , 1715 to 1922', *Africana Notes and News*, 13 (March 1958–December 1959), pp.303–13; Leśniewski, *The Zulu–Boer War*, pp.100–15; Damian O'Connor, 'Dragoons and Commandos: The Development of Mounted Infantry in Southern Africa 1654–1899', *RUSI Journal*, 153: 1 (February 2008), pp.90–3; William Kelleher Storey, *Guns, Race, and Power in Colonial South Africa* (Cambridge: Cambridge University Press, 2008), pp.34–7, 41; Timothy J. Stapleton, 'South Africa', in Ian F.W. Beckett (ed.), *Citizen Soldiers and the British Empire, 1837–1902* (London: Pickering and Chatto, 2012), pp.139–42; Hermann Giliomee, *The Afrikaners: Biography of a People* (Cape Town: Tafelberg; Charlottesville: University of Virginia Press, 2003), pp.26–7, 34, 163; Sandra Swart, *Riding High: Horses, Humans and History in South Africa* (Johannesburg: Wits University Press, 2010), pp.27–9; John Laband, *Historical Dictionary of the Zulu Wars* (Lanham, Maryland: The Scarecrow Press, 2009), pp.2–3, 52–3, 85.

1806. After which, members of a *kommando* had to find their own. A *burger* on *kommando* had no military uniform but continued to wear his ordinary, civilian clothes. Nor, by the early 19th century, was there any structured military training or parade ground drill. Although the British certainly questioned the reliability and effectiveness of the *burger kommando*, for want of a better alternative the British kept the system they had inherited from the Dutch going once the Cape fell under their rule.

The officers of a *kommando*—such as the *veldkornet* (or field cornet) who was responsible for raising and calling out men for service in his ward of a district and for commandeering transport and supplies; and the *kommandant* who led a *kommando* in the field—were elected by the *burgers* in an open, popular vote. The men invariably chose already prominent and charismatic figures in frontier society, such as Piet Uys, whom they were willing to follow. However, because officers were elected by their independently-minded and outspoken men and were merely first among equals, they struggled to ensure obedience, and relied on the *burgers'* voluntary acquiescence and trust in their leadership. There was no punishment for desertion, and officers knew that their men could simply leave service with a *kommando* and go home when they disagreed with plans adopted at a war council that was open to all, or with the way their officers were conducting the campaign. When affairs at home on their farms demanded their attention, they could pack up and go, or simply leave when they had had enough of the hardships of the campaign. The limited authority of officers and the incipient lack of discipline among the rank and file on *kommando* would continue to hamper effective military operations once the emigrating Boers encountered hostile African societies in the interior.

When embodied, a *kommando* was of indeterminate size. In the Cape a mere 20 men were considered in many circumstances a sufficient force to perform their quasi-police, quasi-military role effectively. But no *kommando* was ever a large force. For logistical and recruitment reasons the practical limit for a *kommando's* strength was no more than about 250 men, and to raise even this number required the cooperation of several districts. The 450 mounted *burgers* on *kommando* that served during the Fourth Cape Frontier War of 1811–1812 were as many as would ever take the field in the first half of the 19th century. The combined Boer *kommandos* during the war against Dingane would never reach that figure, and on occasion would be only a quarter that number.

Almost from its inception, the *kommando* system was associated with successful tactics that combined the three pillars of *burger* military supremacy: the musket, the horse and—to a sometimes critical but less frequent extent—the ox-wagon. All three were symbols of settler power, both real and symbolic, over those who did not possess these attributes of a superior civilisation that marked out the colonist from the native inhabitant.

The horse, as opposed to other species of the genus *Equus* like the zebra and quagga, is not indigenous to southern Africa.[2] It had been prevented from migrating south across the Sahara from the Mediterranean littoral on account of horse (or stallion) sickness that is endemic in central Africa and which is caused by the trypanosome parasite injected by the bite of the tsetse fly. In 1653 the Dutch imported the first four 'Javanese' ponies, arguably of Arab-Persian stock, from the Dutch East Indies. But it was no easy matter keeping horses alive in the Cape environment with its alarming array of parasitic and other diseases, including horse sickness

---

2   This discussion on horses at the Cape is based on Swart, *Riding High*, pp. 18–29, 31–3, 35–9.

that had been brought south by the migrating cattle herds from the north. Moreover, horses had to become accustomed to grazing the poor grasses of the Cape, and in the early years were vulnerable to predators like lions before they were shot out.

Faced with these challenges, the colonists created a breed of horse that suited their utilitarian purposes of transport needs and military pursuits such as patrolling their settlements and mounting raids at a considerable distance from base. Over the years, the original Indonesian ponies received an injection of bloodlines from around the world. This fusion of breeds finally produced the iconic *Boerperd* or Cape pony. The *Boerperd* was no elegant English Thoroughbred (later popular with the English at the Cape for horse-racing and smart equitation) and was very homely by comparison. Yet, these compact, short-legged ponies with their undistinguished heads and shaggy coats were extraordinarily hardy, possessing a strong constitution and an ingrown resistance to local diseases. By the eighteenth century the farmers who rode them had developed their own style of riding and, eschewing the trot or even the walk, schooled their horses in a slow, comfortable canter, known as a *trippel*.

When the Dutch settled at the Cape in the mid-17th century, the flintlock mechanism for firing the muzzle-loading musket with its smoothbore barrel and wooden stock was fast replacing the unwieldly matchlock mechanism with its smouldering three-foot-long length of matchcord (rope soaked in a solution of saltpetre). In a flintlock the trigger connects to a hammer, or cock, that holds a flint which (if of good quality) is good for 30 shots or more before needing to be replaced. When the trigger is pulled the cock springs forward and strikes and pushes forward the L-shaped frizzen – or metal plate – which covers the pan that has already been primed with fine black gunpowder poured from the powder flask or horn. The friction causes a spark that explodes the priming powder in the pan and causes the flash that goes through a small hole in the side of the barrel (the touchhole). This ignites the charge of coarser powder that has been poured down the barrel, followed by a lead ball and wadding, and then pushed down firmly with the ramrod.

This is slow procedure, and the flintlock musket is at the mercy of rain or damp weather that prevents the powder charge from detonating. But, at the time, it was a considerable improvement on the matchlock that took between 30 seconds and a minute to load, a procedure requiring 28 distinct actions and considerable training. The flintlock musket takes only seven distinct drill movements to reload and, in practised hands, can fire up to three rounds a minute. However, the flintlock firing mechanism made the musket no more accurate than before. The lead ball, which was often not entirely spherical, bounces when fired down the smooth sides of the barrel, and with no predictable spin given to it from rifling (grooves inside the barrel), tumbles inaccurately through the air. Too little powder in the barrel means the fired shot falls short; too much powder and the barrel can blow up. All this ensured that the flintlock musket is accurate at no more than 70 to 80 yards. Nevertheless, the flintlock in its various models that, over the years, steadily made it shorter, lighter and easier to handle, remained the standard firearm until well into the 1830s.

A musket ball has not nearly the destructive, bone-shattering effect, of a high velocity bullet shot from a modern rifle but, as Boers out hunting knew full well, with a large enough charge and with good aim it could still drop a lion or a hippopotamus. A high velocity bullet leaves a massive exit wound once it has smashed straight through the body, whereas a musket ball is turned easily aside from its straight flight on encountering a bone, or might even run along its length. Thus, if it does not simply lodge in the body, it might make its exit through a modest hole at a considerable angle from its point of entry. The worst danger for the victim is that on its destructive course a musket ball might sever an artery or pierce a vital organ. If it does not, there is some hope of recovery. But in an age before anaesthetics many a person who had received a musket ball died of shock, if not from loss of blood. Since there was as yet no knowledge of germs among either colonists or Africans, no precautions were ever taken against infection, and there was always a considerable risk that the wound would become contaminated—especially if cloth or dirt had been driven into the wound—and that the victim would die of sepsis.[3]

In 1807, the Rev. Alexander Forsyth patented the use of fulminates of mercury as a primer for firearms in place of gunpowder. A brass percussion cap, coated with fulminates of mercury, is placed in a hollow metal 'nipple' over the barrel's touchhole. When the musket's hammer, released by the trigger, strikes it, the fulminates of mercury are detonated and ignite the charge inside the barrel. This is a much more reliable system with fewer misfires than the flintlock mechanism, and has the advantage of not being affected by wet conditions. Moreover, in its simplicity the percussion lock mechanism speeded up the possible rate of fire. The only drawback, as Boers trekking deep into the interior realised, was that manufactured percussion caps could be difficult to procure, whereas flints for flintlock mechanisms were easy to come by wherever they might be.

Percussion caps, which were being mass produced by 1822, were initially developed for sportsmen, and were welcomed by hunters operating in the Cape and from Port Natal. By the 1830s Cape gunsmiths were beginning to adapt the percussion lock to old flintlock muskets. European armies, conservative by nature, were slower to adopt the new technology. The percussion lock, smoothbore musket was not issued to British infantry until it was finally introduced between 1838 and 1842.[4]

Settlers in southern Africa employed a variety of firearms. One type was a military-style musket, similar to the 'Brown Bess'. This was the standard weapon in service with the British Army from 1722, the .750 calibre, 46 inch-long, muzzle-loading flintlock-action Long Land Pattern Musket, firing a 1.45-ounce ball. Slight modifications were made with the Pattern 1802, and this remained the standard firearm until 1838 when the 'Brown Bess' finally went out of service. Like any other musket, it had no sights and was of low accuracy, emitting abundant clouds of grey-white smoke that could rapidly obscure a battlefield. It had to be cleaned regularly lest moisture and black-powder residue cause erosion to the barrel. As it was, the 'Brown Bess' had a life expectancy of eight to 10 years, after which it could become dangerously unreliable.

The 'Brown Bess' was also known as the 'Tower musket' after the mark of the Tower of London system that subcontracted manufacture to many gunsmiths, primarily in London and Birmingham. The muskets of this type available in the Cape were assembled by local gunsmiths who imported the components such as barrels and locks and hybridized their own versions of the muskets to suit local conditions. Some were almost identical to the standard military

---

3   Storey, *Guns*, pp.18–22, 25–6, 28; John Laband, *Bringers of War: The Portuguese in Africa during the Age of Gunpowder and Sail from the Fifteenth to the Eighteen Century* (London: Frontline Books, 2013), pp. 7–10, 239; Timothy J. Stapleton, 'Firearms Technology', in Timothy J. Stapleton (ed.), *Encyclopedia of African Colonial Conflicts*, vol. 1 (Santa Barbara and Denver: ABC-CLIO, 2017), pp. 287–289; Richard Holmes (ed.), *The Oxford Companion to Military History* (Oxford: Oxford University Press, 2001), p.305.
4   Holmes (ed.), *Military History*, pp.704–5; Laband, *Historical Dictionary*, p. 214; Storey, *Guns*, p. 86.

musket, but some idiosyncratic designs emerged such as the Cape gun that was favoured by hunters. It had two barrels, one a smoothbore to be used as a shotgun, and the other rifled for greater accuracy. (Rifled barrels with machined spiralled grooves had to be repeatedly cleaned on account of the fouling left by black powder. Rifled muskets were therefore not suitable as general infantry weapons, but had been in use since the late 18th century by sharpshooters who were not required to keep up a high rate of fire. The Enfield rifled percussion-lock musket was only introduced in the British army in 1853.)[5]

Settlers at the Cape employed firearms first and foremost for hunting, both for the pot and for animal ivory and hides for sale and trade. Their hunting gun came to be known affectionately as the *sanna*, a word derived from the Dutch for the snaphaunce, or *snaphaan*, an early type of flintlock. During the 1830s this last term was the favoured one employed for referring to a muzzle-loading musket, or *voorlaier*. A musket was also known as a *roer*, the Dutch word for gun, and the phrase, *die boer en sy roer* (the farmer and his gun) became a familiar trope in the frontiersman's gun society. Cape gunsmiths assembling the *roer* provided it with an unusually long and heavy wooden shoulder stock fashioned with a special bend. This idiosyncratic stock was nicknamed the *bobbejaanboud*, or baboon bum, because it resembled the hindquarters of a baboon. Local gunsmiths tended otherwise to follow Dutch custom in decorating a musket, and on the barrel often engraved a twelve-pointed star, a Dutch folk symbol for prosperity and freedom. Boers called a gun decorated in this fashion a *sterloop*, or star barrel.

Single and double-barrelled fowling pieces firing buckshot were in common use among Boers. A smoothbore musket could also be used as a powerful shotgun when firing buckshot slugs set in cylinders of hard fat, or a *loper*. A *loper* consisted of 10 to 12 lead pellets inserted down the barrel in an oiled buckskin bag that would explode at about 40 yards. This made for a vicious anti-personnel projectile, as did a musket ball cleft down the middle that broke apart in flight.

Hunting large and dangerous game animals with a *voorlaaier* required an assessment of the quality of the gunpowder so that the correct amount was loaded depending on the type of game or the distance of target. A hunter carried his powder—a pound-and-a-half to two pounds—in an ox or buffalo horn attached to his waist belt. It was sawn off at the tip and either plugged or fitted with a measure. Experienced hunters dispensed with the measure and shook out as much powder as they required into their hand.

Hunting also demanded outstanding marksmanship, and to earn the title of marksman among the Boers required hitting the small knucklebone of an ox at 80 paces. Yet marksmanship alone was not enough. When hunting large and dangerous game like buffalo, elephant, lion, rhinoceros, or hippopotamus—and not unthreatening creatures such as antelope or birds—it was essential to have a musket that was powerful enough to kill or disable the animal with the first shot. There was no time to reload if the hunter missed. A skilled and fearless marksman could kill an elephant at short range with a well-placed shot to the brain or heart from a regular Brown Bess type musket. Nevertheless, a larger musket that fired a heavier, more destructive ball was preferred for elephant and other big game since it inflicted terrible damage on a wide

---

5 Col. H.C.B. Rogers, *Weapons of the British Soldier* (London: Sphere Books, 1968), pp.90–6, 100–1, 143–6, 170; Richard Holmes, *Redcoat: The British Soldier in the Age of Horse and Musket* (London: HarperCollins, 2001), pp.194–9, 200–2; Storey, *Guns*, pp.81, 83; Laband, *Historical Dictionary*, p.238. The 'Tower' musket was fitted with a 16-inch-long bayonet of fluted steel attached to its muzzle. Boers made no use of the bayonet.

swathe of tissue and made absolute accuracy less essential. The distinctive 'four-bore' *roer*, or elephant gun, was such a weapon. It was a 1.052 calibre flintlock muzzle-loading musket that fired a ball weighing 4 ounces propelled by a charge of 20 drams (1.25 ounces) of black powder. The 'four-bore' had a tremendous kick and if you overloaded it you were likely to be knocked to the ground. As it was, every shot left a bruise on the shoulder, and some Boers therefore shot from both shoulders. Its tremendous detonation made the shooter temporarily deaf.[6]

All who ventured onto the veld carried a sheath knife with a steel blade from seven to 18 inches long. It had a short cross guard modelled on the Bowie knife and a handle four to five inches long. Such a knife was called a *herneuter* or *herneutermes* after the Herrnhutters, or Moravian Brethren, who first made them in the early 19th century at their mission station at Genadendal in the Western Cape. *Herneutermesse* were used for skinning game, cutting up carcases and eating. They could also be wielded as a weapon for fighting at close quarters. In the same vein, some hunters and travellers might carry a pair of the highly inaccurate, short-ranged flintlock pistols of the day for personal protection against thieves and robbers, and not animals.[7]

Unlike later, machine-tooled, breech-loading rifles that were too complex to be mended in the field, both flintlock and percussion lock muskets, whose barrels and firing mechanisms were made of wrought iron, could be repaired over a hot fire. By the same token, soapstone bullet moulds in which lead hardened by tin was melted over a fire to make musket balls and pellets, could be extemporised in the field from clay or the fine dirt from anthills. This ability to repair his musket or mould his shot when away from the presence of a gunsmith was an invaluable boon for the hunter on a distant hunting expedition. So it was too for Boers when they trekked away into the interior, far from the centres of manufacture in the Cape and their associated craftsmen. However, those on trek still required the lead and tin for their musket balls (even if, at a pinch, a musket could be loaded with tacks, scrap metal, iron pot legs and the like), along with the ingredients for the black powder that fired the musket: a mixture of 75 percent potassium nitrate (saltpetre), 15 percent charcoal powder (carbon), and 10 percent sulphur powder.[8] These metals and chemicals could not be found on the veld, but they were absolutely essential for the Boer's very existence, for his food and his security. Running out of these necessities was the ever-present concern that haunted hunter and emigrating farmer alike.

By the 1830s, the length of Cape gun barrels started to shorten as gunsmiths realized that they were sufficiently powerful for big game hunting (previously, 44-inch barrels had been popular). Hunters normally fired from the saddle, but with the older, long musket they had to dismount to reload, and the *Boerperd* was schooled to stand without being held during this operation. With a shorter musket it was possible for a skilled rider to load from the saddle. To speed loading and to free his hands for the reins, he would pour powder down the barrel and then insert one of the musket balls that he carried in his mouth instead of keeping it, along with wadding and *lopers*, in the pockets of his broad leather bandolier. His spit on the ball helped seat it on the powder without having to use wadding. A few taps down the barrel with the ramrod, a pinch of power in the pan or the insertion of a percussion cap, and the weapon was ready to fire.

---

6   Storey, *Guns*, pp.81–5, 87–8; Laband, *Historical Dictionary*, p.85; Eric Walker, *The Great Trek* (London: Adam and Charles Black, 1938), p.39.
7   Walker, *Great Trek*, p. 39; Laband, *Historical Dictionary*, p.112.
8   Storey, *Guns*, pp.84, 87.

The trigger on a Cape musket usually required an especially heavy pull to prevent an accidental discharge should the hunter fall from his horse.

For the Boer, it was but a step from hunting to fighting on *kommando*. The lightly encumbered riders made rapid and unexpected thrusts against the enemy thanks to the mobility and resilience of their sturdy ponies. Once scouts had located the enemy and reported back, the *kommando* would take a circuitous route, keeping out of sight of the adversary until ready to attack. When the foe was in sight, the armed horsemen formed a line and charged. Once they were in effective musket range, but themselves still out of range of the enemy's spears—and in the case of warfare against the Khoisan, arrows or stones—they dismounted (and we have seen that the *Boerperd* was trained to stand still) and fired a volley, often resting their muskets across their horses' backs or necks. They then remounted and fell back to reload, and the procedure was repeated. If two ranks of horsemen had been formed, when the first retired to reload the second took its place and fired its volley, thus keeping up a pretty continuous fire. In this sense, a *kommando* fought like mounted infantry, not cavalry, only employing their horses to bring the firing-line into position. Of course, as they did when hunting, members of a *kommando* might also fire from the saddle, but this tended to be only during an emergency such as an ambush when they had lost formation and become involved in a melee. Generally, though, being without sabres or lances, they were reluctant to charge home and engage hand-to-hand with their spear-carrying adversaries as British cavalry would have done.[9]

It was foolhardy for a mounted *kommando* to seek out an enemy on his own ground unsupported by supply wagons. In the Cape, the vehicle preferred by explorers, hunters, traders, farmers, missionaries, soldiers, and men on *kommando* when making long journeys over many days or even months was the *ossewa*, or ox-wagon, which doubled as a mobile home.

The basic design of the *ossewa* was established by the late seventeenth century, although it naturally went through various modifications over the next two centuries in which it was in use. By the 1830s the *kakerbeenwa* was ubiquitous. This was the 'jawbone wagon', so named because it was long in proportion to its breadth and carried a load of up to 3,960 lbs. Basically, it was a sturdily built, wooden wagon on four spoked, wooden wheels shod with iron half an inch thick, those at the back being considerably larger than those in the front. Wagons were held together by angle-blocks and leather raw-hide thongs (*rieme*) so there was less chance of the parts breaking in an upset. Most of the load-carrying and living area was covered by a double canvas canopy (one canopy thickly painted to keep out the wet, the other left white to reflect back the sun's hot ray) supported on a dozen semi-circular wooden hoops. The body of the wagon was usually painted dark green and the wheels red, while the wooden side-panels were often decorated with hand-painted flowers. There were four wooden chests inside the wagon: one at the back, one along each side, and a fourth in the front, in the open. This served as the seat for the driver who drove the span of eight to 16 oxen by calling to each by name or by urging them on with a long whip. Oxen were normally of the 'Afrikander' strain of the 'Sanga' breed. They were red and white or black and white. No Boer, if he could help it, would put up with plain white or slate-grey oxen. The ideal was always to have a well-matched span. The two most powerful oxen were yoked either side of the shaft, or *disselboom*, which was attached to the swivelling front axle, and the rest were yoked in pairs (the straight wooden yoke fitted over

---

9   Storey, *Guns*, p.86; Laband, *Historical Dictionary*, pp. 52–3.

An ox-wagon negotiating a mountain pass. Anonymous engraving. (Anon., *Pictorial History of South Africa* (London: Odhams Press, *c*.1937))

the necks of each pair) and attached by a long chain or a thick rope of twisted leather strands (a *trektou*) to the *disselboom*. A young African boy (*voorloper*) led the front pair of oxen by a *riem* attached to their yoke, and the rest followed.

Oxen had to be regularly rested and given time to graze during the day, which meant that journeys were often undertaken by night. When the going was level and easy, oxen could drag a wagon at a walking pace, or three miles an hour, but that rate slowed down at every incline and over broken ground. Distances were reckoned in *skofte*, or the distance covered in one day's trek. A *skof* averaged at best about 20 miles, so that (for example) it might take two months to travel to the distant Eastern Frontier from Cape Town. The sandy, deeply rutted tracks were appalling, there no bridges, so a river had to be crossed at a negotiable *drift*, or ford, or (on rare occasion) on a pontoon. Mountain ranges—of which there were any number in the Colony—inevitably presented the greatest challenge, and wagons made their perilous and exhausting way over fearsomely steep and rugged passes, or through beetling gorges along the rocky banks of rivers. Spans of oxen might have to be doubled going up a pass and rested every 300 yards or so. When (as often happened) even a double span of oxen was unable to pull a wagon up a pass, the wagon would have to be taken to pieces, carried up piecemeal and reassembled on the other side.[10] If in the Colony a journey by ox-wagon was truly daunting, how much more taxing was it to travel along unknown ways—such as Piet Uys had on his *kommissietrek*—where there were no tracks, where *driwwe* across rivers had to be sought out and mountain passes identified. Dr Smith, it will be remembered, averaged only three-and-a-half miles a day in 1832 on his journey from Grahamstown to Port Natal.

Wagons could be formed into a mobile, fortified camp, or laager (*laer*), and this was first attempted by settlers during the Second Cape Frontier War of 1793. Indeed, by the 1830s the laager had become indispensable for Boer survival on the frontier and constituted a vital element in the conduct of war by *kommandos*. A *kommando* campaigning with a supply train of wagons could draw them into a laager that served as a defensive base deep in enemy territory from which mounted expeditions could be sent out on punitive raids to destroy enemy property and capture or recover livestock. The speed and unpredictability of these mounted thrusts were calculated to keep the foe off-balance; while in any armed clash the manoeuvrability of the Boers on their horses and the superiority of their firepower gave them a considerable advantage over their foes who were on foot and armed almost entirely with edged weapons.

In a laager, the wagons were drawn into a circle, rough triangle or whatever shape best fitted the terrain and took advantage of natural features that might impeded the enemy's advance. They were lashed together with *rieme* and chains end to end, with the *disselboom* of each wagon fitting between the rear wheels and under the chassis of the one next to it. Poles might be planted behind the wagon wheels and similarly secured. Branches from thorn trees or wooden hurdles filled the openings underneath the wagons and the spaces between them, and ox-skins were stretched over the spoked wheels. An entrance was constructed by putting two wagons end-to-end with an opening just wide enough for a horseman to pass through, and heavy branches were pulled across it when it needed to be shut. If there was time, an outer perimeter

---

10 Walker, *Great Trek*, pp.36–8; J.L. Smail, *From the Land of the Zulu Kings* (Durban: A.J. Pope, 1979), p.65; Laband, *Historical Dictionary*, p.212; Swart, *Riding High*, pp.34–5. For detailed descriptions of Cape roads and passes, see E.E. Mossop, *Old Cape Highways* (Cape Town: Maskew Miller, 1927), *passim*.

of thorn trees, branches, and other entanglements—an *abattis*—would be constructed to disrupt and slow down an attack and expose it to defensive fire. The non-combatants, draught oxen and horses sheltered inside the laager during an attack. Sometimes, four wagons were parked in a square inside the laager and were roofed over with planks and raw hides to protect the women, children, and the elderly. The canvas canopies of the other wagons might be covered by reed mats and tarpaulins to prevent cast spears from penetrating them. The defenders were positioned in the approximately two-yard-wide gap between each wagon and ideally fired in ordered rotation to maintain an uninterrupted rate of fire. A laager would have been very vulnerable to artillery fire, but no enemy the Boers encountered during the 1830s possessed any. Consequently, a laager could withstand the heaviest of assaults and the defenders could keep the enemy at bay until reinforcements arrived to relieve them, or until the enemy abandoned the futile attack and retired. That was the moment, if they had the pluck and enough horses, for the defenders to sally out and transform the enemy's retreat into a rout.[11]

It must not be supposed that *kommandos* were made up exclusively of white settlers. It is an aspect of South Africa's racialised history that people of colour who always formed part of a *kommando* have more often than not been painted out of the picture or, because their ubiquity on campaign was taken so much for granted, were simply not mentioned. Consequently, there is often scant reference to them in the sources, and their presence on campaign must be inferred. Yet, the ironies and complexities of the paternalistic relationship between white *burgers* on one hand, and their acculturated black servants on the other, allowed for the latter to bear arms on *kommando* alongside their masters. This was hardly unusual in the annals of colonial conquest. The colonial recruitment of locally raised forces was a very old practice, dating back in sub-Saharan Africa to the first arrival in the early sixteenth century of the Portuguese in the kingdom of Kongo, in what is now northern Angola.[12] Likewise, from the very outset of Dutch rule at the Cape, Khoikhoin, slaves and '*Bastaard Hottentotten*' (men whose fathers were slaves and mothers Khoikhoin) served as an integral part of the *kommando* system,[13] sometimes even outnumbering the *burgers* they accompanied and always making up a substantial proportion of the force.

These *agterryers* (or 'attendants on horseback') served in two different capacities, although any distinction between the two overlapped or dissolved as circumstances dictated. In one role they offered menial support to the firing line, driving the *kommando's* wagons, herding its draught animals and horse, slaughtering and cooking livestock, and tending the sick and wounded. In their other, purely military role they were the equals of the frontier farmers, riding fully armed beside them on their punitive expeditions, guarding ammunition stores and, by the end of the 18th century, helping them defend their wagon laagers.

Agterryers were naturally considered collaborators by those fighting against a *kommando*, traitors working with the white enemy. Yet, to think of them as clients is probably more appropriate, for that term applies where an individual (or, indeed, a community) that is destitute, socially adrift, or politically vulnerable seeks the protection of a patron and serves him in return

---

11 George Tylden, 'The Wagon Laager', *Society for Army Historical Research*, 41: 168 (1963), pp.200–1; Walker, *Great Trek*, pp.122–3; Laband, *Historical Dictionary*, pp.136, 270.
12 Laband, *Bringers of War*, 199–202, 208–9.
13 In Dutch the term '*bastaard*' means 'mongrel' rather than 'illegitimate', and was applied without further qualification to those with a white father and a Khoikhoi mother.

for security and a livelihood. In any case, there were always those who opportunistically saw the common sense of aligning themselves with the demonstrably winning side when resistance was no longer feasible, and of taking whatever rewards were on offer. Besides, there were many in Africa as a whole—and not just in the Cape—who, when they found themselves under colonial rule, perceived how they could maintain their warrior traditions (which included hunting) and uphold their concepts of masculine honour through military service alongside their new masters. They would have been encouraged, moreover, by the knowledge that the stock captured on a *kommando* raid was always divided, and even if an *agterryer's* share was less than a *burger's*, it was nevertheless a substantial one for an impoverished people who still counted their wealth in livestock.[14]

14 Pieter Labuschange, *Ghostriders of the Anglo-Boer War (1899–1902): The Role and Contribution of Agterryers* (Pretoria: University of South Africa Press, 1999), pp.7–8; Giliomee, *Afrikaners*, pp.61, 63; Bouda Etemad, *Possessing the World: Taking the Measurement of Colonialism from the 18th to the 20th Century* (New York and Oxford: Berghan Books, 2007), pp.39, 42–3. See also Iliffe, John, *Honour in African History* (Cambridge: Cambridge University Press, 2005), pp.227–45: chapter 5, 'The Honour of the Mercenary'.

7

The House of Bondage

The Sixth Cape Frontier War ended in September 1835 with the thorough defeat of the amaXhosa. Piet Uys, while on his way home from his *kommando* service, learned on 26 October 1835 that his wife Alida had been arrested on a charge of slapping her indentured Khoikhoi servant-woman, Rosina.[1] Although Alida was acquitted and Rosina jailed for perjury, the affair was a deep affront to Uys's deeply engrained sense of racial superiority that he shared with all his settler neighbours on the Cape eastern frontier. He was already disgruntled, for along with many others who had served in the *kommandos* during the recent war, Uys would already have been resentful that during the campaign the British military authorities had treated them with humiliating disdain despite the vital role they played in the fighting. Now, to add injury to insult, they were resisting compensating them properly for their service. This fresh slight only compounded the bitter sentiment already entertained among many *burgers* in the frontier districts that under British rule they had been progressively marginalised. They were under the growing impression that they had been turned into foreigners in their own land where the command of the English language, along with the adoption of English dress and manners, had become the prevailing indictors of civilization. And, perhaps most of all—as the Rosina case exemplified—they were deeply aggrieved that they had been put on an equal footing legally with their servants and Christian converts of colour. It was this social levelling under the British administration they took deep exception to, quite as much as the affront to established racial hierarchy it entailed

In January 1836 Uys laid a civil charge for wrongful arrest against the Special Justice Sherwin (formerly a British officer) who had brought the charge against his wife. The case dragged on and Uys lost patience. He sold his farm Brakfontein and set about organising a large party among his Dutch speaking neighbours to trek out of the Colony with him. By March 1836 officials were reporting the widespread reluctance of the disaffected settlers of the eastern districts to comply with official directives and the intention of some to *trek*, or migrate. Four months later, in mid-1836, alarmed officials became aware that 'a considerable number' of frontier settlers had their farms up for sale, that they were buying large stocks of gunpowder, mustering their

---

1   For the Rosina affair and its consequences, see Uys, 'Petrus Lafras Uys', pp.32–3 and Uys, 'Boer Family'.

livestock, and loading their valuables into wagons, all with the intention of at last carrying out their 'long projected scheme' to 'quit the colony' for the interior.[2]

Some later Afrikaner historians adduced a conspiracy to *trek* that was secretly devised by a network of key Boer leaders determined to throw off the yoke of British rule. However, more recent scholarship has demolished this misleading impression of a co-ordinated movement planned years in advance, even if an interest in the possibility of emigrating was of long standing. The 'Great Trek', as the exodus has come to be known since the late 19th century, was altogether more haphazard. It took the form of a gradual landslide with the departure of one party dislodging the ground, so to speak, for the emigration of the next from the Cape. A typical group consisted of a handful of families travelling together under the leadership of a senior male, such as a prominent local official or a family patriarch, and tended to be known by his name, such as the Uys Party, the Potgieter Party, and so on. Probably, each of these leaders regarded their party as forming part of a single community of emigrants (*trekkers*) sharing a common goal, but they were stalwart individualists, and unity of purpose would prove difficult to achieve over the coming years. Even so, the cumulative effect was a mass migration, or *trek*, a popular movement that was nothing less than a peaceful rebellion against British rule.

Between 1836 and 1838 perhaps as many as 8,000 *burgers*—men, women and children—along with their flocks and herds, left the Colony for the interior, this number growing closer to 14,000 by 1845. By 1840 about 10 percent of the Colony's whites had joined the Great Trek and some districts of the Eastern Cape had lost as many as 20 percent of their *burger* inhabitants. Freed of British control, they planned to set up home in the interior and to regulate society as they chose, and that meant replicating Cape society and its racial hierarchies as they had been before the British began reforming them. They had no intention of ceasing to use dark-skinned people as shepherds, cattle-hands, field-workers, and domestic servants. They took with them as many servants as they could from the Colony, men, women, and children, and these racially inferior dependents swelled the number of white *trekkers* by nearly half again. By the end of 1837 there were probably about 4,000 of them—but they have largely been ignored in the narrative. Precisely how many of them were so-called 'apprentices' is unknown, but the indications are that they numbered several hundreds.[3] These 'apprentices' were former slaves, who, with the abolition of slavery in 1834 (see below), had become indentured to their former masters until 1 December 1838. It did not seem to concern their emigrating masters that it was now illegal to remove 'apprenticed labour' from the Cape.

Critically for the indigenous inhabitants of the interior, this wave of invaders—who intended either to displace them or reduce to them servitude—came heavily armed with muskets and a few small cannons. By mid-1837 they could field a total of a thousand or more mounted men on *kommando*, a new and formidable fighting force that threatened the entire region.[4]

---

2   *RN 3*, pp.27–9, no. 15: Duncan Campbell to Secretary to Government, 25 March 1836; pp.47–8, no. 32, annex. 1: Campbell to Secretary to Government, 29 July 1836.
3   See the discussion in C. Venter, 'Die Voortrekkers en die Ingeboekte Slawe Wat die Groot Trek Meergemaak Het', *Historia: Journal of the Historical Association of South Africa*, 36: 1 May (1991), pp.17, 21, 26–9.
4   Norman Etherington,, *The Great Treks: The Transformation of Southern Africa, 1815–1854* (Harlow, England: Longman, 2001), pp.243, 244, 246; Leonard Thompson, 'Co-operation and Conflict: The High Veld', in Monica Wilson and Leonard Thompson (eds), *The Oxford History of South Africa, Volume 1: South Africa to 1870* (Oxford: Oxford University Press, 1969), pp.405–8; Leonard Thompson, 'Co-

These Pioneers, or *Voortrekkers* as they have been known for somewhat over a century, or *Emigranten* as they called themselves in Dutch (rendered into English as Emigrant Farmers), were not the same as the *trekboere*, or 'migrant farmers' who dated back to the early 18th century. These were individual families of poor, landless *burgers* and the simply adventurous who gradually moved out in an uncoordinated way beyond the initial limits of white settlement in the Cape Peninsular. They went in their wagons wherever prospects of a livelihood beckoned, driven ever forward by the increase in their herds and the search for unexhausted pastures. The VOC had no option but to follow in their wake, setting up new administrative posts to ensure that its laws were obeyed and its taxes paid. This in turn provoked the *trekboere* to move on to escape the irksome controls of government, and the consequence was an unsystematic colonisation of the Cape interior, the extension of the Colony's boundaries, and a paper-thin layer of settlers spread over a vast area.

As stock farmers, the *trekboere* lived the simple life, content to dwell with a few sticks of furniture in a rudimentary homestead of two rooms with walls of clay, roof of reeds, and floor of dung and clay. Some *trekboere* simply preferred to stay on the move and to live in their wagons all the year through, extending their cramped accommodation by erecting canvas awnings alongside. With Khoisan retainers or slaves to tend his flocks and herds, a *trekboer* was often downright idle. He was therefore free to spend much of his time hunting with the easy advantages his *Boerperd* and his *snaphaan* afforded him, not merely for the pleasure of the sport, to secure meat for the table or to protect his livestock from predators, but to acquire valuable ivory and skins to exchange for necessities on his infrequent visits to a distant village.[5]

But by the 1830s when the *Voortrekkers* were preparing to move off in their organised parties under recognised leaders, circumstances had changed. The Emigrant Farmers were no longer individuals like the *trekboere* looking to eke out a rudimentary livelihood in the wilderness. If they did not live in gracious gabled homesteads as *burgers* did in the sophisticated Western Cape, their homes were comfortable *langhuise*, oblong, barn-like structures, thatched and whitewashed. There was little evidence of the handsome Cape-Dutch furniture of Cape Town and its environs, but there were strong wooden bedsteads and feather-beds, wooden chests, tables and chairs, iron pots, copper jugs, earthenware dishes, plates, and mugs. Orchards and fields of crops surrounded the homestead, while their numerous flocks and herds grazed their spreading pastures as far as the horizon. They were self-reliant in all the staples, while small luxuries like coffee, tea, brandy, clothing, crockery, and medicines in bottles were regularly available from itinerant *smouse*, or pedlars.[6] Why then would the *trekkers* sell off their farms and other fixed property—often at great financial loss—and abandon their familiar and relatively well-off way of life in favour of a cramped, itinerant, disagreeable and hazardous existence in their ox-wagons? Their resolve to accept such material sacrifice in exchange for an uncertain future in untamed lands far away to the north requires further explanation.

---

    operation and Conflict: The Zulu Kingdom and Natal, in Monica Wilson and Leonard Thompson (eds), *Oxford History of South Africa, Volume 1*, pp. 355–357; Giliomee, *Afrikaners*, p.161.
5 Giliomee, *Afrikaners*, pp.20–1, 27, 30–3; Storey, *Guns*, pp.38–40; Christopher Saunders (ed.), *Reader's Digest Illustrated History of South Africa: The Real Story*, 3rd edition (Cape Town: The Reader's Digest Association South Africa, 1994), pp.56–9.
6 Walker, *Great Trek*, pp 39–43.

The *trekkers* believed (as we have seen) that they were suffering from cultural marginalisation under the British, but more was at stake than that. As Hermann Giliomee has pithily suggested, the other causes of the Great Trek 'can be summarized as a lack of land, labor and security.'[7] It was all very well for those prosperous Boers who owned their own farms, but with the natural growth in the *burger* population, by the 1830s the shortage of land still available in the Eastern Districts for new farms was becoming acute. If *burgers* had been prepared to farm more intensively and efficiently all might nevertheless have been well, but they were wedded to their traditional subsistence farming, and that way of life depended on continuing expansion rather than on the better usage of the land. In the past, over two centuries, land-hungry *trekboere* and frontiersmen had (as we have seen) pushed north and east, driving away the indigenous inhabitants or subduing them. But under British rule any further expansion eastwards seemed to have been terminated.

On 10 May 1835, in the midst of the Sixth Cape Frontier War, Governor D'Urban annexed a huge swathe of territory lying between the Keiskamma and Kei Rivers to the Cape Colony, and named it the Province of Queen Adelaide after King William IV's consort, Princess Adelaide of Saxe-Meiningen. It was D'Urban's intention to expel all the amaXhosa currently living in the newly annexed province east beyond the Kei, and to throw the territory open to occupation as farms. Needless to say, land-hungry settlers and speculators in land were extremely gratified. But they were destined to be thwarted by the rising swell of humanitarian and Evangelical unease in Britain concerning how indigenous people were being treated in the expanding empire. Lord Glenelg, the Whig Secretary for War and Colonies, was an Evangelical Christian and ill at ease with the many questionable consequences of colonial conquest. On 26 December 1835 Glenelg fired off a despatch to D'Urban ordering the immediate retrocession of the Province of Queen Adelaide. Glenelg's bombshell of a despatch only reached Cape Town on 21 March 1836. Mortified and indignant, D'Urban stonewalled, but Glenelg was not to be moved, and on 2 February 1837 the Province of Queen Adelaide was formally de-annexed. During the protracted process of retrocession, land-hungry frontiersmen had time to reflect that any possibility of expansion east under the aegis of British rule was being terminated, and that the only remaining alternative lay north, over the Orange River and beyond the boundaries of the Colony.[8]

If the desire to procure new lands in which to settle was a strong motive among those contemplating trekking out of the Colony, then the shortage of labour on their farms in the Cape was another, related issue. This had long been a problem, made worse by the promulgation of Ordinance 50 of 1828 that reflected the current 'liberal' approach to imperialism and its concern for the rights of indigenes under British rule. The Ordinance repealed the existing vagrancy laws that required the Khoisan to obtain a pass if they left the farms where they worked, outlawed any form of coerced labour, protected workers against arbitrary punishment, and specifically reaffirmed their rights and those of all free people of colour to buy and own land and property on the same basis as white people. The unintended consequence of this liberalising legislation was the immediate flight of emancipated Khoisan from farms to the towns and to mission stations. No longer abler to retain and control their labour in the old way, farmers

---

7   Giliomee, *Afrikaners*, p.144.
8   Laband, *Land Wars*, pp.191–2.

complained of a sudden upsurge in stock thefts and pilfering by wandering Khoisan unfettered by the former vagrancy laws.

The abolition of slavery within the British Empire was a related matter. On 1 August 1834 the Slavery Abolition Act (1833) came into effect and commenced in the Cape on 1 December 1834. All slaves in the Cape were emancipated, although under terms that left them indentured for four years to their former owners in the so-called 'apprenticeship' system that finally came to an end on 1 December 1838. The release (according to official figures) of 38,742 slaves in the Cape – where the population as a whole was approaching 250,000—had a far greater impact in the Western Districts of the Colony where most slaves were held than on the Eastern Frontier where few *burgers* were slave-owners and where slaves numbered 8,196, or 21 percent of the total.[9] Nevertheless, emancipation was another psychological blow to the old paternalist order. It hardened the resolve of the Emigrant Farmers to perpetuate traditional—and oppressive—labour relations on the new farms they planned to stake out for themselves in the far interior beyond the reach of British interference.

Pressing as these land and labour shortages were for those *burgers* planning to abandon the Colony, it was the breakdown of security on the frontier which they found the most distressing. Frontier farmers had long complained about the nuisance posed by those they characterised as 'vagrants' (the wandering bands of Khoisan or amaXhosa begging for food and stealing when they could), and by the graver threat presented by armed parties of stock-thieves. Loss of property and life had always spiked during the successive frontier wars, sometimes significantly. But the Sixth Cape Frontier War came as an extreme shock to all colonists along the Eastern Frontier since it was so unexpected, and since the loss of life suffered was so unprecedented, and the material damage inflicted by the amaXhosa so particularly severe. The subsequent annexation of the Province of Queen Adelaide had seemed at first to promise greater security, but its retrocession and the reappearance of plundering Xhosa bands shattered any such hope. Settlers along the entire frontier zone were reduced to a state of nervous apprehension, and the resentful notion was widespread that the British government was indifferent to their fate. To those joining the Great Trek, it seemed that their future security lay in taking responsibility for it out of British hands, and in placing it squarely in their own.

And topping these discontents and apprehensions was the drought of 1836–1838, considered almost unprecedented in its severity, even in the frontier districts where water was scarce at the best of times. For those already considering migrating out of the Colony, the repeated failure of their crops and the withering of their pastures was another incentive to move on in search of better-watered lands.[10]

Despite finding the prospective *trekkers* 'in a state of great excitement and irritation', the local British authorities believed they had 'no means to prevent emigration',[11] even though it was technically unlawful for British subjects to leave the Cape without permission. It was the

---

9 See Alan F. Hattersley, 'Slavery at the Cape, 1652–1838,' in Eric A. Walker (ed.), *The Cambridge History of the British Empire, Volume VIII, South Africa, Rhodesia and the High Commission Territories* (Cambridge: Cambridge University Press, 1963), p.275.

10 For a systematic setting out of the reasons for the Great Trek as perceived at the time, see *RN 3*, pp.291–4, no. 154: Maj. Gen. Sir George Napier (Governor of the Cape, 1838–1844) to Lord Glenelg, 18 May 1838.

11 *RN 3*, p.113, no. 48: Andries Stockenstrom to D'Urban, 27 September 1836.

opinion of the Cape Attorney General, A. Oliphant, that the laws currently in force in the Colony could not 'prevent persons discontented with their condition to try to better themselves in whatever part of the world they please.' In any case, he rhetorically enquired, what could be done to prevent 'persons determined to run away, short of shooting them as they pass the boundary line?'[12] In fact, since most of the *trekker* parties crossed the Orange River on their way north by way of six or seven *driwwe* close by the later village of Aliwal North, it would not have been a difficult matter for troops to guard the crossings and stem the exodus.[13] But the will was lacking among officials daunted by the strength and scope of the popular movement. Norman Etherington is therefore probably right to conclude that the *Voortrekkers* 'barged through an open door' when they abandoned the Cape.[14] But, as it turned out, even if the Cape authorities washed their hands of them, and were no longer prepared to consider Emigrant Farmers who permanently quitted the Colony to be subject to its laws as British subjects, the government in London disagreed. Lord Glenelg, motivated by the growing humanitarian concern in many circles in Britain for the wellbeing of indigenous peoples, suspicious that the Boers would resort to slavery beyond the Cape's borders, and apprehensive that their activities would stir up wars that would threaten the Cape' security, introduced legislation that was approved by the British Parliament on 13 August 1836.

The Cape of Good Hope Punishment Act, as it was commonly called, was promulgated in the *Cape of Good Hope Government Gazette* on 27 January 1837.[15] As Glenelg explained to D'Urban, the law was intended 'to enable the tribunals at the Cape to take cognizance of, and punish, offences committed by British subjects, within the Kaffre territory in the same manner as if they had been perpetrated within the limits of the colony.'[16] In other words, for purposes of the Act, the *trekkers* (*pace* Oliphant's legal opinion) were to be considered British subjects, subject to the Cape's laws, and the 'Kaffre territory' was arbitrarily defined as being 'to the Southward of the Twenty-fifth Degree of South Latitude'. This line of latitude runs just north of Delagoa Bay, so the Zulu and Swazi kingdoms, and many of the African polities of the highveld fell into the region where the Act was in effect—as did Port Natal. Glenelg sternly reminded D'Urban it was his 'duty' in terms of the Act to exercise his authority 'to take the necessary steps' in the 'Kaffre territory' to bring offenders to justice.

How the Cape authorities were to implement this injunction was not spelled out. For the moment, therefore, the *trekkers* could afford to ignore the Act as a dead letter in the lands beyond the boundaries of the Cape, even while they regarded it as an affront to their newly-won independence. In only a few years' time, however, the Act would come to bite them when the British invoked it as justification for taking military action against them.[17]

12 *RN 3*, pp. 48–9, no. 32, annex. 2: Report by A. Oliphant, 13 August 1836.
13 Thompson, 'High Veld', p.409.
14 Etherington, *Great Treks*, p.246.
15 *RN 3*, pp. 92–3, no. 40, annex. 1: An Act for the Prevention and Punishment of Offences committed by His Majesty's Subjects within certain Territories adjacent to the Colony of the Cape of Good Hope, 13 August 1836.
16 *RN 3*, p.91, no. 40: Glenelg to D'Urban, 12 September 1836.
17 Thompson, 'High Veld', pp.409–10.

8

A Chosen People

Piet Uys was unique among the *Voortrekker* leaders in personally visiting D'Urban in Cape Town to secure his permission to leave the Cape. When his party, under the nominal leadership of his 66-year-old father, 'Koos Bybel' Uys, did finally set off from Grahamstown in April 1837,[1] it was following in the wake of several other major groups and many smaller ones.[2] The wagons in these trek parties were packed with household goods. The more prosperous families might have several wagons filled with clothes, dress materials and bedding, fine sets of furniture, precious items of silver and porcelain. But all carried supplies of tobacco, coffee, flour, sugar, and salt, along with stools, chests and small tables. Agricultural implements such as ploughs, picks and spades were taken along, as well as seed and carefully wrapped fruit trees. Gunpowder was one absolute essential, and any amount up to 300 lbs might be packed into a wagon. The real wealth of the Emigrant Farmers or *Trekkers* (as we might now capitalise them as members of a coherent movement), that is, their horses, cattle, and sheep, went with them alongside their wagons. The migrants' leisurely speed of travel was dictated by their livestock's grazing needs, and that of their draught-oxen. Naturally, no matter how much the *Trekkers* had taken with them, much would have been left behind or disposed of for a mere song – or *'n appel en 'n ei*, as they would have regretfully put it, for 'an apple and an egg.'[3]

The men in these parties of *Trekkers* would have been dressed in their characteristic frontier costume that, to the eyes of sophisticates from Cape Town, would have appeared eccentric at best. Metropolitan fashions took years to reach the frontier, and because clothes were usually home-made, they rarely followed the new patterns accurately. Moreover, since many frontiersmen could not in any case afford new clothes, styles ranged over those of a quarter-century or more. Whatever the details of style, though, men wore jacket, waistcoat and trousers. The latter were of the *klapbroek* variety with a flap that buttoned up the front, and were kept up with belt or braces. Jackets were of variable length, sometimes reaching down nearly to the ground. The poorer among them wore clothes of leather that were almost as soft as cloth. But if they got wet, they could dry hard and be very uncomfortable. Many men wore waistcoats of calfskin with

---

1 Uys, 'Petrus Lafras Uys', pp.33–4.
2 C.F.J. Muller, *A Pictorial History of the Great Trek* (Cape Town: Tafelberg, 1978), p.9.
3 Ivor Pols, 'The Voortrekker Museum', in John Laband and Robert Haswell (eds), *Pietermaritzburg 1838–1988: A New Portrait of an African City* (Pietermaritzburg: University of Natal Press and Shuter & Shooter, 1988) pp.162–4; Walker, *Great Trek*, pp.102–4.

the dappled hair outwards, although the flashier among them might sport ones made of satin, silk, or flowered velvet. The usual material for men's workaday clothes (when not leather) was moleskin and, more rarely, smooth or ribbed corduroy, black, green, brown or dark yellow in colour. Overcoats were of duffel and week-day shirts of wool. Every man would have a suit or two of carefully-tended clothes for special occasions: a linen shirt and corduroys for ordinary people, or a broad-cloth coat and waistcoat with cashmere trousers for the well-to-do. The latter might even keep a pair of white gloves for weddings. Most people, men as well as women, had their leather boots or shoes made for them by cobblers who stitched them together with fine leather thongs and did not use nails. Men very often did not wear stockings and children (who usually went barefoot) never. No man was ever without his hat, and these came in a great variety of styles. Some were the broad-brimmed, flat-crowned felt ones favoured by the *trekboere* of old. Broad-brimmed straw hats with green linings were popular. There were high-crowned felt hats with brims of every variety of width turned out by the hat factories of Cape Town. A few dandies even flaunted pale, dust-coloured 'bell' tops hats of the latest fashion that widened out at the crown. Most men would have sucked a pipe, often made of soft stone, artfully carved and coloured with a boss below the bowl to hold it by when it grew hot.

Trekker women's clothing can best be described as plain and sober. Like their menfolk, they did possess clothes for special occasion such as brightly-coloured silk dresses, dainty little hats and white shoes, stockings, and gloves. Everyday dresses, though, followed a common pattern of turn-over collar, wide sleeves fastened at the writs and flounces around the lower part of the full-length skirt. These dresses, in plain colours or checks, could be made of any conceivable material from silk and linen to thick woolly baize and leather. Petticoats were usually of red or white flannel. Women never wore their hair loose. They parted it in the middle and fastened it at the back with a comb. A few of the more fashion-conscious tortured their hair in front into little plaits they kept in place with pins, ribbons, or combs. Little hats with streamers were for special occasions. Otherwise, a woman wore her big sun-bonnet of black or fine white linen, or sometimes of dull-coloured merino or even silk. These *kappies* with their tucks and embroideries were elaborately made, and were a matter of considerable pride for the wearer. Besides being becoming (or so they believed) they shielded the face and neck from the sun and preserved the white complexion in which women took such pride. Indeed, when travelling in their wagons they wore light goatskin masks to protect their faces, and sometimes gloves as well. Some women carried parasols to shade themselves. It grows very cold on the highveld in winter, and women had muffs as well as shawls of wool or silk to help keep them warm.[4]

Physically, the *Trekkers* were muscular and long-limbed with many men – and women too – over six feet tall. For the most part they were fair-haired and light skinned. The men sometimes went clean-shaven, but more often they were fully bearded, usually with the upper lip shaven. Some considered the *Trekkers* 'rather good looking',[5] but to the eyes of an unsympathetic sophisticate like the young French naturalist, Adulphe Delegorgue, who in 1839 observed a party of Boer men, they were 'great gangling … fellows, with clumsy gestures, awkward bearing, dull faces,

---

[4] Walker, *Great Trek*, pp.32–5, 42; Pols, 'Voortrekker Museum', p.164.
[5] Cited by Walker, *Great Trek*, p.31.

faltering speech, gaping mouths, men made to drive oxen and to hold converse with them.' (He did concede, however, that they were the boldest and most skilful wagon drivers in the world.)[6]

There was no denying, though, that the Boers of the frontier districts generally lacked education. Only the children of the most well-to-do attended the government schools the British had established in some villages in the mid-1820's. Otherwise, Boer children learned what their mothers—and sometimes fathers—and the infrequent wandering tutor could teach them. This went little beyond instilling basic reading and writing skills, sufficient for their pupils to read the Bible, along with the occasional newspaper, and to put their pens to official documents and perhaps a short letter or two. Their lack of book-learning, beyond what was contained in the Bible, meant that most *Trekkers* were remarkably ignorant of the world beyond the circumscribed orbit of their own and neighbouring farms, and the nearest village with its magistracy. They were often at the magistrate's because they were a legalistically-minded, litigious people with sufficient leisure to mull over their grievances, constantly poring over their title deeds and interminably feuding over land-ownership and water and grazing rights.[7]

What held these *Trekkers* together – besides a commonly held distrust and dislike of the British administration – was *kommando* service and their religion. They were all Calvinists, members of the Nederduits Gereformeerde Kerk. Their speech was filled with Scriptural allusions and injunctions since the Bible, which they took literally, was the one book they could all at least pick through and recite. When the *Trekkers* were still living on their farms in the Cape, every morning and evening the household would gather for prayers and a reading from the Bible or a book of sermons, the Boers seated around the table, their Khoisan servants and 'apprentices' squatting against the wall. This practice continued in wagons or out of doors while on *trek*. The *Trekkers* were especially drawn to the Old Testament because it told the story of a semi-nomadic, pastoral people like themselves, especially chosen by God. Church buildings and ministers of religion (*predikante*) had been very scarce in the frontier districts, and the faithful had resorted to them only for the ceremonies of baptism, marriage, and burial. It was incumbent, however, for all to partake of *Nagmaal*, or Holy Communion, at least once a year, or quarterly if possible. Then the whole community would have gathered in the nearest village in their wagons, not only for religious observances, but for merry-making, shooting competitions, trading and bartering, and for energetic discussions about topical events. How *Nagmaal* would continue to be celebrated once the *Trekkers* were in the distant interior was a problem to be faced.

Although all the *Trekkers* had their strict Calvinist beliefs in common, they were nevertheless fractious in their faith in a way common to many Protestant sects. An extremely conservative and austere Calvinist religious movement had developed in the Netherlands in the early 1830s that preached a fundamentalist Biblical literalism and objected to hymns, church organs, candles, or fripperies of any kind. It caught on in the frontier districts of the Cape where its adherents came to be known as *Doppers*. These *Doppers* rapidly came to represent principled resistance to all things British, to unnecessary refinement of manners, and to innovations generally. Little, wonder, perhaps, that in popular speech having '*Dopper* manners' became a synonym for being uncouth. Not that the *Doppers* took any notice of this slur. They believed they had a special understanding

---

6   Adulphe Delegorgue, edited by Fleur Webb, Stephanie J. Alexander and Colin de B. Webb, *Travels in Southern Africa, Volume One* (Durban: Killie Campbell Africana Library; Pietermaritzburg: University of Natal Press, 1990), pp 87, 174.
7   Walker, *Great Trek*, pp.47–52.

of God's purpose, that it was their bounden promise—their covenant with Him—to fulfil His will, and that to fail to do so was to condemn oneself to eternal punishment. They signalled their distinctiveness as *Doppers* by adopting a unique manner of dress, different from that of other Boers. The women always shrouded their faces with plain *kappies* and wore their hair pulled back behind their ears, while the men placed broad-brimmed hats on their closely cropped heads. Men's jackets were worn so short that they invariably displayed an expanse of shirt at the back between the hem of the jacket and the unusually wide trousers favoured by *Doppers*. These sagged because they were held up by draw-strings rather than by new-fangled belts or braces, or were pinched up at the back with a strap and buckle. Despite their small numbers, the *Doppers* would nevertheless prove disproportionally influential during the Great Trek because of their strongly held belief they were fulfilling God's manifest purpose in whatever they did.[8]

The synod of the Nederduits Gereformeerde Kerk in the Cape—composed mainly of Scottish Presbyterian ministers to make up for the local shortfall—disapproved of the Great Trek, insisting that it would lead to godlessness among the Emigrant Farmers wandering so far from the nearest church. As a consequence, and to the dismay of the *Trekkers*, no *predikant* could be persuaded to join any of the emigrating parties. Yet, for the *Trekkers*, it was precisely their deeply-held religion that would save them from sinking (with or without a *predikant*) to the perceived degraded level of the heathen peoples who inhabited the interior of the subcontinent. On the Cape frontier in the 1830s it was still the supposed savagery, licentiousness, and godlessness of Africans that distinguished them from civilized Europeans, rather than their dark pigmentation as such. The pseudo-scientific concept of a hierarchy of races that justifies the domination of whites over blacks was a late-19th-century aberration based on a perversion of Darwin's theories. It played no part in the formulation of the racial attitudes of the *Trekkers*, but their Bible, which they took absolutely literally, did precisely that. Noah's curse on Canaan, the son of Ham, that 'a servant of servants shall he be' was the divine explanation for those born with a black skin, and was the justification for their subordination or enslavement.[9]

As Eric Walker has expressed it, the *Trekkers* 'went out of the Old Colony in a state of mind that ranged from a fury of suspicion against the British Government to a dull resentment.'[10] For, however brave a face they put on it—and putting aside the allure of adventure, the promise of new lands and opportunities, and the prospect of ruling themselves without British interference —all would have felt the Great Trek to have been a great physical and psychological uprooting. Yet most – and not just the *Doppers* among them—saw themselves in the same light as the Children of Israel whom God brought 'out of the land of Egypt, from the house of bondage.' They too were a Chosen People engaged in their own divinely ordained Exodus, and were justified by God in seizing the land from those who already dwelt there. For, as the Bible proclaimed, 'the Lord thy God bringeth thee into a good land … A land wherein thou shalt eat

---

8   John Laband, *The Transvaal Rebellion: The First Boer War 1880–1881* (London: Pearson Longman, 2005), pp. 25–6; Rev. H.F. Schoon and W.G.A. Mears (eds), *The Diary of Erasmus Smit* (Cape Town: C. Struik, 1972) (*Smit's Diary*), pp. 175–8: 'The Dutch Reformed Church and the Great Trek'; Walker, *Great Trek*, pp.32, 55–9. In 1859 the Doppers would break away from the mainstream Calvinists with the formation of the Gereformeerde Kerk van Suid Afrika.
9   *Genesis* 9: 25. See Giliomee, *Afrikaners*, pp.13–14, 34–8; Thompson, 'High Veld', p.407.
10 Walker, *Great Trek*, p.104.

bread without scarceness ... Thou art ... to go in to possess nations greater and mightier than thyself.'[11]

Yet, even though armed with this divine mandate, the *Trekkers* hoped they could find a place to dwell without having to fight for it. Piet Retief, who was destined to become the most charismatic leader of the Great Trek, stated the *Trekkers'* position unambiguously in a manifesto he published in the *Graham's Town Journal* on 2 February 1837, just as he was about to depart for the interior. 'We will not molest any people,' he declared, 'nor deprive them of the smallest property; but, if attacked, we shall consider ourselves fully justified in defending our persons and effects, to the utmost of our ability, against every enemy.' Nonetheless, Retief went on to assure his readers, 'We purpose in the course of our journey, and at arriving at the country in which we shall permanently reside, to make known to the native tribes our intentions, and our desire to live in peace and friendly intercourse with them.'[12] In practice, though, would it be possible to settled down peaceably in territory already inhabited by other people? The Bible indicated not, for the Israelites took Canaan bloodily by the sword. And, far closer in time and space, the *Trekkers* knew that the six wars of conquest and dispossession already fought along the Cape Eastern Frontier pointed strongly against the likelihood.

---

11   *Exodus* 20: 2; *Deuteronomy* 5: 6; 8: 7, 9; 9: 1.
12   John Centlivres Chase, *The Natal Papers: A Reprint of All Notices and Public Documents Connected with That Territory Including a Description of the Country and a History of Events from 1498 to 1843 in Two Parts*, facsimile reprint (Cape Town: C. Struik, 1968), Part 1, pp.83–4: Manifesto of the Emigrant Farmers by P. Retief, 2 February 1837.

9

Transorangia

Despite its great size, Africa is a continent with only limited tracts of territory suitable for human habitation. Much of it is desert or semi-arid scrubland, and its open grasslands are periodically afflicted by drought. Where rainfall is more plentiful and rivers flow the whole year through, then there are dense forests—but these harbour virulent insect-borne diseases. Most of the soil thinly covering the continent's ancient, rocky skeleton is lacking in nutrients and would have given the pioneering Bantu-speaking farmers working their way south from central Africa aeons ago a poor return for all their labour. Later on, when these African settlers acquired cattle, the search was on for suitable summer and winter grazing for their livestock. However, adequately watered regions low in disease that were fit for both farming and herding were restricted and patchily situated. And difficult as it is to imagine today after the unrelenting slaughter of Africa's wildlife over the last two centuries, wherever people ventured they were potential prey for great beasts such as lions and crocodiles, as were their livestock, while their fields were ravaged by elephants and hippos. All these pitfalls and dangers meant that great stretches of the continent were left uninhabited by African farmers and pastoralists who naturally concentrated in those select regions where they could best sustain themselves.[1]

For the *Trekkers* venturing into the interior, this likewise meant that localities suitable for permanent settlement were circumscribed. Once they crossed the *driwwe* of the middle Orange River into what was known to the British authorities as Transorangia, they had before them a vast parallelogram of grasslands suitable for pastoralism and limited agriculture. But to the west the grass faded away into the uninhabitable Kalahari Desert; while to the east the highveld was bounded by the Maloti Mountains and the great chain of the Drakensberg Mountains that drop down abruptly to the coastal lowlands. To the north the grasslands were bordered first by the mountain chain of the Soutpansberg, and then by the valley of the Limpopo River that harboured both the tsetse fly whose bite causes the deadly horse sickness, and the malaria-carrying mosquito, debilitating if not fatal to humans.[2]

Despite the subsequent *Voortrekker* legend of the 'empty land' that was theirs to claim, the highveld was indeed populated. Not that it ever had been heavily so. Confronted today by Africa's roiling population explosion, it is hard to imagine a time, only two centuries ago, when

---

1   John Iliffe, *Africans. The History of a Continent* (Cambridge: Cambridge University Press, 2000), p.1.
2   Eric A. Walker, *A History of Southern Africa* (London: Longmans, 1968), pp.201–2.

sub-Saharan Africa was noticeably under-populated. Even the largest kingdoms such as that of the amaZulu encompassed only about 250,000 subjects. During the decade before the Great Trek every African community on the highveld had been severely disrupted by the violent turmoil of the *Difaqane*. Thousands of people had been slaughtered or displaced and old polities crushed and broken up. But by the mid-1830s when the *Trekkers* were entering the area, new chiefdoms were putting down secure roots under strong rulers who provided protection for their adherents and allowed them to return to a settled way of life.[3]

When they crossed the Orange River, the *Trekkers* initially found themselves among various culturally and racially intermixed peoples whose way of life was little different from their own, and to whom the vague term of '*métis*' might be appropriately applied.[4] Settled since the early 19th century along a line of springs in the valley of the lower Orange River beyond its confluence with the Vaal River were a group of people know as the Korana or Kora. These Korana were the descendants of Khoisan who had been progressively pushed out from the fertile south-western Cape by Boer pastoralists trekking north in search of new hunting grounds and lands to settle. In their new home outside the Colony, the Korana regularly intermarried with the small, wandering bands of hunter-gatherer San, the original people of the land, and with the Setswana-speaking Batlhaping of the region. In the process of their enforced migration across the Orange, the Korana had adopted elements of the culture of their enemies, peppering their speech with Dutch words, adopting Dutch names, and wearing items of Dutch clothing. Most significantly of all, they took to riding horses and carrying muskets, and exploited them to become highly efficient and mobile raiders, preying on neighbouring settled communities.[5]

Towards the end of the 18th century another group of colonial outcasts had settled along the northern bank of the middle Orange River.[6] These were people of mixed-race origins, the offspring of white male colonists and Khoisan women or female slaves imported from the East Indies, Madagascar, or East Africa, as well as of intermarriage with the Batlhaping. They spoke a dialect that was the simplified form of Dutch that in the later 19th century would become the Afrikaans language, wore only European-style clothing, and were equipped like the Boers with muskets, horses, and wagons. They were known as the Oorlams, a word derived from Malay that refers to riding and shooting skills. Although they had lived at first among stock-farming Boers on the far northern margins of the Cape, these dark-skinned versions of the colonists found themselves increasingly rejected on racial grounds. Squeezed out, they made their home among the Korana and, like them, sought their fortunes in Transorangia.

There the Korana and Oorlams lived in semi-nomadic, heavily armed hunting communities, or gangs, sometimes called *drosters* (meaning deserters or absconders from servitude) raiding far and wide for cattle and taking slaves from other communities. When raiding, they operated just

---

3   See Wright, 'Turbulent Times', pp.213–19, 234–6, 239–247.
4   Paul S. Landau, *Popular Politics in the History of South Africa* (Cambridge: Cambridge University Press, 2010), pp.4 n.8, 5, 17, 145.
5   Robert Ross, 'The !Kora Wars on the Orange River, 1830–1888', *Journal of African History*, 16: 4 (1975), pp.561–3, 575.
6   For the early history of the Griqua, see Hermann Giliomee and Bernard Mbenga, *New History of South Africa* (Cape Town: Tafelberg, 2007), pp. pp. 68–9; Nigel Penn, *The Forgotten Frontier: Colonists and Khoisan on the Cape's Northern Frontier in the 18th Century* (Athens: Ohio University Press; Cape Town: Double Story Books, 2006), pp. 157–69; Kevin Shillington, *Luka Jantjie: Resistance Hero of the South African Frontier* (London: Aldgate Press, 2011), pp. 4–5, 8–9, 92; Storey, *Guns*, pp. 89–93.

like the mounted Boer *kommandos*, skilfully managing their old Tower muskets. By the early 19th century, they were established as the most mobile and feared fighters on the highveld, terrorizing the wide plains as far north as the country of the Bapedi. There the amaZulu encountered the 'yellow people on horses', [7] who would have been dressed in their familiar costume of 'white fustian jackets, leather pantaloons, striped waistcoats, white hats, with broad edges, shirts, neck-cloths, stockings and shoes.'[8]

Several main *droster* bands emerged, the Korana and Oorlams proper, the Bergenaars, the Hartenaars and the Basters (self-proclaimed 'mongrels') led by Adam Kok and Barend Barends (also known as Berend Berends). The Basters were nominally Christian, and Barends saw how the evangelical missionaries of the Protestant London Missionary Society [LMS] could help bring his people around to 'civilized' occupations instead of living by raiding. Indeed, missionaries in the interior were establishing themselves as the principal intermediaries for ideas and materials from the outside world and, since they traded to earn a living, the Cape government used them as its agents with the interior. The LMS were invited in 1804 to establish a mission station at Klaarwater, and the roving Basters began to settle around it. In 1813 the Rev. John Campbell persuaded the Basters to change their rather too explicit name to Griqua,[9] and Klaarwater was renamed Griquatown, which developed as an important trading centre well-known to the *Trekkers*.

As part of their drive to convert the Griqua to more civilized behaviour, the missionaries persuaded them to adopt a written constitution for a fledgling, independent statelet governed by a *Kaptein* (Chief) and advised by a council. Adam Kok II and Barend Barends were the first *Kapteins*, but political stability was not easy to impose. The Kok and Barends families were soon at odds with one another and with a further grouping led by Andries Waterboer. Waterboer was of Khoikhoi descent and gained respectability by closely allying himself with the missionaries. By the early 1820s he had established his political predominance in Griquatown. The British found they could deal with Waterboer's stable little state, and in 1834 concluded a treaty recognizing his sovereignty and the right to the land his people occupied. Adam Kok II, Waterboer's main rival, conveniently left the picture when, in 1826, he moved upstream along the Orange with his followers to settle at Philippolis. By the early 1830s the settlement had schools, a court house and magistracy, and a legislative council; in other words, the whole apparatus of government built in imitation of Cape institutions.[10]

To the north-west of the Korana and Griqua, in the parched terrain on the margins of the uninhabitable Kalahari Desert, lived the Setswana-speaking Batswana. The scarcity of water meant they could not settle in scattered household communities like the amaZulu and amaXhosa in their well-watered lands to the east. Instead, they packed into compact, dense settlements of round wattle-and-daub and thatched huts in those rare places where there were springs and sufficient water for their crops and herds. They worked iron acquired through trading the ivory

---

7   Isaacs, *Travels and Adventures*, p.100.
8   John Philip in 1825, quoted in Etherington, *Great Treks*, p. 133.
9   The name Griqua was derived from the Khoisan Cha-guriqua clan from which the former Basters were partly descended through Adam Kok I's marriage in the 1750s (Shillington, *Luka*, p.9 n.9; Landau, *Popular Politics*, pp.4, 13.
10 Landau, *Popular Politics,* p. 200; Giliomee and Mbenga, *South Africa*, pp. 143–144, Etherington, *Great Treks*, p.227.

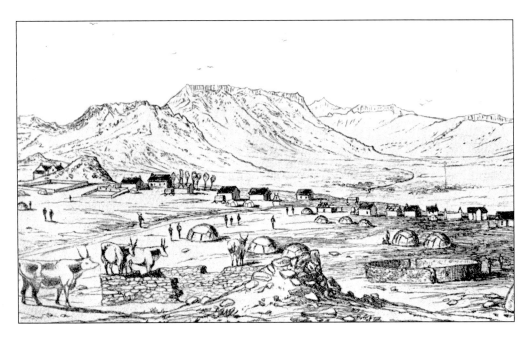

Philippolis, the capital of the Griqua *kaptein*, Adam Kok II. Anonymous drawing *c*.1830. (Anon., *Pictorial History of South Africa* (London: Odhams Press, *c*.1937))

and skins garnered in great game drives when they stampeded wild animals into pitfall traps to be killed.[11]

Shortages of agricultural land and pasturage, along with competition for trade, kept the Tswana chiefdoms in a state of endemic warfare with each. Succession disputes meant that chiefdoms were subject to regular splintering, and the vast stretches of unoccupied land made it easy to secede and move away. The Batswana consequently seldom succeeded in forming large, enduring states. One that lasted better than most others was that of the Batlhaping, established in the late 18th eighteenth century west of the Vaal River on the Ghaap plateau where, as we have seen, some intermarried with the *drosters*. (At its height, the chiefdom numbered no more than 10,000 people, an indicator of how low the population of any one of the polities of Transorangia was.) In 1812 Mothibi succeeded as chief and in 1820 permitted the Rev. Robert Moffat, a Scottish Congregationalist missionary and future father-in-law of the famous missionary and explorer, David Livingston, to settle at Dithakong, his capital.

By the 1820s the Batlhaping were under increasing pressure from Griqua raiders. Tlhaping warriors were traditionally armed with a bundle of long-shafted throwing-spears, and often carried a battle-axe with a crescent blade set into a stout, knobbed stick. For protection they had a small, light, cowhide shield cut distinctively into a pattern resembling an H turned on its side, the four wings designed to deflect cast spears rather than for tough, close combat.

---

11 Shillington, *Luka*, pp.22, 26; Paul Maylam, *A History of the African People of South Africa: From the Early Iron Age to the 1970s* (London: Croom Helm, 1989), pp.42–4.

Mothibi grasped that his warriors and their time-hallowed way of warfare were no match for the Griqua raiders with their muskets, and that future survival depended on acquiring guns for war and hunting, along with horses and ox-wagons.[12] Then, in 1823 Dithakong was threatened from the east by masses of refugees displaced by the turmoil of the *Difaqane* on the highveld. The Batlhaping were fortunate that Robert Moffat persuaded Andries Waterboer and the Griqua—lured on, it is true, by the prospect of booty and captives—to come to their aid with 200 horsemen.[13]

Victory at the battle of Dithakong on 23 June 1823 did more than save the Batlhaping from being overrun. It confirmed that the Batlhaping, as well as other Tswana chiefdoms, must adopt the Griqua way of war, and that it was necessary to forge alliances with the various *droster* groups. The *drosters*, and particularly the Griqua who traded colonial goods with the Batswana for their hunting products, became the middlemen in the illicit arms trade between the Colony and the African people to the north, and put pressure on the missionaries to supply the arms and ammunition necessary for hunting and raiding.[14] Soon the Batswana were joining the *drosters* in raiding and counter-raiding for cattle, women for wives, and children as menials, thus adding to the widespread disruption of the highveld.

Mothibi rewarded Moffat for securing victory at Dithakong by granting the LMS a fertile site in 1824 for their mission on the Kuruman River south of Dithakong. Kuruman duly became the missionaries' base from where they progressively eroded the traditional practices of the Batlhaping. Under their influence the Batlhaping abandoned their former dress of skins, along with the red-clay ochre they smeared over their bodies as protection against sun and parasites. Instead they took to wearing broad-brimmed hats, jackets and trousers in the Boer style, and became indistinguishable in dress from the Griqua.[15]

North-east of the Griqua at Philippolis, between the fertile valley of the Caledon River (which drains into the Orange River) and the Maloti Mountains, lay the Sotho kingdom of Moshweshwe. By the 17th century Sesotho-speaking people were living in the Caledon valley, but by the late 18th century they were being pressed by their Tswana and San neighbours and by raiding *drosters*. Then, in the late 1820s when Shaka began consolidating the new Zulu kingdom, wandering bands of desperate, displaced migrants began pushing into Sotho territory. Under intolerable pressure from the intruders, the southern Sotho chiefdoms collapsed and there was an almost complete breakdown of the existing social order. However, a leader of superior military and political talents arose out of this turmoil. He was Moshweshwe, the son of an undistinguished minor chief. Gathering together the remnants of various shattered Sotho chiefdoms, and under constant attack, in 1824 he led them south to safety on Thaba Bosiu. This was a flat-topped mountain with an area of about two square miles in the valley of the Phuthiatsana River. It was topped by sheer cliffs with a few easily defensible passes to the summit where there were many springs capable of supporting enough cattle to provision Moshweshwe's people during a siege. Over the next several years Moshweshwe beat off repeated

---

12 Shillington, *Luka*, pp.5–6, 11, 12–13; Ian Knight, *Warrior Chiefs of Southern Africa* (Poole: Firebird Books, 1994), pp 61, 65, 70, 71.
13 Maylam, *African People*, pp.59–60; Giliomee and Mbenga, *South Africa*, p.130; Shillington, *Luka*, pp.9, 11, Wright, 'Turbulent Times', p.235; Laband, *Zulu Warriors*, pp.160–1.
14 Storey, *Guns*, pp.90–3; Etherington, *Great Treks*, pp. 54, 223.
15 Shillington, *Luka*, pp.11–13.

attacks on Thaba Bosiu. From this natural fortress he fostered a cult of his superior leadership, attracted growing numbers of adherents, built up alliances and increased his cattle holdings. He also forged a common identity among his followers, the disparate victims of the upheavals of the *Difaqane*, who by the early 1830s were coming to be known as the Basotho.

Repeatedly threatened by the *drosters* with their muskets and horses—although they found that their *kommando* tactics of mounted charges, firing and retreating to reload did not work well in the mountainous terrain—Moshweshwe recognised that to be secure he had to follow suit.[16] He purchased his first horse in 1829 and his first firearm shortly thereafter from the *drosters* who continued to be a main source of supply since the British prohibited direct arms sales from gun-dealers in the Cape. Those of his adherents who worked as migrant labourers for white farmers in the neighbouring northern Cape were encouraged to bring home the cattle, guns and horses they bought with their wages. In 1830 Moshweshwe inflicted his first defeat on a band of raiding Griqua, thus demonstrating that the Basotho had successfully adopted their enemies' weapons and tactics. Moshweshwe continued to accumulate guns and horses and to use them to expand his chiefdom. To assist him in forging alliances with his neighbours to secure peaceful co-existence—but also to help him to acquire firearms with which to defend himself—Moshweshwe invited Christian missionaries to his kingdom. In 1833 the first to arrive were members of the Calvinist Paris Evangelical Mission Society who quickly proved useful in his negotiations with the Cape authorities.[17]

Immediately to the north of Moshweshwe's kingdom were his inveterate enemies the Batlokwa. They were located near the strategic passes down the southern Drakensburg to the lowlands of the Zulu kingdom, and were destined to play a significant role in the coming war between the Boers and the amaZulu. In around 1815 the Tlokwa chief, who ruled over maybe as many as 40,000 people of mixed Sotho, Tswana and Nguni origin, died. He left a son, Sekonyela, who was too young to rule so his mother MaNthatisi became queen-regent. She was a most capable and intelligent woman who succeeded in keeping the chiefdom together during the upheavals of the *Difaqane*, secure in her inaccessible mountain fortress of Kooaneng on the northern side of the Caledon River.

Once Sekonyela reached late adolescence, he asserted himself and thrust MaNthatisi aside. He was described as tall, like his elegant mother, but utterly lacking in her agreeable charm and tact. He was of surly demeanour with a taciturn way of speaking, relying on his impressively muscular physique and aggressive personality to browbeat all those who opposed him. There was no denying, however, that he was a very capable war leader, and it was he who had forced Moshweshwe south to Thaba Bosiu in 1824. In the on-going fighting between Sekonyela and Moshweshwe, the prize was the Caledon River valley that offered water, pasturage and defensible strongholds. The Batlokwa prevailed in the upper reaches of the valley, pushing the Basotho out. By early 1830s Sekonyela was emulating Moshweshwe in forming periodic alliances with the *drosters* and was likewise mounting his men on horses and equipping them with muskets. He deeply distrusted the missionaries entering the region because of their influence over his Griqua, Korana and Sotho rivals, and was happy to entertain British overtures of friendship.[18]

---

16 Etherington, *Great Treks*, p.169.
17 Thompson, 'High Veld', pp.394, 398–402; Etherington, *Great Treks*, pp.129, 131, 195; Storey, *Guns*, pp.96, 211–12, 215.
18 Thompson, 'High Veld', pp.394, 398, 400; Etherington, *Great Treks*, pp.79, 128–30, 195, 226, 243.

'Medicine man blowing counter charms towards the enemy.' Charles D. Bell, who accompanied Dr Andrew Smith during his expedition to the interior in 1834–35, drew Rolong warriors being 'doctored' before battle. (MuseumAfrica, Johannesburg, with permission)

The rivalry between Moshweshwe and Sekonyela for the control of the Caledon valley and its environs was complicated by the arrival in December 1833 of 5,000 or so newcomers. These were the Seleka branch of the Barolong (a Tswana people) who had been living in the environs of the Vaal River to the north-west. Beset by droughts and by raiding enemies, and wishing to be closer to supplies of firearms and ammunition essential for their self-preservation, they were persuaded by two Wesleyan Methodist missionaries, John Edwards and James Archbell, to migrate to the plain below Thaba Nchu (or Black Mountain) at the headwaters of the Modder River. There they formed a large, Tswana-style concentrated settlement under their chief, Moroka II, and were soon joined by more Setswana-speaking people and small allied groups of Korana and Griqua. Moroka converted to Christianity, built up local alliances and, like Sekonyela, looked to closer relations with the British to curb raiding by some of the *droster* groups and other enemies, especially Moshweshwe with his French, rather than British, missionaries.[19]

These developments in Transorangia meant that when the *Trekkers* began pushing onto the highveld they were at first not entering some unknown wilderness. This, as we have seen, was a

---

19   Thompson, 'High Veld', pp.401–3; Etherington, *Great Treks*, pp.204–5, 226–7, 308.

territory affected by long-standing linkages to the Cape and its institutions and by missionary endeavour. Everywhere in the little states in the process of consolidating themselves were people anxious to buy firearms, to trade goods and to establish positive relations with the colonial authorities. Many people wore colonial clothing, lived in settler-style houses and spoke a local form of Dutch evolving into Afrikaans. Colonial and non-colonial space merged here; people intermingled. The Griqua in particular were used to the incursion of Boer hunting parties, and to the hundreds of Boer men, women and children and their servants who ranged over their pastures and camped near their rivers and springs during time of drought. The *Trekker* parties would find no difficulty in securing people willing to act as interpreters or serve as guides, especially since their way of life differed so little from that of the heavily armed *drosters* already roaming the highveld.[20]

Nevertheless, all the societies in Transorangia were taken aback by the increasing number of parties of *Voortrekkers*, along with their retainers and livestock, who from 1835 began entering their territory. And when they realised that the newcomers were shrugging off British control and intended to settle on the highveld further to the north, they foresaw that these interlopers would inevitably clash with the powerful amaNdebele beyond the Vaal River, a warlike people with whom all these communities, as well as the *drosters*, had had several unsuccessful passages of arms.

---

20 Etherington, *Great Treks*, pp.50–3, 227–8, 340–4.

10

I Had to Keep Open Veld around Me

The Sotho, Tlokwa, Tlhaping, and Rolong chiefdoms of Transorangia that had been forged in the crucible of the *Difaqane* were essentially defensive in nature. They were held together by persisting outside threats and by effective diplomatic manoeuvring on the part of their rulers. Elsewhere, in several other new kingdoms spawned in this time of troubles, rulers had established firm, centralised control over their subjects and were able to deploy large military forces that aggressively dominated their rivals and extracted tribute from subject peoples. East of the Drakensberg, the Zulu kingdom was the preeminent militarised and expansionist state, followed by Soshangane's Gaza kingdom in the environs of Delagoa Bay. On the northern highveld, Mzilikazi kaMashobona's restless and aggressive Ndebele kingdom was created in the same mould, although it was probably responsible for more violence and disruption than either of these other two other predatory states.[1] It stood menacingly in the path of the *Trekker* parties pushing north across the Vaal River, and a confrontation appeared unavoidable.

The Ndebele kingdom arose from small beginnings. In the late 18th century several Khumalo chiefdoms emerged in the region of the sources of the Black Mfolozi in north-western Zululand. In around 1820 (the chronology is very uncertain) a group of about 300 young warriors and women of the abakwaKhumalo were led by their young chief Mzilikazi away from the hazardous zone of conflict between the abakwaNdwandwe and the amaZulu towards the upper reaches of the Vaal River on the highveld.[2] Evidence of Khumalo movements and raiding over the next six or so years is fragmentary and inconclusive. What is certain is that during their peregrinations Mzilikazi was steadily building up his chiefdom by seizing cattle and by incorporating refugees from the Sotho and Tswana chiefdoms that were falling apart during the disruptions of the *Difaqane*. By 1823 Mzilikazi's people were becoming known among Sesotho-speakers as 'Matabele' (amaNdebele in isiZulu), that is, 'marauders', although Mzilikazi always insisted on calling his adherents amaZulu.[3] With Shaka's final crushing

---

1   Wright, 'Turbulent Times', pp.242, 249–50.
2   *JSA* 5, pp.12–13: Norman Nembula, 8 February 1905; *JSA* 6, p.24: Socwatsha, 30 December 1901; William F. Lye, 'The Ndebele Kingdom South of the Limpopo River', *Journal of African History*, 10, 1 (1969), p.88. For a detailed account of the rise of the Ndebele kingdom, see R. Kent Rasmussen, *Migrant Kingdom: Mzilikazi's Ndebele in South Africa* (London: Rex Collings; Cape Town: David Philip, 1978), *passim*. For a succinct and up-to-date account, see Wright, 'Turbulent Times', pp.240–43.
3   Knight, *Warrior Chiefs*, p.107; Etherington, *Great Treks*, pp.165–66, 256.

victory over Sikhunyana kaZwide of the abakwaNdwandwe at the battle of the izinDolowane hills in October in 1826, the amaNdebele were augmented by many of the defeated Ndwandwe remnants who gave Mzilikazi their allegiance.[4]

It was not until a few years later that whites first encountered Mzilikazi and recorded their impressions of a man who was clearly an effective ruler and evidently an attractive personality. In 1829 the missionary Robert Moffat described him as an athletic, courteous man in his early thirties, with a pleasing, soft expression and an unexpectedly soft and feminine voice. There seems to have been no agreement on Mzilikazi's height, but he evidently had a round forehead, his body bore the scars of war and, as he grew older, he tended to corpulence. In 1836 an English hunting party found him manly, grave, and reserved in public assembly, but given to joking and laughing in private, familiarly pulling the hunters' full beards which he admired with surprise. On that occasion he was wearing an ample black leather cloak that reached to his heels. Like the Zulu king, Dingane, he loved to lead the dance and took especial pleasure in music. His bodyguard sang as they escorted him to and from his morning wash, and in the assembly the common people sang, rather than spoke their feelings, reciting his praises, and calling him the Elephant, the Great Lion.[5] There was certainly no doubting his personal charisma, and in 1833 a missionary reported:

> When he converses with a stranger he seems as if he penetrated into their very thoughts and when he wishes to please there is an ease and openness in his manner, and he can put on so fascinating a smile that it would be next to impossible for anyone not acquainted with his character not to be gained over to have a good opinion of him.[6]

'Machaka (warriors) conducting a train of tributary Baquains [Bakwena] with supplies for Matzelikatzi – 1835', by Charles D. Bell, 1835. (MuseumAfrica, Johannesburg, with permission)

4   Laband, *Assassination*, pp.78–9.
5   Lye, 'Ndebele', p.88; Etherington, *Great Treks*, pp.163, 166.
6   *RN 2*, p.216: no. 185: W.C. van Ryneveld to Chief Secretary to Government, Cape Town, 3 January 1833.

Indeed, Mzilikazi's undoubted magnetism should not be allowed to veil a harsher reality. As with Dingane, he ordered regular public executions—even his close relatives were not exempt—to underline his authority over his subjects. And there was no denying that his kingdom, as it expanded, developed into the major marauding power of the highveld. His warriors raided in all directions and drove away defeated enemies who would not submit to his rule and consent to be absorbed into his chiefdom.

In 1827/1828 Mzilikazi led the amaNdebele south-west to the good cattle country on the northern slopes of the Magaliesberg, territory where the Bakwena (a Sotho people) had been the original inhabitants. There he built two *amakhanda* on the Apies River, enDinaneni and enKungwini, and a third, enHlahlandlela, at its confluence with the Crocodile River. From this base, the amaNdebele continued to raid long distance for cattle, even venturing north across the Limpopo River into Shona country, and south over the Vaal into Transorangia where they attacked the Sotho communities. To the west, all the Tswana groups within closer raiding distance were broken up, subjugated, forced to pay tribute, or compelled to move away altogether into the Kalahari Desert where the Ndebele found it unprofitable to follow. The only major Tswana group to escape Ndebele raids were the Batlhaping because of the presence at Kuruman of the missionary Robert Moffat whom Mzilikazi did not wish to alienate.[7]

As in the Zulu kingdom, Mzilikazi's word was law, but his authoritarianism was checked by his inner council that advised him, and by a general council of chiefs that reflected popular opinion. The ruling group in Mzilikazi's socially stratified kingdom that formed his councils and provided his chief officers of state was drawn from the abakwaKhumalo and other families that had accompanied him when he first began his wanderings. They referred to themselves as *abasenzani*, 'those from down below', meaning the low-lying countryside east of the Drakensberg, and their language, isiZulu, was that of the court. Ranking under the *abasenzani* were the primarily Sesotho- and Setswana-speaking groups that had given their allegiance to Mzilikazi during the early stage of his migrations. They were collectively referred to as *abasenhla*, 'those from the higher country'. They were expected to learn isiZulu, build their huts in the Zulu way, and to dress in the Zulu fashion, even though the skimpy costume outraged Tswana modesty. In the outlying districts of the kingdom lived the low-status tributary groups, or *amahole*, people who had been subjugated in the later stages of the Ndebele migration and expansion.[8]

Mzilikazi's military system echoed those of other northern Nguni-speakers, and had much in common with those of the abakwaNdwandwe and amaZulu. Once an age-grade of youths —confined to those descended from the *abasenzani* and the *abasenhla*—who had been tending livestock at military stations since around the age of ten reached sexual maturity, Mzilikazi formed them into a new *ibutho*. Members of a young *ibutho* (known as *amajaha*) required his permission to marry, and this was granted only once they had distinguished themselves in battle, usually between five to 10 years after their *ibutho* had been formed. As in the Zulu kingdom, the members of an *ibutho* who had married undertook fewer military duties than the unmarried *amajaha*. These mature warriors with their many wives and children (including the sons who would be the next generation of *amajaha*), their accumulated herds of cattle and their captives taken in war settled down to raise their families in closely related clusters of small villages (what

---

7   Lye, 'Ndebele', pp.88, 90.
8   Julian Cobbing, 'The Evolution of Ndebele Amabutho, *Journal of African History*, 15, 4, (1974), p.629; Lye, 'Ndebele', pp.87, 91; Knight, *Warrior Chiefs*, p.108; Etherington, *Great Treks*, p.166.

white colonists referred to as 'towns'). However, the unmarried *amabutho* were stationed in *amakhanda* that held the kingdom's choice breeding cattle and were concentrated defensively in easy reach of Mzilikazi's own great place. Each *ikhanda* could house several hundred warriors, and differed from a typical Zulu one in that the *isigodlo* stood in its own stockade in the middle of the parade ground. One of the king's wives would reside there as his representative, but shared power with an *induna* who was both the military commander of the *ibutho* and the civil administrator of the district to whom all its village headmen reported.

Outside the central ring of *amakhanda*, settlement was less dense and military posts were positioned facing the direction from which an enemy was likely to mount an attack. Their garrisons guarded the villages in-between and tended the less valuable cattle. Beyond this outer ring of settlement, the population thinned out yet further, and there it was the function of the tributary *amahole* to guard the marches of the kingdom, to man the most outlying royal cattle posts, and to keep their rulers informed of any hostile activity. The ceaseless movement of *amabutho* on raiding expeditions helped screen these peripheral cattle stations, and ensured that more distant tributary chiefs remained true in their allegiance to Mzilikazi.

The Ndebele *amabutho* were armed and dressed in much the same style as their Zulu counterparts. They wore a penis sheath below their kilt or skimpier front and back covering of tails, and cow tails were tied above the elbows and below the knees. Although the headdress differed in detail from *ibutho* to *ibutho*, it was formed typically of a pom-pom made from a mass of ostrich, guineafowl, or crow feathers stitched to a string net, and ornamented with additional feathers. Officers wore distinctive, coloured feathers from blue cranes and the like. On ceremonial occasions (although not on campaign), warriors wore a cape around their shoulders made of cows' tails or ostrich feathers. Like the amaZulu, each warrior carried a great cow-hide shield fixed to a central stick that covered him down to the knees, and that, by its colour and patterning, identified to which *ibutho* he belonged. As with the amaZulu, each warrior carried several throwing-spears, a fearsome stabbing-spear, and often a knobbed stick as well. A warrior was expected to be courageous, to win or die, and was punished if he wavered.

When the Ndebele *amabutho* raided an enemy settlement, their preferred tactic (identical to the Zulu one) was to surround it before mounting a surprise attack at dawn. Then they would cast their throwing spears over the stockade to sow panic as they rushed in, and with firebrands blazing finished off the assault with their stabbing spears. In a field engagement their tactical intention was always to outflank and surround the enemy in the Zulu fashion, and to press home the attack in a fearsome hand-to-hand encounter with the stabbing-spear, sparing nothing except the cattle they took as booty.[9]

The tight cluster of settlement at the centre of Mzilikazi's kingdom north of the Magaliesberg occupied a well-watered, diverse, and defensible pasture land, and from there the amaNdebele dominated the open plains of the highveld, their roving *amabutho* (as we have seen) ensuring that subordinate chiefs remained loyal in their allegiance. The *amabutho* also raided cattle throughout a still wider zone extending several hundred miles in every direction from the kingdom's heartland. Nevertheless, despite the widespread projection of Ndebele power,

---

9 Cobbing, 'Ndebele Amabutho', pp.610–11, 613, 616, 618–19, 621–4, 629–31; Lye, 'Ndebele', pp.97–100; R. Summers and C.W. Pagden, *The Warriors* (Cape Town: Books of Africa, 1970), pp.20–8, 36–52. For a contemporary missionary account of Ndebele accoutrements and battle tactics, see *RN 2*, p.217, no. 185: W.C. van Ryneveld to Secretary to Government, Cape Town, 3 January 1833.

Mzilikazi felt insecure. And ironically, he knew that his people's success in accumulating vast herds of cattle through their incessant raiding would attract those who believed they in turn could predate off the amaNdebele. He continued to fear attack by Dingane's armies even though hundreds of miles of sparsely occupied grassland separated him from the Zulu kingdom to the south-east. To the south, Mzilikazi faced the *drosters* and their allies whose raiding had for a generation dominated the highveld from the Orange River to the Magaliesberg.[10]

For their part, the *drosters* recognised that ever since the amaNdebele had moved to the environs of the Magaliesberg that they presented a growing challenge that demanded to be countered, even though they were without guns or horses. In July 1828 Jan Bloem, the leader of the Links Korana,[11] assembled a *kommando* of mounted Korana, Bergenaars, and Griqua armed with muskets and supported by Taung and Rolong foot soldiers under Molitsane, the Taung chief. Seizing the opportunity while most of Mzilakazi's *amabutho* were away on campaign to the west against the Bangwaketse, Bloem's *kommando* attacked the Ndebele frontier cattle posts from the south-west and made off with 3,000 cattle. The Ndebele pursued and overtook the retiring *kommando* and succeeded in regaining most of their cattle. In July 1829 Mzilikazi took his revenge when he counterattacked across the Vaal, crushed Moletsane and the Bataung, and ravaged the Caledon River valley before being finally driven off by the Basotho and Batlokwa.[12]

The Griqua *Kaptein*, Barend Barends, who had attracted Methodist missionaries to his base at Boetsap on the Harts River, resolved that it was his Christian duty to take the war back against the godless amaNdebele. In June 1831 he recruited a grand coalition of Hartenaars, Bergenaars, and Griqua (led by Hendrik Hendriks and Cornelis Kok). These 300 or so horsemen were supported by about 1,500 Tswana spearmen. As with Bloem's raid of 1828, Barends struck deep into the Ndebele heartland while most of Mzilikazi's *amabutho* were away (this time raiding the Shona people to the north), and drove off great herds of captured cattle. And, as before, with their superior discipline and strong command structure the Ndebele tracked down the retiring *kommando*. While its members slept, the Ndebele *amabutho* surprised their unguarded camp at Kena near modern-day Sun City, killed several hundred of the raiders and recaptured most of the cattle. For years afterwards the site was littered with whitened bones and broken muskets that had proved useless in the hand-to-hand melee when the Ndebele overwhelmed the defenders before they could reload. The victorious amaNdebele then pushed on across the Vaal, scattered several more Griqua parties and captured muskets, horses, wagons, and some children.

The amaNdebele had little time to enjoy their second victory over the *drosters*. The amaZulu, perhaps supposing that Mzilikazi would be weakened after these two encounters, and taking advantage of the absence of the bulk of the Ndebele *amabutho* in renewed raiding towards the north, struck in August 1832. Ndlela kaSompisi, one of Dingane's two great *izinduna*, led a large Zulu army deep into Mzilikazi's territory. In fierce fighting along the Apies River, the amaZulu defeated Mzilikazi himself and the small force he had on hand, and destroyed a number of his *amakhanda*, including enHlahlandlela, his great place. With the rushed return of the main Ndebele army the amaZulu withdrew with disappointingly few cattle as booty, but well pleased with the resounding success of their strike against their inveterate enemy and rival.

---

10 Etherington, *Great Treks*, pp.196, 198, 253.
11 The future town of Bloemfontein, the capital of the Orange Free State, was named after him.
12 Lye, 'Ndebele', p.91; Etherington, *Great Treks*, p.196.

Soon after the Zulu attack, in late 1832, Mzilikazi moved the core of his kingdom some 125 miles west to the headwaters of the Marico River where he established one great place at Mosega (10 miles south of the modern town of Zeerust) surrounded by a cluster of *amakhanda*, and another, eGabeni, 40 miles to the north of it. This was the heart of the well-watered, fine grazing country ruled by the Hurutshe chiefs who had already submitted to him. Many Bahurutshe remained and gave their allegiance to Mzilikazi; but others scattered south into the territory of the Batlhaping and Griqua, destabilising the region around the lower Vaal. Mzilikazi's intention in setting up his headquarters in the Marico valley was not only to distance himself further from Zulu attacks. He also wished to make it easier to confront the Tswana communities that had combined with Bloem and Barends in their raids of 1828 and 1831. Wasting no time, no sooner had Mzilikazi moved to the Marico than he launched a series of raids against those who had been complicit in Barend's great *kommando*, forcing the Bangwaketse further west. Many of the Rolong and Hurutshe chiefs who would not bow to him moved south (as we have seen) to Thaba Nchu with the remnants of their cattle herds in the hope that they would obtain revenge in the future with the help of Barends or Bloem.

And, indeed, in May 1834 Bloem organised a major expedition of mounted Korana and Griqua, supported by Tswana footmen, to raid Mzilikazi's poorly defended cattle posts for the third time. His attack followed the same pattern as the previous raids of 1828 and 1831: the surprise seizure of cattle, a successful Ndebele counterattack and the recovery of their livestock. This success might have encouraged Mzilikazi to push further south and eliminate the *droster* threat once and for all. But he did not wish to over-extend himself militarily. Nor did he wish to annoy the British at the Cape with whom (as we shall see) he was hoping to forge friendly relations, by intruding into their sphere of interest. So Mzilikazi adopted the policy of maintaining an empty buffer zone beyond the southern marches of his kingdom, and contented himself with chasing out any hunting or trading parties that ventured into it without his prior permission.[13] As he told the elephant hunter, Jan Viljoen, for fear of attack 'I had to keep open veld around me.'[14]

It had become increasingly obvious to Mzilikazi that the best way to neutralise the continuing threat posed by the *drosters* was to enlist the support of the British in restraining them. It was for that reason that from 1829 he fostered good relations with the missionaries among the Batswana in the hope that they would act as sympathetic intermediaries between him and the Cape authorities. In the event, it was not the missionaries who were instrumental in cementing an alliance between the British and the amaNdebele, but Dr Andrew Smith.

In 1834 Governor D'Urban supported a new government-sponsored expedition of exploration into the interior under Smith's leadership. Ostensibly, Smith was simply on 'an expedition of discovery and scientific research', but his real brief was to gather information about the important chiefs of the highveld, and to cultivate a 'good understanding' among 'surrounding native tribes' with the purpose of establishing 'a consequent influence' among them.[15]

---

13 Lye, 'Ndebele', pp. 91–4, 102; Etherington, *Great Treks*, pp.196–8, 227; Knight, *Warrior Chiefs*, pp. 112, 115.
14 Quoted in Lye, 'Ndebele', p.91.
15 *RN 2*, p.268, no. 202: D'Urban's passport for Smith and his party, 1 July 1834; *RN 3*, p.35, no. 23: D'Urban to Glenelg, 23 April 1836.

Smith set out in July 1834 in a number of fine wagons with a bevy of companions, assistants, and servants, escorted by well-armed British soldiers. In his baggage he carried several large marquees and elaborate presents. Indeed, everything was calculated to overawe and win over those African rulers he encountered. Smith's expedition coincided with the Sixth Cape Frontier War of 1834–1835, and he made sure that all these chiefs were thoroughly informed of dire fate befalling the amaXhosa who had dared to cross swords with the British.[16]

After visiting, among others, Moshweshwe and Sekonyela, in March 1835 Smith entered Mzilikazi's domain. Thanks to Moffat's good offices, Smith presented Mzilikazi with a medal and a cloak as symbols of D'Urban's desire for a treaty of friendship. Mzilikazi responded by sending Mncumbathe, one of his very top advisors, to Cape Town to enter into a formal treaty with the British. After being entertained for six weeks when every effort was made to impress Mncumbathe and his companions with the power and sophistication of colonial life, on 3 March 1836 Mncumbathe drew his cross for his master, 'Umsiligas' on the treaty between the Ndebele ruler and D'Urban. The treaty bound Mzilikazi to be a friend of the Colony, to preserve order in his land, to abstain from war except in self-defence, to protect all white men who visited him, to defend any missionaries who might settle among his people and to refrain from interfering with other chiefdoms in his vicinity. For his part, D'Urban engaged to grant Mzilikazi periodic gifts and to arrange for a missionary to settle with him to forward the intentions of the agreement.[17]

As a result of this treaty between the Cape and the Ndebele kingdom, D'Urban confidently anticipated 'very beneficial results to the peace and good order of the country without our Northern border, and consequently of that border itself.'[18] In London, Lord Glenelg declared himself extremely gratified by 'the propriety' of the steps D'Urban had taken in eliciting a desire among the 'neighbouring tribes' for developing 'an amiable intercourse with the colony' essential for 'retaining peace.'[19]

Although Dr Smith reported Mzilikazi equally 'very anxious for peace',[20] the Ndebele ruler nevertheless made it clear that he would resist any hostile intrusion onto his territory.[21] For the truth of it was that while Mzilikazi was ready to employ diplomatic means to secure his future security, he knew he would very likely still have to resort to arms to defend himself. And in doing so, he was prepared to adopt the new military technology.

The laws of the Cape forbade the export of firearms to the interior, but the illicit trade persisted in Transorangia nonetheless. When discussing firearms with missionaries, Mzilikazi affected to despise them, saying correctly enough that they 'would be very good things if they did not require to be reloaded'. He added that if those who attacked him were armed with guns but were not mounted and so could not 'run away', then his warriors would not fear them. Yet, the truth was that he did not doubt the efficacy of firearms, and firmly intended to use them against the *drosters* should they attack him again. In early 1833 he stated that he had 'about 400 in his possession which he took from the *kommandos* of Bloom and Barends', and that in

---

16 *RN 3*, p.24, no. 12: Dr Smith, 16 January 1836; Lye, 'Ndebele', pp.87, 93–4; Etherington, *Great Treks*, pp.192, 221, 223, 236–8.
17 Lye, 'Ndebele', p.103.
18 *RN 3*, p. 5, no. 23: D'Urban to Glenelg, 23 April 1836.
19 *RN 3*, p.88, no. 36: Glenelg to D'Urban, 3 September 1836.
20 *RN 3*, p 31, no. 18: Statement by Dr A. Smith, *c.*March 1836.
21 Etherington, *Great Treks*, p.237.

addition he had obtained 'three hundred horses and abundance of ammunition which has been furnished to him by the traders'.[22] But before Mzilikazi could integrate guns and horses into the Ndebele military system, events overtook him.

Despite his fearsome reputation and the havoc he had perpetrated on the highveld, Mzilikazi's kingdom was not nearly as powerful as it appeared, even if by 1836 it was at its widest extent. The core remained at Mosega and eGabeni on the Marico River. To the west the amaNdebele continued to maraud among the Batswana in the environs of the Malopo River, but not beyond. The Limpopo River was Mzilikazi's natural boundary to the north, and he did no more than raid the Shona people beyond. He never occupied the land to the east in order to keep a space between him and the amaZulu. The Vaal continued to serve as his southern boundary, and for fear of the *drosters* the amaNdebele patrolled it and left the land denuded as another cordon sanitaire. That meant the territory Mzilikazi firmly controlled was only about 200 miles across from north to south and from east to west, and only part of that was settled.

Nor were the military forces at his command nearly as large as their formidable reputation seemed to warrant, and were nowhere near the 50,000 men imagined by the military authorities in the Cape.[23] In fact, in March 1836 Dr Smith reported: 'The male population between the ages of 15 and 60 have been estimated by me at 4,000. About 2,000 are regularly trained and kept as warriors, the remaining 2,000 are occupied in taking care of the cattle and performing the other duties of the state.'[24] No wonder, then, that when Mzilikazi mobilised his army for a major raid that he had to leave his territory largely unguarded—a situation that (as we have seen) the *drosters* and amaZulu had repeatedly exploited.

Above all, Mzilikazi feared further raids by the mounted and well-armed *drosters*. He hoped, however, that his treaty of friendship with the Cape would serve as a restraint and deter any further attacks from south of the Vaal. What he did not anticipate was that a new group of people who came in large numbers, who were dressed, armed, and equipped exactly like the *drosters*, and who were constrained by no treaty with the British that bound them to keep the peace, would invade his territory with the clear intention of staying.

22   *RN 2*, p.217, no. 185: W.C. van Ryneveld to Secretary to Government, Cape Town, 3 January 1833.
23   *RN 2*, p.234, no. 191, annex. 1: Remarks on the military defence of the Eastern frontier of the Cape by Col. Henry Somerset, 20 March 1833.
24   *RN 3*, p.31, no. 18: Statement by Dr A. Smith, *c.*March 1836.

11

They Came with Wagons

The first two parties of *Trekkers* that left to settle in the interior quit the Colony surreptitiously, and would hardly be remembered were it not for their ultimately tragic wanderings that, in retrospect, seemed heroically to foreshadow the vicissitudes endured by those who came after them. One group was led by Louis Tregardt (later spelled 'Trichardt' by the family), the lawless eastern frontier son of a father of Swedish descent who had a long record of resisting both Dutch and British authority. In 1834 he and 30 Boers families had settled outside the Colony along the White Kei River in territory still ruled by Hintsa, the chief of the amaGcaleka and the Xhosa paramount. There Tregardt and his companions traded firearms illegally and took slaves despite the Slavery Abolition Act of 1833.[1] When a government patrol finally swooped on his settlement in November 1834 he fled with a price on his head, along with a party of nine men who could bear arms. Once across the Orange River, Tregardt joined another party of 10 men led by 'Lang Hans' Janse van Rensburg. Almost all the men in both parties were married and had their wives with them, as well as about 30 children in each group. An unrecorded number of Khoisan slaves and Xhosa servants accompanied them. The two small trek parties slowly made their way to the Soutpansberg in the far north, their pace determined by their flocks of sheep that could go no further than five miles a day. Their ultimate goal was Portuguese Delagoa Bay where they intended to settle beyond British jurisdiction. Van Rensburg's party eventually disappeared without a trace in June 1836 near the Limpopo valley, seemingly wiped out by Soshangane's Gaza warriors or their allies. Tregardt's party stayed in the Soutpansberg for more than a year before slowly moving eastwards in November 1836, finally crossing over the northern reaches of the Drakensberg to reach Delagoa Bay in April 1838. There, most of the party—including Tregardt himself and his wife—soon succumbed to malaria.[2]

Andries Hendrik Potgieter led the first significant trek north. A resolute and single-minded farmer, he left the Cradock District in the Eastern Cape in December 1835 with a group consisting mainly of his extended family, neighbours and friends travelling in about 50 wagons. His party included 33 full-grown men and seven lads of over 16 who were also capable of bearing arms. His party grew along the way and was joined by that of Charl (Sarel) Celliers (or

---

1 Laband, *Land Wars*, p.194.
2 Walker, *Great Trek*, pp.109, 111–13; Etherington, *Great Treks*, pp.246–8. See Jackie Grobler (ed.), *Louis Tregardt se Dagboek 1836–1838* (Pretoria: Litera Publikasies, 2013), *passim*.

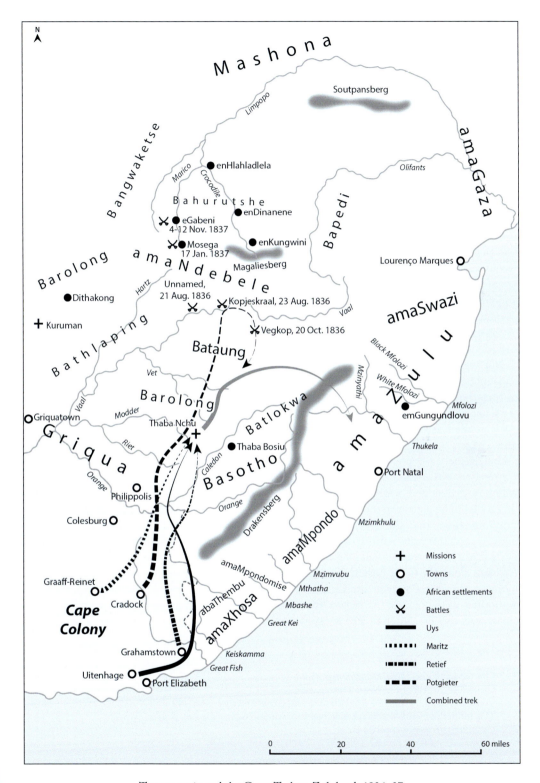

Transorangia and the Great Trek to Zululand, 1836–37

Cilliers) from the Colesberg District with 25 adult men, augmented by Caspar Kruger's small group including the 10-year-old Paul Kruger who would one day be the last president of the Zuid-Afrikaansche Republiek (or Transvaal Republic) founded in 1852.

The two parties separately crossed the Orange with their horses and oxen swimming the flooded river, while their wagons, small stock, domestic belongings, and the *Trekkers* themselves were all floated over on rafts made of the willow trees that grew along the river bank. The women, whom a British settler described as fancying they were 'under a divine impulse' in undertaking their trek,[3] joyfully raised their voices in sacred song as, with psalm-books in hand, they stepped onto their Promised Land.

The two parties passed Philippolis and journeyed on through Adam Kok II's territory without hindrance. The Griquas profited by the intruders' need to buy supplies and, in any case, felt unthreatened by the *Trekkers* whom they closely resembled in language, religion and customs. Indeed, they could readily accept Potgieter's assurance that 'We are emigrants together with you … who dwell in the same strange land, and we desire to be regarded as neither more nor less than your fellow-emigrants.'[4] To the chiefs of the Barolong, Bataung, Batlhaping, and Batlokwa to the north of the Griquas, the Trekkers would appear at first to be just one more set of Griqua families on the move, potentially dangerous because of their muskets, horses, and wagons, but people with whom they could likewise come to terms and recruit as allies. In particular, those who had suffered from Mzilikazi's depredations believed they could harness *Trekker* aid in regaining their lost cattle and territory, and hoped the *Trekker kommandos* would succeed where Barends's and Bloem's *drosters* had previously failed.[5]

Nor were the Boers unwilling to enter into treaty relations with the African chiefs they encountered. Even if it was their ultimate intention to dispossess the Africans of the interior and to turn those they did not drive away into labourers on their farms—precisely what settlers in the Cape had been doing since the mid-17th century—they initially needed the help of as many African allies as they could secure against those rulers who decided to oppose their advance. The *Trekkers* were legalistically-minded and Gerrit Maritz, a wagon-maker whose party left Graaff-Reinet in September 1836, took numerous legal works along with him. Included was *On the Law of War and Peace* by the 17th-century Dutch humanist and jurist, Hugo Grotius, in which he deliberated in what circumstances it was legitimate to wage war, and canvassed what limits should be placed on the conduct of belligerents.[6] It was as part of their culturally-defined thinking, then, that the *Trekkers* were anxious to enter into verbal agreements and—even better—formal treaties with African rulers in order to legitimise what they seized by violence or by its threat. Such treaties had long been an important element in relations between settlers and Africans along the Cape Eastern Frontier where most *Trekkers* hailed from.[7] Indeed, at the very moment when the Potgieter and Celliers parties were moving through Transorangia, the Cape authorities were preparing to replace their recent policy of military coercion against the Xhosa chiefs with the institution of a treaty system regulated through resident diplomatic agents.[8]

---

3   Quoted in Walker, *Southern Africa*, p.200.
4   Quoted in Etherington, *Great Treks*, p.249.
5   Walker, *Great Trek*, pp.114–15; Etherington, *Great Treks*, pp. 244, 249.
6   This influential work was first published in Latin in 1625 as *De Iure Belli ac Pacis*.
7   Giliomee, *Afrikaners*, pp.162–3.
8   Laband, *Land Wars*, pp.192, 196.

In early 1836 the Potgieter and Cellier parties converged on Thaba Nchu, which they referred to as Blesberg, or Bald Mountain. It seemed a good place to halt and take stock for a couple of months since, as the base of so many people who had been dispossessed by the amaNdebele and who were burning for revenge, they were given a warm welcome as potential allies. Moroka II of the Barolong became their close friend, and relations were opened up with Sekonyela of the Batlokwa. Knowing that when they moved on from Thaba Nchu into unknown and potentially perilous territory that proper military organisation was required, the members of Potgieter's and Celliers's parties drew on their long experience on *kommando* in the Cape to set up a command structure. The 65 men in the two parties able to bear arms voted that Potgieter should be the *Kommandant* of the combined trek and Celliers his deputy. Potgieter's men were in the majority so the outcome of the vote was inevitable, but the choice was the right one, nevertheless.

Sarel Celliers photographed in *c*.1855. (Gustav Gerdener, *Sarel Cilliers* (Pretoria: J.C. van Schalk, 1925))

Potgieter, who had been born in 1792, was a veteran of both the Fourth (1811–1812) and Fifth (1818–1819) Cape Frontier Wars. His was a powerful personality. He was easy with children, but there was no disguising that he was a natural leader, active and energetic. A tall, lanky man, but strong and wiry, he had long darkish hair and wore a closely-cropped, brown scrubby beard with his upper lip clean-shaven. As a *Dopper*, he wore the characteristic short jacket of his sect, and his wide-brimmed straw hat with its green lining shaded his blue eyes and his deeply line face with its broad cheekbones. In sharp contrast, Celliers was short and thick-set with a ruddy complexion and fair hair. He too shaved his upper lip and wore a short beard. Where Potgieter was dauntingly taciturn, Celliers was lively, self-confident, and an eloquent speaker, a skill he was more than happy to display when leading prayers (he was an orthodox Calvinist) or indulging in vigorous theological debates. Some found him unctuous and self-centred, but he was warm-hearted and served the combined trek well as a conciliator.[9]

Potgieter was anxious to move his party away from the British zone as soon as possible. The territory of Makwana, the Taung chief, lay beyond Thaba Nchu, and once Willem Pretorius had made an alliance with him, in mid-May 1836 he led the joint trek some 80 miles north to a new encampment at the Sand River. This was intended as but a temporary halt because Potgieter was determined his people should settle even further north, across the Vaal River. Once they were there, it would be essential to establish a viable route to Portuguese Delagoa Bay where they

---

9   Walker, *Great Trek*, pp.115–16; Etherington, *Great Treks*, pp. 249–50.

could regularly resupply themselves, without hindrance from the British, with sugar, coffee, tea, and other groceries, and (above all) with gunpowder and lead for their muskets. With the objective of finding a viable route to Delagoa Bay, on 24 May 1836 Pretorius set out from the Sand River encampment with a scouting party, or *kommissietrek*, of 11 men. He intended along the way to inspect the territory across the Vaal for good grazing country and for likely spots for permanent settlements. The *Kommandant* also planned to make contact if he could with the Tregardt and van Rensburg parties.

In June 1836 Pretorius did indeed visit Tregardt in the Soutpansberg, but searched in vain for van Rensburg, pushing north-east across the Limpopo in his quest. Failing to discover a good route down the northern Drakensberg to Delagoa Bay, and deterred by the vast distances and the deadly diseases that could kill people as well as livestock (as Tregardt would discover to his cost) Pretorius decided he had done enough. In August 1836 he and his small party began their ride back to join the combined trek on the highveld, little suspecting what they would find there.[10]

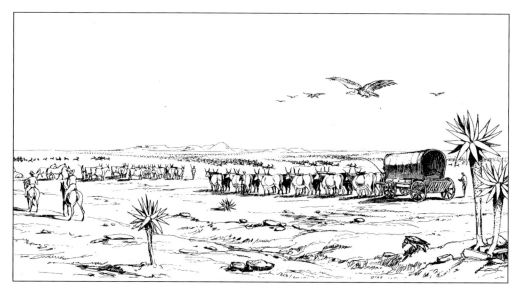

Boers trekking over the open plains north of the Orange River with herds of wild game in the distance. Anonymous drawing. (Western Cape Provincial Archives and Records Service, by permission)

During Potgieter's absence, members of the joint trek had spread northwards, scattering in temporary camps along the south banks of the Vaal. By August 1836 two groups with 40 wagons had crossed the Vaal near the present town of Parys and moved westwards down its northern bank. There they found themselves moving through vast grasslands empty of human habitation and apparently free for the taking. They did not grasp that while large chiefdoms clustered their main settlement in desirable locations, they pastured their herds more widely and

---

10 Walker, *Great Trek*, p.118.

projected power further still. Such, as we have seen, was the practice of the Ndebele kingdom into whose territory the unwary *Trekkers* had strayed. Luck had been with the Tregardt and van Rensburg treks, and with Potgieter's reconnaissance too, because when they journeyed north, they unintentionally skirted east of the usual range of Ndebele operations, through the depopulated buffer zone they left between the amaZulu and themselves. However, it was not long before Mzilikazi's scouts informed him on 15 August 1836 of the *Trekkers* encamped in considerable numbers either side of the Vaal on land he considered part of his domain.

Afterwards, Mzilikazi assured two British officers who visited him that his ensuing attack on the encampments of the joint trek had been provoked by their entering his territory from the direction always taken by *droster* raiders. Had they come by way of Kuruman, Moffat's mission station, which was the route he had sanctioned for traders and travellers entering his domain, then (so he declared) he would have known that the Trekkers came with the missionary's blessing and he would have accorded them a safe passage through his kingdom. As it was, he was especially concerned that the Boers who were encamped along his sensitive southern border were not a typical mounted *droster kommando* but came with wagons, women, children, herds, and servants. Clearly, this was not a raid but a full-scale invasion with the objective of settling permanently in Ndebele territory. In confirmation, Mzilikazi's spies reported that the *Trekkers* had been negotiating with African rulers south of the Vaal to be allowed to settle. There could be only one response to this naked challenge, and that was to expel the would-be settlers by force of arms. Military success usually attended on speed and surprise, and Mzilikazi resolved to strike first, and hard.[11]

The first Boers attacked by the amaNdebele were not strictly members of a trek party. On 28 June 1836 Stephanus Petrus Erasmus had left his farm Mooiplaats in the north-eastern corner of the Cape Colony as leader of a party of eight white men, eight Khoisan servants, five wagons, 80 oxen and 50 horses. He was a local *veldkornet* and had official permission to go elephant-hunting beyond the Orange River. But the truth of it was that he was also investigating the possibilities of emigration and was on a *kommissietrek*.

On the morning of Sunday, 21 August 1836, Erasmus and his son Pieter left their camp on the northern side of the Vaal at Coquis Drift (now known as Scandinavia Drift), about 30 miles south of modern town of Potchefstroom, to go hunting. Two of Erasmus's other sons went out to collect the carcases of antelope shot the previous day. Except for Carel Kruger who remained in the camp, the other Boers likewise set off to hunt and explore. Unbeknown to Erasmus and his party, a war party of about 500 amaNdebele was rapidly approaching from the direction of the Marico River. As an indication of the importance Mzilikazi invested in this operation, the Ndebele force was under the command of no less a personage than Kaliphi, his leading general who was also was in charge of Mosega itself and of all the country to its south.[12]

When Erasmus and his son Pieter returned to their camp that evening, they found the wagons and livestock gone and the speared bodies of five of their servants on the ground. Members of the American Missionary Society [AMS] settled close by Mosega since 1832 later interviewed three of Erasmus's servants who had been taken prisoner. They reported that Kaliphi's men had pulled Erasmus's five wagons back to Mosega, and that his two other sons and Carel Kruger

---

11   Lye, 'Ndebele', pp.94, 102; Etherington, *Great Treks*, p.249.
12   Lye, 'Ndebele', p.98.

had been captured alive in order to demonstrate to the amaNdebele how to *inspan* (yoke) oxen to the wagons. However, when the three Boers attempted to escape Zethini, Kaliphi's second-in-command, had them summarily executed. Nothing else was ever heard of the other white members of the party who had been out hunting, and they were presumed to have been tracked down and killed.

A party of amaNdebele were lying in wait for Erasmus and his son when they returned to the site of their devastated camp. The two horsemen managed to break out of the ambush and gallop off in the direction of two groups of the joint trek that were encamped on the north bank of the Vaal 30 miles away, just across the river from the modern-day town of Parys. Early on the morning of 22 August, the two exhausted fugitives reached the south-westerly of the two group. It consisted of members of the Kruger, Steyn, Bronkhorst, and other families who were scattered in the vicinity of what was later to be the Kopjeskraal farm. They had no expectation whatsoever of being attacked but, on hearing Erasmus's grim tale, the scattered families congregated in their wagons as quickly as they could and formed a circular laager.

However, no Ndebele attack occurred that day, and early the following morning, 23 August, Erasmus set out from the Kopjeskraal laager with 11 mounted men to search for the missing men of his hunting-party, his wagons and livestock. After an hour's ride, which would have taken them about six miles, they encountered a force of about 500 amaNdebele advancing in the direction of the Kopjeskraal laager. In accordance with their *kommando* training, Erasmus's group immediately conducted a fighting retreat to the laager, dismounting, firing a volley, then remounting to retire and reload before repeating the same procedure.

The mounted men regained the laager just ahead of the Ndebele attack, swelling the number of the defenders to 35 men. They were under the command of Johannes Lodewikus Petrus Botha whom Potgieter had appointed to act as *Kommandant* in his absence. The amaNdebele had never encountered a laager before, but they were not deterred. Deploying as usual with their horns thrown out, they surrounded the laager and dauntlessly threw themselves at it. They attacked again and again between 10:00 a.m. and 4:00 p.m. but were unable to break in and finally withdrew. Only one of the defenders was killed in the affray, as well as several Khoisan herdsmen who had been tending the Boers' livestock and were not able to make it into the laager in time. The amaNdebele seem to have lost about 50 men in what is sometimes called the Vaalrivierslag (battle at the Vaal River), as well as the battle of Kopjeskraal.[13]

During the battle, at about 10:30 a.m., several horses as well as an *inspanned* team of oxen dragging a *disselboom* came into sight from the north-east. Ominously, the second of the two *Trekker* groups north of the Vaal was encamped in that direction, its nine waggons scattered around a conspicuous little hill about three miles north of the river where the modern bridge crosses over. This party was under the leadership of the patriarch Gotlieb Liebenberg Snr of the Colesberg District and was made up of his wife, four sons and a daughter—all of whom were married—their 21 children, a Scottish *meester* (schoolmaster) called MacDonald, and a dozen or more Khoisan servants. Warning of the Ndebele attack on the Kopjeskraal laager was carried

---

13 For the battle at the Vaal River, see Johannes J. Retief, 'The Voortrekkers and the Ndebele. Part One: Attacks on the Vaal River and Liebenbergskoppie, 21 and 23 August 1836', *Military History Journal*, 16: 1 (December 2015), <samilitaryhistory.org/vol166jr.html>, accessed 30 July 2020; Chase, *Natal Papers*, Part 1, p.74: account by J.G.S. Bronkhorst; Summers and Pagden, *Warriors*, p.80; Walker, *Great Trek*, p.122.

to them—on his mother's urging—by a youth called Rudolph Bronkhorst. Nothing more was ever seen of the unfortunate messenger, and only his riderless horse with a spear-wound in its hindquarters returned to the Kopjeskraal laager. Liebenberg's party were still desperately *inspanning* their wagons preparatory to forming a laager or possibly attempting to fly, when they were overrun by a section of the Ndebele force that had split off from the fight around the laager.

All six of the men in the Liebenberg party were killed, along with 12 of their Khoisan servants. Two of the women also perished, and six of the children. The others were miraculously saved by the fortuitous arrival of Herman Jacobus Potgieter, the *Kommandant's* brother, and five companions who had pushed on ahead from the rest of Hendrik Potgieter's returning *kommissietrek*. The six intrepid horsemen charged those amaNdebele still ransacking the camp, took them completely by surprise, and scattered them. They found one of the women and four of the children still unharmed in the wagon where they had hidden themselves. Eleven other children survived, as well as three more of the women, even though all of them had received multiple wounds from Ndebele spears—one women had been stabbed no less than 21 times.

The survivors of the battle of Liebensbergkoppie (as it was named) were left grief-stricken, destitute and in horrible pain from their wounds. They joined the Trekkers in the Kopjeskraal laager who were in an equally poor state. The amaNdebele had rounded up many of their livestock when they retired, allowing Kaliphi to claim at least a partial victory, and a detachment had driven their booty back to Mosega.[14]

---

14 For the battle of Liebensbergkoppie, see Retief, 'Voortrekkers and the Ndebele. Part One'; Chase, *Natal Papers*, Part 1, p.74: account by J.G.S. Bronkhorst.

12

We Are Here to Kill You

For fear of another Ndebele attack, the demoralised *Trekkers* remained in their laager at Kopjeskraal 'in a deplorable state' for about a week after the two battles of 23 August 1836 and buried their dead.[1] They eventually re-crossed the Vaal on around 31 August. The *Trekker* movement had suffered a severe and deeply troubling setback that brought the whole enterprise into question. When Hendrik Potgieter finally returned on 2 September to resume his command, he found the members of the joint trek in two minds as to how they should proceed. Some split away and returned south to Thaba Nchu; the rest decided to stand their ground in northern Transorangia, and Potgieter led them east along the Rhenoster (Rhinoceros) River towards its source. There they encamped at a little hill called Doornkop (Thorn Hill) between the Rhenoster and Wilge (Willow) Rivers, later to go down in the annals of the Great Trek as Vegkop (Combat Hill).

At Doornkop the families scattered to obtain pasture and water for their livestock. They seemed for the moment to have lost any concern that the amaNdebele might attack them again, but they were soon disabused. It appears that Mzilikazi was determined to eliminate the new threat posed by the *Trekkers* once and for all. He therefore despatched his main army, estimated by Daniel Lindley, the AMS missionary at Mosega, to be about 2,000 strong (later *Trekker* estimates unrealistically doubled or even trebled that figure). It marched under Kaliphi's command, and his orders were apparently to kill all the *Trekker* men and boys, but to capture and bring back all the women and girls, as well as all Emigrants' herds and flocks.

As with the accounts of the battles of Kopjeskraal and Liebenbergskoppie, contemporary sources describing the battle of Vegkop are scarce, and the few relevant memoirs were penned decades later when the participants were old men. Consequently, many details are uncertain.[2]

---

1 *Annals* I, pp.238: Journal of the Late Charl Celliers.
2 The following account of Vegkop is based on M.C. Van Zyl, 'Die Slag van Vegkop', *Historia: Journal of the Historical Association of South Africa*, 3: 21 (October 1986), pp. 65–70; Johannes J. Retief, 'The Voortrekkers and the Ndebele. Part Two: The Battle of Vegkop', 20 October 1836', *Military History Journal*, 17: 1 (June 2016), < samilitaryhistory.org/vol171jr.html>, accessed 30 July 2020; *Annals* I, pp.23 –2: Narrative of Willem Jurgen Pretorius; pp. 238–40: Journal of the Late Charl Celliers; Chase, *Natal Papers*, Part 1, pp.74–5: account by J.G.S. Bronkhorst; Walker, *Great Trek*, pp.122–5; Etherington, *Great Treks*, pp.249–52; Knight, *Warrior Chiefs*, pp. 17–18; Summers and Pagden, *Warriors*, p.64.

On the 18 or 19 October 1836 (the date is debated, but the later one is generally preferred) two Tlokwa scouts brought in the news that the whole of Kaliphi's army was at the Vaal and was advancing on the encampment. Flight was not an option since the dispersed wagons and livestock presented an easy target, and there was no alternative but to form a laager in a strong position on a low ridge south of Doornkop and fight it out. It was late on the same day while the laager was being constructed that a three-man reconnaissance reported back that the Ndebele army was only a few hours on horseback away, or at a distance of between 12 and 18 miles. That night the defenders of the laager slept ill, keeping apprehensive vigil. Many spent the hours of darkness in prayer, and all were kept awake by fear of an imminent attack.

It is not absolutely definite who commanded the laager. Was it Sarel Celliers as some insist, or was it *Kommandant* Hendrik Potgieter? It seems most likely, though, that it must have been Potgieter, the experienced and trusted military commander, and that Celliers confined his role to acting as the party's spiritual leader and inspiration.

The size and shape of the laager is also open to debate, but it was clearly formed in the classic way. Seemingly, it was made up of about 46 wagons drawn up in a circle with another four wagons in the middle as a refuge for the non-combatants. With a diameter of about 60 yards it was large enough to accommodate all the *Trekkers'* precious horses, but not the cattle and sheep that had to remain outside. The terrain roundabout was flat, offering no tactical advantage to either side. However, so that the long grass surrounding the laager offered no cover to the amaNdebele, the defenders flattened it by driving livestock across it and dragging branches over it.

As it turned out, there was no Ndebele pre-dawn attack, and at first light on 20 October Hendrik Potgieter and Sarel Celliers led out between 25 and 33 able-bodied men from the laager. This was a mounted reconnaissance, and the objective was to locate the Ndebele army. Potgieter nursed the faint hope that he would be able to ward off an attack through negotiation. If that failed, as it probably would, he and his men could at least disrupt the rhythm of the Ndebele onslaught.

The amaNdebele had continued their advance since spotted by the Boer patrol of the previous day, and Potgieter came upon them when now only little more than an hour's ride from the laager. It would seem that it was Kaliphi's intention to mount the standard Ndebele pre-dawn attack the following morning (21 October) once his army had taken the day to rest. Consequently, the amaNdebele were not preparing to attack when Potgieter's *kommando* unexpectedly rode into sight. The Ndebele commanders hastily assembled their men from their scattered overnight bivouacs and sat them down in a line, side-by-side and close together. Potgieter intrepidly continued to lead his *kommando* forward until only 50 paces separated him from the waiting amaNdebele. Accounts of what happened next are not consistent. It would seem, though, that Potgieter, heartened by the apparent passivity of the Ndebele army, brusquely enquired of Kaliphi through a Khoikhoi servant of Celliers's (who was fluent in isiZulu) why the amaNdebele wished to harm his people who had done them no evil, and why they had 'come to murder us and rob' the Trekkers of their property?[3] Kaliphi responded with spirit that 'Mzilikazi alone issues commands, we are his servants, and we do his behest, we are not here to discuss or argue,

---

3   *Annals* I, p.239: Journal of the Late Charl Celliers.

we are here to kill you.'⁴ The parlay was already going nowhere when (so it has been claimed) a nervous Boer fired inadvertently into the Ndebele ranks. If he did, that probably made little difference to the already edgy and indignant amaNdebele. They jumped to their feet with a loud hiss, shouted 'Mzilikazi', and charged, throwing out their tactical horns with the intention of surrounding the small group of horsemen.

Employing their habitual *kommando* tactics for a fighting retreat – just as Erasmus and his horsemen had done before the battle of Kopjeskraal – Potgieter's men skilfully avoided encirclement and pulled back to the laager in a running battle that lasted nearly three hours. Sarel Celliers later recalled that he fired 16 shots during the encounter, seldom missing. Even if that was an exaggeration, the *kommando* probably fired over 500 shots at the pursuing amaNdebele, undoubtedly inflicting significant casualties – even if their later estimation of 200 amaNdebele killed was undoubtedly considerably inflated. It does seem, though, that many of the Ndebele commanders who were in the forefront of the pursuers were among the fallen, and their leadership must have been missed in the subsequent Ndebele attack on the laager. What is without doubt, is that by intercepting the amaNdebele army before it was ready to advance, Potgieter had deprived Kaliphi of any advantage of surprise, and that by goading his men into an attack before they intended to fight, he had disrupted their commander's plan to attack at dawn the following day, and had forced his men into battle before they were properly rested or fed.

With their ammunition almost exhausted, Potgieter's horsemen finally neared the laager with the amaNdebele close behind. Just before they galloped in through the open gap between two wagons, which was hastily barricaded behind them, three of their number broke away in panic and rode off for their lives. (They shame-facedly drifted back unharmed a few days after the battle, and were forever afterwards scorned as the *lafaards*, the cowards.) Those horsemen who returned to defend the laager promptly took up their positions at their designated posts around the perimeter with dishes handy to hold their powder and bullets. There they were joined by the men who had remained in the laager during Potgieter's mounted sortie and by seven or so youths who knew very well how to shoot, making a total of about 40 defenders. They were augmented by a few of their womenfolk and *agterryers* who could also handle a musket. Other women helped to load for them and to rinse the dirty barrels of their *voorlaiers* to make for smoother loading. With two muskets serviced by an assistant, an experienced marksman (as all the Boers were) could maintain a firing-rate of four shots a minute. And, as had been demonstrated time and again on the Cape Eastern Frontier, even a small force of men with firearms in a solid, well-prepared defensive position could hold off greatly superior numbers of assailants armed only with spears.

While these final preparations were taking place, Sarel Celliers called everyone in the laager together and had them pray humbly on their knees to God not to forsake them but to give them strength to resist their enemies. He then offered further encouragement by loudly reading from Psalm 50, verse15: 'And call upon me in the day of trouble: I will deliver thee, and thou shalt glorify me', while Potgieter went quietly among the women, encouraging them. Then all the men and as many as were old enough of the estimated 160 women and children in the laager joined Martha van Vuuren in singing Psalm 130, verse 1: 'Out of the depths have I cried unto

---

4   Quoted in Knight, *Warrior Chiefs*, p.118.

thee, O Lord'. When they had done, Celliers warned that 'not a voice of woman or of child should be heard' until the battle was over.[5]

Meanwhile, having been drawn onto the laager, Kaliphi had no option but to order an assault. He broke the pursuing amaNdebele army into three groups—the classic chest and two horns— and surrounded the laager. The amaNdebele were in no hurry to attack after the extended skirmish with Potgieter's *kommando*. The majority sat down to rest in the full heat of the day at a distance of about 500 yards from the laager, safely out of range of musket fire. While they caught their breath, some eagerly honing the blades of their spears on convenient stones, a few small groups were set to rounding up the *Trekkers'* livestock left outside the laager. They immediately butchered several oxen which they and their ravenous comrades devoured raw. Then, needing to be sure-footed when they attacked the laager, the amaNdebele took off their sandals and heaped them in a great pile. Inside the laager, the defenders waited in an agony of trepidation. Some accounts mention Potgieter's attempt to end the unbearable tension by bringing on the Ndebele attack by tying a white or red rag to a long whipstock and provocatively waving it.

Suddenly, at about noon, at Kaliphi's command the Ndebele warriors (whom Potgieter described as 'black devils' when recounting the day's fighting to Erasmus Smit) leapt to their feet 'with an infernal alarming yell', and charged at the laager from all sides, beating in unison with their spears 'on their hide shields like a roll of thunder from the clouds', hissing and shouting the name of their king.[6] So began the first full-scale battle between an African army of the interior and *Trekkers* sheltering in a defensive laager. No accounts mention the amaNdebele using the firearms Mzilikazi had begun collecting (and some explicitly deny they carried any),[7] and their tactics were entirely conventional, aimed at breaking into the fortified enclosure and killing all those within in hand-to-hand fighting.

As the amaNdebele converged on the laager, they naturally bunched ever closer together until they were should-to-shoulder, offering nigh unmissable targets. For the defenders who were under orders not to fire until the amaNdebele had advanced to within 30 or 20 yards of the laager, this was a supreme test of nerve and discipline. But once the attackers were within close range, the defenders opened fire with their *lopers* (each man had prepared about a dozen beforehand), the spraying buckshot striking several men with each shot. Undeterred, the warriors pushed on over the bodies of their fallen comrades until they reached the abattis of felled thorn trees staked to the ground that formed the outer ring of the laager's defences. As intended, this obstacle slowed the charge and gave the defenders an almost stationary target. Those who pushed or cut their way through the abattis, or climbed over it on the shields thrown onto the branches, were confronted by the wagons themselves. Some tried to sever the leather *rieme* and break the chains binding them together, or to push them over. Others attempted to climb onto the wagons and others to creep under them. The Boer women were waiting for them, and 'with the courage of despair' killed those who wriggled through 'with hatchets and knives' before they could rise to their feet.[8] Inside the laager the frenzied horses that had been tied to several wagons to prevent

---

5   *Annals* I, p.239: Journal of the Late Charl Celliers.
6   The Rev. H.F. Schoon and W.G.A. Mears (eds), *The Diary of Erasmus Smit* (Cape Town: C. Struik, 1972) (*Smit's Diary*), p.2: 20 November 1836.
7   *Annals* I, p. 231: Narrative of Willem Jurgen Pretorius.
8   *Annals* I, p. 231: Narrative of Willem Jurgen Pretorius.

them from stampeding, nevertheless kicked up a cloud of dust that combined with the billows of dirty white smoke from the muskets to form an almost impenetrable haze.

After about 15 minutes (but no longer than 30), during which not one Ndebele warrior succeeded in entering the laager alive, the amaNdebele pulled back to loud hosannahs from the defenders. Many amaNdebele were left lying on the ground, dead, wounded or waiting to join a new attack, and Boer marksmen, knowing that the dead do not sweat, picked off those still perspiring. With the failure of their direct assault, the amaNdebele now changed tactics and began casting their throwing spears – which they could do effectively from about 40 yards away – over the wagons and into the laager in such numbers that they seemed to the defenders like a heavy swarm of locusts. (After the battle 1,172 of them were found inside the laager and caused almost all the casualties the *Trekkers* suffered that day.) At 40 yards, however, the amaNdebele remained well within effective range of musket fire and suffered accordingly.

The final phase of the battle remained a blur in the memory of the participants. After perhaps another half-an-hour, the amaNdebele gave up their assault and began leaving the battlefield under gradually diminishing long-range fire from the defenders. There is some suggestion that, in accordance with customary *kommando* tactics in such a situation, the *Trekkers* then sallied out in a mounted pursuit. But Willem Pretorius stated categorically that the 'handful of men in the camp could not venture to pursue the retreating enemy, or leave their hastily-formed place of safety.'[9]

Once the amaNdebele had withdrawn, Celliers predictably conducted a thanksgiving service for the victors. Only two of the defenders had been killed, and they were *Kommandant* Potgieter's brother and brother-in-law. Fourteen others—or every third man—was wounded (including Celliers), along with several horses. The number of amaNdebele killed is unknown, but with 184 bodies found around the laager—although some claimed that as many as about 430 lay dead—and with (as Potgieter estimated) 'well above 200 persons fallen wounded or dead along the route' home,[10] losses must have amounted to at least 300. A missionary who witnessed the return of the defeated army reported that 'there was nothing but lamentation heard in the land for weeks on account of those slain in battle.'[11] For Mzilikazi, this was an unprecedented defeat and it augured ill for the future.

Potgieter's party had victoriously survived the heaviest attack Mzilikazi could throw at them, but they had nevertheless suffered crippling material losses. Many of their wagons had been severely damaged, with some of their canopies pierced in up to a hundred places by spears. Far worse than that, the amaNdebele had driven off all the cattle, sheep and goats left outside the laager, and a *kommando* that set out three days after the battle to recover them was unsuccessful. The only cattle they found—about 1,000 of them—had been left by the amaNdebele 'killed and skinned'.[12] Just over a year later, when the *Voortrekker* leader, Pieter Retief, addressed a letter to King Dingane, he attached a postscript specifying the total losses the *Trekkers* had suffered at Mzilikazi's hands in the three battles culminating in Vegkop. The very specificity of the figures renders them suspect, especially with regard to the livestock, but the scale is undeniable: 'Twenty white and 26 coloured people killed, of whom nine were women and five children. Twenty-seven

9 *Annals* I, p.232: Narrative of Willem Jurgen Pretorius.
10 *Smit's Diary*, p.3: 20 November 1836.
11 Quoted in Rasmussen, *Migrant Kingdom*, p.124.
12 Chase, *Natal Papers* Part 1, p.75: account by J.G.S. Bronkhorst.

persons were robbed of cattle: 51 saddle and 45 untrained horses; draught oxen 945; breeding cattle, 3, 726; sheep and goats, 50,745; also nine guns and four wagons.'[13] Potgieter alone, who was reckoned a rich man among the *Trekkers*, lost 400 cattle (of which 100 were draught oxen) and 5, 000 sheep.[14]

Most disastrous of all for the *Trekkers* at Vegkop was the loss of their draught-oxen, because without them their wagons were stranded. When it proved urgently necessary to move camp 400 yards closer to the Rhenoster River because of the pestilential Ndebele bodies lying unburied around the laager, they had to *inspan* their horses to the wagons or to manhandle them themselves.

Potgieter knew that he could not remain at the Rhenoster River for much longer since, without cows to milk or sheep to slaughter for meat, and without corn or millet, his people were in real danger of starvation with many (especially children) already crying from hunger. Besides, the marooned laager was vulnerable to a renewed Ndebele attack. But if they were to rejoin those members of the joint trek who had earlier fallen back to Thaba Nchu, they required help. Fortunately for them, other *Trekker* groups came to their rescue with 200 draught-oxen, and Gerrit Maritz sent along a guard of *burgers* from the large trek party that he had just brought into Thaba Nchu. By the middle of November all the survivors of the battle of Vegkop were back with their wagons in Thaba Nchu where Moroka of the Barolong and the Methodist missionary, James Archbell, were generous with supplies.

The battle of Vegkop, as the Boers called it, was a critical moment in the Great Trek. If Kaliphi had succeeded in wiping out Potgieter's party, the whole movement might have received such a check that it would have proceeded no further, and there would have been no *Trekker* invasion of the Zulu kingdom. As it was, the *Trekkers* regarded Potgieter's victory over overwhelming odds as a clear sign of divine intervention. God, it was manifest, approved of their venture and they were encouraged to persist in it with confidence.

---

13 *Annals* I, p.364: P. Retief to Dingaan, King of the Amazulu, 8 November 1837.
14 Van Zyl, 'Vegkop', p.70.

13

Our God Delivered Mzilikazi into Our Hands

The *Trekkers* were loosely organised into family parties that became larger groups when, as we have seen, they accepted the leadership of a man of proven ability, character and military reputation, such a one as Hendrik Potgieter. After the trauma of Vegkop and the military challenge they had only narrowly survived, it was obvious to the *Trekker* parties huddled together at Thaba Nchu that some form of over-all unity with clear lines of leadership was required. Yet, as events would prove, no external danger was ever enough to damp down for long the divisions and squabbles between the various leaders that repeatedly threatened to scupper the *Trekker* movement.

There was a brief moment of unity at the end of 1836. Gerrit Maritz left Graaff-Reinet for Transorangia in September 1836 with more than 700 people, some 100 of them white male adults. Maritz was the leading wagon-maker at Graaff-Reinet, a prosperous and locally prominent individual with more than the usual level of education. Still in his middle-30s, he was a strongly-made, big man, with tawny hair cut short and with a darker beard (as was common, his upper lip was clean-shaven). He was something of a dandy with long coat and trousers in the latest mode and a fashionable, roughly-textured top hat. Everyone in the neighbourhood was familiar with his wagon jauntily painted light blue rather than the usual green, and knew him as a cheery, convivial fellow. But Maritz was also an orthodox pillar of the Dutch Reformed Church, and held *Doppers* in the deepest contempt. Although not a fighting man like Potgieter, he was an ambitious one, and believed that outside the constraints of the Colony he would find his destiny.[1]

When the Maritz trek joined Potgieter and Celliers at Thaba Nchu, the men of all the groups there held a general meeting on 2 December 1836 and elected a *Burgerraad* (Burgher Council) of seven members to supervise the making and enforcement of laws. Maritz was voted in as the President and Judge to head the civil administration, and Potgieter as Chief Commandant, or military commander, with his own War Council. Even though yoked together, Maritz and Potgieter represented opposed views on the purposes of political organisation among the Trekker groups. Maritz regarded the Trek as a common enterprise, a *verenigde maatskappy* (united community) or a *volk* (nation), and called for the leaders' submission to the *Burgerraad*. Potgieter only reluctantly complied. He remained an irredeemably patriarchal figure, ultimately

---

1   Walker, *Great Trek*, pp.91–2.

concerned with the welfare of only his own party that he and his close family continued to lead in a fiercely autocratic fashion.[2]

Sarel Celliers later recorded that the united *Trekkers* concentrated at Thaba Nchu 'were very desirous that a *kommando* should go against our enemy', Mzilikazi.[3] Their motives, besides the primordial desire to punish the amaNdebele, were the recovery of their looted livestock and wagons, and the need to ensure that Mzilikazi would never again be in a position to endanger them. In this enterprise they had the support of those African and *droster* societies in Transorangia that had been displaced or were threatened by the amaNdebele, and who wished to drive away their old enemy and regain their lands.

On 4 January 1837 a *kommando* under the command of Potgieter and Celliers set out from Thaba Nchu for Mosega in the Ndebele heartland, 325 miles away, guided by their Barolong allies. The *kommando* was made up of 107 mounted Boers, supported (although this was not mentioned by Celliers in his account) by 40 Griqua horsemen under Peter David, five or six of Gert Taaibosch's Korana, a few Tlokwa horsemen contributed by Sekonyela along the way, and about 60 Barolong on foot. The allies crossed the Vaal at a place still called Kommando Drift, and proceeded north to the Makwassie River. There they left their wagons and moved to the Harts River before turning north-east for the Marico valley. The amaNdebele least expected an attack from this direction. This was the road of missionaries and traders to Kuruman, and all previous *droster* raids had come from the south. Cannily, by taking this unexpected route, the *kommando* was almost certainly assured of achieving surprise.

And, as Potgieter and Celliers had hoped, Mzilikazi's scouts and spies gave no prior warning of their advance. At dawn on 17 January 1837 the kommando charged into the valley, opening a heavy fire on the Mosega complex that consisted of a cluster of 15 homesteads. As usual, many of Kaliphi's warriors were away raiding, and he himself was with Mzilikazi at eGabeni further down the valley. Taken completely by surprise, there was no time for the limited number of warriors scattered around Mosega to concentrate and mount an effective defence. The *kommando* attack consequently turned into a massacre with the Boers even gunning down the women who had taken refuge in the house of the AMS missionaries. It was not until about midday that the Boers finally gave up their pursuit of the scattering fugitives. As Celliers, expressing himself as one of the self-appointed Chosen People, stated with intense satisfaction, 'our God delivered him [Mzilikazi] into our hands.'

Once they had put all of Mosega to the torch, the victorious *kommando* retired towards Thaba Nchu. In the past, the amaNdebele had always successfully pursued the raiding *droster kommandos*, but this time they were too stunned to stir. So, the *kommando* got away with about 6,000 cattle and the wagons the amaNdebele had previously captured. The three AMS families, seeing four years of missionary work among the amaNdebele destroyed in the course of a single morning, withdrew with the *kommando*. Celliers later crowed that all this and been achieved 'without the loss of a man from our number', disregarding two of his Barolong allies who had

---

2   Thompson, 'Zulu Kingdom', pp. 355–57; Giliomee, *Afrikaners*, pp 162–4; Walker, *Great Trek*, pp.126–7; Etherington, *Great Treks*, p 252.
3   *Annals* 1, p.240: Journal of Charl Celliers.

been killed. The amaNdebele losses are not known, but probably about 400 or more were slaughtered, many of them non-combatants: women, children, and the elderly.[4]

The battle of Vegkop had demonstrated that a properly prepared laager could withstand a massed attack in daylight by an overwhelming number of warriors armed with traditional weapons such as spears, and without firearms. The *kommando* raid against Mosega showed that, with the advantage of surprise, a mobile *kommando* was more than a match for warriors in the open field. The lesson to be drawn was that the *Trekkers*, if they were properly prepared and competently led, were capable of defeating any African society that attempted to block their advance into the interior by force of arms. The inevitable corollary was the perception that their future safety lay more in the hands of effective military leaders than in those of civil administrators.

By the time Potgieter's and Celliers's victorious *kommando* returned with its booty to Thaba Nchu in early February, about 300 *Trekker* wagons were assembled there. During their absence, there had been a steady stream of small parties along the by now clearly defined *Trekkers*' Road from Norval's Pont across the Orange to Blesberg, a wide, churned-up scar snaking across the veld. Now, perhaps because with Mzilikazi's defeat they felt more secure, the *Trekker* leaders allowed their rivalries to surface openly. Potgieter and Maritz fell to arguing about the distribution of the Ndebele loot, and when Potgieter secured control over most of it, Maritz was left feeling distinctly aggrieved.

Then, another issue arose that encapsulated the simmering rivalry between Maritz and Potgieter. No *predikant* had accompanied the *Trekkers* because of the opposition of the Dutch Reformed Church in the Cape to the Great Trek. Maritz consequently turned to Erasmus Smit, a former mission teacher with the LMS and subsequently a *meester* in the Eastern Cape. Smit, who had been born in Amsterdam, was short, stout, and ruddy with a close-clipped grey beard and a cast in his left eye. As it happened, he was married to Susanna, Maritz's managing and outspoken sister. But Smit was not ordained, and until Maritz could persuade the *Burgerraad* to install him as their official *predikant*, he could neither baptise nor conduct a marriage ceremony. Moreover, he seemed to his detractors to be weak and sickly, and was rumoured to be an alcoholic. The Potgieter circle simply would not accept him, and instead ostentatiously attended the services of James Archbell, the Wesleyan missionary at Thaba Nchu. Undeterred, Smit continued assiduously to minister to Maritz's adherents, preaching in the space between three or four wagons roofed over with a bucksail that served as his church.[5]

Their confidence greatly restored, the *Trekkers* were slowly beginning to fan out again from Thaba Nchu. In March 1837, as an indication of his discontent, Potgieter moved his party north to the banks of the Vet (Fat) River (a tributary of the Sand River that runs into the Vaal) and the *Trekker* movement seem about to split. At this critical moment, on 8 April 1837, Pieter Retief crossed to the north bank of the Orange River at the head of a large party of 100 wagons and 120 men. There he was met by a deputation of *Trekkers* led by Maritz who saw in him a new leader whom all factions could accept.

---

4   For the Mosega campaign, see *Annals* 1, p.240: Journal of Charl Celliers; the Rev. A.T. Bryant, *Olden Times in Zululand and Natal Containing Earlier Political History of the Eastern-Nguni Clans* (London: Longman Green, 1929), p.435; Summers and Pagden, *Warriors*, p.64; *Smit's Diary*, p. 20: 26 and 28 January 1837; Walker, *Great Trek*, pp.127–8; Etherington, *Great Treks*, pp.252–4.

5   Walker, *Great Trek*, pp.128–31; Giliomee, *Afrikaners*, p.164.

At 57 years of age, Retief was the oldest of the leaders of the Great Trek, his dark brown hair and beard shot with grey. He had been born on a wine farm in the Western Cape, the scion of a family long established at Stellenbosch. Well-educated, he lived in Cape Town for a number of years acquiring business experience. Becoming bored in these settled surroundings, he moved to a farm in the Eastern Cape in 1814 and married a widow. He soon settled in Grahamstown where he employed his business acumen to raise capital and made a fortune selling grain at inflated prices to the 1820 Settlers from Britain who had newly arrived in the Albany District. But Retief was a speculator and a gambler. He lost his fortune in 1824 when he failed to deliver on a contract to build government offices and was bankrupted. He retired to the Winterberg District at the northern end of the eastern frontier to lick his wounds, and won a new reputation in public office as *veldkornet* of the Winterberg District. During the Sixth Cape Frontier War, he performed effectively as the field-commandant of the Winterberg. He

Erasmus Smit, minister to the *Trekkers*. (Photo: uMsunduzi Museum, Pietermaritzburg, with permission)

had become a familiar and respected figure in his district, always friendly and tactful, and normally dressed in his round felt hat, short black jacket and light-coloured trousers.

As before, Retief soon became restless, and with the eye of a speculator saw that the trekking movement promised great rewards for those who could establish a legal title to newly-opened lands. However, he had hesitated to risk life and worldly goods until the victory at Vegkop convinced him that the *Trekkers* could successfully defend themselves if necessary. A born publicist, constantly writing to the newspapers and government officials to present his views cogently and clearly, he announced he decision to trek in November 1836, projecting a beguiling narrative of gallant pioneers opening up the savage interior to eventual British rule. Finally, in February 1837 he set out from the Albany District with his party.[6]

---

6 Walker, *Great Trek*, pp.104–5.

Piet Retief by an anonymous artist. (Pietermaritzburg Archives Repository, with permission)

Retief held his own capabilities in high estimation. On the strength of his education, coupled with his military experience and the public offices he had held in the Cape, he confidently expected to take charge of the *Trekker* movement. He was hardly surprised, therefore, when on 17 April 1837 a full public meeting unanimously elected him *Goewerneur*, or Governor. In his speech accepting the 'immense responsibility' placed upon him, he was not shy in recognising 'the hand of God in what had taken place.'[7] Indeed, as events unfolded, with ineffable self-confidence Retief would again and again declare that he was God's instrument. Maritz was elected Judge President of the Council of Policy and Deputy Governor at the same meeting. However, Potgieter was left firmly out in the cold when his post of Chief Commandant was taken away and given to Retief.[8]

Potgieter's loss of influenced was firmly signalled when, despite his remonstrances, and after anxious negotiations, on 21 May 1837 Retief inducted the controversial Erasmus Smit as Minister of the Congregation of the Reformed Church.[9] Potgieter's exclusion from power was confirmed when, on 6 June 1837, a meeting of about 140 *burgers* at their united camp at the Vet River (near the site of the future village of Winburg) adopted nine Articles of Association. These had to be accepted on oath by all those who would be members of the collective society of *Trekkers*, the *verenigde maatskappy*. All the existing office-holders were confirmed with Retief as *Goewerneur*. The meeting also adopted a name in Dutch for 'the country to which they travelled', *De Vrye Provincie van Nieuw Holland in Zuid Oost Africa* (The Free Province of New Holland in South East Africa).[10]

Meanwhile, in April 1837 the blond and shaggy-bearded Piet Uys, accompanied by more than 100 members of his family and connections in 23 wagons, had finally set out from the Uitenhage District of the Cape. He proudly carried a handsome Bible presented before he left by

---

7   Chase, *Natal Papers*, Part 1, p.87: eye-witness account.
8   Walker, *Great Trek*, pp.92–4, 131–2; 134–5; Giliomee, *Afrikaners*, pp.162, 164; Etherington, *Great Treks*, pp.257, 259–60.
9   *Smit's Diary*, p.28: 21 May 1837.
10 *Smit's Diary*, pp.30–2: 6 June 1837; Walker, *Great Trek*, pp.136–7; Giliomee, *Afrikaners*, p.164.

his English-speaking neighbours. When Uys arrived on 29 June 1837 at the combined *Trekker* laager at the Sand River, it was only three weeks after the Articles of Association had been adopted. He at once found that he, like Potgieter, would hold no office. Mortified, and with a poor opinion of the other leaders, Uys refused to accept resolutions in which his party had exercised no voice, and that represented the will of only a section of *Trekkers*.[11] The exclusion of eminent leaders from the governing body of the *Trek* was certainly a factional miscalculation, one that ensured enervating resentments and jealousies that continued to grow and fester. And it was not only that the frozen-out Potgieter and Uys parties that were at loggerheads with the ruling Retief and Maritz followings. Maritz was becoming increasingly suspicious of Retief's accumulation of offices and dictatorial leanings, and warned the other leaders against him.[12]

Certainly, Retief intended to rule. With his experience of the war-torn Cape Eastern Frontier and the need for orderly conduct and effective defence, he laid out strict rules of comportment for his followers.[13] And wielding his pen with great skill, he made sure his words appeared in the Dutch and English newspapers across the Colony, investing him with the obvious authority unlettered leaders like Potgieter could not similarly claim. To ensure the security of the *Trekkers* in Transorangia, but also to reassure the British that they were not stirring up conflicts that would have repercussions along the Cape's frontiers, Retief set about entering into treaties of friendship with his African neighbours Moroka, Sekonyela and Moshweshwe, assuring D'Urban that 'it is not … our intention unlawfully to molest any of the native tribes.'[14] To make sure that such agreements would carry weight with the British, he framed them in careful, legalistic phraseology they would recognise as valid.

These treaties, however, were not agreements between equals, as was made very clear when on 18 July 1837 Retief offered the two principal Griqua *Kapteins*, Adam Kok, and Andries Waterboer, a treaty a friendship between them and the Chosen People couched in terms of pure menace. 'I am fully convinced,' he declared, 'that such who may stubbornly refuse to enter into these desirable relations, will soon see and feel that they are contending with a mighty GOD!' And, with sublime arrogance, he added that he recognized 'the hand of God in placing me at the head of my countrymen.'[15]

The winter of 1837 on the open, treeless highveld which the *Trekkers* called the *kaalveld*, or naked veld, proved uncomfortably cold with snow and bitter rain. To make matter worse, fever ravaged the 2,000 or so *Trekkers* living in the five or six large camps between the Orange and Vaal Rivers. By the time spring came, all felt that they would have to find a better place to settle, but where was that to be? And inextricably tied up with that question were the issues of *Trekker* leadership and unity, as well as the fate of Mzilikazi.

The members of the Potgieter party, who had borne the brunt of the war with Mzilikazi and who had taken the initiative in defeating him in January 1837, favoured the temperate grasslands across the Vaal River and advocated opening up of a trade route to Delagoa Bay

---

11   Uys, 'Petrus Lafras Uys', pp. 33–5; Uys, 'Boer Family'; Walker, *Great Trek*, pp.139–40.
12   Giliomee, *Afrikaners*, p.162; Etherington, *Great Treks*, p.258.
13   See Chase, *Natal Papers*, Part I, pp. 116–18: Retief's Instructions to the Commandants and for the Field-Cornets, 21 June 1837.
14   Chase, *Natal Papers*, Part I, p.101: Retief to D'Urban, 21 July 1837.
15   Chase, *Natal Papers*, Part I, pp. 113–16: P. Retief, Commandant of the United Encampments to the Griqua Captains, 18 July 1837; Walker, *Great Trek*, pp.138–39.

where the Portuguese were free of British control. That agenda required the final elimination of Mzilikazi as a threat to any trans-Vaal settlement. Retief and Maritz, on the other hand, preferred the fertile lowlands east over the Drakensberg and the closer (and less disease-ridden) outlet to the sea at Port Natal. Uys too regarded the same region as his prime objective, but considered he had the prior right to command there on account of his *kommissietrek* of 1834. But 'Natal' too had its drawbacks. Close relations between the Port Natal settlers and the Cape authorities meant that the port was still very much within the sphere of British interest. And then there was Dingane and the Zulu kingdom. Would his reaction to a *Trekker* incursion be any different from Mzilikazi's?[16]

On 4 July 1837, Retief sent out a scouting party to find a suitable pass over the Drakensberg from the highveld. They reported a month later that there were five places to the east of the *Trekker* encampments where the mountain range could be crossed with reasonable ease, and that the *trek* would not have to round the far-away northern tip of the Drakensberg. This intelligence confirmed Retief in his decision to lead his people into the God-given 'place of our destination', the Promised Land. He did indeed foresee that there might be problems with Dingane but, believing as ever in his divinely-sponsored mission, he was certain that all would be well since his intentions were 'not evil but good'. Nevertheless, even though he assured D'Urban (who was following the *Trekkers*' activities with mounting unease) that he could thank God that he 'did not possess a thirst for blood', he went on to add that he had not 'been taking lessons' on the Cape Eastern Frontier for 22 years without learning 'what should be done or what should be left undone.' By that he meant only prompt, severe action against African foes would serve, and he would not flinch from going to war with the amaZulu if the situation required it.[17]

Yet, even if Retief's mind was made up that the Zulu territory was to be the *Trekkers*' destination, could he carry the United Encampments with him? When he set off eastwards along the valley of the Sand River, the parties of the other leaders followed unenthusiastically. Then, on 14 August, Potgieter announced that he and his people would have nothing further to do with United Encampments as they were currently constituted and led. For his part, Retief knew he must keep the *Trek* together if it were face down Dingane. More trek parties were coming in every day, so that soon the *verenigde maatskappy* would number close to 4,000 *Trekkers* (apart from their servants and retainers). Coherent and unified governance was required more than ever. At Retief's urging, between 13 and 14 September 'a great gathering of the people' (as Smit recorded) thrashed out the matter at Tafelberg. Predictably, the followers of Retief and Maritz faced off those of Potgieter and Uys with much shouting and flourishing of firearms. When asked at the close of the stormy confrontation, 'How will things go with the journey now?' Uys gnomically shot back: 'Each one goes his own way: these go before in front; others go to the flank; none of them will come in the rear.'[18] When the dissidents then rode away, those remaining in Retief's camp settled down to reflect pointedly on the anathema proclaimed in Psalm 109: 'Let his days be few; and let another take his office. Let his children be fatherless, and his wife a widow. Let his children be continually vagabonds, and beg: let them seek their

---

16 Giliomee, *Afrikaners*, pp.162, 164.
17 Chase, *Natal Papers*, Part I, pp. 111–12: Retief to D'Urban, 9 September 1837; Walker, *Great Trek*, pp.140–1.
18 *Smit's Diary*, pp.52–3: 13, 14 September 1837; Walker, *Great Trek*, pp.144–7.

bread also out of their desolate place.'[19] The Great Trek was united no longer and the *verenigde maatskappy* was riven.

While most of the *Trekkers* journeyed eastwards towards the Drakensberg passes with the Retief party in the van, Potgieter turned his eyes firmly towards the lands north of the Vaal. There he intended to encompass Mzilikazi's final destruction. Indeed, after his disastrous defeat at Mosega in January 1837, Mzilikazi had felt himself to be on the defensive. He made no further attacks on the Boers south of the Vaal and concentrated instead on preserving his precious herds from all his old enemies who now scented the smell of blood.

Dingane was the first to strike when he launched a bold and risky long-distance raid in force during the frosty winter months. The iziNyosi, uDlambedlu and imVoko *amabutho* under the command of Ndlela kaSompisi set out in May 1837 when the people were threshing the ripe sorghum. None of the other, older *izikhulu* went on the expedition; nor did Dingane.

Guided by an Ndebele deserter, the *impi* reached the environs of Mosega at the end of June or beginning of July. The long march had taken its toll. There was no firewood on the open plains of the highveld, so the *amabutho* had to make their exiguous fires of eland-, hartebeest- and elephant-dung. Many had fallen out on the way through illness or hunger, or because they had been incapacitated by torn feet or other injuries. The amaZulu discovered that Mzilikazi had already withdrawn most of his people and stock north towards eGabeni in the lower Marico River valley. The two sides engaged in a number of sharp skirmishes, during one of which Mzilikazi's crack *ibutho*, the izimPangele, with whom he had originally set out from Zululand, perished almost to a man. Even so, Ndlela's *amabutho* did not manage a decisive victory and the amaZulu eventually withdrew with two of Mzilikazi's sisters as captives and with thousands of cattle and sheep, many of which (with dire, unforeseen consequences) were the remnants of those the amaNdebele had seized from the *Trekkers* at Vegkop. The amaNdebele rallied and pursued the retiring amaZulu, succeeding in recovering an appreciable number of their livestock. The Zulu *impi* nevertheless still managed to carry off such substantial herds and flocks that driving them along considerably slowed down the pace of their march home along a different, more southerly route. Ndlela finally arrived in triumph at emGungundlovu in September 1837 when the maize was ripe. He over-optimistically claimed a complete victory over Mzilikazi, but the extent of the booty he had brought home was enough to please Dingane mightily. The Zulu king distributed the largesse among the *amabutho* who had gone on campaign, as well as among the great men of the kingdom, and could be satisfied that the campaign had unambiguously asserted his ascendancy over his African neighbours.[20]

The Griqua and Korana too were emboldened by Mzilikazi's defeat at Mosega in January 1837, and temporarily put aside old rivalries to mount a combined *kommando* against him. In May 1837 they met at the Vaal under Abraham and Cornelis Kok, Peter David, Barend Barends, and Jan Bloem. By the time they were ready to advance in late July—when Mzilikazi was busy fighting off the Zulu raid—their forces included unmounted Batlhaping and Bahurutshe allies. During August they mounted a series of hit and run raids, carrying off large herds of cattle

---

19 *Psalms* 109: 8–10.
20 *Annals* 1, p.325: Captain Gardiner to Colonel Bell, 9 September 1837; p.331: Owen's Diary, 31 October 1837; *JSA* 2, p.176: Mandhlakazi ka Ngini, 21 May 1916; *JSA* 3, p.205: Mkebeni, 19 September 1919; *JSA* 4, p.274: Ndukwana, 15 September 1900; *JSA* 5, pp.5–6: Nduna, 24 and 25 April 1910; pp.77, 79–82, 88–9: Ngidi, 18, 22, 23 October 1905; Bryant, *Olden Times*, pp. 436, 438–9.

and killing maybe hundreds of amaNdebele, leaving Mzilikazi feeling even more vulnerable than before.[21]

It was against a severely weakened Mzilikazi, therefore, that Potgieter determined to deliver his *coup de grace*. He was unaware that Mzilikazi had lost so many men and cattle to the Zulu and *droster* raids of 1837 that he had already decided (as he had done throughout his career when threatened) to withdraw north out of reach of his enemies in order to recuperate and repair his fortunes.[22] Yet, even if he had known of Mzilikazi's intention to relocate his people, it is unlikely that Potgieter (known to the amaNdebele as 'The Attacker')would have let the opportunity to wreak vengeance on the amaNdebele slip. Potgieter was joined by Piet Uys who, even though he did not intend to settle in the trans-Vaal, was eager both to prove his mettle and to collect booty. Between them, during October 1837 the two *Trekker* leaders gathered a force of between 330 and 350 mounted *burgers*—the largest *kommando* the Trekkers had yet mustered—supported by numbers of Barolong on foot enthusiastically contributed by Moroka. (Every year until his death, Potgieter henceforth sent a complimentary message and presents to the Barolong chief with thanks for his help 'when in time of distress.')[23]

When the Potgieter-Uys *kommando* reached Mosega on 2 November, they found the place deserted. But it pressed forward, and 45 miles to the north-east, at eGabeni (which the Boers called Kapain), it caught up on 4 November with the migrating host of amaNdebele. In nine days of running skirmishes, the Boers attacked and torched settlement after settlement, gunning down warriors when they tried to form up to resist, and harrying the mob of refugees that fled before them. Mzilikazi himself attempted to make a stand, but was forced to withdraw. The *kommando* killed as many as 500 amaNdebele and captured some 6,000 head of cattle. A few Barolong died in the fighting, but not a single mounted *burger*.[24]

When the elated Potgieter finally called an end to the carnage and the amaNdebele had fled, he declared 'the whole territory which that chief had overrun and now abandoned, forfeited to the emigrants.'[25] It is true, as Norman Etherington has pointed out, that the various peoples who had been displaced by the amaNdebele quickly moved back to repossess their lost lands, and that they were welcomed by their kinsmen who had never left and now threw off their allegiance to Mzilikazi.[26] Nevertheless, the fact is that in their own eyes the Boers had taken the northern highveld by right of conquest and, in Celliers' words 'that which had been his [Mzilikazi's] became ours'.[27] It was on this proposition that, once they had gathered the military strength to effect it, that the Boers subsequently based their territorial claims to the entire region between the Vaal and Limpopo Rivers.

As Mzilikazi retreated north, sending out an *ibutho* ahead of him to reconnoitre a suitable place to settle, he permitted many of his subject people to remain behind. Between 10,000 and 20,000 adherents nevertheless followed him over the Limpopo in long, straggling columns, driving along what livestock they had managed to salvage. Once across the Limpopo, the

---

21   *RN 3*, pp.183–185, no. 86: P. Wright to D'Urban, 6 August 1837; Etherington, *Great Treks*, p.254.
22   Bryant, *Olden Times*, p.437; Summers and Pagden, *Warriors*, p.65.
23   *Smit's Diary*, p. 181.
24   Summers and Pagden, *Warriors*, pp.64–5; Knight, *Warrior Chiefs*, pp.121–2.
25   Bryant, *Olden Times*, p.437.
26   Etherington, *Great Treks*, p.255.
27   *Annals* I, pp.238: Journal of the Late Charl Celliers.

amaNdebele wandered in several rival groups, and it was not until 1842 that Mzilikazi had finally reasserted his authority and re-established his kingdom north of the Matobo Hills, far away from the events playing out south of the Limpopo where he was no longer a contestant.[28]

While Potgieter and Uys were laying their plans to destroy Mzilikazi, Retief was continuing to head east to the Drakensberg passes, his following dwindling as the other parties hung back in indecision. On 2 October 1837 Retief reached the top of the escarpment with its stunning views of the Promised Land spread out below. There his party of 50 wagons laagered next to a huge rocky outcrop they dubbed Kerkenberg (Church Mountain). On 6 October Retief led a small party of 15 men and four wagons out of the laager and descended the Drakensberg by way of what is now known as Retief's Pass. He lingered for several days at the base of the mountains in the hope that Maritz would join his party. When he did not, Retief and his small expedition set off in the direction of Port Natal. Retief knew enough about the situation in the Zulu country to understand that if the *Trekkers* were to settle there in peace and security that he should first seek accommodation with the Port Natal traders to forestall possible British intervention. It was even more imperative that he negotiate with King Dingane to secure his permission to settle in the lands where he was acknowledged as ruler. Otherwise, the *Trekkers* could expect to be attacked with even greater force and determination than they had been by the amaNdebele.[29]

---

28 Summers and Pagden, *Warriors*, pp.66–73; Lye, 'Ndebele', p.96; Cobbing, 'Ndebele Amabutho', pp.622, 624; Knight, *Warrior Chiefs*, pp.122–4; Etherington, *Great Treks*, pp.255–6.
29 Thompson, 'Zulu Kingdom', p.358: Walker, *Great Trek*, pp.147–8.

14

The Chief of Port Natal

After 90 exhausting hours on horseback, Retief and his small party rode into Port Natal on 20 October 1837. There they found '53 Englishmen; no white women, only black ones.'[1] Many of the 'Englishmen' welcomed the *Trekkers* heartily, for the events of the past few years had caused them to despair of securing British protection while leaving them as distrustful and apprehensive as ever of Dingane's intentions towards them. The two concerns were tightly intertwined.

Dingane, as much as he distrusted the Port Natal settlers (whom the amaZulu called the *ababomvana*, or 'little red ones'),[2] remained as dependent as ever on their commercial network, not only for desirable trade goods, but for firearms. As regards the latter, he had his eye fixed uneasily on military events along the Cape Eastern Frontier and in Transorangia, and was fast coming to the conclusion that for his *amabutho* to maintain their ascendancy over the Zulu kingdom's neighbours, they must have firearms. Not for nothing was Dingane celebrated in his *izibongo* as 'Jonono who is like a fighting-stick of thunder [a gun]!'[3]

While the Port Natal settlers remained Dingane's main source for firearms, and were essential too for training his warriors in their use, he also obtained firearms and gunpowder from the Protestant missionaries of the (British) Church Missionary Society and the American Board Mission operating in his territory since 1835. The missionaries reluctantly supplied these dangerous items to curry favour with Dingane, but gained little from the transaction, admitting that the Zulu elite evinced no interest in the word of God, but only in their instructions on how best to use the onomatopoeic 'issibum', or musket.[4]

Tununu kaNonjiya, a member of the of umKhulutshane *ibutho* and an *isilomo* of Dingane (that is, a courtier holding no official position but whose personal friendship with the king gave him much influence) was directly involved in the firearm issue since he was a gun-holder of the king, an *isithunyisa*. He recounted how in September 1836 Dingane sent him to the Rev. Aldin Grout's mission on the banks of the Msunduze River to learn how to handle a musket for hunting purposes only. When he returned after a year, Tununu tapped his new-found expertise to

---

1 *Annals* 1, p.368: Daniel Pieter Bezuidenhout's narrative, December 1879.
2 *JSA* 6, p.281: Tununu, 6 June 1903.
3 Rycroft and Ngcobo (eds), *Praises*, p.75.
4 Capt. Allen Francis Gardiner, *Narrative of a Journey to the Zooloo Country in South Africa, Undertaken in 1835*, (facsimile reprint, Cape Town: C. Struik, 1966), p.68. The Zulu word for gun is *isibamu* (pl. *izibamu*). See also *Annals* 1, p.314: Captain Gardiner to Colonel Bell, 18 March 1837.

instruct others in the use of firearms for war as well as hunting. He remembered how the settlers and missionaries carefully packed the muskets and double barrelled elephant guns they were dealing in, along with a regular supply of powder and percussion caps, into boxes for delivery to Dingane's *izinceku*, and that they were paid with oxen and young bullocks, and sometimes with ivory.[5] Nor, despite alarmed warnings by some missionaries that supplying firearms to Dingane was sure to cause dangerous problems in the future, did the Cape authorities do anything to hinder the gun trade. The position taken by the Cape officials was that it was beyond their power to 'prevent or control' the importation and sale of gunpowder and arms at Port Natal.[6]

What made Dingane more determined than ever to obtain firearms was his campaign in early 1836 against the neighbouring Swazi kingdom to recover raided cattle and, in the process, to teach King Sobhuza's people a lesson they would not forget. Yet, despite being a major military effort involving most of the Zulu army under the joint command of Ndlela and Nzobo kaSobadli, his two chief *izinduna*, the expedition was a humiliating failure. The amaSwazi, as was their usual practice, avoided pitched battle and took instead to their mountain caves and strongholds, from where they defied the Zulu *amabutho* and rolled rocks down on the attackers. Thwarted, the Zulu army withdrew and Dingane called on Port Natal for assistance in winkling out the amaSwazi. The settlers were his tributaries and were thus under obligation to comply, but the lure of loot also motivated them. In June 1836 about 30 settlers under the command of John Cane ('Jana') mustered at emGungundlovu along with some 40 of their African retainers, all of whom were experienced hunters adept in the use of firearms. Indeed, at that time this was the most considerable force of musketeers ever fielded in the Zulu country. Cane's musketeers unequivocally demonstrated their worth when the Swazi campaign was renewed in August 1836 and their firepower subdued the Swazi strongholds. The now triumphant Zulu army was able to withdraw with 15,000 captured cattle but, as Dingane fully appreciated, only the muskets of the Port Natal contingent had made it possible.[7]

That military capacity on the part of the settler was a standing threat to Dingane's rule even if, on occasion, he could harness their firepower for his own purposes. And he could not but notice that Port Natal was growing. Not only were more traders coming in from the Eastern Cape, but they were bringing numerous Khoisan with them whom they employed (and armed) as hunters, transport-riders and interpreters. Yet what made the burgeoning settlement an immediate danger for Dingane was the persistent flight there of refugees from his rule. By the mid-1830s their numbers had swelled to about 2,500, meaning that the Port was becoming a significant nest of Zulu malcontents. Many of these entered the traders' service and were trained in musketry, so that, if ever Dingane decided to take military action against Port Natal, he would be confronted by a force of anything up to 300 men bearing firearms. Daunted by the

---

5   *JSA* 6, pp.255, 268, 269: Tununu, 1 June 1903; Anthony Edward Cubbin, 'Origins of the British Settlement at Port Natal, May 1824–June 1842' (unpublished Ph.D. thesis, University of the Orange Free State, 1983), pp.107–9. When staying with Grout, Tununu also learned how to drive a wagon.
6   *RN 3*, p 130, no. 62: John Bell, Secretary to Government, 20 March 1837.
7   *JSA* 5, pp.71, 89: Ngidi, 9 November 1904, 28 October 1905; *Annals* 1, pp. 377–8: William Wood, *Statements Respecting Dingaan, King of the Zulus*, 1840; Bryant, *Olden Times*, pp.321–3; Cubbin, 'Port Natal', p.106; Philip Bonner, *Kings, Commoners and Concessionaires: The Evolution and Dissolution of the Nineteenth-Century Swazi State* (Johannesburg: Ravan, 1983), pp 40–41; Tabler, *Pioneers*, p.18.

prospect, Dingane was prepared—if he could manage it—to adopt a policy of containment, rather than confrontation, with Port Natal.⁸

Agreement between Dingane and the Port Natal settlers was brokered though Allen Gardiner, a retired captain in the Royal Navy. When his wife Julia lay dying in May 1834 he promised 'to give himself wholly to God' and accordingly arrived in Port Natal on 29 January 1835 in the service of the Church Missionary Society.⁹ As he later informed the Select Committee on Aborigines (British Settlements) when giving evidence before it, he quickly discovered that Dingane 'was much perplexed to know what to do with the English at Port Natal. They were frequently breaking faith with him and troubling him very much … and he wished to set the matter at rest.'¹⁰ Since the success of Gardiner's missionary activities depended on Dingane's good will and on his peaceful relations with Port Natal, in early May 1835 he travelled to kwaKhangela, the *ikhanda* where Dingane was then residing, to see what he could achieve. Dingane was eager to negotiate and summoned Ndlela and Nzobo, his two chief councillors, from emGungundlovu. After some 'little deliberation' an agreement was hammered out and Dingane declared of its terms: 'they were good words – that they had made his heart glad.'¹¹ The settlers would cease to provide sanctuary to disaffected amaZulu (although those already at Port Natal were permitted to remain) and undertook to repatriate all future Zulu refugees. In return, Dingane promises to respect the right of Port Natal to continue as a trading settlement, and to respect the settlers' lives and property. On 6 May 1835 Gardiner signed the treaty at kwaKhangela on behalf of the residents of Port Natal, and it was witnessed by Ndlela, Nzobo and George Cyrus, the interpreter.¹²

Engraving of Captain Allen Gardiner, RN, missionary at Port Natal. (Campbell Collections, with permission)

8 Laband, *Zulu Nation*, pp.74–6.
9 Cubbin, 'Port Natal', p.80; Tabler, *Pioneers*, pp.48–9.
10 *RN 3*, p.72, no. 34, annex. 6: Minutes of Evidence before the Select Committee on Aborigines, 9 May 1836, # 3998, Captain Gardiner.
11 *RN 3*, p.11, no. 10, annex. 1: Gardiner to D'Urban, 4 June 1835.
12 *RN 3*, p.15, no. 10, annex. 1, enc. 2: A treaty concluded between Dingaan, King of the Zulus and the British residents at Port Natal, 5 May 1835.

Even so, Dingane knew the Port Natal settlers well enough to doubt their good faith. In his parting words to Gardiner, Dingane gave him the assurance that 'I shall hold fast to my word,' but, he presciently continued, I know that the white people will be the first to break the treaty.'[13] Gardiner stiffly responded that an Englishman never broke a treaty, but the Zulu king was soon proved right. Gardiner's authority was not generally recognised at the Port, and some traders continued to encourage amaZulu—particularly young women—to move to the settlement. Dingane retaliated by prohibiting all commerce between Port Natal and his subjects, and by forbidding any white people (with the exception of Gardiner) from crossing north of the Thukela.[14] Gardiner was therefore compelled to go back to Dingane only two months later to salvage the treaty of 6 May 1835.[15]

As Gardiner later reported to Governor D'Urban,[16] when in discussion with Dingane he suggested that on account of the 'bad faith of my own countrymen' it was necessary to establish some 'recognised authority' at the Port to enforce compliance with the treaty. Ndlela and Nzobo urged that Gardiner himself should be invested with the necessary powers, and he in turn rather rashly assured them that he would secure 'equal sanction' from his own government to make the treaty work.

The upshot was that:

> On the 13th of July when I took my last leave of Dingān, he of his own accord said: 'You must be the chief of Port Natal. I shall look to you to preserve order.' Before I could make any reply he continued by declaring that on this day he gave to me the whole of the Issibūbūlūngu country and that henceforth he should neither receive teachers nor traders unless they had previously received my permission to enter his territory.

Gardiner thereupon asked Ndlela and Nzobo what he was to understand by 'the Issibūbūlūngu country'? They replied that they meant all the country between the Thukela River to the north and the Mzimkhulu River to the south, and between the Drakensberg Mountains and the sea. This was the territory that would later form the British Colony of Natal, and esiBubulungu (the name in isiZulu for the Durban Bluff) is what the amaZulu then called it.[17]

Gardiner was understandably embarrassed to be made chief of such a large territory, and in his report hastened to assure D'Urban that he intended immediately to transfer the entire grant to the British government 'should they be willing to recognise it as a colony of the British Empire.' But Gardiner knew this was unlikely, and we have seen how on 29 March 1836 Lord Glenelg would firmly veto the possibility.[18] Even so, Gardiner set off for England in September

---

13   *RN 3*, p.14, no. 10, annex. 1, enc. 1: Gardiner to the British Residents, Port Natal, 7 May 1835.
14   Cubbin, 'Port Natal', pp.95–6.
15   See Bryant, *Olden Times*, pp. 675–77; Lugg, H.C. *Historic Natal and Zululand* (Pietermaritzburg: Shuter & Shooter, 1949), pp. 21–22; Etherington, Norman, 'Christianity and African Society in Nineteenth-Century Natal', in Andrew Duminy and Bill Guest (eds), *Natal and Zululand from Earliest Times to 1910: A New History* (Pietermaritzburg: University of Natal Press and Shuter & Shooter, 1989), pp.275–7.
16   See *RN 3*, pp.19–20, no. 10, annex 2: Gardiner to D'Urban, 24 November 1835.
17   *JSA 5*, p.92: Ngidi, 29 October 1905. The amaZulu also called Natal esiLungwini, 'the Place of the Whites' (*JSA 6*, p.270: Tununu, 1 June 1903).
18   *RN 3*, pp.30–1, no. 17: Glenelg to D'Urban, 29 March 1836.

1835 to lobby for the annexation of Natal. Gardiner failed in his attempt, and instead had to settle for a nebulous official appointment to sanction his position at the Port.[19] In terms of the Cape of Good Hope Punishment Act of 13 August 1836, on 21 April 1837 D'Urban appointed him Justice of the Peace at Port Natal with authority over the entire territory Dingane had granted his as chief.[20]

On his return from England, Gardiner landed at Port Natal on 24 May 1837 with his new wife and set about establishing his fortified mission, Hambanathi, on the banks of the Thongathi River, 25 miles north of Port Natal.[21] He knew he would be exercising only the 'faint shadow of British jurisdiction', and that with no active support from the government at the Cape he would be powerless to restrain further clashes between the settlers and Dingane.[22] Even his modest request for some muskets, ammunition, '2 bell tents' and '1 Union Jack, with block and haulyards' with which to advertise and assert his status was turned down.[23] The Cape Executive Council was especially determined that it would not permit the establishment of 'an authorized armed force where Her Majesty's Government has determined that no British settlement shall be formed or even countenanced.'[24] Nor did the residents of Port Natal take kindly to Gardiner's newfound authority, and on 12 June 1835 formally protested at his being set as 'Magistrate over them'.[25]

Undeterred, and following D'Urban's instructions to do so, Gardiner set about restoring relations with Dingane. In mid-June 1837 he arrived at the kwaNobamba *ikhanda* where the Zulu king was residing and presented him with gifts the Governor had supplied: 15 yards of scarlet cloth, a pair of gold epaulettes of the 98th Regiment, five dozen gilt military buttons and a silver watch with chain and seals, all of it worth £26 10s 6d.[26] Dingane was 'much pleased' with the watch and epaulettes, but disappointed in not receiving more cloth and no beads.[27] Even so, on 21 June 1837 he signed a new treaty with Gardiner. In return for Gardiner sending back all the Zulu refugees in Port Natal, Dingane declared that he gave 'the ground on which the white people live about Port Natal' to 'the King of England', William IV. (Neither he nor Gardiner would have known that the king had died the very day before, and that the teenaged Queen Victoria now sat on the throne.) Dingane went on to specify that by his grant he meant 'the whole country' between the Mgeni River just to the north of Port Natal down to the Mzimkhulu River in the south, and from the sea to the Drakensburg Mountains.[28] Excluded

---

19 Cubbin, 'Port Natal', pp.97–104.
20 *RN 3*, pp.131–3, no. 62, annex. 1: D'Urban to Gardiner, 21 April 1837; *RN 3*, p.109, no. 47: Glenelg to D'Urban, 7 September 1836.
21 Cubbin, 'Port Natal', pp.117–18.
22 *RN 3*, p.176, no. 82, annex. 1: Gardiner to Col. Bell, 14 April 1837.
23 *RN 3*, p.135, no. 62, annex. 3, enc. 1: Gardiner to Bell, 14 March 1837: List of articles requested for the public service at Port Natal.
24 *RN 3*, p.130, no. 62: John Bell, Secretary to Government, 20 March 1837.
25 *RN 3*, pp.179–80, no. 82, annex. 6, enc. 1: Protest of the inhabitants of Natal against the appointment of Capt. A. Gardiner, R.N., as a Magistrate over them, 12 June 1837.
26 *RN 3*, p.136, no. 63: Bell to Chief Clerk, Colonial Office, 22 March 1837.
27 *RN 3*, p.187, no. 87, annex. 1: Gardiner to Bell, 28 June 1837.
28 *RN 3*, p.188, no. 87, annex. 1, enc. 1: Dingarn, King of the Zoolus X His sign to the King of England, 21 June 1837.

was the territory between the Mgeni and the Thukela Rivers that had formed the northern part of the chiefdom Dingane had first granted Gardiner on 13 July 1835.

Considering the legal weight the *Trekkers* subsequently laid on the witnessed treaties they entered into with Dingane, treaties that apparently ceded them similarly vast tracts of territory, this is the moment to explore what the Zulu king understood by such grants. Crucially, the European concept of the permanent alienation of land through a treaty was entirely foreign to the amaZulu. They held that all the land belonged to the king, not personally, but as the representative or guardian of the nation as a whole. In him was vested the power of allotting the land to his subjects through his subordinate *amakhosi* and *izinduna* who gave them permission to build their *imizi* on it and to use it for their agriculture and grazing.[29] Consequently, when Dingane made Gardiner a chief or 'gave' territory to King William IV, he never imagined for a moment that he was surrendering the sovereign rights over the land. Rather, he was permitting others (such as Gardiner) to exercise power over the land in his name, a prerogative that could be extended, transferred, or terminated. Moreover, he expected these subordinates to perform whatever actions he required in return for their delegated privileges, and in Gardiner's case that meant handing over the Zulu refugees at Port Natal, even though it entailed abandoning them to summary execution. We shall soon see how Dingane tested Retief's compliance and loyalty in similar fashion.

The Port Natal settlers were unimpressed by Gardiner's latest treaty with Dingane and its terms, and had done with him as a Justice of the Peace. On 9 September 1837 Gardiner wrote in consternation to the authorities in the Cape that the settlers had 'set my delegated authority at defiance … and have declared themselves independent of all British control … a few days since.'[30] The government back in Britain was entirely unimpressed by this move, Lord Glenelg dismissively stating that the Port Natal settlers had 'not ceased to be subjects of the Queen,' and that the 'pretension they make to constitute a free independent state is so extravagant that I can hardly suppose that it has been seriously put forward … whatever may be the light in which these settlers may be regarded by the chiefs of the rude tribes with whom they are living.'[31]

Yet for Gardiner, who was on the spot, the settlers' petulant if meaningless declaration of independence was imbued with 'a more serious aspect,'[32] because he had known for many months of that *Trekker* parties were intending to cross over the Drakensberg and settle in Natal.[33] It was his not unfounded fear that the Port Natal settlers would 'very likely … coalesce with the Boers and invite them to make that neighbourhood the seat of their projected government.'[34] However, the English settlers were divided over that very issue. British loyalists like Gardiner believed that if the Boer succeeded in taking control of the Port and imposing their laws, they would have no choice but to depart since the Cape authorities were 'utterly precluded' from taking

---

29 A.T. Bryant, *The Zulu People as They Were before the White Man Came* (Pietermaritzburg: Shuter & Shooter, 1949), pp.464–5; Eileen Jensen Krige, *The Social System of the Zulus* (2nd edition, Pietermaritzburg: Shuter & Shooter, 1974), pp.176–7; J.S.M. Maphalala, 'The Re-interpretation of the War of Ncome, 16 December 1838', in DACST, *Blood River/Ncome*, p.57.
30 *RN 3*, p.200, no. 99, annex. 1: Gardiner to Bell, 9 September 1837.
31 *RN 3*, p.206, no. 174: Glenelg to the Officers Administering the Govt of the Cape of Good Hope, 29 October 1837.
32 *RN 3*, p.200, no. 99, annex. 1: Gardiner to Bell, 9 September 1837.
33 *RN 3*, p.21, no. 10, annex. 2: Gardiner to D'Urban, 24 November 1835.
34 *RN 3*, p.187, no. 87, annex. 1: Gardiner to Bell, 28 June 1837.

possession of the settlement.³⁵ Many others, however, saw the *Trekkers* as vital reinforcement against Dingane's perennial threats and had, in any case, already unilaterally thrown off their unrequited attachment to Britain.³⁶

Most influential in this latter group were John Cane ('Jana') one of the original settlers, and Alexander Biggar, know to the amaZulu as 'Mazingensasa'.³⁷ The Scottish Biggar had arrived in Port Natal on 7 May 1836 with his brother George and several Khoisan.³⁸ A former soldier and Peninsular veteran with a wife and 11 children, he had been an 1820 settler in the Eastern Cape. Ruined as a farmer and transport rider by the Sixth Cape Frontier War, he had decided to seek his fortune in Natal. On account of his military experience, the other residents had appointed him in May 1837 as Commandant of Port Natal and commander of the very short-lived Port Natal Volunteers, raised during yet another passing crisis in relations with Dingane.³⁹ These two, along with 12 of the other leading settlers, wasted no time in signing an address publicly informing Retief that they desired to receive the Trekkers 'as friends, and perhaps, in the course of events, as neighbours'. Retief responded in the same vein, expressing the desire that 'the Almighty … may bring us together for our mutual welfare.'⁴⁰

Believing that he had secured the necessary support of the majority of the Port Natal settlers and that they would not appeal to Britain for aid against the *Trekkers*, Retief prepared to embark on the second and much more uncertain leg of his mission: his visit to Dingane to obtain the Zulu king's permission to settle within his domain. As a first step he made contact with Dingane through the good offices of the Revd Francis Owen of the Church Missionary Society.

Owen, accompanied by his wife, sister, his interpreter, the artisan Richard Hulley, the latter's wife and three children, and Jane Williams, his servant, had arrived at emGungundlovu only a short time before, on 10 October 1837. He set up his mission in some huts on the upper end of the Matiwane ridge on the eastern side of the *ikhanda*, but not so far along so as to overlook the king's private enclosure, or *isigodlo*.⁴¹ Owen, who had been recruited by Gardiner, knew he had come to the Zulu kingdom without the 'sanction' or protection of the British authorities,⁴² and that the future of his ministry depended entirely upon Dingane's goodwill. Short as Owen's four months at emGungundlovu would be, his sojourn there has proved invaluable to historians since he recorded in obsessive detail what he witnessed there in his diary.⁴³

Dingane sent Owen some *umndlunkulu* (maids-of honour from his *isigodlo*) to form his congregation—and to learn how to sew—and allowed people from the *umphakathi*, or general

---

35 *RN 3*, p.243, no. 119: Cape Executive Council, 16 December 1837; p.255, no. 120: Bell to Gardiner, 22 December 1837.
36 Cubbin, 'Port Natal', pp.135–8.
37 *JSA 5*, p.62: Ngidi, 8 November 1904.
38 *RN 3*, p.36, no. 24: Names of party proceeding with Mr Biggar to Port Natal, 7 May 1836. See Laband, *Historical Dictionary*, p.15.
39 Tabler, *Pioneers*, pp.12–13; Cubbin, 'Port Natal', pp.111–13.
40 *Annals* 1, p.360: Address by A. Biggar and others to Retief, n.d.; Retief's reply to the Address, 23 October 1837.
41 *JSA* 1, p.20: Baleni, 10 May 1914.
42 *RN 3*, p.118, no. 59: George Grey to D'Urban, 11 November 1836.
43 Sir George E. Cory (ed.), *The Diary of the Rev. Francis Owen* (Cape Town: Van Riebeeck Society, 1926) (*Owen's Diary*), pp. 38–120: 10 October 1837–12 February 1838.

assembly, to attend his services.[44] But Owen, known to the amaZulu as uMshumayeli (Preacher), proved himself both unbearably earnest and involuntarily condescending, and his grasp of isiZulu remained weak. Dingane had little time for him personally, or for his theology. Once, after stopping Owen half an hour into his interminable sermon, he roundly declared:

> I and my people believe that there is only one God—I am that God. We believe there is only one place to which all good people go—this is Zululand—we believe there is one place where all bad people go, there said he, pointing to a rocky hill in the distance [kwaMatiwane, the place of execution]. There is Hell, where all my wicked people go.[45]

Yet, for all Owen's shortcomings as a missionary, Dingane quickly grasped how useful he could prove as a conduit for written communications between him on the one side, and the *Trekkers* and residents of Port Natal on the other, even though he could not understand those written in Dutch.[46] Knowing this, Retief wrote to Owen in English on 19 October 1837, informing Dingane through him of the *Trekkers'* desire to live at peace with the amaZulu. Pointedly, he also reminded the Zulu king of Mzilikazi's defeat by the Boers in January 1837 (Potgieter's and Uys's final victory at eGabeni would not take place until the following month).[47] This missive, with its superficially conciliatory sentiments underlaid by the barely veiled and ominous threat of force, set the tone for all of Retief's future dealings with Dingane. It could not have failed to put Dingane and his councillors instantly on their guard.

Protocol required Retief to wait for Dingane's reply to his letter permitting him to proceed to emGungundlovu. However, it was characteristic of the man, and an indication of the fundamental disdain in which he held African rulers, that he did not do so. Instead, he set off on 24 October for Dingane's great place with his party of 15 Boers and two settlers, the influential John Cane and Thomas Halstead. Halstead, tall and of slight build, whom the amaZulu called Damuse, had been living in the Zulu country for a dozen years and was now 26 years of age. He lived next door to Cane and was employed by him, and had served in his expedition of 1836 against the amaSwazi. Known personally to Dingane, Halstead was fluent in isiZulu and had considerable experience as an interpreter.[48] It was in that capacity that he would serve Retief until he was killed alongside him three months later.

---

44 *JSA* 6, p.256, Tununu, 29 May 1903.
45 *Owen's Diary*, p.174: R.B. Hulley's account.
46 *Owen's Diary*, p.60: 4 November 1837.
47 *Annals* 1, pp.359–60: Retief to Dingaan, 19 October 1837.
48 *JSA* 1, pp.110–11: Dinya, 3 and 5 April 1905; Tabler, *Pioneers*, pp. 55–6.

15

The Place that Encloses the Elephant

Retief and his small party reached emGungundlovu on 5 November 1837. The vast *ikhanda* itself was a spectacular and daunting sight, and it was the stage for intricate royal rituals and ceremonies, some of which the white visitors would have witnessed. As the seat of royal power, and the barracks of several *amabutho*, of it was intended to awe and intimidate all those who entered it. We do not know what Retief and his companions made of it all, but there can be little doubt that they did their best to seem unimpressed, even though they had never before seen its like and must have been overawed.

The Zulu kings would regularly progress from one *ikhanda* to another, but the one where each preferred to live for most of the time was regarded as his capital, his 'great place'.[1] It was the setting for his domestic routine, the place where he exercised his royal authority and made his decisions of state, and where he performed the great ceremonies and rituals of the nation. KwaBulawayo, built in 1824, had been Shaka's initial 'great place', followed by kwaDukuza where he moved in 1827. EmGungundlovu was Dingane's, and he ruled from there. Its name means 'the place that encloses the elephant', and since the king was referred to as 'the elephant' (honoured as the greatest of all the beasts), it translates in effect as 'the royal capital'. Dingane established it in 1829 on the southern side of the White Mfolozi River in the emaKhosini valley (the 'Valley of the Kings') where his ancestors of the House of Zulu were buried. The location was in cool lowveld country that abounded with patches of acacia bush in the rolling grassland, and where aloes and euphorbias stood sentinel. With its mixture of summer and winter grazing, the valley and its environs were ideal for pasturing cattle the whole year round. To allow for drainage, emGungundlovu was constructed on the northern slopes of the stony iSingonyama, or Lion Hill, in the fork between the Mkhumbane stream to the east, where Dingane and his household drew their drinking water, and the much smaller Nzololo stream to the west, both of which flowed into the White Mfolozi.[2]

From contemporary descriptions of emGungundlovu, from Dr Andrew Smith's sketch taken in April 1832 of its ground plan, from recorded recollections,[3] and from archaeological

---

1 For an account of emGungundlovu and daily life there, see Laband, *Zulu Nation*, pp.64–71.
2 *JSA* 1, p.20: Baleni, 10 May 1914.
3 For Smith's sketch, see Kirby (ed.), *Smith*, p.53. Smith's account of his visit—when taken in conjunction with the published memoirs of two Port Natal traders, Nathaniel Isaacs, and Henry Francis Fynn, the only slightly later reports and diaries of missionaries, notably those of Captain Allen Gardiner and the

The Place that Encloses the Elephant 121

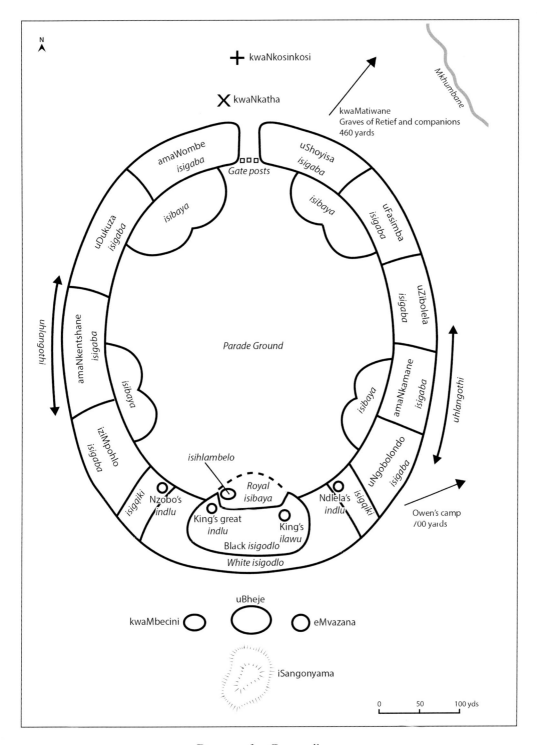

Diagram of emGungundlovu

excavations at the site in 1974 and 1975 that have uncovered the floors of huts, post-holes, grain-pits and middens,[4] we know the *ikhanda's* layout followed that of Shaka's kwaBulawayo and kwaDukuza. This was a pattern that would be maintained at kwaNodwengu, King Mpande's capital established in 1843, at oNdini, King Cetshwayo's 'great place' built in 1873, and at every other *ikhanda* of whatever size in the Zulu kingdom. In turn, all these *amakhanda* mirrored in colossal form the tens of thousands of humble circular clusters of thatched, beehive *izindlu* dotting the undulating Zulu countryside. Each was a self-sufficient family homestead, or *umuzi*, its half-dozen or so huts arranged around a circular cattle byre, or *isibaya*, protected by a wooden palisade. It was only appropriate that the *isibaya* should form the core of every *umuzi* or *ikhanda* because the Zulu were above all a pastoralist people. Nguni cattle with their spreading horns, multi-coloured skins and black-tipped noses were their favoured indigenous strain.[5] Dingane favoured those that were light reddish-brown, black, or red with a white patch along the back.[6] These cattle were central to Zulu culture and religious ritual when they were sacrificed to honour and appease the *amadlozi*, and possession of them was the prime indicator of wealth in a society that had little others means of accumulating it. Daily, their milk provided food, as did their flesh when they were slaughtered or sacrificed, while their hides when scraped became shields for warriors or skirts for women. Their fat softened hides such as those that covered people when they slept on their narrow grass mats with their heads supported on a carved wooden headrest, or was smeared on the body and shaved head as a salve.[7]

EmGungundlovu was bigger than any other of Dingane's *amakhanda* and was considered the largest ever built by a Zulu king.[8] To Captain Gardiner who first saw it in 1835, it looked like a cross between a 'distant racecourse' and 'an immense assemblage of haystacks'.[9] Covering nearly 56 acres and with a circumference of a mile, it was so extensive that it was said that a man would not be heard if he tried to shout from one side to the other. When filled to capacity at the great national ceremonies, it could accommodate between 5,000 and 6,000 people. Approximately 1,100 *izindlu*, protected by a stout outer palisade of timbers, enclosed an elliptical, open parade ground some 1,640 feet wide and 1,870 feet long. Men of status were permitted to cross this

    Revd Francis Owen, and when reinforced by the extensive Zulu oral testimony James Stuart recorded in the first years of the twentieth century—provide us with a rich and detailed picture of Dingane and his world. See too sketches of emGungundlovu according to Lunguza in *JSA* 1, pp.309 and 340, n.d. [1909], and according to Tununu in *JSA* 6, pp.294–6, 14 June 1903.

4   John E. Parkington and Mike Cronin, 'The Size and Layout of Mgungundlovu 1829–1838', *South African Archaeological Society Goodwin Series*, No. 3. Iron Age Studies in South Africa (1979): pp.133–48; Natal Provincial Museum Service, *uMgungundlovu* (Melmoth: uMgungundlovu Museum, n.d.), pp.8–9, 14–16.

5   The Zulu language contains hundreds of cattle terms by which to identify the distinctive shapes of horns, the presence or absence of a hump, and the numerous different colours and patterns. Favourite cattle had praise-names and were trained to respond to whistled commands. For descriptions of 42 cattle colours and of myriad names for types of horns and other characteristics, see *JSA* 6, pp.40–1: Socwatsha, 24 January 1904. See Marguerite Poland, David Hammond-Tooke, and Leigh Voight, Leigh, *The Abundant Herds. A Celebration of the Nguni Cattle of the Zulu People* (Vlaeberg, South Africa: Fernwood Press, 2003), *passim*.

6   *JSA* 6, p.295: Tununu, 14 June 1903.
7   *JSA* 6, p.38: Socwatsha, 24 January 1904.
8   *JSA* 6, p.259: Tununu, 30 May 1903.
9   Gardiner, *Journey to the Zooloo Country*, pp.28, 199.

open space, but women had to go up the side, close to the inner palisade of timbers, reeds and thatching grass that cordoned it off from the encircling huts.[10] Dingane insisted that the *izindlu*, whose entrances all faced the central parade ground, were well built and properly thatched, and used regularly to inspect the whole *ikhanda*, giving orders for repairs.[11] As was customary in every *umuzi* and *ikhanda*, grain-pits were dug and covered in the central parade ground where a number of cattle enclosures were built against the inner palisade. Access to the parade ground was through narrow openings at several places in the inner and outer palisades (which also allowed men to go outside to relieve themselves, or to bask in the sun), and through the main entrance to the *ikhanda* on its northern, lower side. This entrance, which was 20 feet wide, could be closed by laying wooden poles across it.

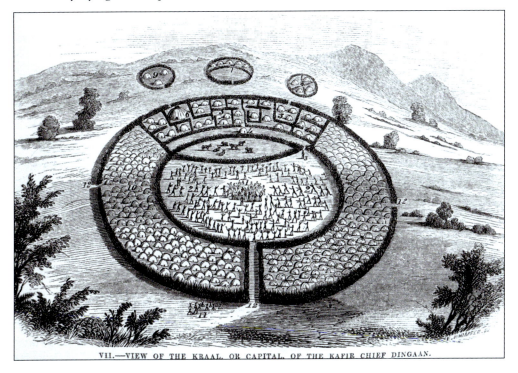

'View of the Kraal, or Capital, of the Kafir Chief Dingaan'. An accurate representation of emGungundlovu, incidentally showing the execution of Retief and his companions in the parade ground. (Engraving in the Rev. William C. Holden, *History of the Colony of Natal, South Africa* (London: Alexander Heylin, 1855))

Directly opposite the main entrance, at the higher, southern side of the parade ground, was the royal cattle enclosure, the *isibaya*, sacred to the king. There Dingane and his councillors would

---

10   *JSA* 6, p.296: Tununu, 14 June 1903.
11   *JSA* 6, p.296: Tununu, 14 June 1903.

discuss matters of state and administer justice. It was also the place where he would ablute in a special enclosure, the *isihlambelo*,¹² perform the religious rituals required of the monarch, and officiate over the great national ceremonies. Adjoining the *isibaya* and higher up the slopes of the iSingonyama Hill, was the private royal enclosure, or *isigodlo*, sacred to the king. Retief and none of his companions would ever have been allowed to enter it.

The *isigodlo* was divided into two sections of close to 150 huts in all, accommodating about 500 women. The central, 'black' section of the *isigodlo* was divided into numerous triangular compartments of about three *izindlu* each, demarcated by fences of intertwined, flexible branches some two yards high. The huts, which archaeologists have found to have varied greatly in size (13 to 20 feet in diameter) and to have exhibited individuality in their design,¹³ were lit by black candles about a foot in length made of ground dried cattle dung and beef fat with strips of cloth for wicks. Fires for warmth or cooking were made in broad, shallow flat-bottomed earthenware basins and the inside of the huts were always black with smoke.¹⁴ About a hundred women lived in the black *isigodlo*. At first, they were under the charge of Langazana kaGubetshe, one of Senzangakhona's widows, remembered as being short and stout and 'lightish in colour', and celebrated for her open hospitality.¹⁵ When Dingane despatched her to rule over the nearby kwaKhangela (royal women were often put in charge of *amakhanda*), she was succeeded by Mjanisi, another of Senzangakhona's widows.¹⁶ If Dingane had ever married, his wives (*amakhosikazi*) would have lived in the black *isigodlo*. Since he never took a wife, the only *amakhosikazi* there were Senzangakhona's widows and Dingane's aunts and sisters. As senior married women of the royal house (or with the honorary status of married women) their hair was worked into intricate topknots 'greased and clotted with red ochre clay'.¹⁷ They wore leather skirts reaching to the knees but hanging low over the buttocks so that a few inches of the cleft could be seen.¹⁸ They decorated themselves with multi-coloured beads around the forehead, ankles and arms. Some varieties of beads only the king himself and the members of the *isigodlo* were permitted to wear. These included the small opaque dark red ones with white insides and the small white beads that came from Delagoa Bay, and the dun-coloured polished ones and the dark blue ones imported by sea from Cape Town through Port Natal. Like all Zulu people, women as well as men, their earlobes had been pierced just before puberty as the first of the rituals marking the transition from childhood to adulthood, and they wore small ear plugs of carved, polished wood.

Alongside the *amakhosikazi* in the black *isigodlo* lived the king's favoured maids-of-honour, the *umndlunkulu* who had been given to him as tribute and who served as his concubines. Unmarried girls across the kingdom had a front covering of beadwork or leaves to shield their nakedness, or perhaps a fringed waistband of skin, but these *umndlunkulu* wore only a slight loin cover about two inches square, and strings of the prestigious opaque red- and amber-coloured beads and wristlets of the pure white ones. The most favoured *umndlunkulu* also sported brass or

---

12   *JSA* 6, p.12: Socwatsha, 28 December 1901.
13   Parkington and Cronin, 'Mgungundlovu', pp.136, 138–42.
14   *JSA* 6, pp.375–6: Xubu ka Luduzo, 26 May 1912; Kirby (ed.), *Smith*, pp. 89–90.
15   *JSA* 5, p.53: Ngidi, 5 November 1904.
16   *JSA* 5, p 76: Ngidi, 18 October 1905.
17   Stuart and Malcolm (eds), *Fynn's, Diary*, pp. 293–94.
18   *JSA* 6, p.45 Socwatsha, 26 June 1904.

copper coils around their left upper arms as well as four hollow brass rings around their necks, worn one above another and so tight that it made it almost impossible to turn the head. The rings chafed the wearer and heated up in the sun causing blisters, and it was necessary to pour water over them to cool them down and to rub fat and gall onto the irritated skin. Nevertheless, these ornaments conferred such prestige that they were displayed with pride.[19] It was death to look upon these *umndlunkulu* when they left the *isigodlo* under armed escort to bathe or to relieve themselves. The only male who could freely enter the black *isigodlo* was the king himself. Trusted attendants who filled the milk gourds and cut up the meat for the women were allowed in past the huts that guarded the entrances to the *isigodlo*, and councillors like Ndlela might enter when especially summoned. But the life of any other man who tried to penetrate the *isigodlo* without specific permission—even the king's own brothers—was forfeit, as was that of any man who slept with one of the *umndlunkulu*.[20]

In the 'white' section of the *isigodlo* that surrounded the black *isigodlo* on all sides except that abutting the *isibaya*, lived a further 400 or so women under the charge of Bhibhi, Senzangakhona's widow and Ndlela's sister. Royal children were normally reared in the white *isigodlo*, but Dingane had none. With no children to look after, the women quartered there were the younger or less attractive *umndlunkulu* who had not attracted the king's eye, and the *izigqila*. The latter were women who had been captured in war or were the wives or daughters of men the king had executed. Their status was slave-like, for they could never be ransomed or freed. Not only were they obliged to be at the sexual disposal of men of the royal house, but they performed all the menial domestic chores in the *isigodlo*. Their days were filled cultivating vegetable gardens, fetching water, gathering firewood, cooking food and waiting on the women of high status whose clay chamber pots they emptied.[21]

Dingane especially favoured fat young women with pretty faces. The secluded, sedentary life of the *isigodlo*, with nothing much to occupy the *umndlunkulu* except to keep their bodies anointed to a fine sheen with sheep-fat and to entertain the king with interminable song and dance of an evening, combined with the staple fare of the *isigodlo* that consisted of blood-clots and fat cooked into a rich soup and washed down by whey, ensured that they did indeed grow as corpulent as their lord desired. (The rich diet of the *umndlunkulu* was in stark contrast to that of ordinary people who ate meat only when they had sacrificed a beast and who subsisted on sour clotted milk (*amasi*), beer made from sorghum (*utshwala*), pounded grain boiled as porridge, and fresh vegetables.)

All the gates of the *isigodlo* were shut tight when darkness fell, and the king was the only male permitted to spend the night there. Dingane, being without any wives, slept in an *ilawu* (the small private *indlu* of an unmarried man) in one of the triangular enclosures on the eastern side of the black *isigodlo*. The *ilawu* had a single, central wooden post beautified from top to bottom by the *umndlunkulu* who had entwined it with intricate patterns of the red and white beads restricted to the *isigodlo*. When Dingane wished to have sex, the chosen *umndlunkulu* were

---

19 Frans Roodt, 'Zulu Metalworking', in Wood (coordinator), *Zulu Treasures*, pp.95–7.
20 *JSA* 5, pp. 49–50, 54, 90: Ngidi, 28 October, 5 November 1904; p. 379: Sivivi, 14 March 1907. For a discussion on the *umndlunkulu* and *izigqila* in the *isigodlo*, see Shaun Hanretta, 'Women, Marginality and the Zulu State: Women's Institutions and Power in the Early Nineteenth Century', *Journal of African History*, 39 (1998), pp. 397–403, 408–409.
21 *JSA* 3, p. 162: Mkando, 10 August 1902.

summoned one at a time to his *ilawu*.[22] Since, like his brother, Shaka, Dingane was afraid that any sons he sired would grow up to kill or depose him, none of the *umndlunkulu* he penetrated and made pregnant was permitted to bring the child to full term.[23] Each 'had a pot [of *imxukuzo* medicine] cooked for her ... which she was made to drink to bring away the pregnancy.'[24]

The king also possessed a great hut in the extreme north-western corner of the *isigodlo* abutting the *isibaya* where he held audiences during the daytime. In its size it dominated all the surrounding *izindlu*. It was a monument to the hut-builders' art, uniquely lofty with ten poles to support it and large enough to accommodate 50 people. Its greeny-black floor that was made of cow-dung mixed with sand from anthills—as were the floors of every *indlu* in Zululand—was polished until it glowed like marble.

Behind the *isigodlo* and higher up the slopes of iSangoyane Hill, were three small *imizi*. Ranged from east to west, these were eMvazana, uBheje and kwaMbecini, the last of which housed artisans who worked in copper.[25] The biggest, uBheje, consisted of eight large *izindlu* and was named after after Bheje kaMagawozi, the Khumalo chief whose stronghold Dingane had successfully stormed in 1827 during one of Shaka's campaigns. This was where the women of the *isigodlo* could isolate themselves when menstruating, bask outside in the sun under the trees planted nearby, and generally relax.[26] The *induna* of Bheje was Vumbi kaMkhele who cooked for the women in six great pots that could stew a whole beast in one day. Besides the king, only he and several *izinceku*, his trusted body servants, were allowed inside. Dingane's great *inceku* was Masiphula kaMamba (afterwards King Mpande's chief *induna*), a man notorious for his cruelty and likened in his violent rages to a wild animal.[27]

When visiting uBheje, the king liked to sit there in the shade on his great, European-style chair.[28] Shaka had always sat on an *umqulu*, or rolled up mat, but Dingane favoured the type of chair Cayana kaMaguya fashioned out of a single block of the marula tree (Sclerocarya caffra), a wood normally used for carving pots or meat trays. (Such items, Smiths noted, were not used by the common people.)[29] Like many of these items, Dingane's chairs were decoratively marked with spots burned onto them.[30] Under Dingane, only the king might sit on a chair, and he often did so on ceremonial occasions. (A number of chairs of different design conserved in various museums are said to have been Dingane's, but their provenance is difficult to establish.)[31]

Dingane's daily life in the *isigodlo* was hedged around by rigid etiquette that signalled his royal status and made it difficult to approach him. Among the many duties of the *izinceku* who served him (and for which they were lavishly rewarded with meat, *amasi* and cattle) was

22 *JSA* 5, pp.370–1: Sivivi, 7 March 1907.
23 *JSA* 6, p.43: Socwatsha, 24 January 1904.
24 *JSA* 6, p.270: Tununu, 1 June 1903.
25 Parkington and Cronin, 'Mgungundlovu', pp. 137, 142–3, 147–8.
26 *JSA* 5, p.374: Sivivi, 10 March 1907.
27 *JSA* 2, p.208: Mangati ka Godide, 15 June 1920; *JSA* 6, p.254: Tununu, 28 May 1903; Magema M. Fuze, edited by H.C. Lugg and A.T. Cope, *The Black People and Whence They Came: A Zulu View* (Pietermaritzburg: University of Natal Press; Durban: Killie Campbell Africana Library, 1979), p. 94.
28 *JSA* 6, pp.255, 262–3: Tununu, 28, 31 May 1903.
29 Kirby (ed.), *Smith*, p.83.
30 *JSA* 5, p.369: Sivivi, 6 March 1907; *JSA* 6, p.271: Tununu, 1 June 1903.
31 Gillian Berning, '*Indaba Yamakhos' Ayibanjelwa Mlando* / The Matter of Kings in Not Kept', in Wood (coordinator), *Zulu Treasures*, pp. 47–51, 59–60.

the cooking of the king's meat in the royal *isibaya*, meat that was preferred very well matured, almost rotten. The *izinceku* were also responsible for milking the hundreds of cows kept in the cattle enclosures in the great parade ground, and then, with arms uplifted, carrying the milk into the *isigodlo* in wooden buckets covered with a basket.[32] Despite the status enjoyed by the *izinceku*, Smith noted that—like any of Dingane's subjects who did not carry out his orders with 'proper alacrity'—they were subject to 'the liberal bestowal of kicks and blows.'[33]

Dingane would be summoned to his meal by an *umndlunkulu* striking together the shanks of two hoes in very rapid succession. While the king was at his meal, and until he had finished rinsing out his mouth afterwards, the blows would ring on, although not as fast. While the hoes were sounding, no one in the entire *ikhanda* might spit or cough on pain of death. If you had to cough, you threw yourself on the ground and buried your face in your hands to smother all sounds of coughing. (Breaking wind or having an erection in the king's presence, Smith learned, also led to execution.)[34] Only the *umndlunkulu* beating the hoes together was present with the king in his hut while he ate. Any food left unconsumed in the *isigodlo* the *izinceku* distributed to destitute people and commoners who were encouraged to visit emGungundlovu to *ukukhonza*, and by demonstrating their allegiance and loyalty to the king, thereby to 'warm themselves' by his presence.[35]

When the king sent for a man to visit him in his hut in the *isigodlo*, he instantly ran to obey, shouting out Dingane's *izibongo* as loudly as he could. An *inceku* posted at the gate to the *isigodlo* and known as *ugayinyange* ('he who watches the moon') would take the person, who was stooping low in respect, to the royal hut and would sit outside until the interview was over. Once the summoned man had crawled into the king's hut, he would remain lying subserviently in front of Dingane like a dog. The interview over, he would crawl out backwards, never turning his back on the king and praising him as before.[36]

Declaiming the *izibongo* of the king was essential in honouring him correctly and in invoking the favour of his royal *amadlozi*. Magolwana kaMkatini of the amaWombe *ibutho* was Dingane's chief *imbongi* (praise-singer).[37] Stout and tall, Magolwana was a man of considerable status and considered it his right to help himself to cattle seized in war. He had his own hut at emGungundlovu where—as a special concession—his women were allowed to live with him. Magolwana would get up at dawn, go into the great parade ground, and begin to praise the king to waken him in the *isigodlo*, not leaving off until late in the morning. Not even a thunderstorm could deter him. When he finally had done, Dingane would come out and give him a large pot of *utshwala* to refresh his dry throat. Magolwane was accompanied by two other *izimbongi* whom Dingane treated as jesters and enjoyed cruelly teasing. Duda was physically impaired and went about on his hands and knees, while Mhaye was only three feet six inches high with little

---

32 *JSA* 5, pp.75–7: Ngidi, 6 March 1907; *JSA* 6, pp. 253, 254: Tununu, 28 May 1903.
33 Kirby (ed.), *Smith*, p.54.
34 Kirby (ed.), *Smith*, p.92.
35 *JSA* 5, p.379: Sivivi, 14 March 1907.
36 *JSA* 5, pp.370–1: Sivivi, 7 March 1907; Laband, *Zulu Nation*, p.68.
37 Mpande executed Magolwana once he came to the throne.

bow legs. Considered a simpleton, the latter was permitted to enter the *isigodlo* to make rude jokes about the women's private parts to the merriment of all.[38]

Dingane kept a number of dogs in the *isigodlo* and favoured the large, powerful *igovu* breed that originated in the Cape and was brought back by Shaka's armies that raided the amaMpondo in 1824 and 1828. Of various colours—black and white, light brown, reddish—and almost always neutered if male, they seem to have been vicious animals, and the king was in the habit of setting them on people for his amusement. His favourite was Makwedlana, fat and large and slow on his feet.[39]

Dingane's *insila*, or body dirt—nail clippings, phlegm and the like—was a matter of concern lest an evil *umthakathi* (a wizard or witch) employ it to concoct *umuthi* (occult medicine) to bring death or misfortune down on the king. Thus, the *inceku* cutting his hair below the *isicoco* or shaving him—and showing proper deference when doing so by stealthily approaching Dingane and then running off for a moment after daring to touch him—would catch the hair in a basket and give it to another *inceku* to burn and scatter the ashes in a running stream.[40] The king's phlegm would be ground underfoot into the dirt, and the water from his washing place (*isihlambelo*) in a special enclosure in the royal *isibaya* surreptitiously disposed of.[41] Where the king defecated, whether inside or outside the hut, was kept secret, but it was known that he always did so accompanied by a favoured *inceku*.[42]

---

38 *JSA* 5, p.32: Ngidi, 12 August 1904; *JSA* 6, p.12: Socwatsha, 29 December 1901; pp.266–7: Tununu, 16 January 1903.
39 *JSA* 6, pp. 262, 299: Tununu: 31 May, 1 June 1903. Tununu listed and named Dingane's favourite dogs. At that time there were no domestic cats in Zululand.
40 *JSA* 5, p.370: Sivivi, 7 March 1907.
41 *JSA* 6, p.12: Socwatsha, 28 December 1901.
42 *JSA* 5, p.378: Sivivi, 14 March 1907.

16

Do You Hear the King?

The main entrance at emGungundlovu, through which Retief and his companions would have passed, separated the two great wings (*izinhlangothi*) of four to six undulating rows of close to 1,000 *izindlu*. These huts were of uniform size (12 feet in diameter), each with a single central post. They were evenly spaced, but not linearly aligned.[1] The *izinhlangothi* adjoined the *isigodlo* on its eastern and western flanks and swept around the great parade ground. When taking their turn to serve the king for several months a year, or when congregating for the great national festivals, this is where the *amabutho* were accommodated. The two wings were divided into sections (*izigaba*) connected by openings in the fence. In terms of the structure of an *ibutho*, an *isigaba* was a section, varying in size from 10 to 40 *amaviyo*, or companies. An *ibutho* such as the uFalaza, for example, had four *izigaba*, each with its own name.[2] In an *ikhanda* there would be accommodation for only one *isigaba* of an *ibutho* when its members came to serve the king, and it was in that section of an *uhlangothi* assigned to their *ibutho* that they would be quartered. (When there was a full mobilisation, such as in time of war, the other *izigaba* of an *ibutho* would be accommodated in neighbouring *amakhanda*.)

At emGungundlovu there were five *izigaba* in the left-hand (eastern) *uhlangoti* commanded by Ndlela, whose hut was in the 'headrest', or *isigqiki* section against the fence of the *isigodlo*. This is where half the *izinceku* slept so as to be close to the king's quarters in the *isigodlo*. These arrangements were mirrored in the right-hand (western) *uhlangoti* where Nzobo, living in his own *isigqiki* area, was in command of its four *izigaba*. It seems, as noted by Dr Andrew Smith in 1832, that there were three rectangular buildings in each *uhlangothi* where shields and spears were stored,[3] and likely more were kept in huts close to those belonging to Ndlela and Nzobo, but this has not been confirmed archaeologically.[4]

Life for members of an *ibutho* at emGungundlovu was rigorous despite generous servings of beef, otherwise reserved for the conspicuous consumption of the elite and members of the *isigodlo*. It was easy to become disorientated in the confusing maze of almost identical *izindlu*, and when a man wandered into an *isigaba* occupied by another unit, he risked being beaten up

---

1   Parkington and Cronin, 'Mgungundlovu', pp.142, 147.
2   *JSA* 5, p.171: Nsuze, 19 May 1912.
3   Kirby (ed.), *Smith*, p.53.
4   Parkington and Cronin, 'Mgungundlovu', pp. 136, 143–5, 147.

and chased away. Because members of each *ibutho* were always being rotated in and out, huts would be left periodically empty. Then they would be filled with wood ash and excrement by those living in neighbouring *izindlu* and required much cleaning to be made habitable again. For lack of supervision, when warriors did not relieve themselves in empty huts, they did so very close by the outer palisade and in the streams where others drew their water. Consequently, in the *ikhanda* 'the stench was very bad'.[5]

As the Retief party would have witnessed, the young warriors' day of labour began at dawn, and none were exempted—except perhaps an *induna*'s favourites who might cry off pleading diarrhoea (easy enough to contract in the insanitary *ikhanda*) or other ailments. Their regular tasks included gathering wood and grass to repair the huts and palisades, tending the king's fields of crops—they used the shoulder-blades and ribs of cattle as implements since there were so few metal hoes available—and guarding his extensive herds of grazing cattle.[6] Through the custom of *ukusisa* (pasturing cattle in the care of a subordinate), royal cattle such as these were entrusted to the care of all the *amakhanda* (and often to *imizi* as well). They remained the property of the king, but their carers had the right to make use of them for milk or dung and to keep their offspring.

While herdsmen at *amakhanda* carried arms against cattle thieves, other warriors going about their chores stowed away their *izihlangu* or great cowhide war shields, tall enough to cover the body from ground to shoulder, in huts raised on wooden stilts to preserve these valuable items (only two could be cut from the hide of a cow) from the rats; while their menacing stabbing-spears, or *amaklwa*, that were issued by the king and remained his property, were piled out of sight in their huts. Likewise laid aside on a routine working day was the warriors' superb and intricate ceremonial dress, and only the basic loin-cover was retained. Woven blankets, which became an increasingly favoured item of outer wear in cool weather, had been introduced in 1824 with the arrival of the first white traders at Port Natal. Initially, they were luxury garments or coverings confined, as Smith noted, to the elite.[7] The members of an unmarried *ibutho* who had not yet sewn on the *isicoco* and shaved their heads below it wore their hair long and intricately worked into fantastical shapes.

The king entered into the diurnal activities of the *ikhanda* outside the *isigodlo*. Every day he went into the royal *isibaya* to inspect his cattle—every Zulu man's greatest source of pride. And, as unlikely as this may seem, Dingane was often heard to amuse himself clucking like a chicken (still a great rarity in the Zulu country), saying 'Ki ki li gi!'[8] More seriously, he regularly reviewed the *izigaba* of the *amabutho* barracked at emGungundlovu. When doing so, he positioned himself on an anthill or large rock and peered over the palisade of the *isibaya*, encouraging his warriors and their commanders as they sang his *izibongo*, leapt high into the air and rhythmically stamped their feet, showing off their highly disciplined and intricate dancing skills.

Dingane occasionally visited the nearby *amakhanda* in the emaKhosini: esiKlebheni, emBelebeleni, eziNyosini and oDlabendlwini. The furthest he usually went was to kwaKhangela on the lower slopes of the Mthonjaneni heights to the south-east of the valley, and he would

---

5   *JSA* 1, p.344: Lunguza, 22 March 1909.
6   *JSA* 6, pp.74–5: Socwatsha, 17 December 1909.
7   Kirby (ed.), *Smith*, p.87.
8   *JSA* 6, p.266: Tununu: 1 June 1903.

remain there for a while. Once, for ten days, accompanied by the women of his *isigodlo* he stayed at the distant emGumanqeni *ikhanda* near the mouth of the Mlalazi River to see the Indian Ocean. When he ventured into the sea the men of the umKhulutshane *ibutho* ranged themselves in front of him so that he could bathe in safety.⁹

Whenever Dingane embarked on one of these royal progresses (Retief had no opportunity to witness such an event) he was accompanied by all the notables of his court, and was guarded by his *amabutho*, just as if he were going on a warlike expedition. Servants out on the flanks of the column carried household items and supplies. Everyone would know when the king was travelling because one or two *izimbongi* would be shouting his praises throughout the entire journey. As Dingane walked (there were as yet few horses in Zululand and the king never rode one), he was surrounded by his great nobles, his *izikhulu*, who kept a respectful distance of 50 yards or more from him. Those in front thoroughly cleared his way by flattening the grass, removing small pebble and sweeping the ground. His officers would keep the rumbustious *amabutho* back so that they did not crowd the king. Dingane used to become tired on the march and would then sit down on his chair and a large white shield would be held over him to make a shade. His favourite dog, Makwedlana, would lie at his feet. While the king rested, his *amabutho* would perform military exercises to amuse him. As he approached his destination, the inhabitants of the *ikhanda* would come out dancing to welcome him and escort him onto the parade ground. There they formed a circle around him and gave a further exhibition of dancing before Dingane retired to the seclusion of the *isigodlo*.¹⁰

It is doubtful whether Retief grasped the extent to which Dingane's authority as king was based on a combination mystical ritual and naked power politics. He was the great rain-maker, and the fruitfulness of the crops

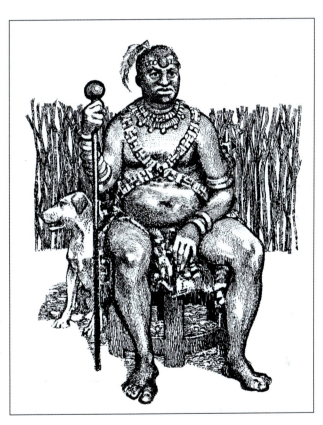

Dingane and his dog Makwedlana by an anonymous artist. (R.C.C Samuelson, *Long, Long Ago* (Durban: Knox, 1929))

---

9   *JSA* 6, p.301: Tununu, 17 June 1903.
10 *Annals* 1, pp.292–4: Capt. Gardiner, 'First Interview with Dingaan', February 1835; *JSA* 5, pp.368–9: Sivivi, 6 March 1907.

and the security of the kingdom depended on his performing the rites at the great national festivals, especially the annual first-fruits *umKhosi* festival that Dingane celebrated with greater magnificence than any other Zulu monarch.[11] The amaZulu believed that in the next world the ancestral shades, the *amadlozi*, maintained the status they had enjoyed in this. Consequently, the king's departed ancestors ruled in the land of the spirits, and it was their powerful aid the king secured when he sacrificed to them on behalf of his people.

Despite the impression formed by white settlers that the Zulu king was a despot, no Zulu monarch could make great state decisions without consulting the leading men of the kingdom— even if, during the reigns of both Shaka and Dingane, they seldom dared to question the king's wishes.[12] A small, select inner council, known as the *umkhandlu*, determined policy in conclave with the king. Some of these councillors would have been *abantwana*, princes of the Zulu royal house, and others *izikhulu*. The latter were hereditary chiefs in their own right whose territory had been incorporated into the Zulu kingdom, and they should be regarded as members of the high nobility.

Alongside these princes and aristocrats were the *izinduna*, the state officials the king had appointed to command the *amabutho*, preside over certain *amakhanda*, or rule over some districts where they administered justice in the king's name. Anyone who was alert, able, active, and intelligent could be made an *induna*, but only after the king had inquired first whether notable men of high birth didn't have sons who could take up the post instead.[13] Because they owed their elevation to royal favour rather than to royal or noble blood, *izinduna* were more amenable to the king's will than the hereditary aristocrats, and Dingane would consult them too on matter of policy. Preeminent among the notables who surrounded the king was his chief *induna*—usually a man of high lineage—the person he had appointed to be his hand and voice throughout the kingdom and the commander-in-chief of the army. Yet, because his office was not hereditary but was the king's gift, it could be withdrawn again at a moment's notice.[14] Throughout Dingane's reign his chief *induna* (as we have seen) was Ndlela, closely supported by Nzobo. Both were of chiefly houses.

All these men of high status grew their fingernails—sometimes an inch-and-a-half long, Smith noticed, especially that on the thumb—to indicate they undertook no manual labour.[15] As did the king, they wore an *ingxotha*, the heavy and excessively uncomfortable brass armlet that reached from wrist to elbow and was conferred as a royal mark of distinction. They girded skin skirts around the loins with blue monkey skins sewn onto them and with twisted thongs of the skins of blue monkey, genet, and mongoose. The long, upright plume of the blue crane, fixed above the forehead, formed their distinctive headdress.[16] Many of the elite, including Dingane, favoured a cloak of the dark-blue cotton salempore cloth imported from Indian and sold by the Portuguese at Delagoa Bay.[17] On days of great ceremony, the elite would don the

---

11   For the *umKhosi*, see Laband, *Zulu Nation*, pp.63–4.
12   Webb and Wright (eds), *Zulu King Speaks*, p. 93. For an analysis of the Zulu power-structure under Dingane, see Laband, *Zulu Nation*, pp. 59–62.
13   *JSA* 6, p. 4: Socwatsha, 17 December 1909; p.275: Tununu, 3 June 1903.
14   *JSA* 4, pp.300–1: Ndukwana, 1 October 1900.
15   Kirby (ed.), *Smith*, p.48.
16   *JSA* 5, p.82: Ngidi, 22 October 1905.
17   *JSA* 6, pp.270–1: Tununu, 1 June 1903.

same intricate dress and elaborate feathered headgear as the *amabutho*. Only the costliness and rarity of their furs and feathers and their greater display of ornaments such as arm bracelets of beads or brass, strings of beads below the knee and around the ankle, and bands of beads slung over the shoulder, indicated their superior status.[18]

Once the king and the *umkhandlu* had agreed on an important policy decision, such as that of going to war or of promulgating new laws, then it would be put for further discussion before the *ibandla*. This was a much larger gathering of notables who were not members of the inner council, and who might voice reservations or suggest amendments. Once they had reached consensus, the general assembly of commoners, the *umphakathi*, would be informed of what their superiors had decreed.[19]

Nzobo kaSobadli and another *induna* ritually challenging each other before King Dingane. Anonymous engraving. (Campbell Collections, Durban, with permission)

There were always many people at emGungundlovu who had thronged there to *ukukhonza* and to be fed milk and meat from the king's bounty—even if he sometime grew impatient with all the hangers-on. The crowd would give praise to the cattle that sustained them by singing and

---

18   Laband, *Assassination*, pp.16–17; Kirby (ed.), *Smith*, p.81.
19   Webb and Wright (eds), *Zulu King Speaks*, pp. 81–4.

dancing when they were brought home in late morning and afternoon for milking. Otherwise, they would hang about waiting for the king to emerge from his *isigodlo*.[20] When he did so, one of his *izinceku* would shout several times for the people to leave their huts and congregate in a general assembly of commoners—the *umphakathi*—at the top end of the parade ground. (Menials who cooked, collected firewood, and did not go on military expeditions, were never invited to attend.)

The king, with his *izinceku* behind him and his major *izikhulu* and *izinduna* ranged in front of him, sat about 25 yards from the *umkhumbi*, the semi-circle formed by the gathered *umphakathi*. Sometimes, when they were no weighty matters to be put before the *umphakathi*, the time would be spent with displays of dancing and accompanying song,[21] boastful talk about glorious deeds performed on campaign, and with the satisfying enumeration of enemy chief the king had 'eaten up'. The tone was far more restrained when there were affairs of state to impart. There was no discussion, however. The people kept quiet while Dingane spoke to Ndlela who wore his distinctive grey feathered headdress of the mousebird and red-faced coly.[22] Ndlela then loudly reiterated the king's words. In turn, the minor *izinduna* who sat in the front rank of the *umkhumbi* repeated what Ndlela had said to the men to their rear. After each statement Ndlela would enquire: 'Do you hear the king?' and the men would all reply, 'Yes, father.' Everybody subserviently laughed when Dingane deigned to do so in his inimitable closed-mouth way, and the whole *umphakathi* shouted out '*Bayede*' when he stood up to leave, and called out his *izibongo*, half stooping as he passed.[23]

Everybody gathered at the assembly knew (as Retief and the *Trekkers* would learn to their cost) that the ultimate decisions over life and death lay with their dread ruler, and that he did not hesitate to overrule the decisions of his advisers and officials.[24] When trying a case in the royal *isibaya*, the *ibandla* sat on the ground in a semi-circle with the offender in the middle facing the king seated on a chair while an *inceku* shaded him from the sun with a shield. The missionary, Francis Owen, witnessed such a trial in 1837. Dingane entered energetically into the proceeding, pacing about, throwing out his arms, snapping his fingers and talking rapidly while his councillors agreed slavishly with everything he had to say.[25] They could hardly do otherwise for, as Smith learned, if they thought differently from the king, they could not show it without disrespect.[26]

Those miscreants found guilty would either have a cattle-fine imposed on them, or be condemned to death. To the right (or west) of the main entrance to emGungundlovu was a deep little valley with gentle slopes down the sides. This was kwaNkatha, the place of execution. The victim was usually killed by a sharp blow to the head or by having his neck broken. Women and men of status were not executed in this way but were throttled to death with a noose around the neck.[27] The bodies of the executed were then dragged across the Mkhumbane stream and

20 *JSA* 6, pp. 300–1: Tununu, 17 June 1903.
21 For various types of warrior dances, see *JSA* 6, p.267: Tununu, 1 June 1903.
22 *JSA* 5, p.82: Ngidi, 22 October 1905.
23 *JSA* 5, pp.278–9: Savivi, 14 March 1907; Kirby (ed.), *Smith*, p.49.
24 Webb and Wright (eds), *Zulu King Speaks*, pp.74, 82.
25 *Owen's Diary*, pp.85, 93: 19 December 1837, 1 January 1838.
26 Kirby (ed.), *Smith*, p.80.
27 *JSA* 5, p.299: John Shepstone, 19 March 1912; *JSA* 6, p.273: Tununu, 1 June 1903.

left as a feast for the waiting vultures on kwaMatiwane, a steep, stony hillock about 500 yards north-north-east of the main gate. (Did Retief take note of it on this, his first visit? For on his second his body would lie there too.) This sinister little hill was named after Matiwane kaMasumpa of the amaNgwane whom Dingane had put to death. Matiwane had made his way back to Zululand after his defeat by the Cape forces at the battle of Mbholompo in 1828, and had begged to die at the new king's hands since he had lost all his following and (as he pitifully put it) no longer had a cloak to wrap himself in.[28]

When large numbers were being put to death, and when the king wished the executions to be performed more visibly, kwaMatiwane was preferred over the relative seclusion of kwaNkatha. Such an event is remembered as having taken place in about 1834, foreshadowing the circumstances of the execution of Piet Retief and his party that would take place on 6 February 1838. On the first occasion, in 1834, Dingane was informed by his guards that commoners who had come up to emGungundlovu to *ukukhonza* were sleeping with the women of his *isigodlo*. Enraged, Dingane deployed the uDlambedlu, iziNyosi and umKhulutshane *amabutho* to round up the miscreants and to carry them off to kwaMatiwane where, over two days, they set about killing them, not with spears but with heavy sticks, or *izinduku*.[29]

Indeed, for all the splendour of its ceremonies and the munificence of the king's hospitality, emGungundlovu was a place of uncertainty and fear for all those who entered it, and none could breathe freely again until they had departed for home. For despite the conciliatory and relative merciful way Dingane had attempted to govern at the beginning of his reign, he soon accepted that to hold together a factious kingdom formed by force and terror only a decade before, he had no choice but to be as implacably ruthless as its founder, his half-brother Shaka. As King Mpande, his successor (who was usually rated a merciful king) would later regretfully admit, 'The Zulu people are ruled through killing.'[30] And this required more than routine executions through judicial procedures. It called for unpredictable violence and apparently arbitrary executions to remind the *abantwana*, *izikhulu* and *izinduna* as well as ordinary people that their lives were entirely in the king's hands.

Certainly, Dingane's closest advisers knew this was essential. We have already met the two men Dingane raised up to be his principal councillors. Nzobo kaSobadli (whose commonly used warrior name was Dambuza),[31] was a portly and notoriously ill-tempered personage always clad in his familiar 'whiteish blanket'.[32] He in particular seemed to have been adept at strengthening Dingane's resolve whenever he was inclined to mercy or compromise, insisting that 'the killing of people is a proper practice, for if no killing is done there will be no fear.'[33] Nzobo was firmly supported in this stance by Ndlela kaSompisi, even though he was reputably a kindly and temperate man inclined to mercy. Ndlela was the brother of Bhibhi, Senzangakhona's favourite wife, and had risen to prominence under Shaka as a much-acclaimed warrior, successful general and fine orator. Older than Dingane and dark-complexioned like Nzobo, he had a shiny skin

---

28   *JSA* 6, p 273: Tununu, 1 June 1903.
29   *JSA* 6, pp.256–7: Tununu, 29 May 1903.
30   *JSA* 5, p 299: John Shepstone, 19 March 1912.
31   *JSA* 6, p.298: Tununu, 14 June 1903.
32   *JSA* 5, p 379: Sivivi, 14 March 1907.
33   *JSA* 1, p.196: Jantshi, 14 February 1903.

and a slight beard, and was tall with thin legs supporting a great belly. He was superior to Nzobo because Dingane had appointed him his chief councillor and commander-in-chief.[34]

Dingane's subjects were not entirely wrong, therefore, to believe that it was his two senior advisers, rather than king himself, who ensured that the vultures were regularly fed with the flesh of those who were summarily put to death. In a telling metaphor in Dingane's *izibongo*, the pair are portrayed as controlling Dingane who is likened to a goat with its proverbially skittish and unpredictable disposition:

> Goat of Dambuza and Ndlela,
> Which they held by the ear and it was patient ...[35]

Yet, for all that, Dingane was his own man. Nathaniel Isaacs, one of the original hunter-traders at Port Natal, early perceived that Dingane was 'deliberative and calculating', indeed, 'reserved, even to the extreme, and in speaking seems to weigh every word before he utters it.'[36] Unnervingly, he never showed his unusually small teeth as he laughed but only nodded his head to and fro and grunted.[37] The amaZulu certainly recognized his unfathomable nature, calling him in his *izibongo* 'Deep one, like pools of the sea!'[38] They also noted his habitually cautious way of proceeding, doubtless born out years of surviving in Shaka's dangerous proximity, describing him as

> He who peeps over dry ravines before crossing,
> Who washed his hands and they dried while he was in council.[39]

As did Isaacs, the amaZulu understood that underneath Dingane's reticent exterior lurked a cunning and brutally dangerous king:

> Ox that encircles the homesteads with tears;
> Mamba who when he was down he was up.[40]

---

34 *JSA* 5, p.82: Ngidi, 22 October 1905.
35 Rycroft and Ngcobo (eds), *Praises*, p. 75.
36 Isaacs, *Travels*, pp.177, 289.
37 *JSA* 1: P. 318: Lunguza, 14 March 1909; *JSA* 5, p. 369: Sivivi, 6 March 1907.
38 Rycroft and Ngcobo (eds), *Praises*, p.91.
39 Rycroft and Ngcobo (eds), *Praises*, p. 83.
40 Rycroft and Ngcobo (eds), *Praises*, p.89.

Die Oorwinning [the Victory] *16 Des. 1838*. Relief by Coert Steynberg on the granite Blood River Monument inaugurated in 1947. (Photo: By kind permission of Elizabeth Rankin and Rolf Schneider, *From Memory to Marble: The Historical Frieze of the Voortrekker Monument. Part II: The Scenes* (Berlin and Boston: Walter de Gruyter, 2020))

The laager of bronzed, cast-iron wagons erected in 1971 at the site of the battle of Blood River (Photo: Talana Museum, Dundee, with permission)

The Ncome monument, unveiled in 1998 by King Goodwill Zwelithini, facing the bronzed wagon-laager across the river. (Photo: uMsunduzi Museum, Pietermaritzburg, with permission)

'Umbambu and Umpengulu, young Zulus in dancing costume.' (George Angas, *The Kaffirs Illustrated in a Series Drawings* (London: G. Barclay for J. Hogarth, 1849))

III

'Kaffir Kraal near the Umlazi River, Natal.' (George Angas, *The Kaffirs Illustrated in a Series Drawings* (London: G. Barclay for J. Hogarth, 1849))

'D'Urban, Port Natal, from the Berea.' (George Angas, *The Kaffirs Illustrated in a Series Drawings* (London: G. Barclay for J. Hogarth, 1849))

'Dingarn in his ordinary and dancing dresses.' (Allen Gardiner, *Narrative of a Journey to the Zooloo Country in South Africa Undertaken in 1835* (London: William Crofts, 1836))

An ox-wagon crossing a drift. Lithograph by unknown artist. (MuseumAfrica, Johannesburg, with permission)

'Encampment of the Griqua Chief Adam Kok on the Riet Modder River Jany. 3. 1835', by Charles D. Bell. (MuseumAfrica, Johannesburg, with permission)

'Sikonelli Chief of the Mantatees – 1834' (Sekonyela, Chief of the Batlokwa), by Charles D. Bell. (MuseumAfrica, Johannesburg, with permission)

'Onset of Matabeli warriors – 1835', by Charles D. Bell, 1835. (MuseumAfrica, Johannesburg, with permission)

'The Battle of Vechtkop, Orange Free State, October, 1836. Lithograph after Heinrich Egersdörfer in *The Press* and *The Johannesburg Times*, Christmas Annuals, 1895. (MuseumAfrica, Johannesburg, with permission)

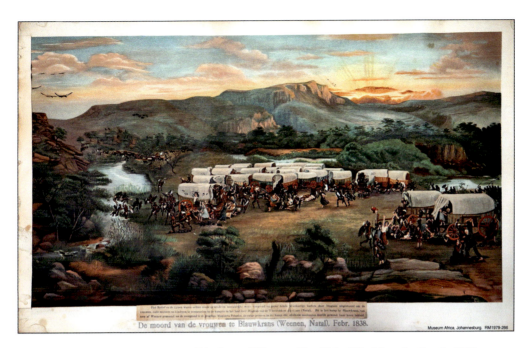

'De moord van de vrouwen te Blaukrans (Weenen, Natal)', by Elia Musschenbroek, 1910. (MuseumAfrica, Johannesburg, with permission)

'Vecht Laager Natal 1838'. Lithograph after Henry Lea. (MuseumAfrica, Johannesburg, with permission)

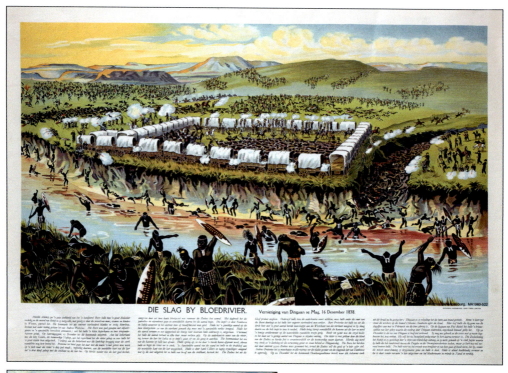

'Die Slag by Bloedrivier', *Cape Times*, 1938. (MuseumAfrica, Johannesburg, with permission)

Andries Pretorius nursing his wounded arm after the battle of Blood River. Artist unknown. (uMsunduzi Museum, Pietermaritzburg, with permission)

Memorial raised in 1922 at kwaMatiwane to Piet Retief and his companions. The unnamed *agterryers* who died on the same day were added as an afterthought. [Photo: By kind permission of Elizabeth Rankin and Rolf Schneider, *From Memory to Marble: The Historical Frieze of the Voortrekker Monument. Part I: The Frieze* (Berlin and Boston: Walter de Gruyter, 2019)]

'Umpande, the King of the AmaZulu'. (George Angas, *The Kaffirs Illustrated in a Series Drawings* (London: G. Barclay for J. Hogarth, 1849))

17

They Desired Port Natal

How aware was Retief of Dingane's reputation for brutality and deviousness? John Cane who rode by his side on the way to emGungundlovu was one of the most influential figures in Port Natal, and his opinions reflected those of the majority of settlers. No sooner had Dingane seized the Zulu throne in 1828 than Cane was describing him to the Cape authorities as 'as weak, cruel, capricious and even more prone to shed human blood than the monster [Shaka] that has been put to death.'[1] Nothing in his subsequent dealings with Dingane would have changed his mind; indeed, Cane's deep dislike and distrust would have been confirmed by the Zulu monarch's periodic and capricious forays against Port Natal aimed at reasserting his authority over the settlers. We must suppose, therefore, that primed by Cane, Retief approached his meeting with Dingane with caution and suspicion, leavened by his habitual disdain for African rulers.

For his part, Dingane too had been cautioned about what to expect from his arrogant and uninvited visitor. On his way to emGungundlovu, Retief stopped to visit Captain Gardiner at Hambanathi, his mission station. Realizing that Retief intended to take possession of the land around Port Natal, Gardiner immediately wrote to Owen to warn Dingane. Owen read the letter to Dingane on 3 November and, much put out, the king instructed Owen to reassure Gardiner that the country already assigned to him by the treaty of July 1835 would remain his.[2]

Forewarned of what Retief wanted of him, Dingane received him and his small party at emGungundlovu on 5 November 1837, at the very moment—unbeknown to both parties—that the Potgieter-Uys *kommando* was victoriously engaging the amaNdebele at eGabeni. The amaZulu dubbed Retief 'Piti' after his first name. They called his people the *amaBunu*, or Boers, and sometimes the *amaqadasi*, the able-bodied ones, 'those with big hats and big trousers and mounted.'[3] The amaZulu also knew them (and their Khoisan *agterryers*) as *imihanga*, ferocious roaming animals or fierce-tempered people with yellowish, tanned complexions that differentiated them from the lighter-skinned, 'white' English at the bay.[4]

Retief left no physical description of the Zulu king with whom he came face-to-face in their edgy and mutually mistrustful conference. Fortunately, other contemporaries recorded their

---

1   *RN 2*, p.52, no. 53: Duncan Campbell, civil commissioner, to Lt. Col. Bell, 19 December 1828.
2   *Owen's Diary*, pp.59 –60: 3 November 1837.
3   *JSA* 6, p.278: Tununu, 4 June 1903.
4   *JSA* 6, p.24: Socwatsha, 30 December 1901.

impressions. Tununu kaNonjiya, who was interviewed when he was 90 years of age, had been one of Dingane's *izinceku* and enjoyed close access to his person. He remembered his master to have been 'good-looking' and described him as 'light brown ... in colour' and about 5 ft 8 inches tall.[5] Lunguza kaMpukane, who had been born in about 1820 and as a child had often seen Dingane, remembered that he had 'the slightest show of whiskers, and a small beard', and that, like many of Senzangakhona's descendants, he had 'very large fat thighs and a large neck'.[6] Indeed, Dingane's 'Prominent buttocks, handsome posterior!' were acclaimed in his *izibongo*.[7] Nevertheless, he was not flabby but, as Isaacs observed, was 'solidly built ... firm and tough', and that despite his heavy frame Dingane regularly 'exhibited his skill and agility' at dancing.'[8] As with Shaka, Dingane had patches of hair on his body, and was hailed in his *izibongo* as

> Hairy-One with hair like a lion's,
> Having hair even on the legs.[9]

Dingane's large, fleshy chin always sweated and he used to scrape off the drops with his snuff spoon which was carried by his *inceku* in a basket along with his capacious snuff box fashioned out of a large gourd. [10] From living in the southern, coastal country in his youth, Dingane used to *ukuthefula*, that is, to speak in the softened accent of the region as opposed to the inland amaZulu who spoke in a harder, stiffer way. Thus, while he pronounced his own name 'Dingana', the latter said 'Dingane'. (This explains why his name was spelled both ways by whites who heard it pronounced differently.)[11] Likely, what would most have struck Retief as he parlayed with him were Dingane's expressive eyes that revealed both his quick apprehension and volatile temperament. Isaacs noted that his fierce glance was 'keen, quick, and always engaged, nothing escaping him,' and admitted that he was quelled by Dingane's exceedingly 'piercing and penetrating eyes' that he rolled 'in moments of anger with surprising rapidity.'[12]

Knowing that his uninvited visitors were dangerous men—*imihanga*—with designs on his kingdom, discourteous men too who did not present him with gifts to show respect as Gardiner would have done, Dingane did his best over the following days to impress and daunt them with his power and wealth. He staged magnificent displays of dancing and military exercise, first by 2,000 young *amabutho*, and on the following day by 4,000 older, head-ringed men. Dingane himself, arrayed in all his finery, took part in the review. With no private property in the Zulu kingdom, personal wealth was measured in cattle. To astonish the Boers with his stupendous riches, Dingane collected a great herd of 2,224 cattle, all of them red with white backs (probably

---

5   *JSA 6*, p.254: Tununu, 28 May 1903.
6   *JSA 1*, p.318: Lunguza, 14 March 1909.
7   Rycroft and Ngcobo (eds), *Praises*, p 93.
8   Isaacs, *Travels*, pp.179, 289.
9   Rycroft and Ngcobo (eds), *Praises*, p.81.
10 *JSA 5*, p.369: Sivivi, 6 March 1907.
11 Laband, *Zulu Kings*, p.104.
12 Isaacs, *Travels*, pp.179, 289.

those known as *izintulo*, or lizards),[13] and had them driven before Retief and his companions to be counted.[14]

Following these displays of his majesty, on 8 November Dingane got down to business with Retief. He assured the Boer leader that he was 'almost inclined' to grant him territory—where precisely he did not specify. Retief had already told him that if he could choose, he would like 'the country near the Natal Bay, as we white people need many things that come from over the sea.'[15] But (as we have seen) in 1835 Dingane had already settled the territory south of the Thukela on Gardiner as its chief, and only a few months before, in June 1837, had 'given' the territory south of the Mgeni River to King William IV. As he assured Gardiner in a letter Owen wrote for him on 9 November, 'he had not told the Dutch *what* country he should give them! He knew that they *desired* Port Natal, but he did not intend to give it to them.' Rather, what he had in mind for Piti and the *amaBunu* was some vague territory far away on the highveld from which he claimed his *impi* had driven Mzilikazi in the recent campaign against the amaNdebele. Owen censoriously noted that 'it appears that Dingarn [sic] has been acting craftily towards the Boers.'[16] So he had, and Retief was fully aware that the Zulu king was being duplicitous, but believed he had no option but to play along and show good will.

Dingane, for his part, seems to have decided to play for time and to put his importunate visitors to the test. Before he could agree to place any part of his domain under Retief's rule, he had first to be sure that he would be as willing as any other subordinate chief to obey his bidding. He therefore set him a task he must perform before he would consent to negotiate further. He explained that 'a people having clothes, horses and guns' had recently rustled cattle from the amaHlubi, a people in the foothills of the Drakensberg who acknowledged Dingane as their king. His implication was that *Trekkers* on the highveld were the culprits—not *drosters*, Basotho or Batlokwa who also operated in that fashion—but that if Retief nevertheless recovered the cattle for Dingane he would thereby prove his loyalty and good faith.[17]

Dingane was fully aware, in fact, that the cattle thieves were indeed Sekonyela's Batlokwa, and not the *amaBunu* at all, and that they had committed the theft two years before. But by sending Retief to seize the stolen cattle he was killing two birds with one stone: he was both testing Retief and punishing Sekonyela. Sekonyela had peremptorily refused Dingane's request for the return of the Hlubi cattle and, with his customary abrasiveness, had added insult to injury. With reference to the Zulu custom of not initiating boys into manhood through circumcision as was the practice among the Batlokwa, he had sent Dingane's envoys packing bearing his unforgivably slighting words: 'Tell that impubescent boy that if he wants to be circumcised let him come and I'll circumcise him.'[18]

Retief knew as well as Dingane that Sekonyela's people were the real cattle thieves. But he was willing to wink, not only to indicate his readiness to comply with Dingane's wishes, but also to demonstrate beyond any doubt that the Boers were innocent of the cattle theft, and that their

---

13   Poland et al., *Abundant Herds*, p.125.
14   *Owen's Diary*, pp.61–2: 5–8 November 1837; *Annals* 1, pp.364–5: letter from Retief in the *Graham's Town Journal*, 18 November 1837.
15   *Owen's Diary*, p.175: Hulley's account.
16   *Owen's Diary*, p.65: 9 November 1837.
17   *Annals* 1, pp. 361–2: Dingaan to Retief (witnessed by Owen), 8 November 1837.
18   *Owen's Diary*, pp.167–8: Rev. D. Ellenberger's account.

intentions were honest and peaceful. Yet, being the man he was, Retief could not leave it there. Although he maintained his outwardly frank, open, and mild demeanour,[19] before he departed on his mission, he could not forbear presenting Dingane with a dire caution. Uncompromisingly, he threw the lesson of Mzilikazi's defeat in the king's face, reminding him that God was with the *Trekkers*, and warning him that, for all the warlike displays by his *amabutho* over the past few days, the Boers possessed the military might to overthrow him: 'The great Book of God teaches us that kings who conduct themselves as Umsilikazi does are severely punished, and that it is not granted to them to live or reign long: and if you desire to learn at greater length how God deals with such bad kings, you must enquire concerning it from the missionaries in your country.'[20]

Dingane did not take kindly to this brazen attempt to intimidate him. There is strong evidence that he decided at that moment to have done with Retief before he threatened him further, and that he gave the order for him to be put to death on his way back to Port Natal from emGungundlovu. Silwebana, the powerful *induna* of the kwaKhangela *ikhanda*, was instructed to invite Retief and his party to stay with him, and while entertaining them with food and dance to take them unawares and put them to death. Luring enemies to a banquet and killing them when unprepared to defend themselves is one of oldest ploys in the book, practiced in all times and places. But, for unknown reasons Silwebana failed to carry out his commission. For fear of the king's retribution, he attempted to flee south over the Thukela with all his people. Dingane's *impi* caught up with them and most of his adherents were killed or drowned in the river, and the captured women were brought back to emGungundlovu and executed. Only Silwebana himself and a few others lived to tell the tale.[21]

This failed plot prefigured the execution of Retief and his companions at emGungundlovu nearly three months later, and indicates that Dingane had already decided that one way or another he must destroy the dangerous *amaBunu* rather than accommodate them. In confirmation, at the *umKhosi* first-fruits festival held on 22 December 1837 the keyed-up *amabutho* assured Dingane that they were prepared to fight and defeat the *amaqadasi*, repeatedly shouting out, 'Who can fight with thee; no king can fight with thee! They that carry fire cannot fight with thee!'[22]

Back at Port Natal, and seemingly unaware that he had narrowly escaped assassination on the way, Retief continued to insist with self-righteous bravado that straight and firm handling of the Zulu king would bring about the desired result of a large grant of territory in his kingdom. Wiser from their many painful experiences in dealing with the devious Zulu king, the settlers warned Retief to be on his guard. Brushing their cautioning aside, Retief addressed their concern about what would happen to them if the *Trekkers* succeeded in establishing their *Nieuw Holland* south of the Thukela. He assured them that as the original settlers they would each be allowed to choose a grant of 6,000 morgen (12,702 acres) of the best land, but that they would have to accept that since the Boers would be in the overwhelming majority most of the land-grants would go to them, and that their republic would be governed in the Boer fashion. Many of the settlers, however, did not relish the prospect of being ruled by the Boers, whom they saw as allies against Dingane rather than as their masters, and sought to reach an alternative

---

19 *Owen's Diary*, pp.61, 64: 5 and 8 November 1837.
20 *Annals* 1, p.362: Retief to Dingaan, 8 November 1837.
21 *Owen's Diary*, pp.158–9: Joseph Kirkman, interpreter for the Rev. Champion. See Cubbin, 'Port Natal', p.143 n. 295.
22 *Owen's Diary*, p.89: 22 December 1837.

accommodation with the Zulu king. In John Cane's letter to Dingane, which Owen read to him on 13 January 1838, Cane suggested the king give the residents of Port Natal a strip of territory parallel to the sea and 20 miles wide stretching from the Mkhomazi River 30 miles south of the Port to the Thukela. All the country west of that line could go to the Boers. Dingane did not take up the suggestion, but Cane's communication was an indication that many residents of Port Natal would continue to play their own game, and that the *Trekkers* could not expect their blind cooperation.[23]

Meanwhile, on his way back from emGungundlovu to confer with his new allies at Port Natal, Retief had sent word to the laagers at Kerkenberg that his negotiations with Dingane had been reasonably successful. His messenger arrived on 11 November, and the anxiously waiting *Trekkers* broke into wild rejoicing. In defiance of Retief's order to stand fast until his return, Retief's party, Maritz's and even some of Potgieter's immediately in-spanned their wagons and headed down the mountain passes into *Nieuw Holland*, their Promised Land. Exulting at leaving the bleak *kaalveld* behind them, women and children walked alongside the wagons as they slithered and skidded down the slopes, and old women and the sick were carried on wagon-beds. The difficult and often hair-raising descent was managed with great skill and there were few accidents, with nothing worse than the breaking of inessentials such as 'a beautiful set of chairs.'[24]

The *Trekker* parties outspanned among the sweet grasses in the rolling, well-watered countryside around the headwaters of the Thukela River and its tributaries, the Bushmans River (Boesmansrivier in Afrikaans or Mtshezi in isiZulu) and the Bloukrans (Blaauwekrans in Dutch) River (so named after the bluish cliff faces along its banks, and known to the amaZulu as the Msuluzi). It was never easy for the *Trekker* parties to remain together for a long time on account of the limited availability of grazing and firewood. Consequently, even though the countryside was lush with the rains of early summer that sometimes became thunderstorms that sent the rivers down in spate, the *Trekkers* broke into small groups and scattered over a wide area along the river banks—as they had earlier (ominous precedent) along the Vaal River. Wild game still abounded in the region. Lions took some of the *Trekkers'* horses, and they organised lion hunts, and went out shooting hippo and eland for food. By the time Retief rejoined the *Trekkers* on 27 November, close to 1,000 of their wagons were scattered amid the streams and foothills of the Drakensberg.[25] In this delectable land the Emigrants went about putting their lives on a more settled, organised footing, creating a proper Church Council. As Erasmus Smit (whose position as *predikant* to the *Voortrekkers* was now at last secure) wrote contentedly, he baptised the 'first of our children born in the country of Dingaan.'[26]

And that precisely was the problem. It was indeed Dingane's country and the *Trekker* encampments were all presumptuously sited on land that was unambiguously part of the Zulu kingdom. Dingane had not given them permission to settle there—or anywhere else yet, for that matter—and Retief had not yet fulfilled his side of the bargain struck on 8 November to

---

23 *Annals* 1, p.370: Bezuidenhout's narrative; *Owen's Diary*, pp.98–9: 13 January 1837; Cubbin, 'Port Natal', p.145; Walker, *Great Trek*, p 154.
24 *Smit's Diary*, p.65: 14 November 1837.
25 *Smit's Diary*, pp.64, 67–9, 73, 82–3: 11, 16, 21, 22, 23, 27, 29 November, 12 December 1837, 22–23 January 1838; Chase, *Natal Papers*, Part II: p.3: J. Boshoff's account; Walker, *Great Trek*, pp.155–6.
26 *Smit's Diary*, pp.70, 71–2: 3 and 10 December 1837.

recover the Hlubi cattle as a preliminary to further negotiations about a grant of territory. To inflame matters further, the *Trekkers* were soon commandeering maize and sorghum from *imizi* abandoned by their terrified inhabitants as if they were the conquerors of enemy territory.[27] Nor was their haul insignificant. On 25 January 1838 alone, '80 heavy waggon loads' were brought in with up to 14 three-bushel bags to a waggon, somewhere in the region of 80 tons or more of grain.[28]

Yet the truth of the matter was that, even though the *Trekkers* had clearly jumped the gun and thereby alarmed Dingane and undermined the negotiations Retief was still conducting with him, it is doubtful whether they would have obeyed their *Goewerneur* if he had tried to stop them coming down the Drakensberg passes. It is too often forgotten that Retief's control over his compatriots was only superficial, and that they would have hived off on their own if they disagreed with his orders. In the final resort, each *Trekker* household moved whenever and wherever it decided, and followed a leader by choice, and not through compulsion.[29]

Indeed, after his return to the main *Trekker* encampment at Doornkop, Retief struggled to hold the *trek* together. Piet Uys arrived from the highveld on 15 December with news of his decisive victory over Mzilikazi and reasserted his claim to assume the leadership in Natal. Maritz again played the mediator and Uys finally agreed on 19 December to take the oath to the constitution of the United Laagers once he had consulted his followers and brought his party down from the highveld.[30] Back on the highveld, though, Uys's attitude hardened, and on 24 January 1838 he dictated a letter to D'Urban in Cape Town reaffirming his loyalty and that of his followers to the Crown. He declared them all 'totally averse' to Retief's 'sinister designs' to found an independent state over the Drakensberg, and assured the Governor that they would employ 'every means in our power' to 'frustrate' them.[31]

Meanwhile, unaware that Uys was planning to break decisively with him, and believing that his position as leader had been reaffirmed, on 5 December Retief prepared to mount a *kommando* against Sekonyela to recover the cattle demanded by Dingane. And while he did so, Dingane and his councillor would have been pondering how to deal with the threat the *amaBunu* posed. It had always proved possible to contain the fractious traders and hunters of Port Natal, but here was a new, warlike people, pastoralists like the amaZulu themselves, come over the mountains in great numbers and already comporting themselves like conquerors. What should be done to meet their threat to the very existence of the Zulu kingdom?[32]

Retief finally set off on 28 December with a *kommando* of 50 *burgers* along with Thomas Halstead the interpreter (whom Dingane had requested to accompany the expedition to ensure that the Boers fulfilled their promises), and two Zulu *izinduna* (one of them Mtweni kaSitibela, a leading *inceku* of Dingane's) and eight more 'officers as witnesses'.[33] The *kommando's* route took it back over the Drakensberg and into the upper reaches of the Caledon River valley where the

27 Smit's Diary, p.84: 25 January 1838.
28 Smit's Diary, p.86: 30 January 1838.
29 Jackie Grobler, 'The Retief Massacre of 6 February 1838 Revisited', *Historia: Journal of the Historical Association of South Africa*, 56: 2 (November 2011), p.130.
30 Smit's Diary, pp.73–5: 15, 16, 18, 19 December 1837.
31 P.L. Uijs (*sic*) to D'Urban, 24 January 1834, quoted in Uys, 'Pieter Lafras Uys', pp. 37–8.
32 Laband, *Zulu Nation*, p.84.
33 Smit's Diary, pp.70, 76, 77: 5, 26 and 28 December 1837; *Annals* 1, p.369: Bezuidenhout's narrative; *JSA* 6, p.261: Tununu, 31 May 1903. Walker, *Great Trek*, p.160.

Batlokwa lived. Backed by his threatening *kommando*, Retief persuaded Sekonyela to meet him at Mpharane in the garden of James Allison, the Wesleyan missionary. There, Retief deployed his disarming social skills to lull Sekonyela's suspicions, and then by a ruse snapped handcuffs onto the astonished chief's wrists. Now in fear for his life, Sekonyela admitted to taking 300 head of cattle from the amaHlubi, and Retief refused to release him until his people had handed them over and paid hundreds more in compensation. Allison tried to instil in Retief some shame for his perfidious act, but with no success. Then Sikonyela's aged mother, MaNthatisi, once the regent of the Batlokwa but now feeble and given over to alcohol, capitulated on Sekonyela's behalf. With 770 head of cattle, plus 63 horses and 11 muskets, she bought her shamed son's freedom.[34]

Retief arrived back triumphantly at his laager on 11 January 1838 with his booty, and wrote to Dingane informing him of his success.[35] The Zulu king was already profoundly shaken by the news Owen had read him on 2 January 1838 that the Boers had utterly defeated Mzilikazi at eGabeni.[36] When he received Retief's letter on 22 January, Dingane was further dismayed to learn how easily Retief had dealt with the formidable Sekonyela, and was considerably put out that he had then let him go. Furthermore (as Owen put it) Dingane was 'disappointed' that while the *Trekker* leader assured him he was going to deliver the stolen cattle, he intended to distribute the captured muskets and horses among his own people. In perturbation Dingane summoned Gardiner to emGungundlovu so he could consult him about what he should do next. But the missionary, hearkening to rumours that Dingane intended to kill him along with Retief, and knowing how unpredictable Dingane could be when he believed himself threatened, refused to go.[37]

On his return from overcoming Sekonyela, Retief had intended to leave immediately for emGungundlovu to claim his anticipated reward that—in his mind if not in Dingane's—was the Zulu king's permission for the *Trekkers* to settle south of the Thukela. But he was running into trouble with his factious compatriots. Maritz was openly complaining that the *Goewerneur* was acting too high-handedly, and Smit noticed that Retief was becoming 'somewhat dispirited'.[38] Where Retief's critics all agreed was in rejecting his plan for a large *kommando* of 200 men to accompany him back to emGungundlovu with the cattle recovered from Sekonyela. They could not ignore messages from Port Natal and the reports of traders selling their wares to the *Trekkers* that strongly suggested that Dingane 'intended to treat the emigrants with hostility.'[39] Maritz in particular argued that, in order to minimise possible casualties, only a small party should return to Dingane with the cattle, and even offered to go in Retief's stead. But Retief remained unmoved, confident as ever in his own judgement. His argument was that a strong *kommando* would intimidate Dingane into carrying out his part of the admittedly nebulous bargain struck in November. Nevertheless, because there was such apprehension among the *Trekkers* and so many objections to what he had in mind, Retief called for volunteers to accompany him to

---

34 *Annals* 1, pp.368–9: Bezuidenhout's narrative; *Owen's Diary*, p.100: 22 January 1838; p.105: 3 February 1838 (Retief's account); pp. 168–170: Rev. Ellenberger's account.
35 *Smith's Diary*, p.79: 11 January 1838.
36 *Owen's Diary*, p.93: 2 January 1838.
37 *Owen's Diary*, pp. 100–1: 22, 23 January 1838; pp.175–6: Hulley's account.
38 *Smit's Diary*, p.82: 20 January 1838.
39 *Smit's Diary*, p.78: 3 January 1938; Walker, *Great Trek*, p.161.

emGungundlovu with the cattle. At length, 69 *burgers* and about 30 *agterryers*, all armed with *voorlaiers*, and with about 200 horses, mustered under Retief's command.[40]

On 25 January the gathered *Trekkers* commended Retief and his departing *kommando* to God and prayed for their 'protection and happy return'.[41] A few days after the *kommando* rode out, Retief wrote to his wife: 'I was deeply affected at the time of my departure ... It was in no way that I feared for my undertaking to go to the king but I was full of grief that I must again live through the unbearable dissension in our Society, and that made me fear that God's kindness would turn to wrath.'[42]

Despite all their trepidations, the *Trekkers* nevertheless seemed to have convinced themselves that Retief would be successful in his mission. In anticipation of Dingane granting them the land where they desired to settle, they planned to break camp within the next few days in order 'to move further along the road to the bay of Port Natal.'[43] Then, on 1 February, news reached Smit's camp that two amaZulu had called across the Bushmans River that 'all the men of the expedition force have been murdered.'[44] As it happened, they were a few days in advance of the event, but knowledge must have been spreading across the Zulu kingdom of what Dingane had in store for Retief and his *kommando*.

---

40 *Annals* 1, pp.401–2: letter by Mr Jacobus Boshof, to the *Graham's Town Journal*, 2 July 1838.
41 *Smit's Diary*, p.83: 25 January 1838.
42 *Smit's Diary*, pp.84–5: 28 January 1838.
43 *Smit's Diary*, p.86: 29 January 1838.
44 *Smit's Diary*, p.86: 1 February 1838.

18

You Thrust an Evil Spear into Your Own Stomach

'All chiefs see war in the water', remembered Tununu kaNonjiya who had been one of Dingane's *izinceku*. What he meant was that when a crisis threatened his kingdom, a king would go into the royal *isibaya* and *ukuphehla*, that is, stir a pot of secret ritual medicine to a foam while the *izinyanga* who had prepared it praised the royal ancestors. After discerning the future in the liquid, he would then wash himself with it, something only the king was permitted to do. Tununu remembered that Dingane often performed this ritual as threats closed in on his kingdom.[1] Naturally, Dingane also had less occult means of discovering what his enemies were planning, and regularly imbedded spies among them. (Spying was a confidential commission, one that carried many dangers. A spy risked death if uncovered, and Dingane was in the habit of putting out the eyes of those who failed to give him effective information.)[2] Typically, the officials Dingane attached to Retief's *kommando* against Sekonyela were expected to observe Boer fighting methods and to report back on how best they could be countered.[3] The Port Natal residents likewise sent out spies to emGungundlovu to give warning of impending danger from that quarter.[4] Only the Boers seem to have had no means of gathering intelligence from the amaZulu. Consequently, when Retief led his *kommando* and the cattle recovered from Sekonyela to emGungundlovu, he had no real idea how Dingane would receive him.

Dingane's advisors were certainly putting mounting pressure on him to deal summarily with the *amaBunu* before he was overtaken by the fate suffered by Mzilikazi and Sekonyela. But how was the undoubted military superiority of the Boers to be neutralised? As we have seen, once already Dingane had conspired to have Retief and his party killed when taken unaware at Silwebana's *ikhanda*. Then the Boer numbers had been small, yet even so the plot had miscarried. Now, as Dingane's spies would have informed him, Retief was approaching in considerable strength, so even more guile and force were required if he were to be overcome.

On 2 February 1838 great numbers of *amabutho* in ceremonial dress began gathering at emGungundlovu in anticipation of the Boers' arrival, and were packed into the huts of the *izinhlangothi*. The Boers appeared the following morning, 3 February, and heralded their

---

1   *JSA* 6, p.285: Tununu, 7 June 1903.
2   *JSA* 5, p.89: Ngidi, 28 October, 1905.
3   Stuart and Malcolm (eds), *Fynn's Diary*, p.315: 'Additional Notes of History and Customs'.
4   *JSA* 5, p.281: John Ogle, 7 March 1914.

coming with an unsettling *feu de joie* before riding right into the great cattle enclosure with their muskets in their hands. Dingane's messengers had challenged them the previous day to compete with the king's *amabutho* in dancing, and the Boers immediately set about demonstrating their skill in 'dancing' their horses. The horsemen separated into two groups and charged each other in sham combat, firing their muskets that had been loaded with powder, but not with bullets. EmGungundlovu was rattled by the unfamiliar noise of gunfire, filled with the stink of exploded gunpowder and enveloped in thick, dirty white smoke that deposited a black, greasy film on objects.[5] Even though many amaZulu were not unfamiliar with firearms, they but must have been daunted by what they experienced. Dingane's forebodings could only have been accentuated. Regardless, the *amabutho* responded to the Boers' display of firepower with their own aggressive war dances and military manoeuvres.

Once these competitive performances were over, the Boers asked for a place to camp, and Dingane assigned them the prestigious quarters abutting the *isigodlo* which were normally allotted to an *isigaba* of a senior *ibutho*. Probably unaware of the honour being paid them, the *amaBunu* insultingly spurned sleeping in huts. Since no 'white people's houses' were available, they insisted on camping instead at a clump of euphorbia trees between the main gate to the *ikhanda* and the Mkhumbane stream. There the amaZulu hospitably supplied them with food: *amasi*, *utshwala*, and oxen to slaughter. But the Boers again slighted their hosts by going out to hunt steenbok and rhebok, thereby seeming to indicate that the rations supplied them were not sufficient.[6] And what their hosts were too polite to tell the *amaBunu* was that they had chosen to outspan at kwaNkosinkulu, the burial place of Dingane's more distant ancestors.[7] This was hallowed ground where no one was allowed to sit, kill an animal (or a person if he took refuge there), or—on pain of death—to touch the ground with a stick because 'it would be said he was stabbing the king'.[8] More than likely, the Boers did not realise they were repeatedly offending their hosts and breaking their taboos. Yet, such was their habitual arrogance when dealing with Africans, one is justified in wondering whether they would have cared if they had in fact known.

About noon that day, when the Boers were seated under the euphorbia trees at their ill-advisedly sited encampment, Owen was witness to Retief's supercilious response to Dingane's messenger who relayed the king's demand that he hand over the firearms and horses the Boer *kommando* had seized from Sekonyela. Brusquely refusing, Retief showed 'the messenger his grey hairs and bid him to tell his master that he was not dealing with a child.'[9] Probably, not since Sekonyela had called him an 'impubescent boy' had Dingane received such a deliberate insult, one that could only have hardened his resolve to have done with his alarming guests.

Nevertheless, over the next two days Dingane maintained an amiable public stance and the amaZulu proceeded to entertain the *amaBunu* with their exuberant spectacles of singing and dancing. Retief's followers even forewent Sabbath service on 4 February to demonstrate their goodwill by attending the festivities, much to Owen's regret that they had not displayed

---

5   *JSA* 3, p.258: Mmemi kaNguluzane, 19 October 1904.
6   *JSA* 6, p.260: Tununu, 30 May 1903.
7   *JSA* 2, p.253: Mayinga ka Mbekuzana, 9 July 1905; Lugg, *Historic Natal*, pp.114, 116.
8   *JSA* 5, p.374: Sivivi, 10 March 1907; James Young Gibson, *The Story of the Zulus* (new edition, London: Longman Green, 1911), p.64.
9   *Owen's Diary*, p.105: 3 February 1838.

their Christian piety instead.[10] All still seemed to be well when, on that same Sunday, Retief presented a previously prepared, legalistically phrased document written in English in an unknown hand to Dingane. It stated that in return for Retief's delivery of the Zulu cattle recovered from Sekonyela,

> I, Dingaan, King of the Zoolas [sic] do hereby certify and declare that I thought fit to resign, unto him the said Retief and his countrymen … the Place called Port Natal together with all the land annexed, that is to say from Dogela [Thukela] to the Omsoboebo [Mzimvubu] River westward and from the Sea to the North as far as the land may be usefull [sic] and in my possession. Which I did by this and give unto them for their Everlasting property.[11]

Dingane put his mark to this deed of cession, as did three other amaZulu, designated 'Great Councillors'. Yet their names are not met with elsewhere among prominent men of the time, and it may be that they were simply *izinceku*, and not councillors at all.[12] In Dingane's previous treaties with Gardiner, agreements he had taken seriously, Ndlela and Nzobo had been witnesses. This time, by employing men of lower status as witnesses, it is conceivable Dingane was obliquely invalidating a document he had no intention of honouring, and was only mollifying the Boers even while planning their destruction. And there is a crucial detail in his cession of territory that confirms Dingane's lack of sincerity. By stipulating the Mzimvubu as the southern boundary of the territory he was ceding to the Boers, he was giving away territory neither he, nor even Shaka, had ever ruled. Both accepted that the Mzimkhulu River marked the southern limits of the Zulu kingdom. Beyond it lay the kingdom of the amaMpondo that had its heart along the Mzimvubu River and was ruled over by King Faku kaNgqungqushe. Twice, in 1824 and 1828, Shaka had raided Faku's kingdom, but had never conquered it.[13]

Regardless of how Dingane viewed the document, the *Trekkers* subsequently based their legal claim to their future Republiek Natalia on its terms. Yet exactly what it stated is open to dispute. The Boers claimed that they later retrieved it, miraculously preserved, when 'on or about' 23 December 1838 they identified Retief's remains on kwaMatiwane.[14] Five of the Boers leaders then vouched for its authenticity under oath, and Erasmus Smit, as he recorded in his diary, was shown it on 9 January 1839.[15] Edward Parker, an English adventurer who attached himself to

---

10   *Owen's Diary*, p.105: 4 February 1838.
11   The wording and punctuation are taken from the lithographed tracing of the purported original made in about 1891. For slight variants in spelling and punctuation, see Dr B.J.T. Leverton (ed.), *Records of Natal, Volume Four July 1838–September 1839* (Pretoria: The Government Printer, 1992) (*RN 4*), p.207: no, 119, annex. 1, enc. 5: Edward Parker, A True Copy of Treaty, Unkuningsloave, 4 February 1837 (*sic* for 1838); and *Annals* 1, p.366: Cession of Port Natal to the Boers by Dingaan, 4 February 1838. Certified copy of the original.
12   On enquiry at the beginning of the 20th century, Gibson, *Story of the Zulus*, p.64, discovered that 'Nwara' [Mnwana kaCelo] was a 'private servant' (or *inceku*), and that 'Manondo' [Magonondo kaKondlo] was 'a medicine man in attendance' (or *inyanga*). Gibson could not trace 'Juliwane'.
13   Laband, *Assassination*, pp.74–6, 109–10.
14   *RN 4*, p.207, no, 119, annex. 1, enc. 5: Parker, 4 February 1837 (*sic* for 1838).
15   *Smit's Diary*, p.161: 9 January 1839.

the Boers in Natal,[16] made 'A True Copy' on 4 February 1839 which Karel Landman presented to the British military authorities at Port Natal on 15 January 1839.[17] A tracing was made of the original in about 1891 and the facsimile lithographed. However, the original disappeared in 1900 during the Second Anglo-Boer War and can never now be verified.[18] Several authorities insist that lithographed document was in any case a fake, but there is little doubt that a treaty of some sort was indeed signed, certainly one that was sufficient to satisfy Retief and his companions.[19] It is perhaps a measure of the *Trekker'* belief in their God-given right to the land that they found nothing strange in Dingane's apparent willingness to cede them so much of his territory, including lands south of the Mzimkhulu he did not rule over. Instead, they congratulated themselves that that they had gained what they had come for without the trouble or violence they had been more than half anticipating.

Consequently, with the signing of the treaty the Boers relaxed. Over that Sunday and the following Monday, they took their ease, wandering inquisitively around emGungundlovu. Some of them approached too close to the *isigodlo* which, they probably did not entirely appreciate, was absolutely out of bounds and reinforced the impression that they were *abathakati*, 'wizards' full of evil intent against the king's household.[20] As a result, the unusual precaution had to be taken of shutting the gates to the *isigodlo* during daytime in order to bar them entrance,[21] and Dingane notched up a further Boer provocation against him, one that directly affected his honour as king.

Retief resolved to depart on the morning of 6 February once the proper courtesies had been observed. The Boers had little rest the night before on account of a violent summer storm (some said it was an omen) during which lightning struck and killed 12 of their horses and they had to borrow hoes to bury them.[22]

On the morning of 6 February, a fine and very hot day, while Owen sat in the shade of his wagon reading his Bible, a messenger came from Dingane to tell him not to be alarmed, but that it was his master's intention to kill the Boers since they were going to kill him. Overcome by horror, Owen turned his telescope on kwaMatiwane and spied a great crowd on the hill, with groups of nine or ten Zulu each dragging a Boer or one of their *agyerryers* to its summit. Owen and his terrified wife set up an appalled cry and threw themselves trembling and fainting to the ground. They only roused themselves when they heard the exultant cries of acclimation when the crowd returned to the king, who sat in earnest conversation with Ndlela and Nzobo. The following morning two *izinduna* came to Owen to amplify Dingane's reasons for killing the *amaBunu*. The king, they told the quaking Owen, declared that while he could live in peace

---

16 Tabler, *Pioneers*, p.86–7.
17 *RN 4*, p.208, no. 119, annex. 1, enc. 6: Major Samuel Charters, 15 January 1839.
18 Laband, *Zulu Nation*, pp.102–3; Smail, *Land of the Zulu Kings*, p.53. For an exhaustive and authoritative examination of the treaty, its provenance and authenticity, see Rankin and Schneider, *Memory to Marble, Part II*, pp. 231–64.
19 See Maphalala, 'War of Ncome', p.62; Jay Naidoo, *Tracking Down Historical Myths: Eight South African Cases* (Johannesburg: Ad. Donker, 1989), pp. 82–105. Anthony Edward Cubbin, 'A Study in Objectivity: The Death of Piet Retief' (MA dissertation, University of the Orange Free State, 1980), p.127, has argued that the treaty was signed on 6 (not 4) February 1838, just before Retief's execution.
20 Grobler, 'Retief Massacre', pp.128–9.
21 *JSA 6*, p.260: Tununu, 30 May 1903.
22 *JSA 6*, p.260: Tununu, 30 May 1903.

with the Port Natal traders and missionaries because they were few in number, he could not do so with the Boers. They had come in such force, 'like an army,' that he had to defend himself and kill them—as would be the fate of 'all armies' that invaded his kingdom.[23]

As the historian Sifiso Ndlovu reminds us, Dingane could be dangerous and unpredictable when he believed his authority was being undermined.[24] And it does seem clear that the Boers' aggressive and insolent behaviour while at emGungundlovu had confirmed his conviction that he must kill them to preserve his kingdom.[25] Ndlela continued to urge him into taking action, arguing that Piti 'deserved to be killed, because he had really come only to oust Dingane from his land and his possessions.'[26] Some oral sources suggest that it was Mnkabayi, Dingane's powerful, king-making aunt, who was putting pressure on Ndlela from behind the scenes to nudge Dingane into taking this course.[27] Be that as it may, in his own suspicious state, Dingane believed he had accumulated sufficient evidence to prove that the Boers intended to kill him while he slept. On two successive nights the guards stationed at the top end of the *ikhanda* reported that mounted Boers had been seen moving around the outside of emGungundlovu while the people slept. They were detected measuring its size with the apparently sinister intention of surrounding the *ikhanda*, although they did not have the numbers to do so successfully. A wide track made by hoof-marks discovered in the morning, along with many horse-droppings, verified his guards' observations to Dingane's satisfaction. The Boers' earlier prowling around the *isigodlo* only served to confirm the case against them. When taxed with their suspicious activities, the Boers insisted that they had simply been in search of their horses that had broken loose and strayed in search of grazing. But they were not believed, and Dingane, with Sekonyela's fate in mind, feared the Boers intended to seize him as a hostage (why else were they attempting to survey the *isigodlo* where he slept?), and probably kill him too. Certainly, it became pervasively established in Zulu oral tradition that the Boers' attempt to encircle emGungundlovu was an act of war, and fully justified their subsequent execution.[28] As Owen subsequently noted in his diary, 'The story that they [the Boers] intended to kill the king has been propagated, and is confidently believed by the natives.'[29] Zulu tradition also holds that people who move surreptitiously around at night are

---

23 *Owen's Diary*, pp.107, 110–11: 6 and 7 February 1838.
24 Sifiso Mxolisi Ndlovu, '"He Did What Any Other Person in His Position Would Have Done to Fight the Force of Invasion and Disruption": Africans, the Land and Contending Images of King Dingane ("The Patriot") in the Twentieth Century, 1916–1950s', *South African Historical Journal*, 38 (May 1998), p.108.
25 For a discussion on Dingane's motives for killing Retief and his party and making war on the *Trekkers*, see Leśniewski, *The Zulu–Boer War*, pp.72–81.
26 Paulina Dlamini, edited by H. Filer and S. Bourquin, *Servant of Two Kings*, (Durban: Killie Campbell Africana Library; Pietermaritzburg: University of Natal Press, 1986), p.13.
27 Sifiso Ndlovu, 'Zulu Nationalist Representations of King Dingane', in Carton, Laband and Sithole (eds), *Zulu Identities*, pp.102–3.
28 *JSA* 3, pp.205–06: Mkebeni, 19 September 1921; *JSA* 4, p.73: Mtshapi, 6 April 1918; p.112: Mtshayamkomo, 11 January 1922; p.276: Ndukwana, 15 September 1900; *JSA* 5, p.118: Meshach Ngidi, 29 November 1921; p.149: Nozulela ka Hlangwana, 30 January 1922; p.201: Ntshelele, 27 February 1922; *JSA* 6, p.260: Tununu, 30 May 1903; Fuze, *Black People*, p.170 n. 5.
29 *Owen's Diary*, p. 112: 8 February 1838.

abathakati, intent on causing disaster for the king and his people: hence Dingane's subsequent order to 'kill the wizards.'[30]

If all this were not enough to alarm and antagonise Dingane, on the day before he intended to depart Retief peremptorily demanded the return of Boer livestock that was among the booty the amaZulu had brought back from their recent campaign against Mzilikazi. These were beasts the amaNdebele had captured at the battle of Vegkop and which, the Boers insisted, could be identified because they had 'marks cut on them.'[31] It was certainly impossible for Dingane to return them at such short notice because he had already distributed them as war booty, and they were scattered all over the kingdom. However, he could have substituted cattle of his own, but he refused to comply with Retief's demand because the amaZulu considered that the *amaBunu* had forfeited any claim to their cattle the moment the amaNdebele had captured them.[32] It was, in any case, the proud Zulu stance that 'no cattle ever left Zululand after once getting here.'[33] For the Boers even to make such a demand was considered a hostile act. The Zulu rank and file, who were not party to Dingane's negotiations with Retief, believed the restitution of their cattle to have been the main purpose of the Boers' visit to emGungundlovu, and 'knew nothing' of their 'wanting to ask or land.'[34]

It was in these provocative circumstances that Dingane held an emergency meeting of his *umkhandlu* to discuss how to proceed. Added to the growing fear of what the *amaBunu* intended and the need to eliminate them before it was too late, was perhaps the temptation to seize the opportunity to secure their muskets and horses. Be that as it may, Nzobo is credited with putting forward the suggestion that the Boers should be invited to a display of dancing and be killed while unsuspectingly watching on. Otherwise, to attack them while they were armed and mounted would lead to terrible casualties.[35] The council required little convincing. Dingane summoned his *amabutho* from the surrounding *amakhanda*, and crammed as many as would fit into the huts of the *izinhlangothi* at emGungundlovu, while others were concealed close by in the gulley near kwaMatiwane.[36] So as not to alarm the Boers, those selected to dance before them were ordered to carry neither *amaklwa* (stabbing-spears) nor *izihlangu* (war-shields). Instead, they were to appear with *izikhwili*, stout, short fighting-sticks about 2 foot 6 inches long without knobbed heads, and with *amahawu*, small shields carried when dancing or travelling.[37]

With his plans laid, early in the morning of 6 February Dingane invited the departing Boers and their *agterryers*, whose horses were already saddle up, into the great cattle enclosure to take leave of him. The Boers then unwittingly confirmed all of Dingane's worst apprehensions when they declared that they wished to fire a parting salute with blank charges, as they had done on their arrival. Dingane immediately construed this as a plot to kill him, a suspicion that was later confirmed to his satisfaction when the dead Boers' muskets were found to be loaded with

---

30 Oscar D. Dhlomo, 'A Zulu Perspective of the Battle of Blood River', *The Daily News*, 21 January 1988, quoted in Grobler, 'Retief Massacre', p.124.
31 *JSA* 5, p.2: Nduna, 27 April 1910.
32 *JSA* 6, p.261: Tununu, 31 May 1903.
33 *JSA* 1, p.318: Lunguza, 14 March 1909.
34 *JSA* 6, pp.261–2: Tununu, 31 May 1903.
35 *JSA* 3, pp.257–8: Mmemi, 19 October 1904.
36 *JSA* 4, p.276: Ndukwana, 15 September 1900; *JSA* 5, p.86: Ngidi, 23 October 1905; *JSA* 6, p.261: Tununu, 30 May 1903.
37 *JSA* 5, pp.7–8: Nduna, 27 April 1910.

ball—or that, at least, was what he chose to tell Owen with the request that the missionary impart this compromising information to other white people.[38]

What happened then we know from what Owen spied through his telescope, as well as from the distant observations of the young William Wood, the enterprising 14-year-old son of a Port Natal carpenter and transport rider who was acting as the missionary's interpreter while Hulley was temporarily absent at Port Natal.[39] There is also a body of recorded Zulu testimony. The most compelling is that of Tununu who, as an *inceku*, was positioned close by Dingane as an onlooker and took no active part in killing the *amaBunu*.[40] Ngidi kaMcikaziswa was likewise 'seated with the king, looking on',[41] while Meshach Ngidi's repeatedly heard an account of what had occurred from his father who had been among the *amabutho* who 'killed Piti's people, but was not hurt himself.'[42]

In the event, lulled by securing the treaty now in Retief's leather shooting-bag and by the lavish hospitality they had enjoyed the following day, the Boers were congratulating themselves on their success and suspected no treachery. They ignored young William Wood when he warned them to be on their guard since he perceived from Dingane's glowering looks that he 'meditated some mischief', smilingly assuring him that 'We are sure the king's heart is right with us, and there is no cause for fear.'[43] Not even when their request to fire a departing salvo was refused, and when they were instead requested to pile their arms outside the *ikhanda* under the charge of three *agterryers*, did they smell perfidy.[44]

When Piti and his companions entered emGungundlovu, Dingane was seated at the top of the great cattle enclosure in his great chair, carved all of one piece, with Ndlela and Nzobo standing either side of him.[45] At least, that is what the Boers supposed. Tununu, who was seated near the chair with the other *izinceku*, claimed that Dingane had placed Msongana, the *induna* of kwaDukuza, in front of the assembly to substitute for him, while he himself remained behind the group of courtiers, out of sight.[46] If that was indeed so, Dingane would not have been the only head of state to deploy a double in time of danger. Once Dingane (or his double) had politely greeted the *amaBunu* and wished them a pleasant journey, he invited them to sit and drink *utshwala* and *amasi* with him and receive the cattle he had assigned them for their journey.[47] Retief was seated close by the king and his people sat on the ground a short distance away.[48]

With the Boers in place, the king ordered two crack *amabutho* drawn up either side of him (one of married men, the other of the newly formed iHlaba *ibutho* whose members were about

---

38 *Owen's Diary*, pp.116–17: 10 February 1838.
39 Tabler, *Pioneers*, pp.102–3.
40 *JSA* 6, pp.253, 261: Tununu, 30 May, 1 June 1903.
41 *JSA* 5, p.77: Ngidi, 18 October 1905.
42 *JSA* 5, p.118: Meshach Ngidi, 29 November 1921.
43 *Annals* 1, p.380: William Wood, *Statements Respecting Dingaan* (Cape Town: Collard, 1840).
44 *JSA* 6, p.260: Tununu, 30 May 1903.
45 Based on the account of Zulu eyewitnesses a year later, the French traveller, Adulphe Delegorgue, penned a description of the execution of the Retief party. See Delegorgue, *Travels, Volume One*, pp.63–5.
46 *JSA* 6, p. 260: Tununu, 30 May 1903.
47 *JSA* 5, pp.7–8: Nduna, 27 April 1910; *JSA* 6, pp.260–1: Tununu, 30 May 1903.
48 *Annals*, 1, p.380: Wood, *Statements*.

20 years old)⁴⁹ to dance and sing to entertain his departing guests. Forming themselves into the customary half-moon, the *amabutho* performed an *inkondlo*, a spirited dance with a gradual forward and backward movement.⁵⁰ As they danced, they sang, 'We have two, three *inkondlo* dances; they wind about, they turn all over the place; we shall dance this way, and not that way ... Hi ya ya! Hi ya ya!'⁵¹ During their dance the *amabutho* came closer and closer to their unsuspecting victims, while a mass of other *amabutho* gathered in the great enclosure looked on. Dingane had arranged that at the end of the second song he would wave his left hand over his shoulder as the signal to attack. When the dance had gone on for about a quarter of an hour, he suddenly stood up, and when the Boers asked where he was going, he replied he needed to 'pass his water'.⁵² But as Dingane walked away, he made the agreed signal and cried out, 'Seize them!' He then rapidly left the enclosure and entered the *isigodlo*.⁵³

The *amabutho* then rushed upon the surrounded Boers before they could even get to their feet. Paulina Dlamini, whose father had been a member of the iHlaba, told her: 'We struck the white men, we dragged them down. As we struck them we shouted to one another: "You strike from above!' or "You strike from below!"'⁵⁴ The dust rose as some of the Boers slashed at their assailants with their long *herneutermesse*, ripping open stomachs and killing 20 or so of them. But completely outnumbered they were swiftly overwhelmed and seized. Some were beaten senseless by *izikhwili*, and others had their heads twisted back and their necks broken. But unconscious, already dead or stricken by fear they were all dragged off to kwaMatiwane with their feet trailing on the ground.⁵⁵ With the *amaBunu* overpowered, Dingane took up his seat again in the enclosure. As he watched them being hauled away to the kwaMatiwane, he called out, '*Bulalani abathakathi*!' 'Kill the wizards!'⁵⁶

At kwaMatiwane Retief was held fast and forced to witness his Boer comrades (among them a few boys, some under 11 years old, who had accompanied their fathers), along with their *agterryers*, being finished off before he too was clubbed to death.⁵⁷ Only Lomana, a Khoisan *agterryer* who had been left with the muskets outside the gate, succeeded in escaping on his horse.⁵⁸ Nduna kaManqina ascribed to him the despairing cry that summed up the massacre: 'the chief is dead'!⁵⁹ Thomas Halstead, the Boers' interpreter, died alongside the Boers despite his despairing attempt to plead with the king for his life. His death alone Dingane regretted

49 Dlamini, *Two Kings*, p.13.
50 *JSA* 1, pp.319–20: Lunguza, 14 March 1909.
51 *JSA* 5, pp.7–8: Nduna, 27 April 1910. For another, closely related version, see *JSA* 5, p.86: Ngidi, 23 October 1905. The song's theme of being 'woven together' symbolised Zulu unity.
52 *JSA* 4, p.263: Ndukwana, 18 October 1897.
53 Fuze, *Black People*, pp.74–5.
54 Dlamini, *Two Kings*, p.14.
55 *JSA* 4, p.177: Ndabambi ka Sikakana, 25 March 1909; *JSA* 5, pp.7–8: Nduna, 27 April 1910; p.118: Meshach Ngidi, 29 November 1921; *JSA* 6, pp.260–61: Tununu, 30 May 1903. Gibson, *Story of the Zulus*, p. 65, recorded the Zulu oral tradition that one Boer broke away and was not overtaken and killed by his pursuers until he reached Thala Mountain 15 miles away in the direction of the *Trekker* encampments.
56 *Annals* 1, p.381: Wood, *Statements*.
57 *Owen's Diary*, p.111: 7 February 1828.
58 *JSA* 1, p.312: Lunguza, 14 March 1909. He was still alive and living in Weenen in Natal in 1909.
59 *JSA* 5, pp.7–8: Nduna, 27 April 1910.

somewhat, for he had no wish if he could avoid it to alienate the residents of Port Natal.[60] But he knew that the surviving Boers would now be his irreconcilable enemies, and he ordered Retief's heart and liver to be placed in the path back to the *Trekkers'* encampments to make strong magic against them.[61]

Richard Hulley, Owen's interpreter, arrived back at emGungundlovu from Port Natal on 9 February to observe a large flock of vulture hovering over kwaMatiwane, and to find a pile of saddles at the entrance to the *ikhanda*. With these clues he needed no one to spell out what had occurred.[62] The next few days were excruciating for Owen and his household since they expected every moment to suffer the same fate as the Boers. On 10 February Dingane subjected Owen to a harrowing face-to-face interview, charging him, on the testimony of his servants, with being disloyal and as much his enemy as Retief had been. Fortunately for him, Dingane eventually calmed down, and the next day permitted the missionary and all his party to leave unharmed for Port Natal, later sending after them before they had gone too far with a request for a supply of needles, thread, and green baize.[63]

As they made their way as fast as they could to the relative security of Port Natal, the members of Owen's party knew that the prospects for the *Trekker* encamped in the foothills of the Drakensberg were dire. On the very day that Dingane executed Retief and his *kommando*, Owen had seen the king reviewing several *amabutho*. At about noon, some two hours after the massacre, they had set off at a run in the direction from which Retief had come. There had been no doubt on Owen's mind that they intended to surprise the *Trekker* encampments, and his fears were confirmed on 8 February when he observed more *amabutho* leaving on campaign.[64]

Owen was never in any doubt that Dingane had 'planned the murder in advance since he feared the power of the Voortrekkers.'[65] Nowadays, a postcolonial, Zulu historian such as Sifiso Ndlovu is confident in justifying Dingane's premeditated execution of Retief and his companions as a necessary pre-emptive strike incumbent on a king who 'was expected to protect himself, the land, his people, their customs, traditions, social systems and values from the unscrupulous white settlers.'[66] Naturally, the *Trekkers* never viewed the terrible event in such a light, and colonial-era and Afrikaner-nationalist historians have long condemned it as a 'savage murder by a barbaric African monarch.'[67] Dingane's own position was that echoed by Sifiso Ndlovu 160 years later. When Hulley hurried to see him on his return to emGungundlovu, the Zulu monarch received him most affably, and complacently enquired of him, 'Don't *you* think I have done a good thing in getting rid of my enemies in one stroke?' But Hulley refused to play along, and dourly warned Dingane that he had begun a war whose end none could predict.[68]

Indeed, in the view of many amaZulu who lived through the bitter fighting, destruction, and political dislocation that were to be the direct consequences of Dingane's strike against the unwary *Trekkers*, he had set in motion events that came close to destroying the kingdom, rather

---

60 *Owen's Diary*, p.111: 7 February 1838.
61 *Annals* 1, p.381: Wood, *Statements*.
62 *Owen's Diary*, p. 79: Hulley's account.
63 *Owen's Diary*, pp.113–120: 10–12 February 1838; pp. 178–79: Hulley's account.
64 *Owen's Diary*, pp.108, 112, 117: 6, 8, 10 February 1838.
65 *Owen's Diary*, p.111: 7 February 1838.
66 Ndlovu, 'King Dingane', p.108.
67 Grobler, 'Retief Massacre', p.131.
68 *Owen's Diary*, p. 77: Hulley's account.

than saving it. When in the years to come, Magolwana kaMkhathini, the royal *imbongi* serving Mpande, Dingane's successor, praised the line of Zulu kings, he always included the following dirge:

> Alas, O Hairy one of Mgungundlovu!
> You killed the Boers!
> You thrust an evil spear into Zululand!
> You thrust in an evil spear!
> You thrust it into your own stomach, did you not? [69]

---

[69] Rycroft and Ngcobo (eds), *Praises*, pp. 7, 202, 203; *JSA* 4, p.107: Mtshayankomo, 10 January 1922.

19

O My God, Shall the Blood of the Sucklings Be Unavenged?

Once Retief and his companions lay dead on kwaMatiwane, at about noon on 6 February 1838 several *amabutho*, having undergone the rituals to protect them against danger in time of war,[1] prepared to set out to surprise the unsuspecting *Trekkers* in their encampment along the Bloukrans and Little Bushmans Rivers. As they paraded before Dingane, they shouted out their ferocious promise to him: 'We will go and kill the white dogs!'[2] From a Zulu perspective, they were embarking on the normal follow-up operation *amabutho* always undertook when a chief was disgraced and executed. His family and adherents were 'eaten up' so that none were left alive to avenge him, and his livestock were brought back for the king to redistribute to this *amabutho*, favoured courtiers and *amakhosi*.

It has not been recorded who commanded the Zulu forces that left emGungundlovu that day and marched south-west. Two days later they were reinforced by several more *amabutho*. Their total number is unknown, although it was probably at least 5,000. The *impi* forded the Mzinyathi (Buffalo) River near what is now Rorke's Drift, and moved along the Helpmekaar Heights towards the confluence of the Bloukrans and Thukela Rivers.[3] Unaware of what had befallen Retief and his *kommando*, and putting aside their niggling forebodings, the *Trekkers* were going about their daily business in their camps pitched under the large, flat-topped trees in the grassy river valleys. A few of the more wary Boer leaders possessed the foresight to establish defensible wagon laagers, but most of the Emigrant Farmers were scattered in little family encampments of three or four wagons over a considerable area. Many of the men who had not been members of Retief's ill-fated *kommando* were off buffalo hunting or away assisting further parties of *Trekkers* down the Drakensberg passes, thus leaving their families and Khoisan dependents

---

1   *JSA* 6, p.286: Tununu, 7 June 1903.
2   *Annals* 1, p.381: Wood, *Statements*.
3   For a general account of the Weenen or Bloukrans 'massacre', see Adulphe Delegorgue, edited by Fleur Webb, Stephanie J. Alexander and Colin de B. Webb, *Travels in Southern Africa, Volume Two* (Durban: Killie Campbell Africana Library; Pietermaritzburg: University of Natal Press, 1997), pp.65–6; Manfred Nathan, *The Voortrekkers of South Africa* (South Africa: Central News Agency, 1937), pp.216–28; Walker, *Great Trek*, pp.166–9; Smail, *Land of the Zulu Kings*, pp.56–60; and (most recently) Leśniewski, *Zulu–Boer War*, pp. 120–33.

156 The Zulu Kingdom and the Boer Invasion of 1837-40

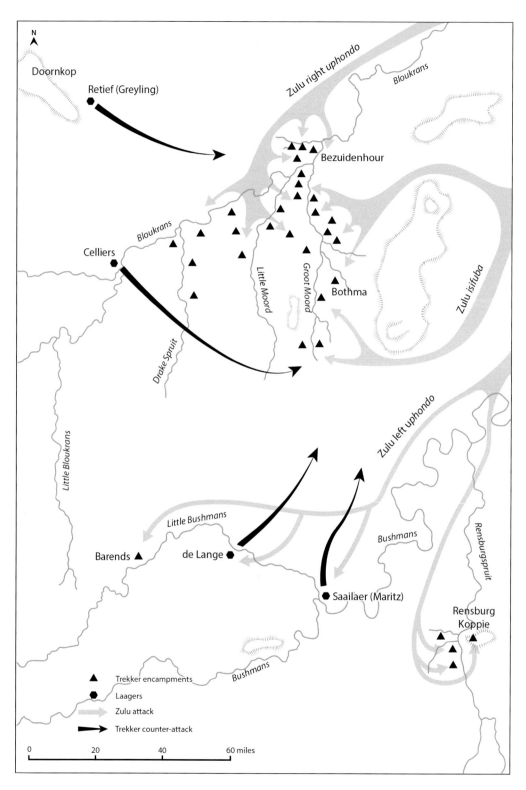

Battle of Bloukrans, 16–17 February 1838

unprotected.[4] It was all too similar to the situation along the Vaal River in August 1836 when the amaNdebele had made their attack. The consequence, as Erasmus Smit expressed it in his diary on 17 February 1838, was to be 'the saddest night and present day of our long journey.'[5]

Relying on the information of their spies who had been mingling freely with the Boers in their encampments,[6] the right and centre divisions of the Zulu army—the chest and right horn—opened their attack just before midnight on 16 February, striking the Boer camps along the Bloukrans and its two tributaries which the *Trekkers* would later grimly dub the Great and Little Moord (Murder) Rivers. The *Trekkers* were taken completely by surprise. Daniel Bezuidenhout, for one, thought his dogs were barking at a leopard, and was dumbfounded to discover that they were alerting him to the approaching *impi*. The amaZulu rapidly overran the encampments, ripping up the tents, breaking the wagons and stabbing to death the dogs and poultry (the amaZulu did not then eat chicken). Whole families of Boers were wiped out before they could offer any resistance.[7] Others managed to fight back for a while. The Bothma family group, for example, attempted to retreat down the Great Moord to where other Boers were encamped. Hemmed in and cut off, they made their last stand on a small koppie where the amaZulu, driving captured cattle before them as a shield, finally overwhelmed them.[8]

Trekkers in their encampments further away to the west heard the distant musket fire and thought at first that volleys were being fired to celebrate the return of Retief's *kommando*. The arrival of desperate refugees and the faraway flames of burning wagons soon disabused them. They were more fortunate than their comrades to the east because they were at least granted some time to improvise a defence. And, as it turned out, the haphazard dispersal of their encampments was in their favour. The *amabutho* of the Zulu chest and right horn, committed to all the uncertainties and confusions of a night attack and having underestimated the sheer extent of their target, rapidly lost cohesion and their commanders were unable to control them. Moreover, as so often happens in war in such situations, the *amabutho* were diverted from their main objective to pillage, and broke up into small groups to secure what loot they could. Laden with portable booty and more concerned with driving along captured livestock than in hunting down Boer fugitives, the impetus of their attack faltered, and finally petered out beyond the Little Moord.

Meanwhile, the Zulu left horn was achieving less success in its attack than the chest and right horn. Gert Maritz at the confluence of the Bushmans and Little Bushmans Rivers was one of those who had established a proper wagon laager known as the Saailaer. Another who had done so further west on the southern banks of the Little Bushmans was Johan Hendrik de Lange, a farmer from the Grahamstown District nicknamed 'Hans Dons' ('Orphan Fluff') after his sparse beard. In the early 1830s he had hunted and explored the interior, and had accompanied Uys on his *kommissietrek* to Port Natal. Firmly committed to the aspirations of the Great Trek, he and his party had joined Retief when he crossed over the Drakensberg. As a

---

4   *Annals* 1, p. 370: Bezuidenhout's narrative; p. 463; Anne Elizabeth Steenkamp (*née* Retief), 'Record or Journal of Our Migration from Our Mother Country to Port Natal', in the *Cape Monthly Magazine*, September 1876.
5   *Smit's Diary*, p. 88: 17 February 1838.
6   *Annals* 1, p. 404: Jacobus Boshof to the editor, *Graham's Town Journal*, 2 July 1838.
7   *Annals* 1, p.372: Bezuidenhout's narrative.
8   *Annals* 1, p.373: Bezuidenhout's narrative.

veteran of the Cape Frontier Wars, he had considerable military experience and would emerge as one of the *Trekkers'* most expert scouts and ablest commanders. He had learned while fighting the amaXhosa to put his faith in the defensibility of the wagon laager, and that conviction stood him in good stead now.[9]

He and Maritz were able to throw back the amaZulu when they attacked their laagers, unable to penetrate the all-round defensive perimeters. Further west down the Little Bushmans, Gert Barends had his wagons drawn up in an open half-moon and was consequently far more hard-put to defend his camp. To the east of Maritz's laager, Johannes van Rensburg's family, along with several other small family groups—14 men and 20 women and children—fled from their overrun camps to make a desperate stand on a steep *koppie* (hillock) protected to the west by the gorge through which the Rensburgspruit flowed. When almost out of ammunition they were finally extricated by Sarel Celliers and a small force of about a dozen men who fought from horseback.[10]

During the morning of 17 February, pathetic little parties of fugitives Boers, mainly women and children, after having walked for many hours, took refuge in Maritz's and De Lange's laagers. To the north, they also found sanctuary in Celliers's laager on the west bank of the Bloukrans and, even further away to the north-west, in Retief's own laager below the Doornberg where he had left Piet Greyling in command. There they were safe, for none of the Zulu forces penetrated that far west to threaten either laager.[11]

On the afternoon of 17 February, the *Trekkers* launched mounted counter-attacks from all four laagers. They inflicted heavy casualties on the exhausted *amabutho*, and by evening the amaZulu were all in full retreat, lashed by a heavy thunderstorm during which several individuals were killed by lightening.[12]

However, as had the amaNdebele after the battle of Vegkop, the *impi* retired driving about 25,000 head of cattle and thousands of sheep and horses before them. Individuals such as Daniel Bezuidenhout, who had been a rich man with 7,000 sheep to his name, were ruined, left with nothing but shirt and pantaloons to cover him and with four stricken orphans consigned to his care.[13] At dawn on 18 April a *kommando* of about 50 mounted men under Maritz set out in pursuit of the amaZulu and caught up with them on the west bank of the Thukela as they were beginning to cross the river with their captured livestock. The Boers fired on the amaZulu bunched up on the banks of the river which was in spate from the heavy rains, but did not close with them. So, despite taking casualties from the Boer musketry, and with others drowning in the swirling, flooded river, the *amabutho* successfully crossed to the far bank with most of their booty. The members of the *kommando* did not risk following and turned back, tears of frustration and grief pouring down their faces.[14]

---

9   Laband, *Historical Dictionary*, p.61. De Lange's fate was an unfortunate one. Living as a farmer in Natal after the British annexed it as a colony, in December 1860 he shot and killed an African in circumstances that were never properly clarified. He was found guilty of murder and hanged on 26 March 1861.
10 *Annals* 1, pp.241–3: Journal of Charl Celliers.
11 *Annals* 1, p.464: Steenkamp, 'Record'; p.372: Bezuidenhout's narrative.
12 *JSA* 5, p.86: Ngidi, 23 October 1905.
13 *Annals* 1, p.373: Bezuidenhout's narrative.
14 *Annals* 1, p.405: Boshof's letter, 2 July 1838; p.463: Steenkamp, 'Record'; *Owen's Diary*, p.125: 11 March 1838.

While Maritz's *kommando* was away pursuing the retiring *impi*, the stunned *Trekkers* conducted a search of the countryside attacked by the amaZulu. When later in 1838 the Boer laid out a little village on the west bank of the Bushmans River, they called it Weenen (Weeping) after the bitter tears they shed and their lamentations over what they found in that region of devastation.[15] 'Ach God! Ach Lord! How severe, how great are Thy judgments upon us!' wrote Erasmus Smit who, in his anxiety and sorrow, sleep 'entirely deserted' for four nights in a row.[16] Overturned wagons were literally awash with blood. The grass was matted with gore, household possessions were scattered in all directions, and carrion birds—vultures and crows—were gathered for the feast. Not untypically of many survivors, Daniel Bezuidenhout lost his father and mother, his wife and their two infants, his little brother and four sisters, his mother-in-law, and a little niece. Only his 14-year-old brother escaped, although wounded.[17] Confronted by the sight of infants lying in their blood in the arms of their dead mothers, Sarel Celliers cried out in anguish, 'O my God, shall the blood of the sucklings be unavenged?'[18]

Of the Boers, according to the list of casualties—perhaps some 10 or so names might have been missing—40 men, 56 women and (hardest to bear) 185 children lay dead. About 250 of the Khoisan servants, 'apprentices' and *agterryers*, along with some Zulu herdsmen, had been killed alongside them.[19] Large burial parties were sent out to inter them, and every day more of the wounded died and were buried to unending 'lamentation and weeping'.[20] Yet some of the desperately wounded, such as a child who had been stabbed 30 times or the man with 32 wounds, eventually recovered, although injured for life.[21]

In making their surprise attack, Dingane and his councillors had underestimated the *Trekkers*' fighting spirit and their gritty ability to defend themselves, even when taken at such a disadvantage. The amaZulu had lost up to 500 men in the campaign, far too many against a scattered and unprepared foe. Moreover, their withdrawal with their booty had been a strategic error, even if it was the norm for a punitive raid such as the recent ones against the amaSwazi and amaNdebele. The enormous number of livestock the victorious *amabutho* drove back to Dingane could not disguise the uncomfortable fact that, like the amaNdebele had at Vegkop, they had left the Boers badly battered but still intact. They had squandered the advantage of surprise in an incomplete victory, leaving the Boer survivors aflame to avenge their slaughtered kinsfolk. Far from the war being over, as Dingane had intended, it had just begun.

The surviving *Trekkers* drew together in several large laagers for their mutual protection. Between the destruction of Retief's *kommando* and the Bloukrans massacre, they had lost close to 10 per cent of their total numbers and, critically, some 110 of their fighting men—a figure that did not include the dozens of *agterryers* who had perished, men who also bore arms. Fears grew that now they were weak Sekonyela might come down over the Drakensberg to recoup the cattle Retief had taken from him although, in the event, he did not act on his threats

---

15　*Annals* 1, p.233: Narrative of William Jurgen Pretorius.
16　*Smit's Diary*, pp.89–90: 18, 19, 21, 22 February 1838.
17　*Annals* 1, pp.372–3: Bezuidenhout's narrative.
18　*Annals* 1, p.243: Journal of Charl Celliers.
19　*Annals* 1, pp.406–8: Jacobus Boshof's report of 31 July 1838 in the *Graham's Town Journal*, 9 August 1838.
20　*Annals* 1, p.464: Steenkamp, 'Record'.
21　*Annals* 1, p.405: Boshof's letter, 2 July 1838; p. 71: Bezuidenhout's narrative.

of retaliation being too involved in his own conflicts in the Caledon River valley.[22] It was a particularly rainy summer, and life under canvas in muddy encampments full of flocks and herds was hard to bear. Many had been left destitute with the loss of their wagons, household possessions, draught-oxen and other livestock and had to rely on the charity of others. Under these stressful conditions people's health began to give way. Supplies of food ran very low. There was no grain available, and those whose livestock the amaZulu had driven away were almost entirely dependent on hunting game.

In desperation, the *Trekkers* sent messages over the Drakensberg to other parties of Emigrant Farmers still on the highveld begging for assistance in recovering their looted livestock and in avenging 'the innocent blood so treacherously shed'. But, to their astonishment, almost no reinforcements arrived because most of those still west of the mountains thought it prudent not to risk themselves against the amaZulu. The only exceptions were Piet Uys, who immediately came back over the Drakensberg with all his people to help his compatriots in distress, arriving on 1 March; and Hendrik Potgieter, who came a week or so later (the date is uncertain) accompanied only by men ready to take the field as a *kommando*.[23]

The advent of these two stalwart leaders, the joint victors over the amaNdebele, gave the *Trekkers* fresh heart. However, when planning to strike back against Dingane, they fully understood that their chances of success would be enhanced if they could do so in coordination with the Port Natal settlers who would open up a second, diversionary front. Not that the Port Natal settlers needed much persuading. By the first days of March, many—even if by no means all—were indeed determined to attack Dingane.[24] Here was a chance to settle old scores against the capricious Zulu king while he was preoccupied with the *Trekkers*, and the lure of easy plunder beckoned. There was also the genuine desire to aid the Emigrant Farmers with whose plight they greatly sympathised, along with the urge to avenge the death of Thomas Halstead. Dingane, learning from his spies which way the wind was blowing in Port Natal, sent to the settlers, warning them that they 'had made themselves his enemies', and that he would 'come down some night … in a more sudden way than he had attacked the Boers [and] drive all the people away.'[25] After receiving this menacing message, attacking Dingane was no longer simply a matter of 'plunder and revenge' for the settlers. As they vehemently assured the Rev. Owen when he finally made it back to Port Natal, they were now actuated by 'self preservation, the first law of nature.'[26]

On 13 March John Cane (Jana) and John Stubbs—the child of an 1820 Settler who had been one of Alexander Biggar's captains in his short-lived Port Natal Volunteers in 1837—led a small army out of Port Natal.[27] It was made up of at least 1,000 or more of their African clients and Khoisan retainers, and could possibly have been of nearly twice that number. Cane's and Stubbs's objective was to raid the amaZulu living along the middle reaches of the Thukela. On

---

22 Leśniewski, *Zulu–Boer War*, p. 140.
23 *Annals* 1, pp.408–9: Jacobus Boshof to the editor, *Graham's Town Journal*, 31 July 1838; *Smit's Diary*, pp.91, 92–3: 23, 28 February, 1 March 1838; Michał Leśniewski, 'Deconstructing the Myth of the Deaths of Piet and Dirk Uys: A Reconstruction of the Battle of eThaleni, 10 April 1838', *Journal of African Military History*, 2 (2018), pp.3–4.
24 *Owen's Diary*, p.123: 4 March 1838.
25 *Owen's Diary*, p.124: 8 March 1838.
26 *Owen's Diary*, p.124: 11 March 1838;
27 Tabler, *Pioneers*, pp. 2–13, 97–8.

the way, while encamped at the Mgeni River (some miles north of where Pietermaritzburg would later be founded), their retainers and those led by Henry Ogle (Wohlo) came to blows in a protracted brawl over whose detachment would take precedence in leading the column. Cane's people prevailed, and Ogle's were left swearing to be revenged.

Some days later in the fourth week of March—the precise date is unknown—the fractious 'Army of Natal' (so it called itself) attacked and destroyed several large and populous *imizi* belonging to the powerful *inkosi* Nombanga kaNgidli on the southern banks of the Thukela at Ntunjambili, or Kranskop, where a great spur of the Drakensberg ends precipitously above the river. Cane's attack was well-timed because Dingane had summoned away all the local *amabutho* and cattle guards to repel a *Trekker* attack his spies had informed him was in preparation, and would indeed take place in the first week of April, culminating in the battle of eThaleni (see the following chapter). Consequently, the raiders met almost no opposition, killing five or six amaZulu in the raid. They suffered only two themselves: one the victim of snake-bite and the other summarily shot by Cane for attempting to conceal some of the plunder for himself before it had been divided. Indeed, the spoil was considerable. As well as carrying off as many as 4,000 head of cattle, numbers of them royal cattle which, though the practice of *ukusisa*, Dingane was pasturing with Nombanga, the raiders also took some 500 women and children captive. These were a considerable prize because the captors would initially have the benefit of their labour, and would later receive *ilobolo* (bride-wealth) for them from the families of the men to whom they duly married them off. All in all, the Army of Natal returned triumphantly to Port Natal on 2 April, very well pleased with its easily acquired plunder—but also uneasily trying to put out of mind what retribution Dingane was likely to exact.[28]

During the Army of Natal's absence, there had been another small strike against Dingane's subjects calculated to raise his ire still further. Captain and Mrs Gardiner set sail on 25 March from Port Natal. A deeply disappointed man, on 20 March he had resigned his commission as Justice of the Peace for Natal since he believed he had no means of carrying it out.[29] Moreover, he felt that 'the ground was swept from under him' and saw no purpose in staying in Natal if the Boers took over because (even less than the British settlers) they were not inclined to encourage missionary activity among the amaZulu.[30] No sooner had he departed than some of his abandoned African adherents decided to embark on a raid of their own, intending (if called to account) to pin the blame on the Port Natal settlers. On some date between 26 and 30 March, they raided several Zulu *imizi* along the lower reaches of the Thukela and seized a considerable number of cattle. However, in unconscious repetition of several of the *drosters*' raids against the amaNdebele, they took no proper military precautions on their return. The pursuing amaZulu surprised them one night, killing most of them and recapturing their cattle.[31]

---

28 For the Ntunjambili raid, see *Owen's Diary*, pp.127, 130–1: 13 March, 2 April 1838; *Annals* 1, pp.383–4: Wood, *Statements*; pp.551–2: D.C. Toohey's evidence to the Kafir Commission, 1852; *JSA* 5, p.218: Ogle, 7 March 1914; Rev. William C. Holden, *History of the Colony of Natal, South Africa* (London: Alexander Heylin, 1855), pp. 63–5; Cubbin, 'Port Natal', p.154; Laband, *Zulu Nation*, p.93; Laband *Historical Dictionary*, p.206; Leśniewski, *Zulu–Boer War*, pp. 136–9.
29 *RN 3*, pp.270–1, no. 135: Gardiner to Bell, 20 March 1838.
30 *Owen's Diary*, p.128: 25 March 1838; C. de B. Webb (ed.), 'Captain Allen Gardiner: A Memoir by His Wife' *Natalia*, 4 (December 1974), p.33.
31 *Owen's Diary*, p.129: 1 April 1838; Cubbin, 'Port Natal', p.154.

Even as these two raids seriously raised the stakes and put Port Natal in increased jeopardy, the Boers (as Dingane was anticipating) took their own initiative. On 24 March Hans de Lange led out a patrol of 30 men to attack nearby *imizi*, killing a number of their inhabitants and driving away the rest. The *kommando* brought back 261 cattle, many fat sheep and a 'superabundance' of sorghum and maize to feed the Emigrants.[32]

These three pinpricks were enough to enrage Dingane without much hurting him, and the Boers and Port Natal residents very much needed to act in concert to confront him. And, in fact, on 13 March, the day the Army of Natal had begun its march, an embassy had set out from Port Natal to the Boer laagers to formulate a joint strategy. While on the road, on 17 March, they came upon a Boer delegation travelling to Port Natal with the identical purpose, and the two parties came to an agreement. Together, the *Trekkers* and Port Natal settlers would carry the war back to Dingane.[33] As Francis Owen had reflected on quitting emGungundlovu, if Dingane had grasped 'the character of his antagonists' he would have known 'how dreadful it is to provoke their wrath and what determined and powerful enemies he has made himself.'[34]

---

32   *Smit's Diary*, p.97: 24 March 1838.
33   *Owen's Diary*, p.127: 17 March 1838; Cubbin, 'Port Natal', pp.150–52.
34   *Owen's Diary*, p.119: 11 February 1838.

20

I Will Die with My Father!

Who in the Boer camp was to take command of a retaliatory offensive against Dingane to recover as many as they could of their precious livestock? Piet Retief's death was finally confirmed to great communal distress only on 18 March 1838,[1] and the question of who was to succeed him became urgent. Gert Maritz was eager to step in, but Uys (as we have seen) had his Natal ambitions and would not accept his leadership. At length, on 28 March an agreement was reached whereby Maritz continued as the civilian leader of the *Trekkers*. He would remain behind in laager when Uys, who was voted in 'as the Chief Commandant for the war against the treacherous enemy, Dingaan', led the campaign against the Zulu king. Lukas Meyer was elected on 4 April as Uys's Assistant War Leader. They, Potgieter, and the other commanders were all enjoined to 'consult each other' in the coming operations.[2]

Yet it seems that Potgieter, whose focus was on the highveld, and who saw himself as an independent ally of the Natal *Trekkers*, chafed at being consigned to a subordinate position. For the sake of unity, and to damp down festering ill-will, Uys ultimately 'consented' to Potgieter being 'equal in command with him.'[3] After all, Uys and Potgieter had cooperated perfectly well together in their final victory over Mzilikazi, so inherently there was no military problem in this arrangement. It was only after the campaign in which they jointly commanded had come to grief that their 'rivalry' was seized upon as the reason for their defeat. As Michał Leśniewski has effectively argued, though, the supposed conflict between the two is 'an historiographical creation' and was not a decisive factor in their lack of military success in the battle to come.[4]

On 6 April the *kommando* set off north-east from the *Trekker* laagers in the direction of emGungundlovu.[5] It was divided into two sections, riding in separate columns, with Potgieter

---

1   *Smit's Diary*, p.93: 18 March 1838.
2   *Smit's Diary*, pp.98–100: 28 March, 4 April 1838; *Owen's Diary*, p.129: 26 March 1838.
3   *Annals* 1, p.409: Boshof's letter, 31 July 1838.
4   Leśniewski, 'Piet and Dirk Uys', pp.8–9.
5   For the battle of eThaleni, see *Owen's Diary*, pp.134–6: 23 April 1838; *Annals* 1, pp. 233–4: narrative of Willem Jurgen Pretorius; pp. 409–12: Boshof's letter, 31 July 1838; Delegorgue, *Travels, Volume One*, pp. 109–10; *Travels, Volume Two*, pp. 66–8; Fuze, *Black People*, p.75; Nathan, *Voortrekkers*, pp.230–6; H.C. De Wet, 'Die Grafte van Piet en Dirkie Uys', *Historia*, 8: 3 (September 1963), pp.166–74; H.C. De Wet, 'Waar het Piet Uys en sy Seun Dirkie Geval?', *Historia*, 4: 2 (June 1959), pp.75–88; Ian S. Uys, 'The Battle of Italeni', *Military History Journal*, 4: 5 (June 1979), <samilitaryhistory.org/vol045iu>.

commanding the larger force of 200 men, and Uys the smaller one of 147. As was customary, *agterryers* must certainly have accompanied the expedition to look after the pack horses and spare mounts and to perform duties in the camp, but their presence was taken for granted and their number is mentioned in none of the sources. Unusually, the *kommando* brought along no wagons carrying its supplies and took only such stores, powder, and shot as could be carried on their pack horses. The reason was that the two commanders intended to move as rapidly as possible to surprise the amaZulu, exactly as they had done when attacking the amaNdebele at eGabeni in 1837. Unfortunately for the Boers, whereas Dingane with his extensive and effective network of spies and informants was fully appraised of the composition of their *kommando* and of the route it planned to take to emGungundlovu, they were woefully in the dark about Zulu dispositions and intentions. Indeed, this time the boot was to be on the other foot, and it was Potgieter and Uys who were going to be taken by surprise.

The rivers of Zululand were flooded by the unusually heavy late summer rains. With no other option open to it, the *kommando* forded the Mzinyathi at what Natal settlers later called Rorke's Drift. Once across the Mzinyathi, the Boers turned due east and made for emGungundlovu. They passed through a countryside disconcertingly empty of all livestock and inhabitants because Dingane, warned of their coming, had ordered it to be evacuated to deny the Boers either supplies or plunder. Unnerved and anxious, the Boers nevertheless pushed on. On 9 April they sighted a large Zulu force at a distance away to their left, in the region of Babanango Mountain to the north. Their patrols captured a number of Zulu scouts ('spies' to the Boers), quite probably deliberately planted to feed them the intelligence that the main Zulu army was concentrated at emGungundlovu, and to guide them there by a route that would lead them straight into the trap the amaZulu were laying for them.

Riding on, following cattle paths, the *kommando* passed along under the southern lee of the great, flat-topped Thala Mountain about 18 miles WSW of emGungundlovu and halted for the night on the banks of the upper reaches of the Mhlathuze River. Before daybreak the following morning, 10 April, the crossed the river and halted on the plateau below a conical hill, Katazo Kop. From its summit they could see the enormous ellipse of emGungundlovu itself, some four miles away to the NNE. The route to the emaKhosini valley and the *amakhanda* clustered there lay first down a narrow defile (or *poort*) from the plateau and then across a valley, its rugged, rocky floor intersected by dongas and covered by tall, yellowing grasses and patches of thick bush. The boulder-strewn Nzololo River flowed through the valley, squeezing through a narrow cleft to the north between two low hills that flanked it on either side. The path to emGungundlovu, which lay about three miles further on, passed through the same *poort* as the river, a trying route for the *kommando* to negotiate. It was here that the Zulu *impi* had taken up position.[6]

> html>, accessed 18 May 2020; Laband, *Historical Dictionary*, pp.284–5; Leśniewski, 'Piet and Dirk Uys', pp.10–20; and *Zulu-Boer War*, pp.142–57.
>
> 6 The accurate identification of the site of the battlefield has caused historians some problems. The persuasively detailed map in Smail, *Land of the Zulu Kings*, p.61 is based on the wrong site entirely, and the two hills closing in the valley to the north are depicted to the west, resulting in a tortured and inventive depiction of the movements of the various military units. Leśniewski, 'Piet and Dirk Uys', pp.12–17 has confused the orientation of the battlefield, writing of 'northern' and 'southern' hills instead of western and eastern ones and in *Boer-Zulu War*, p. 152 has confused the Nzololo River with Mhlathuze. Uys, in 'Italeni' has mistaken the Nzololo River for the Mkhumbane which flows to its east

I Will Die with My Father! 165

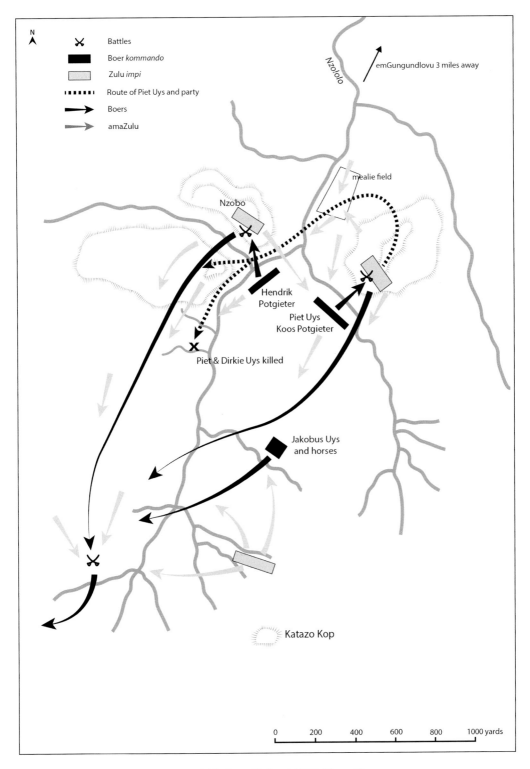

Battle of eThaleni, 10 April 1838: Phase One

Dingane had placed Nzobo himself in command of several thousand warriors—perhaps as many as 5,000 to 7,000 of them. They were made up primarily from the umKhulutshane and isiGulutshane (young *amabutho* the king had enrolled in 1833), along with smaller elements of other *amabutho*, all of them incorporated into the imVoko (or imVokwe), the large, composite unmarried *ibutho* created by Dingane. Their great *izinduna* were Mjobo kaBangu and Nduvana kaNkobe.[7] In planning how best to counter the Boer *kommando* effectively, Nzobo was able to draw on his knowledge of the tactics typically employed by the enemy. He had seen the Port Natal musketeers in action in 1836 against the amaSwazi, and had witnessed the mounted *amaBunu* showing off their fighting skills as they 'danced' their horses before Dingane at emGungundlovu. He would doubtless have learned how they had twice defeated the amaNdebele, and his *amabutho* would have reported back how the *Trekkers* had comported themselves during their surprise attack in February on their encampments. As a canny, experienced commander, Nzobo would have realised that to diminish the Boers' undoubted advantages of firepower and manoeuverability he had to make every use he could of surprise and difficult terrain to disrupt their usual pattern of combat. With that objective Nzobo had posted a division of his *impi* on each of the two hills commanding the defile through which the route to emGungundlovu passed. Banking on the *amabutho* being able to hold the *poort* against the *kommando*, he concealed a third division in the broken terrain and high grasses of the valley to cut off the Boer retreat or to attack them from the rear. (As we have seen, this was a classic Zulu disposition for an ambush, and it is mistaken to suppose that an *impi* was always deployed in the chest and horns formation suitable for a pitched battle in the open field.)[8]

To ensure that the *kommando* rode into the trap he had laid for it, on the morning of the battle Nzobo had a herd of cattle driven as a decoy across the valley towards its northern end where his *amabutho* waited. Unable to resist the lure (after all, the recovery of cattle was the *kommando's* chief objective) and with too little caution the Boers gave pursuit. But they were not chasing the likes of the amaNdebele at eGabeni, easy prey already in the process of withdrawing and not prepared to offer much resistance. As they entered the valley, to their shock the members of the *kommando* saw the amaZulu posted in battle array on the two hills at the far end. Nevertheless, they decided to attack and hastily made their plans.

Jakobus Uys, Piet Uys's elder brother, in command of 40 men, was detailed to remain in the rear guarding the 60 or so pack horses and the *kommando's* spare riding horses. Piet Uys and Potgieter agreed to divide the remaining forces more or less equally, with Uys's being the slightly larger group of between 150 and 170 men. As Leśniewski has pointed out, this decision to redistribute their forces in the face of the enemy indicates that there was indeed no serious disagreement between the two commanders and that they jointly planned the operation.[9] As they had done at eGabeni, one division was to attack while the other protected it from

---

towards its confluence with the White Mfolozi, not through the *poort*, and passes emGungundlovu on the opposite side of the *ikhanda*. Ds H.C. de Wet, in 'Grafte' and 'Piet Uys en sy Seun' undertook extensive and thorough fieldwork based on his knowledge of the primary sources to identify the site correctly, but his work (which is in Afrikaans) has often been overlooked.

7   *JSA* 2, p.92: Magidigidi, 8 May 1905; *JSA* 5, pp.74, 82–3: Ngidi, 17, 22 October 1905; *JSA* 6, p.278: Tununu and Ndukwana, 4 June 1903.
8   See Leśniewski, 'Piet and Dirk Uys', pp.12–13 and 15 for efforts to make Nzobo's dispositions for an ambush conform with those for a set-piece battle.
9   Leśniewski, 'Piet and Dirk Uys', p.13.

encirclement or counterattack. The plan was for Uys to attack first, driving the larger of the two Zulu divisions off the eastern hill on their right. Once he had done so, he would support Potgieter in his attack against the western hill on their left. Having cleared the *poort* between the two hills, the *kommando* would be free to continue its advance into the emaKhosini valley.

The *amabutho* remained sitting among the rocks on the south-eastern hill, waiting for Uys's men to commit themselves. At about 40 yards from the Zulu position, Veldkornet Koos (Jakobus) '*Grootvoet*' (Bigfoot) Potgieter, Uys's second-in-command, gave the order to halt and dismount. Thereupon, the *amabutho* sprang up and charged. They were met by a deadly volley of buckshot at close range, and before they could recover the Boers had time to reload and discharge a second, equally lethal volley. The Boers then started firing at will, and after only five minutes or so the amaZulu, who had taken heavy casualties, began to fall back in disorder. Whether they did so because they could take no more of the devastating fusillade, or whether this was a deliberately planned manoeuvre to draw the *amaBunu* out of position, is ultimately immaterial because the consequences were identical. Instead of staying on the hill they had cleared of amaZulu and, as was the plan, supporting Potgieter's assault on the hill to the west, a few of Uys's men remounted and foolhardily pursued the amaZulu down the farther side. There they fell into a carefully laid Zulu ambush in a field of mealies along the banks of the Nzololo.

Seeing their danger, Uys immediately resolved to ride down to extricate them, but most of the *kommando* considered the enterprise too risky, and Uys had to call for volunteers to accompany him. With about 15 of them, including his 15-year-old son Dirkie,[10] he rode off down the northern side of the hill, leaving the bulk of his force where they were under Koos Potgieter's command. As they approached, the amaZulu showered Uys and his party with their *izijula* (throwing-spears) and manoeuvred to cut them off from moving back up the hill to where Koos Potgieter remained stationed. Uys and his small party were left with no choice but to retire south through the *poort* to the valley beyond. As they fell back, some of their horses were killed and their riders had to be taken up behind their comrades. Uys himself was struck in the back by a hurled spear, to the left of the spine, and the point penetrated through his groin. He pulled the *isijula* out and continued to lead his surviving men as they struggled with difficulty through the boulders and bushes of the valley floor. But he was bleeding profusely and could barely keep in his saddle. One by one his fleeing companions were cut off by pursuing amaZulu and speared to death.

Meanwhile, as planned, on seeing that Uys's men had gained their objective and taken the eastern hill, Potgieter led his men halfway up the western hill to make his assault in turn against the *amabutho* holding the summit. But then, he suddenly changed his mind and ordered his men to fall back to the valley despite the vigorous protests of a few of them who continued for a while to advance to the attack before also withdrawing. Why Potgieter retreated is a matter of dispute since he never explained his reasons. He has been charged with cowardice, but this hardly accords with his record as an experienced and determined commander. As we have seen, the *kommando* tradition placed a premium on avoiding unnecessary losses. Koos Potgieter (it should be noted) did not venture to lead his men off the hill they had captured to rescue Piet Uys struggling with the amaZulu in the *poort* below. Quite possibly Potgieter calculated that to continue his assault uphill over treacherous, broken ground against a large, determined enemy

---

10 His age has been recorded as being as young as 12, but 15 is the most likely.

force was overly risky, especially since Uys's party on the opposite hill was distracted by the skirmish in the *poort* and was unlikely to lend him their full support. Moreover, the fact that he had already firmly decided that his future lay in the highveld doubtless made him less willing to endanger his men in a struggle not properly in his own interests, and that influenced his decision to disengage. Yet, it is also conceivable that Potgieter calculated that if he withdrew to the valley, he would be in a better position both to support Koos Potgieter if he attempted to retire, and perhaps to lend Piet Uys his assistance too.

In the event, Potgieter's withdrawal was a tactical disaster and achieved neither of these putative objectives. Seeing Potgieter beginning to fall back, the amaZulu charged down the western hill with such a rattle of shields and shouting of war-cries that the Boers turned tail and made off, any thought of assisting the other half of the *kommando* forgotten. The third Zulu division that had remained concealed in the valley until that moment sprang up and manoeuvred to cut them off, but Potgieter's horsemen managed to evade them and, keeping up a good pace, outdistanced their pursuers as they headed southwards towards the drift across the Mhlathuze. Veldkornet Karel Landman, a prosperous farmer from the Uitenhage District who had experience in the Cape Frontier Wars and had led his *Trekker* party over the Drakensberg in February 1838,[11] volunteered with a small party to stay back and cover Potgieter's retreat. They at least had the satisfaction of shooting dead an *induna* mounted on a horse they recognised as having belonged to Piet Retief. But it was not possible to lead away the pack-horses, and Jakobus Uys and the contingent under his command abandoned them to the enemy as they also made their escape.

The amaZulu broke off their pursuit of Potgieter's force to prevent Koos Potgieter's men on the eastern hill from breaking out, and occupied the dongas and footpaths around its base. As for Piet Uys, when he realised that the amaZulu had cut him and his surviving companions off from rejoining the bulk of his contingent on the eastern hill, he was left with no choice but to try and follow the direction of Potgieter's retreat up the Nzololo stream. The going was extremely difficult, and Uys was repeatedly fainting and falling from his horse from loss of blood. Now through the *poort* and in the valley, the party of fugitives split up to by-pass a small hill. Uys and some of his men who kept to it eastern side along the Nzololo, were prevented from joining up again with the others by a steep, stony ridge held by the amaZulu. It was there, among the boulders and bushes that Uys and his son Dirkie were finally surrounded and killed.[12]

The rest of Uys's contingent on the eastern hill under Koos Potgieter's command was left completely in the lurch by Hendrik Potgieter's flight. Surrounded by the amaZulu, it was in a perilous situation. For an hour or more the Boers held off Zulu attacks with effective musketry that kept their enemies out of spear-throwing range. They could not continue to do so indefinitely, however, and resolved to break out. Suddenly concentrating all their firepower on the southern section of the Zulu encirclement, they blasted a gap through the Zulu ranks and rode off with amaZulu clinging to their horses in an attempt to prevent their escape. They then conducted a fighting retreat across the valley, alternately dismounting, firing and retiring

---

11   Laband, *Historical Dictionary*, p.139.
12   In December 1838, after the battle of Blood River, a burial party interred the remains of the Boers who had been killed at the battle of eThaleni. Piet Uys's were identified by six small, hand-beaten silver buttons on his waistcoat. They were later donated to the Voortrekker Museum in Pietermaritzburg (now the Msunduzi Museum).

I Will Die with My Father! 169

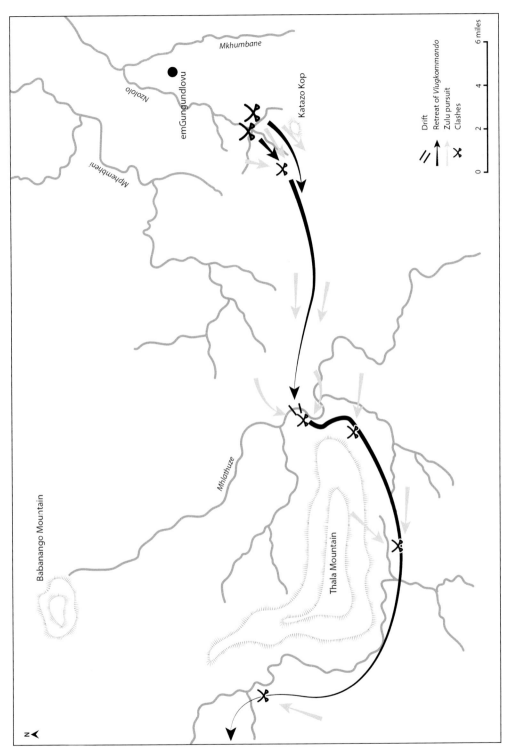

Battle of eThaleni, 10 April 1838: Phase Two

in classic *kommando* fashion, changing direction numerous times under Zulu pressure. Many amaZulu had managed to regroup at the drift across the Mhlathuze and tried to cut the Boers off there. But they charged and shot their way through, eventually rejoining Hendrik Potgieter's men who had finally halted and had been waiting for them on the plateau beyond. But the battle was not yet over. For the next two hours, the amaZulu pursued and harried the reunited *kommando* as it retired westwards as fast as it could manage along the southern flank of Thala Mountain. It is for this reason (and because it is the most prominent natural feature in the vicinity of the battlefield) that the amaZulu called the encounter the battle of eThaleni,[13] a running fight that extended over nearly 15 miles from the two hills held by Nzobo's men in the valley of the Nzololo to the western end of Thala Mountain.

The Boers did not extricate themselves unscathed. Besides Piet Uys and his son, they lost eight men killed (only one of whom was of Hendrik Potgieter's division) and a few dozen wounded, as well as all of the 60 or so pack horses along with their baggage, spare ammunition, and a number of muskets. The amaZulu must have suffered many casualties themselves—perhaps several hundred—since they had been compelled to brave well-disciplined, heavy musket-fire at close range in order to get close enough even to throw their *izijula* with any effect. Even so, the battle had been a decided Zulu success in which—in contrast to the amaNdebele at Mosega and eGabeni—they had prevailed over the mounted Boers and their fearsome muskets. Zulu morale would have received a decided boost, and it now remained to be seen whether Dingane could capitalise on Nzobo's victory and drive the *amaBunu* out of his kingdom.

As for the *Trekkers*, they were left aghast that Uys and Potgieter, the two victorious commanders against the amaNdebele, should have suffered such a significant reverse, only mitigated by the defeated *kommando's* success in breaking out of the Zulu ambush and making its escape. After all, it was one thing for the Emigrant Farmers to be taken by surprise in their unprepared encampments at the Bloukrans and Bushmans Rivers, but it was quite another to be trounced in the open field. The chastened *kommando* returned to the Boer encampments on 12 April, and the extent of their setback unleashed terrible consternation in camp. 'O God! help! help! help! still now protect, preserve our camps' cried Erasmus Smit in his deep distress. Over the next two days the wagons of four different camps were brought together in heavy rain for greater protection, concentrating at the western foot of Doornkop at what came to be known as the Modderlaer (Mud Camp).[14] Under this new adversity the old dissensions flared up with a new intensity. The disastrous expedition began to be referred to derisively as the *Vlugkommando*, or Flight Commando. For, indeed, it had indubitably fled. The *Trekkers* cast about to assuage their dismay by raising up heroes they could celebrate in order to gloss over the shock of defeat, and (the opposite side of the same coin) to identifying villains on whom they could pin the blame for the disaster.

Piet Uys and his son Dirkie provided the desired hero-figures. The emerging myth related how the mortally wounded Uys, when he fell from his horse for the last time, nobly urged his companions to leave him and save themselves, exhorting them to 'fight like brave fellows to the last, and hold God before your eyes!'[15] In a further, poignant touch that has passed into legend, Dirkie was said to have been so moved by the sight of his father abandoned on the ground and

---

13 Spelled 'Italeni' in older secondary sources.
14 *Smit's Diary*, p.102: 13, 14 April 1838.
15 *Annals* 1, p.411: Boshof's letter, 31 July 1838.

surrounded by the enemy that, even though he could have saved himself, he wheeled his horse about and rode back to protect Uys. To those who tried to hold him back he courageously declared in Dutch, '*Ik zal by myn vader sterven*! (I will die with my father).[16]

Potgieter, by contrast, was openly accused of cowardice and treason for having fled the battlefield. Indignant at what he considered the unfounded criticism, and impressed moreover with the military strength of the amaZulu, he huffily withdrew across the Drakensberg taking his invaluable group of horsemen along with him. Back on the highveld, he resumed his endeavours to found a republic where he could achieve his ideal of liberty. As for the *Trekkers* who remained east of the Drakensberg, they had to accept that overthrowing Dingane and settling in his former kingdom would be a far more difficult and uncertain enterprise than defeating Mzilikazi. They would have to adjust their strategy and tactics and prepare for a prolonged campaign. One thing, though, was certain. Henceforth they would risk engaging the amaZulu only from within the sure protection of a wagon laager.

---

16 Testimony of J.H. Steenkamp who took part in the battle, quoted in De Wet, 'Piet Uys en sy seun Dirkie', p.81.

21

The Great Elephant Will Trample You Underfoot!

A week after Nzobo ambushed the Boer *kommando* at eThaleni and put it to flight, the amaZulu under the nominal command of Mpande kaSenzangakhona, Dingane's half-brother, comprehensively routed the forces of Port Natal at the lower Thukela River. From a mixture of motives, the Port Natal residents had taken the fatal decision to follow up their rewarding raid at Ntunjambili in the last week of March 1838 with a fresh punitive expedition against the amaZulu. On the one hand, an offensive up the coast would honour the agreement concluded with the *Trekkers* in late March to support each other in the war against Dingane. Accordingly, the strike was timed to coordinate with Uys's and Potgieter's *kommando* raid towards emGungundlovu and, by opening a second front, was intended to split the Zulu riposte. Alongside that honourable intention, however, was a more venal one. The Ntunjambili raid had whetted the Port Natal settlers' greed for plunder. As Dingane astutely remarked when he learned of the Ntunjambili raid, 'They will return because they have tasted good things.'[1]

Greed certainly actuated the 26-year-old Robert Biggar, Alexander Biggar's eldest son, who had settled in Port Natal in 1834.[2] He had been absent in Grahamstown at the time of the Ntunjambili raid, and was resentful at having lost his chance for easy plunder. His was therefore a dominant voice, along with those of John Cane and John Stubbs, in arguing for a repeat raid. There were those with cooler heads, especially the missionaries, who questioned the wisdom of a second raid and who pointed out the folly of antagonising Dingane yet further. For them, it was more sensible to prepare against the Zulu king's inevitable attack to recover the cattle lost at Ntunjambili.[3] Robert Biggar and his supporters carried the day, however, and the Port Natal residents agreed to mount a fresh raid. Ogle declined to join the expedition because, according to his son, his daughter was 'exceedingly ill',[4] but perhaps he held off because of the dispute he had had with Cane during the Ntunjambili raid.

The force Biggar and Cane raised, the 'Grand Army of Natal', was larger than the one that had raided Ntunjambili and included a significant number of men with firearms. It consisted of 18 Port Natal residents, most of them mounted, with ostrich feathers in the hats, and all carrying

---

1 *JSA* 4, p.18: Mqaikana, 11May 1916.
2 Tabler, *Pioneers*, pp.13–14; Laband, *Historical Dictionary*, p.15.
3 *Owen's Diary*, p.166: Joseph Kirkman's story.
4 *JSA* 5, p.218: Ogle, 7 March 1914.

muskets of various descriptions, along with swords or cutlasses. Also bearing firearms were 30 of their trained Khoisan hunters, and about 400 of their African retainers whose muskets would have been of inferior quality and of dubious effectiveness. In support were about 2,500 African levies carrying spears and shields. They were men who recognised the settler leaders as their *amakhosi* and who owed them military service. Among them were refugees from Dingane's rule with a score to settle against their former overlord.

When Biggar led out the first contingent of the 'Grand Army' on 10 April, it was already too late to serve the strategic purpose of diverting Zulu attention away from the *Vlugkommando* that was defeated that very same day. And with the Boers temporarily out of the picture, the 'Grand Army' now faced the amaZulu alone. Yet it would be many days before the Port Natal settlers learned of this latest Zulu victory, and Cane followed with the second contingent of the 'Grand Army' on 13 April (which happened to be Good Friday). The two contingents rendezvoused on 14 April and together marched north up the coast. On 16 April the 'Grand Army' reached the banks of the Thukela River that was lazily broadening out towards its mouth in the Indian Ocean some five miles away.[5]

Scouts were immediately sent out and crossed the river a few miles upstream at the Dlokweni Drift (where the John Ross bridge now stands). There they had a slight brush with Zulu scouts and returned to report the that the hilly, bush-covered country on the opposite bank with its deep valleys was full of temptingly unattended cattle. The 'Grand Army's' commanders, whose strategy was never more than hazy, were divided over what to do next. Cane, from his long experience in the region, suspected that the cattle were wandering about in full sight to lure them into a trap. He therefore recommended that the 'Grand Army' remain in a defensive posture on the southern bank of the Thukela. Biggar, on the other hand, feared the army's morale would suffer if it did so, and urged that it advance across the river. He argued that the strong force of musketeers would win the day against any Zulu attack, and that the African levies, who were eager to take on the amaZulu, would provide solid support. And then, of course, there was the irresistible lure of plunder. After much rancorous debate, the imprudent decision was taken to adopt Biggar's counsel and make a foray across the river to seize the livestock roaming there. Accordingly, early on the morning of 17 April the 'Grand Army' forded the river at the Thukela Lower Drift (where the British would build Fort Pearson in 1878). It then advanced a couple of miles north towards a large *umuzi* called Ndondakusuka built on the lower slopes of the high Ndulinde hill.

Warned by their spies and by Captain Gardiner's former African clients of the 'Grand Army's' every movement, the amaZulu, buoyed up by their string of recent victories over the Boers and determined to avenge the Port Natal settlers' raid at Ntunjambili, were ready to take it on. On the evening of 16 April, a Zulu *impi* of 5,000 to 7,000 men—there had been time to redeploy after the battle of eThaleni—hid in the valleys to the north and north-west of Ndondakusuka with the intention (as events were to prove) of enveloping and destroying the 'Grand Army' when it attacked the *umuzi*. One of the Zulu commanders was Zulu kaNogandaya, the *inkosi* of

---

5   For the battle of the Thukela, see *Owen's Diary*, pp.131, 132–4: 13, 16, 17, 19 April 1838; *Annals* 1, pp. 384–6: Wood's *Statements*; p.552: Toohey's evidence, 1852; Delegorgue, *Travels, Volume Two*, p.68; Holden, *Colony of Natal*, pp.65–74; *JSA* 4, pp.18–19: Mqaikana, 11May 1916; Fuze, *Black People*, pp.76–7; Cubbin, 'Port Natal', pp.155–7; Smail, *Land of the Zulu Kings*, p.62; Laband, *Zulu Nation*, pp.93–4; Laband, *Historical Dictionary*, pp.285–6; Leśniewski, *Zulu–Boer War*, pp.157–68.

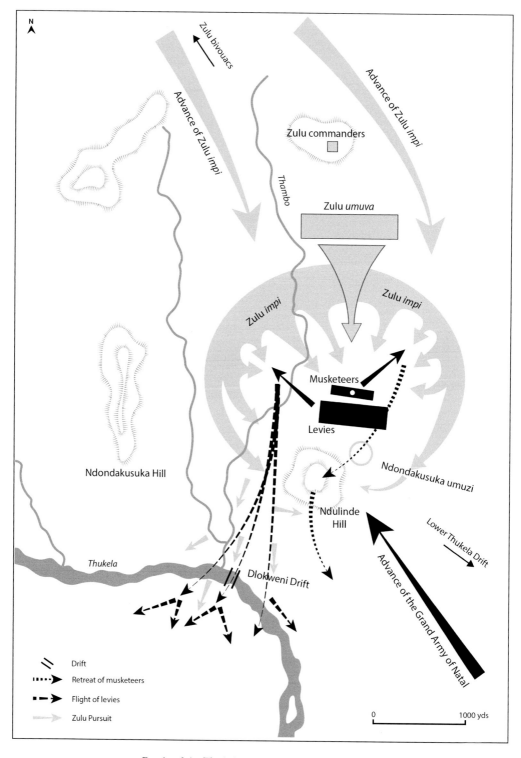

Battle of the Thukela or Dlokweni, 17 April 1838

Ndondakusuka and a famous, battle-scarred warrior of Shaka's time, described by his son as 'a lion of a man'.[6] Other field commanders were Butho, the *induna* of the umKhulutshane *ibutho* quartered at kwaKhangela, Madlebe kaMgedeza and Nongalaza kaNondela. Nongalaza was the *inkosi* of the Nyandwini people, and had been appointed *induna* of the uHlomendlini *ibutho* that Shaka had raised just before his assassination. He was now the principal military officer and favourite of Mpande kaSenzangakhona, the titular commander-in-chief of the *impi* who 'doctored' it before the campaign.[7] Mpande was Dingane's half-brother, and had been one of the few of his siblings whom he had not executed when he seized the throne. As Dingane's possible heir, the *umntwana* had been permitted to live in regal style in his great emLambongwenya *ikhanda* at the Matigulu River, some 10 miles north of the Thukela, and had built up a strong personal following in the region.

Once the 'Grand Army' reached Ndondakusuka, it surrounded and attacked the *umuzi*, burned it to the ground and slaughtered its inhabitants along with several warriors stationed there. It is said one of the dying victims exclaimed: 'Kill me right now, but the great elephant is coming and it will trample you underfoot!'[8] Zulu watched the destruction of his *umuzi* from the top of a nearby hill where, along the other commanders, he had taken up his stand to direct operations. Hard as it must have been for him to witness his home go up in flames, Zulu would have shared with his fellow commanders the grim satisfaction of seeing that the 'Grand Army' had fallen into the trap laid for it. On their orders, the Zulu *amabutho* concentrated into two columns from their several places of concealment and rapidly advanced southwards towards the ruins of Ndondakusuka where the 'Grand Army' was heedlessly milling about. As they approached, the two columns deployed into the classic Zulu battle formation. As became apparent, the Zulu intention was for the *isifuba* (chest) to tie the 'Grand Army' down with a frontal attack. Meanwhile, the two *izimpondo* (horns) were to exploit the broken terrain to mask their outflanking manoeuvre aimed at encircling the 'Grand Army' and cutting it off from any retreat towards the Thukela. The veterans of eThaleni who had come from fighting the mounted Boers were intrigued that the 'English from the Bay' whom they were facing 'had to walk because they had no horses.'[9]

When they became aware of the large Zulu *impi* approaching them in menacing battle array, Biggar and Cane hurriedly drew up their forces below Ndulinde hill to confront the challenge. They deployed all their musketeers near the burning *umuzi* and drew up their African levies behind them in reserve. It would seem (the evidence is sparse) that the plan was for the African levies to advance to the attack once the Zulu chest, shaken by musket fire, began to withdraw. At this stage, Biggar and Cane seem not to have been aware that the two outflung *izimpondo* horns were manoeuvring to outflank them and their attention was concentrated on the *isifuba* facing them.

The body of Port Natal musketeers was under the immediate command of Robert Joyce, an experienced soldier who had deserted from the 72nd Regiment (Duke of Albany's Own Highlanders) in Grahamstown in 1832, and had fled to Port Natal to make his living. He

---

6   *JSA* 3, p.223–4: Mkotana ka Zulu, 10, 11 April 1905. See also *JSA* 1, pp.101–2: Dinya, 2 March 1905; and *JSA* 2, p.272: Maziyana, 22 April 1905.
7   Fuze, *Black People*, p.77.
8   Fuze, *Black People*, p.76.
9   *JSA* 6, p.278: Tununu, 4 June 1903.

would be one of the few white men to survive the battle.[10] Under his direction, well-coordinated salvos—like the Boers, many of the musketeers fired *lopers*—stopped the charge of the Zulu chest with heavy casualties. The *isifuba* did not break up, however, and the *amabutho* fell back in orderly fashion to wait out of effective range of Joyce's musketeers while the encircling *izimpondo* carried out their encirclement.

By this stage the commanders of the 'Grand Army' where aware of the two horns' threatening advance on either flank. To meet this new danger, and misguidedly confident that the repulsed Zulu chest had been knocked out of the picture, Biggar and Cane made the fatal decision to divide their forces. Accordingly, the body of musketeers advanced to their right to deal with the Zulu left *uphondo* coming down upon them from the northeast and east, while the African levies (it has not been recorded who led them) moved out to the left to take on the attack of the right *uphondo* from the northwest. The musketeers' fire successfully stopped and temporarily dispersed the Zulu left horn, while the African levies furiously engaged the Zulu right horn in spear-to-spear combat and likewise drove it back. Apparently, the plan had been for the African levies then to wheel smartly to their right in support of the musketeers and to take the Zulu chest in its flank should it re-enter the fray. But it did not work out like that.

The jubilant African levies could not resist pursuing the fleeing Zulu right horn—or was this a Zulu tactical withdrawal aimed at drawing them out of position? Whatever the case, the result was that instead of the African levies supporting the musketeers to their right, they widened

The battle of the Thukela or Dlokweni, 17 April 1838. Anonymous engraving. (Campbell Collections, Durban, with permission)

10 Tabler, *Pioneers*, p.62.

the gap between them. The canny Zulu commanders on their hill were quick to seize the opportunity that presented itself. Summoning their *umuva* (reserve) to strengthen the *isifuba*, they ordered them to counterattack through the expanding breach in the 'Grand Army's' front. When the African levies realised that the reinforced Zulu centre was advancing to cut them off from the musketeers to their right, their morale collapsed and in panic they sought to escape. In what rapidly became a case of each man for himself, a chaotic flight gathered momentum towards the Dlokwini Drift directly to their rear. The Zulu right wing then rallied, returned to the attack and remorselessly pursued them down to the river.

The flying levies cast off the white calico armbands that had distinguished them as being on the settlers' side, and caused consternation among the musketeers who could no longer distinguish them from the amaZulu. At the same time, the reinforced *isifuba* and the reordered left *uphondo* fiercely engaged Biggar's and Cane's musketeers who fell back up Ndulinde hill. It is known that the imiHaye, one of the *amabutho* incorporated into the imVoko, was part of the advancing *impi* and, as they attacked, they shouted out 'Jaye! Haye! Haye!'[11] Surrounded, the musketeers resisted resolutely for two hours under showers of cast *izijula*, their musket-fire throwing back one Zulu charge after another. But, unlike the *Vlugkommando*, most of them were not mounted and it was impossible to break out of the Zulu encirclement and escape as Koos Potgieter and his horsemen had done at eThaleni. In the end, exhausted, thirsty, their ammunition running out, their over-worked muskets malfunctioning, and all hope lost, they were overrun and all but a few lucky survivors were killed where they stood.

Compared to the *Vlugkammando* in its rout at eThaleni a week earlier, the 'Grand Army of Natal' suffered extremely heavy casualties that can be reckoned only roughly. The slain included 13 to 14 of the 18 white settlers. Cane was mortally stabbed in his back and chest while he sat on his horse with his pipe still in his mouth. Biggar perished close by him, and Stubbs, to his reported indignation, was killed by a mere youth. Of the 30 Khoisan hunters, 10 to 27 of them also succumbed. The defeated African levies were herded down to the river where many were speared along its margins or drowned trying to cross to the opposite bank where they hid among the reeds to avoid detection. The pursuing amaZulu meticulously examined the dead and wounded and finished off those still breathing. The surviving African levies dispersed after being routed, so no tally of their losses was ever taken. But it is likely that between 500 and 700 of them were cut down. In no subsequent battle again the amaZulu would the forces of Port Natal and the Boer allies suffer anything like so many casualties. The Zulu losses would also have been very heavy—probably at least 500 and possibly as many as 1,000—because the battle had been waged for nearly three hours and the *amabutho* had faced repeated volleys of musket fire at close quarters. For a decade or more the heaps of bleached bones were seen to lie thick on that terrible killing ground.

The Zulu called it the battle of Dlokweni after the drift where they had massacred the Port Natal African levies, and sometimes the battle of Ndondakusuka after the *umuzi* where the fighting had begun. The settlers usually referred to it as the battle of the Thukela. By whatever name it is known, though, Mpande was fully justified in claiming that his forces had won yet another great victory in the war against the Boers and their Port Natal allies, even if it had required an unacceptably heavy toll of casualties. For the Port Natal settlers and the *Trekkers*

---

11 *JSA* 5, p.75: Ngidi, 17 October 1905.

(when they learned of it), the battle offered a sobering lesson that reinforced what eThaleni had already taught them: it was foolhardy to engage the amaZulu in the open field without the protection of a wagon laager, and was to be avoided at all costs.

Late on the evening of the battle of the Thukela, several survivors on their exhausted horses brought word to Port Natal of the disaster that had befallen the 'Grand Army', and warned that the victorious Zulu army was fast on their heels.[12] Dismay and panic engulfed the settlement. Providentially, the 120-ton brig *Comet* (a two-masted, square-rigged sailing ship) that had been trading gunpowder and general goods since 1836 between Port Natal, Port Elizabeth and Lourenço Marques, had anchored in the bay on 29 March because its master, William Haddon, was ill and needed to go ashore to convalesce.[13] The *Comet* was still there, and the missionaries and the white settlers and their families were therefore able to take refuge on board from 17 April, but many remained ashore while waiting on developments. The main body of the survivors of the 'Grand Army', many of them with stab wounds, straggled in to Port Natal on 19 April to desperate scenes of lamentation as the extent of the loss of life struck home. The settlement was now defenceless, and the situation was made even worse when on 22 April news finally arrived of the Boer defeat at eThaleni.

Then, the following day, 23 April, an incongruous touch was added to the scene of consternation and collapse when a *Trekker* delegation under Jakobus Uys arrived in Port Natal. It had been despatched by Karel Landman, now the Chief Commandant of the United Laagers, to ascertain the situation in the settlement and to sound out how the residents would react to a Boer settlement there. That afternoon the Boer delegates held a meeting with the principal surviving settlers under the chairmanship of Alexander Biggar. They came away with the impression that the current prospects for Port Natal were grim, but also that the majority of residents were now in favour of accepting Boer protection, even if that entailed being annexed by them.[14]

Meanwhile, where was the victorious Zulu army? The *amabutho*, who had suffered severely in the battle, encamped for a while near the Mngeni River to recoup and to perform the required post-combat purification rituals. On the way there, the imiHaye found two cannons at Gardiner's abandoned fortified mission at the Thongathi. It took six men to carry each of them back to emGungundlovu where they were rolled into the *isigodlo* for the *umndlunkulu* women to admire.[15]

It was only on the evening of 23 April, soon after the Boer delegation had departed, that the firing of two guns from the *Comet* warned all the whites ashore to come on board immediately. Units of the Zulu army had been spotted eight miles away while engaged in rounding up cattle.

12 For the Zulu sack and occupation of Port Natal, see *Owen's Diary*, pp.132–3, 136–9: 17, 23, 26 April, 4, 11 May 1838; *Annals* 1, pp.386–7: Wood's *Statements*; D. J. Kotzé (ed.), *Letters of the American Missionaries 1835–1838* (Cape Town: Van Riebeeck Society, 1950), pp. 243–4: Daniel Lindley to S. Lindley, 5 May 1838; *RN* 3, p.286, no. 148: Fynn to Hougham Hudson, 11 May 1838; Delegorgue, *Travels, Volume Two*, pp.68, 70; Holden, *Colony of Natal*, p.75; Fuze, *Black People*, p.77; Cubbin, 'Port Natal', pp.156–8, 160–1; Smail, *Land of the Zulu Kings*, p.63; Laband, *Zulu Nation*, pp. 94–5.
13 Laband, *Historical Dictionary*, pp.51–2.
14 Cubbin, 'Port Natal', pp.159–60.
15 *JSA* 6, pp. 281–2: Tununu, 6 June 1903. The two cannons were abandoned at emGungundlovu when Dingane ordered the *ikhanda* burned after the battle of Blood River.

At 9:00 a.m. the following morning, 24 April, the long-anticipated Zulu *impi* at last swept down on Port Natal from the Berea heights to its west.

For nine days, while the aghast settlers on board the *Comet* looked on helplessly (but safely) through their telescopes, the amaZulu occupied Port Natal and comprehensively sacked it. The settlers' unfortunate African clients and adherents, for whom there was no room on the brig (not that they were ever invited aboard), took to the bush in fear for their lives. The triumphant amaZulu killed all the African fugitives they could winkle out—maybe as many as 50 women and children—and fired all the buildings and huts in the settlement. They slaughtered all the white people's domestic animals such as dogs, cats, and fowls, destroyed their household furniture, books and clothing, and threw out their comestibles such as coffee, flour, sugar, and brandy. At night they danced and celebrated to the light of the burning settlement, some dressed derisively in looted women's clothing. Sometimes they approached the shore near the ship—although usually deterred by the report of its guns when fired in warning—and shouted to those on board that Dingane intended to kill all the whites living in his domain, Boers and Britons alike.

When the amaZulu at last withdrew on 3 May, driving away the livestock useful to them—Erasmus Smit was told they numbered 4,000 head[16]—and carrying off anything else they deemed of value, such as calico cloth, there was nothing left of Port Natal but debris and the walls of some of the houses. One at least of Dingane's perennial vexations seemed at last to have been eliminated, but the permanence of its removal was only illusory. When the *Comet* sailed out of the bay for Lourenço Marques on the afternoon of 12 May, not all the settlers were aboard.[17] Eight or nine of them elected to remain among the ruins of Port Natal along with numbers of their African adherent who re-emerged from the bush to join them in waving the brig farewell. The settlement had recovered from previous punitive Zulu raids—although never one as devastating as the last had been—and could do so again.

---

16 *Smit's Diary*, p.107: 2 May 1838.
17 The *Comet* reached Lourenço Marques on 20 May and sailed for Port Elizabeth on 16 June, discharging the Port Natal refugees there on 23 June 1838. See *RN 3*, p.314, no. 167: Protocol by J.G. de Villiers, Notary Public, 23 June 1838.

22

The Place of the Game-Pits

Armed with the knowledge that the Port Natal settlers had agreed on 22 April 1838 to accept *Trekker* rule, eight days after the amaZulu had evacuated the Port, Karel Landman rode in at the head of 150 men. On 16 May he 1838 took possession of the harbour and surrounding country in the name of the United Laagers. Having appointed a *landdros* (magistrate) and other officers to take charge, Landman hurried back to the Boer laagers with wagon-loads of urgently required supplies. 'All the emigrants were now cheerful in spirit,' crowd Erasmus Smit, 'on account of the good news that Natal now lies free and open before us.'[1] In the following months, wagon-loads of *Trekkers* moved down to the vicinity of the devasted Port. By early September, some 300 of them were settling down under Landman's command and were busy with ploughing and sowing. The arrival in the same month of the schooner *Mary*, bearing supplies of groceries such as rice, sugar, and coffee collected by a Cape Town committee of well-wishers, was a great comfort for the struggling Boer community.[2]

Inland, following the defeat of the *Vlugkommnado*, the inhabitants of the Boer laagers were afflicted by the fear that Dingane would attack them, and the *Trekkers* became paranoid about the activities of 'spies.' During the last three weeks of April, patrols regularly brought in Zulu captives suspected of spying. After being first interrogated, they were then all shot in cold blood so they could not take information back to Dingane if released. Much to Erasmus Smit's distress, 21 'spies' were executed for this reason during the course of April.[3]

Meanwhile, the *Trekkers* in Natal set about organising themselves administratively. The post of *goewerneur* was allowed to lapse with Retief's death, and on 25 May a general meeting elected Karel Landman military leader. Another general meeting held on 12 June decided to establish a *Volksraad*, or parliament, with Jakobus Boshoff as president. It consisted of 24 elected members with virtually unchecked legislative, executive, and judicial powers.[4] The nascent state the *Volksraad* tenuously governed was dubbed Republiek Natalia, and the name *Nieuw Holland* abandoned.

---

1   *Smit's Diary*, p.108: 3 May 1838.
2   Cubbin, 'Port Natal', pp.162–4; Chase, *Natal Papers*, Part II, p.25.
3   *Smit's Diary*, pp.101–2, 103, 105: 10, 11, 18, 23, 24 April 1838.
4   *Smit's Diary*, p.116: 12 June 1838; Brookes and Webb, *History of Natal*, p.36.

By then, there was a community of about 3,600 *Trekkers* in the Natal laagers, not counting their servants and 'apprentices'. Some of the bigger laagers were becoming untenable for reasons of sanitation and because grazing was giving out and supplies of food were hard to come by. In June 1838 Gert Maritz moved his laager west from Doornkop to the east, or right bank of the Little Thukela. There, under the flank of Loskop Mountain, he established the Sooilaer (Sod Laager), the name derived from the thick wall of sods built to strengthen its defences. Likewise, in July Koos Potgieter and Hans Dons de Lange led their parties southeast out of the big, composite camp at Modderlaer to a new site on the west, or left bank of the Bushmans River. There, 11 miles west of the present town of Estcourt, they established a new laager—the Gatslaer—on a low ridge called the Gatsrand in the river valley with its plentiful supply of firewood. (Today, the site is under the waters of the Wagendrift Dam.)[5] Over the following weeks, several other smaller parties joined them there.[6]

At all the big laagers the Boers began to build huts for shelter against the incessant rains, and set their servants ploughing and sowing to ensure a crop for the next year's season. Supplies of all kinds except meat were running low. Raiding parties went out from the laagers to scour the countryside for food. On 10 July Smit recorded that more than 100 heavily laden wagons from the combined camps brought in maize and sorghum as well as pumpkins and calabashes harvested from the 'Kaffir gardens' of *imizi* that their inhabitants had abandoned for fear of the invaders.[7] Fevers and measles broke out in the crowded, insanitary Boer camps, and disease also spread among the cattle and sheep. Numbers of the *Trekkers*' Khoisan servant began to abscond in fear both of illness and of Dingane's wrath, taking guns, horses, and stores away with them.[8]

Although we cannot be certain for lack of evidence that it was so, it could not have been lost on Dingane and his advisors that the invaders were in a difficult logistical plight and that their morale was faltering. The king's *izimpi* had won three battles in the open field against them and their Port Natal allies, and although the *amaBunu* had not joined the 'English' residents of Port Natal in fleeing the Zulu kingdom, it must have seemed that only one last, determined push was required to dislodge them. Accordingly, in August 1838, Dingane ritually prepared his army for a fresh campaign. Under the command of Ndlela, about 10,000 of the older, more experienced *amabutho* left emGungundlovu on about 10 August,[9] crossed the Mzinyathi and marched towards the Bushmans River (which the amaZulu called the Mtshezi) and the Gatslaer. This was likely to be a hazardous operation because the amaZulu were taking the offensive against an enemy ensconced in their fortified laager rather than operating in the open field. There was little chance of catching them by surprise as they had the Boer encampments in February, although Ndlela calculated that, if he advanced rapidly enough, he still might do so.[10]

Precisely because the *Trekkers* were in great fear of being taken unawares again, the Gatslaer, along with the other main laagers, had been turned into a veritable fort. It was shaped in a

---

5 Leśniewski, *Zulu–Boer War*, p.185, argues that the site of the laager was on the opposite side of the river.
6 *Smit's Diary*, pp.123, 125: 27, 28, 29 July, 1 August 1838.
7 *Smit's Diary*, p.121: 9, 10 July 1938.
8 Walker, *Great Trek*, pp 174–6; Smail, *Land of the Zulu Kings*, pp.58, 78.
9 *JSA* 1, p.322: Lunguza, 15 March 1909.
10 For the battle of Veglaer, see *Smit's Diary*, pp.125–9: 8, 11, 13–17 August 1838; *Annals* 1, p.234: W.J. Pretorius; Chase, *Natal Papers*, Part II, pp.27–8; Nathan, *Voortrekkers*, pp.241–5; Walker, *Great Trek*, pp.176–9; Smail, *Land of the Zulu Kings*, p.64; Lugg, *Historic Natal*, p.69; Laband, *Historical Dictionary*, pp.297–8; Leśniewski, *Zulu–Boer War*, pp.183–93.

rough triangle because of the lie of the ridge where it was situated, and consisted of a double line of 290 wagons lashed together with thornbushes filling all the openings. A 3-inch calibre iron cannon on two wheels was sited at the north-western apex of the laager and was sufficiently light to be easily repositioned if required. Generally, there was a good field of fire from the laager, but dongas to the east and west offered good cover to those attacking it. To entrap an enemy attempting to cross the river at the *drift* across the river on the south-eastern side of the laager, the Boer had dug pits,[11] or *trous-de-loup* as they are called in the technical language of fortifications and siege-craft. On this account the amaZulu would name the coming encounter emaGebeni, the battle of the Place of the Game-Pits, since some of them tumbled in and were trapped like hunted buck.[12]

Boer patrols that had been out hunting returned to the Gatslaer on 8 and again on 11 August bringing no word of Zulu activity, even though Ndlela's *impi* would by then have been on the move. Unaware of the danger in which they stood, parties of Boers kept diligently at work on a defensive ditch six feet broad that they were digging around the camp to the depth of a man's height. Yet, even so, the approaching *impi* failed to catch the Gatslaer as unprepared as Ndlela had hope it would. Very early on the morning of 13 August several of Potgieter's Khoisan herdboys sighted armed Zulu scouts in the neighbourhood of the laager. Potgieter and de Lange immediately led out a mounted patrol to investigate. They had not ventured far when elements of the rapidly advancing Zulu *impi* came into view. The horsemen wheeled their horses about and galloped back to the laager to give warning that the enemy was upon them.

The *impi* came in sight of the laager at about 10:00 a.m., swarming down from the surrounding hills. Ndlela halted his *amabutho* well out of range of the laager and with professional deliberation deployed them in orderly fashion into their traditional chest and horns attacking formation. The Bushmans River was in flood, so while the left *uphondo* forded it at the drift where below the laager where the pits had been dug, the *isifuba* and right *uphondo* approached directly from the east. The right horn then swung around the northern side of the laager to threaten its western flank. Through these well-executed manoeuvres Ndlela had the laager entirely encircled and the defenders were cut off from any possibility of retreat. It took some time for Ndlela's *amabutho* all to be in position, so it was not until noon that he launched them into the attack. They came on in waves, probing first one point of the laager's defences then another, never bunching for fear of the musket- and cannon-fire and doing their best for the most part to keep out of range. As soon as those in the front rank became exhausted and took too many casualties, they fell back to the rear and the next line of *amabutho* replaced them in the assault.

The defenders in the laager realised to their consternation that many of the *amabutho* in the foremost ranks were wearing identifiable items of clothing looted from their companions killed in earlier engagements. They understood only too well that these tattered trophies not only celebrated past Zulu victories, but served as a warning for what lay in store for them should they be defeated. Nor were these flaunted scraps the only tokens of previous encounters between the amaZulu and their white enemies. Boer eyewitness noted that about 100 of the attacking *amabutho* carried muskets they had acquired either through trade or had captured in previous battles against the *Trekkers* and Port Natal settlers. Throughout the battle, they kept up a

---

11 A pit is a *gat* in Afrikaans, hence the name of the laager, Gatslaer
12 *JSA* 5, p.86: Ngidi, 23 October 1905; *JSA* 1, p.77: Christian Cane, 3 October 1907. In isiZulu, an *igebe* (pl. *amagebe*) is a game-pit.

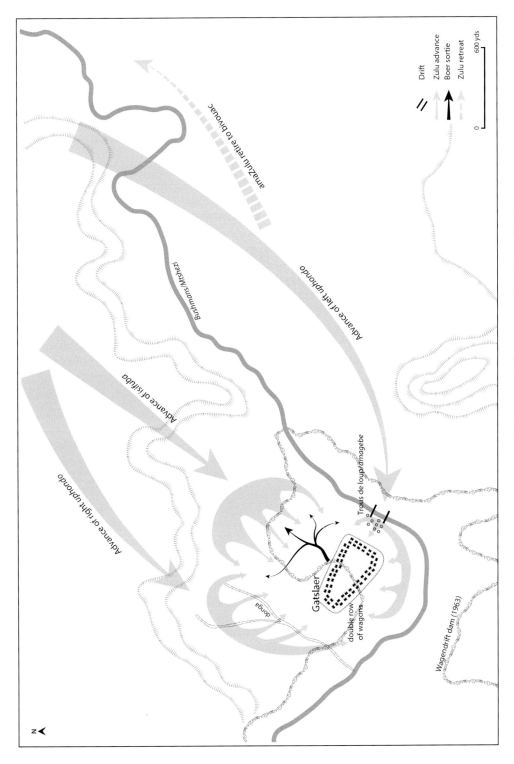

Battle of Veglaer or emaGebeni, 13–15 August 1838: First Day of Battle

constant, but erratic fire. Fortunately for the Boers, most amaZulu so lacked proper training in the use of their new weapons that they haphazardly fired them while still well out of range and neglected to aim, with the result that they failed to hit a single one of the defenders. Numbers of the amaZulu were seen to be mounted on horses they had captured from the Boers, but they played no appreciable part in the battle.

Inside the beleaguered Gatslaer, conditions for the defenders were demanding. As at the earlier battle of Vegkop in 1836 against the amaNdebele, the large number of anxious women and children, many of them the widows and orphans of the war against Dingane, took cover in a spear-proof shelter in the middle of the lager constructed of wagons roofed over with boards. And, once again as at the battle of Vegkop, some of the more intrepid women stayed out in the open to distribute powder and bullets to the men defending the laager. Numbering only 75, the men were too few in number to man the entire perimeter of the large laager, and had repeatedly to move position to reinforce different sectors as they came under Zulu attack. There was rain in the air and the gunpowder was damper than was desirable, but the men, firing and loading in rotation as at Vegkop, nevertheless kept up a constant, impenetrable wall of fire. When the amaZulu ventured into close range they fired the deadly *lopers* that spayed out shot among the attackers, and the over-worked cannon spewed out charges of scrap-iron and pot-legs packed into canvas bags like large *lopers*. So, although the *amabutho* continued to manoeuvre, they could find no vulnerable spot in the laager's defences.

After an hour, at about 1:00 p.m., the amaZulu became discouraged by the Boers' persistent and telling fire, and their attack began to falter. De Lange had brought all the horses inside the laager before the amaZulu had surrounded it, and he decided this was the moment to mount them and make a sudden sally. The amaZulu were surprised and fell back, but they were not sufficiently daunted to give up the fight and withdraw altogether. So Ndlela merely pulled his men out of range of fire from the laager and slowly withdrew north-east to a shallow, open valley downstream the Bushmans River. There the *impi* intended to bivouac for the night. Meanwhile, in another reprise of the Vegkop battle, Ndlela sent out parties to round up livestock that the *Trekkers* had been compelled to leave grazing in the veld outside the laager. That evening the amaZulu made a great feast of some of the cattle and sheep they had captured, not simply to satisfy their hunger, but to taunt the Boers with their loss.[13] The restless activity in the Zulu bivouac convinced the Boers that they intended a night attack. They therefore stood to arms throughout the hours of darkness, the wagons and the ground in front of them lit up by lanterns bound to whipstocks set up all around the laager, and by the blazing Zulu camp fires.

Early on the following morning, 14 August, De Lange led out a mounted sortie to provoke the Zulu *impi* in its bivouac into making another attack on the laager. Having roused the amaZulu, De Langer conducted a fighting withdrawal, drawing the *impi* into the laager's zone of fire. This time Ndlela changed his tactics, and commanded his *amabutho* to set the wagons on fire with burning grass plaited around their *izijula*. But to cast a spear into the wagons required the *amabutho* to approach within short range of their defenders, and under the unremitting fusillade the amaZulu were driven back without achieving their objective. While some of the *amabutho* were making their futile repeated attempt to burn the wagons and break through the

---

13 Erasmus Smit was most distressed that the amaZulu 'cruelly left [the cattle and sheep] lying on the ground half dead and half alive, cutting off a piece here and a piece there, which[sic] stock bellowed and bleated' (*Smit's Diary*, p.126: 13 August 1838).

laager's impregnable defences, others (as at Vegkop) were engaged in rounding up the rest of the emigrants' livestock. Towards evening, the main body of the amaZulu finally gave up their assault on the laager and withdrew to their bivouac. However, those who had been securing the Boers' livestock drove their booty east over the hills towards the heart of the Zulu kingdom, and to deter the *Trekkers* from sallying out in pursuit, set the long grass behind them on fire.

On the third day of the battle, 15 August, Boer reinforcements of about 60 men came up from Maritz's Sooilaer where they had learned of the Zulu attack the previous afternoon. This was enough for Ndlela, and without attacking the laager yet again he gave up the enterprise. Before withdrawing, the *amabutho* performed a defiant war-song. As they made off, they were harried by De Lange who rode out with his mounted men in pursuit. But the Boers' horses were so weak from being kept inside the laager without fodder for three days that the chase could not be kept up for long. Besides, De Lange did not wish to risk his small force in a direct encounter with the Zulu army. His men did manage, though, to scour the veld nearby the laager and kill all the Zulu wounded they came across.[14] And even though they had lost their livestock, the Boers had successfully fought off a major Zulu offensive and won their first victory against Dingane. Very conscious of their achievement, that evening all the Boer men, women, and children in the Gatslaer gathered for an hour to give humble thanks to God for their deliverance.

The battle of Veglaer (Fighting Laager), as the Boers termed it, has generated a scantier body of evidence than the other battles of the Voortrekker-Zulu War, and perhaps for this reason historians have accorded it less attention. They are wrong to brush past it, however, because it marked the turning-point of the conflict. Whereas forays in the open field by the *Vlugkommando* and the Grand Army of Natal had been spectacular failures, the battle of Veglaer re-affirmed that the wagon-laager with its all-round defence was the key to military success against the amaZulu, precisely as it had been against the amaNdebele in 1836. The next time a *kommando* moved forward on the offensive, it would do so only with enough wagons to form a defensive laager as its mobile base.

The lessons the amaZulu drew from the battle were by contrast essentially negative. Over two days of intense fighting they had killed precisely one Boer: Hans Froneman, who, even before the amaZulu began their assault on the laager, was caught outside while tending his sheep and speared to death in the pool where he was trying to hide. An old slave woman out gathering firewood also perished in like circumstances. Zulu casualties, by contrast, were heavy, even if we have no accurate tally of the number cut down by the Boers' deadly fire. For five days after the battle the Boers were kept busy dragging away about 200 Zulu corpses with the help of oxen and tumbling them into a nearby ravine. Doubtless, many other amaZulu would have succumbed to their gunshot wounds on the march home, or have died soon after. That the *impi* had succeeded in driving off so many of the Boers' livestock was no compensation for failing to overrun the laager. The amaNdebele had done likewise at Vegkop, yet in only a short while the Boers had

---

14 The Boers did bring one of the wounded amaZulu back into the camp for interrogation. Over the next 15 days the prisoner, who had been shot through the tibia, answered the questions put to him without dissimulation. But once it was found that he had earlier taken part in the Bloukrans massacre, his captors sentenced him to death for what they regarded as his war crimes, even if he never accepted that what he had done was wrong in terms of Zulu military practice. It fell to Erasmus Smit to attempt to convert him to Christianity before his execution. See *Smit's Diary*, pp.128, 133–5: 15, 16, 31 August 1838.

recovered sufficiently to mount their series of devastating counter-attacks. Crucially, the failure of Ndlela's large *impi* of his most experienced *amabutho* to come even close to breaching the Gatslaer left him and the other Zulu commanders baffled as how to proceed in the future. Another assault against one of the *Trekkers'* fortified laagers was clearly out of the question, so they could do no more than wait to see what move the *Trekkers* would make next, and to hope that they would once again be able to catch them in the open field as they had at eThaleni.

Despite their victory at Veglaer, there was no disguising that the *Trekker* parties were in poor shape and their morale low. The defenders of the Gatslaer were too afraid at first of being caught in the open by the amaZulu to move away from the scene of carnage and the stench of the Zulu dead. They also needed the loan of draught-oxen from the other laagers to draw their wagons. But they eventually trekked away to establish their new laager across the Little Thukela from Maritz's Sooilaer. The Emigrants Farmers, still short of food and crowded in their insalubrious fortified laagers, were dealt another blow when on 23 September Gert Maritz, who had long been ailing from heart disease, died at the early age of 41. Now, of all the principal Natal leaders, only Karel Landman, the Chief Commandant, was left. In their plight, the *Trekkers* turned to Andries Pretorius, whom a deputation approached for help in August 1838.[15]

The 40-year-old Pretorius haled from the Graaff-Reinet District where he was a prosperous townsman and owned several farms in the vicinity. Tall and handsome, with an upright and captivating personality although quick to anger and prone to conceit, he was of the fifth generation of a family of early Dutch settlers at the Cape. Details of his early life are lacking, but he was sufficiently schooled by itinerant teachers to be able to read the Bible and to express himself on paper. He early took an interest in the trekking movement, and in late 1837 made a reconnaissance of the regions traversed by the *Trekkers*, and took part in the fighting against the amaNdebele. He then returned home and organised a *trek* of his friends and relations. His party was on the highveld near the Modder River when the deputation from the Natal laagers set about persuading him to hurry over the Drakensberg with a *kommando* ahead of his wagons and non-combatants.[16]

On 22 November 1838, Andries Pretorius rode into the Sooilaer on the Little Thukela with 60 mounted men and a small ship's bronze cannon. Armed with a musket, a brace of pistols and a heavy naval cutlass, he reminded Erasmus Smit of nothing so much as a 'well equipped dragoon.'[17] He was joyfully received by the Natal *Trekkers* and on 26 November they elected him their Chief Commander. Adept as he was at irregular frontier warfare and proven as a prudent if personally gallant commander, Pretorius immediately began to form a *kommando* to take the war to Dingane. Ahead of Pretorius taking the field, J. Stephanus Maritz, the dead Gerrit's brother, was appointed to command the laagers in his absence. He was ordered to ensure that at every sundown the cattle would be driven into the wagon enclosures and that night patrols would be sent out to guard against a surprise Zulu attack.[18]

There was much need for Pretorius's military preparations to be made in haste, not only to forestall another Zulu strike, but because of likely British intervention. To their chagrin, the *Trekkers* were beginning to grasp that they were still within reach of the hated colonial

---

15 *Smit's Diary*, pp.138–9: 23 September 1838; Walker, *Great Trek*, pp.178–9.
16 Laband, *Historical Dictionary*, pp.220–1.
17 *Smit's Diary*, pp.147–8: 22 November 1838.
18 Walker, *Great Trek*, pp.180, 184; Laband, *Zulu Nation*, p.97.

government from which they believed they had escaped, and that the British would attempt to prevent them from dealing with Dingane as they thought fit.

Since 23 January 1838 there had been a new Governor at the Cape where Major General Sir George Napier had succeeded Sir Benjamin D'Urban. Like his predecessor, Napier was a veteran of the Peninsular War and had lost his right arm in battle. His overriding concern and that of his officials was the security of the volatile Cape Eastern Frontier, and he was especially concerned that once the *Trekkers* had secured a firm foothold in Natal that they would 'embroil themselves with the natives' and destabilise the Cape's hinterland.[19] Lord Glenelg, the Secretary for War and the Colonies, agreed with him that it would be 'expedient' to despatch a 'small body of Troops' to Port Natal to deter the *Trekkers*. However, he added the proviso that it must be on the understanding that such action did not imply the British government's intention to occupy the place permanently, something to which (as we have seen) he had been steadfastly opposed.[20]

There matters had rested while Napier digested the news of the escalating fighting between the Boers and the amaZulu, and learned that Landman had taken possession of Port Natal for the Emigrants and their nascent independent republic. The Governor consequently resolved that it had become imperative to occupy Port Natal since it was the only seaport through which the 'warlike stores' necessary for pursuing the conflict against Dingane could reach the Boers.[21] Accordingly, on 14 November (at the very moment Andries Pretorius was making his way over the Drakensberg to the Sooilaer) Napier issued a proclamation giving notice that is was his intention to seize Port Natal and to build a fort there. However, in accordance with Glenelg's injunction, he stated unequivocally that the military occupation would be only 'of a temporary nature', and that it was not intended to annex Port Natal as a British colony or colonial dependency.[22]

Between 3 and 4 December 1838 a British force of 114 men under Major Samuel Charters (who was Napier's Military Secretary), made up of 12 officers and men of the Royal Artillery with two 9-pounder guns, 95 officers and men of 72nd (Duke of Albany's Own Highlanders) Regiment of Foot and sundry other personnel, landed at Port Natal through very rough seas. All stores were ashore by 12 December.[23] Charters' orders were to build Fort Victoria on the Point commanding the harbour and not to fire on the Boers except to repel an attack. He was also to maintain peace 'with the native tribes.'[24] On 4 December Charters duly proclaimed the 'military possession' of Port Natal, a territory defined by a boundary two miles inland around the bay, and put it under martial law.[25]

---

19 *RN 3*, p.266: no. 132: Lt. Gov. Sir A. Stockenstrom to Maj. Gen. Sir G. Napier, 12 March 1838; pp. 293–4, no. 154: Napier to Glenelg, 18 May 1838.
20 *RN 3*, p.303, no. 161: Glenelg to Napier, 8 June 1838.
21 *RN 4*, pp.46–9: no. 38: Napier to Glenelg, 16 October 1838.
22 *RN 4*, pp.97–8, no. 69, annex. 5: Proclamation by Napier, 14 November 1838.
23 *RN 4*, pp.80–2, no. 69, annex. 1: Return of troops detached for Natal and general orders, 14 November 1838; pp.126–8, no. 86, annex. 1: Maj. Charters to Napier, 12 December 1838.
24 *RN 4*, pp.96–7, no. 69, annex. 4: Military Instructions for Major Charters from Napier, 16 November 1838; pp 94–6: no. 69, annex. 3: Instructions to the Officer in Command of For Victoria in the Harbour of Port Natal from Napier, 18 November 1838.
25 *RN 4*, p.168: no. 101, annex. 2, enc. 8: Proclamation by Charters, 4 December 1838.

But Charters had landed his troops too late to prevent the *Trekkers*, whom he estimated had 800 effective fighting men in their various laagers,[26] from attacking Dingane as planned. Pretorius's *kommando* was already on the move, and on 3 December, Karel Landman had joined him with a contingent of 123 Boers from the environs of Port Natal, supported by 60 or so black levies led by Alexander Biggar (who was burning to revenge the death of his son Robert at the battle of the Thukela). Robert Joyce, who had survived the battle of the Thukela, and Edward Parker accompanied Biggar and served as intelligence officers with Pretorius. On 6 December Charters sent a stiff message to Pretorius informing him that 'having learned that a strong *kommando* of the emigrant farmers had marched under your orders for the purpose of attacking the Zulu chief Dingaan in his own kraal,' that it was his duty in terms of his commission to 'require of you to desist from all offensive measures against the Zulu chief, or any of the native tribes of these regions.'[27] The letter never reached Pretorius but was diverted to the Sooilaer where on 12 December Stephanus Maritz and two of his associates, on behalf of the *Volksraad* of Republiek Natalia, penned Charters an emollient response. 'It has been our wish from the beginning until this moment to live upon good terms with the [British] government,' they declared, 'as well as with our countrymen in the [Cape] colony.'[28] Such sentiment might have been well and good as far as relations with Charters and his troops at Port Natal were concerned, but did not address the critical issue of Pretorius' *kommando* even then approaching emGungundlovu. Indeed, events were taking their course and were out of Charters' hands. Consequently, when on 16 December the British garrison at Port Natal ceremonially hoisted the Union Flag 'under a royal salute and a *feu de joie*,'[29] they were unaware that on the very same day Pretorius had won a great victory over the amaZulu at the Ncome River.

---

26 *RN 4*, p.130 no. 86, annex. 2: Charters to Napier, 12 December 1838.
27 *RN 4*, p.131: no. 86, annex. 2, enc. 1: Charters to Andries Pretorius, 6 December 1838.
28 *RN 4*, p.162: no. 101, annex 2, enc. 1: J.S. Maritz, L.J. Meyer and P.H. Opperman to Charters, 12 December 1838.
29 *RN 4*, p.161, no. 101, annex 2: Charters to Napier, 5 January 1839.

23

At the Ncome We Turned Our Backs

The battle of Blood River, or Ncome, is like no other engagement of the war, not only on account of the significance placed on it at the time by the victorious *Trekkers* and by many Afrikaners since then, but because it has engendered such an extensive but divisive historiography. Interpretations have fluctuated from its being hailed as the triumph of Christianity over barbarism and the justification for specifically Afrikaner rule over Africans, to its being embraced as a symbolic event in the African liberation struggle. Both Afrikaner and Zulu nationalists have taken up the battle as a rallying-cry. The author remembers a seminar at the University of Zululand on 31 October 1998 when he was unequivocally informed from the floor that—despite all the evidence to the contrary—the amaZulu could not have lost the battle since they were an indomitable 'warrior nation'. As discussed in the Preface, in 1998 the post-apartheid South African government appointed a committee of six academics to formulate an interpretation of the battle that fostered understanding and national reconciliation in the 'new' South Africa. As it turned out, Zulu government officials and academics dominated the committee, and the report that emerged was noticeably Zulu-centric. Contemporary professional historians, however, continue to investigate the battle as they would any other military encounter, and attempt to present findings based on the available evidence in as balanced a manner as possible.[1]

The *kommando* under Pretorius's command, soon to be known as the *Wenkommando* (the Victorious Commando), began assembling at Skiet Drift on the Thukela on 28 November 1838. There it waited for all the contingents to come in from the various laagers, daily listening to inspiring sermons. Finally, on 3 December, when Karel Landman's force, which had been detained by rains, arrived from Port Natal, the *Wenkommando* began its march.[2] In planning

---

1   Jabulani Sithole, 'Changing Images of the Battle of Blood River/iNcome', in DACST, *Blood River/Ncome*, pp. 29–42; Jabulani Sithole, 'Changing Meanings of the Battle of Ncome and Images of King Dingane in Twentieth-Century South Africa', in Carton, Laband and Sithole (eds), *Zulu Identities*, pp.322–8; Dlamini, 'Monuments of Division', pp.388–91; Jackie Grobler, 'Afrikaner- en Zoeloeperspektiewe op die Slag van Bloedrivier, 16 Desember 1838', *Tydskrif vir Geesteswetenskappe*, 50, 3 (September 2010), pp.377–80.
2   *Smit's Diary*, pp.148–50: 28 November–3 December 1838. For the Blood River campaign, see *Annals* I, pp. 234–5: Narrative of Willem Jurgen Pretorius; pp. 243–7: Journal of the Late Charl Celliers; pp. 374–5: Bezuidenhout's narrative; pp. 438–50: J.G. Bantjes, Journal of the Expedition against Dingaan; pp. 453–6: Despatches of Commandant A.W.J. Pretorius, 22 December 1838 and 9 January 1839; *JSA* 1, pp.312–13, 320: Lunguza, 14 March 1909; *JSA* 5, pp.71, 72, 77, 94: Ngidi, 9 November 1904,

his counter-attack against the amaZulu, Pretorius took full account of the lessons to be learned from the disaster at eThaleni and the victory at Veglaer. Clearly, to seek out Dingane on his own ground with only a mounted force, such as had the doomed *Vlugkommando*, was out of the question. Instead, Pretorius resolved that his *kommando* would be accompanied by 64 wagons They were to be only lightly loaded with ammunition and supplies so that they could be rapidly drawn up into the infallible defensive formation of a laager. During the coming campaign, the *kommando's* horsemen would be employed for scouting, to defend the laager on foot when the amaZulu attacked, and to follow up any victory with a mounted pursuit.

Pretorius planned the punitive expedition with exemplary thoroughness. He first set about inculcating a sense of obedience and alertness among the undisciplined and disheartened *burgers* he commanded and punished any act of insubordination. He established a coherent chain of command and kept his officers fully informed of his plans. While on the march, scouting parties were unfailingly sent forward, a wagon laager was formed every evening when the *kommando* halted, and sentries were always posted. Above all, Pretorius succeeded in inspiring his men and encouraged them to believe that they were the chosen servants of the Lord in a just and holy cause. Religious services were held every morning and evening to hammer home this exhilarating message.

The related notion of a covenant vow to be taken by the members of the *kommando* to strengthen them spiritually originated with Pretorius and with Sarel Celliers, a veteran of the battle of Vegkop who was acting as chaplain to the *kommando*. In Calvinist theology, a covenant with God has Biblical precedent, and is a community's reciprocal contract with the deity, a binding promise to God to undertake specific commitments in return for divine favour, in this case, victory over the amaZulu. The covenant was made on 9 December at Danskraal on the banks of the Wasbankspruit near modern-day Ladysmith, and was subsequently repeated every evening during the march. J.G. Bantjes, who was acting as Pretorius's secretary during the expedition, recorded that Pretorius requested his followers 'to pray to God for His relief and assistance in their struggle with the enemy: that he wanted to make a vow to God Almighty ... that should the Lord be pleased to grant us the victory, we would raise a house to the memory of His great name.' Pretorius added that should the Deity oblige, he wished the day to be made known to their posterity, so that 'it might be celebrated to the honour of God.'[3]

18 and 30 October 1905; *JSA* 6, p.268: Tununu, 1 June 1903; Delegorgue, *Travels, Volume One*, pp. 109–10; *Travels, Volume Two*, pp. 70–2; Nathan, *Voortrekkers*, pp. 252–60; George Chadwick, 'The Battle of Blood River', *Military History Society Battlefield Tour Notes* (May 1878), <samilitaryhistory.org/misc/bldrvr.html>, accessed 1 November 2020; Grobler, 'Bloedrivier', 367–76; and, most recently, Leśniewski, *Zulu–Boer War*, pp.211–33.

3   *Annals* 1, p.445: Bantje's Journal of the Expedition. In his old age, Celliers recorded a fuller version of the Vow 'as nearly' as he could remember it, adding that the participants had sworn to observe the day of victory 'as an anniversary in each year' and to keep it as a day of thanksgiving, like the Sabbath. See *Annals* 1, pp.244–5: Journal of the Late Charl Celliers. See Rankin and Schneider, *Memory to Marble. Part II*, pp. 425–33 for an exhaustive discussion about the Vow. The Church of the Vow was subsequently built in the *Trekker* town of Pietermaritzburg between 1840 and 1843. After 1861, when a new church was built, the building underwent a variety of uses until it was restored in 1910 and declared a national monument in 1938. In 1912 it was incorporated into the Voortrekker Museum Complex, now part of the uMsunduzi Museum. For a succinct account, see J. Andre Labuschange, 'The Church of the Vow', in Laband and Haswell (eds), *Pietermaritzburg*, p.28; for a full exposition, see Rankin and Schneider, *Memory to Marble. Part II*, pp. 473–501.

The *Wenkommando* advanced north-east from the Skiet Drift by way of what are now the towns of Winterton, Ladysmith, and Dundee. It was the season of summer rains and thunderstorms, and the rivers were full. The *kommando* forded the Mzinyathi River on 12 December and reached the west, or right bank, of the Ncome River on 15 December. Pretorius's patrols had first made contact with Zulu scouts on 11 December, and between that date and the morning of 15 December succeeded in intercepting and killing 32 'spies.' Weeks before 11 December, though, Dingane's intelligence network would have informed him of the military preparations Pretorius was making, and left him and his advisors in no doubt as to the gravity of the threat building up against them. To oppose it, it was necessary to draw on every possible military resource, and the king mobilised his army from every quarter of the kingdom. As Tununu, Dingane's *inceku* who was to fight at Blood River, emotionally expressed it many years later, 'A great campaign was on and therefore the flower of the nation went forth to fight.' [4]

Not all the gathering *amabutho* were earmarked to go against the *Wenkommando*, however. Fearing that the English settlers might advance from Port Natal in its support, just as they had during the April campaign, men from some of the older, less 'crack' *amabutho* were despatched 'to block the way down-country.' [5] Even so, in all likelihood no other *impi* mobilised to face the Boer invaders was as large as this one. Its actual strength is unknown, and estimates made by the Boers fighting it were inevitably inflated. Probably, its size stood somewhere between 10,000 at the least and 15,000 at the very most. It was an indication of the seriousness of the situation that Dingane entrusted the command to both Ndlela and Nzobo. Once the assembled *amabutho* had been ritually prepared for war, the *impi* marched out on about 12 December to confront the *kommando* before it had penetrated too close to the heart of the kingdom and emGungundlovu itself. By the afternoon of 14 December, after three easy stages of march, it bivouacked in two rocky ravines under Mkhonjane Mountain, 10 miles south-east of the future battlefield, and halfway between it and what is now the notoriously tatty village of Nquthu.

Throughout its advance, the *Wenkommando* had sent out patrols far ahead, and on 14 December they made contact with large Zulu scouting parties that indicated that the Zulu army was close. On 15 December, while the *kommando's* wagons congregated on the west bank of the Ncome and some (it seems) began crossing the river, the highly experienced De Lange led a reconnaissance south-eastward towards Mkhonjane Mountain. There he located the Zulu *impi* and rode close enough to identify some of the *amabutho* that made it up. He hastily reported back, and Pretorius (or Potolozi, as the Zulu called him) went forward himself with about 200 mounted men to assess the situation. Despite the urging of some of the more hot-headed among his *kommandants*, he refused to attack that day. It was already late afternoon, the countryside was broken and unfamiliar, and the fate of the *Vlugkommando* was doubtless in Pretorius's mind. He therefore decided to stick to the tactics he had planned, that is, to avoid a battle in the open, and prepare his laager to repel a Zulu assault.

While Pretorius was out on patrol, 'Rooi' ('Red') Piet Moolman formed up the 64 wagons on a gently sloping, boulder-free spit of land near the west bank of the Ncome. Its shape has ever since been a matter of controversy with all sorts of configurations suggested. The sources would

---

4   *JSA* 6, p.268: Tununu, 1 June 1903.
5   *JSA* 5, p.72: Ngidi, 9 November 1904.

seem to indicate, however, that it was rough oval with a more flattened side on its south flank, and that it had a circumference of just over 400 yards and a diameter of 70 yards.

Just to its south, about 50 yards away and out of range of cast spears, the laager was protected by a deep donga that ran into the Ncome with banks some four yards high. The eastern side of the laager facing the Ncome about 100 yards away was even more secure. The muddy banks of the river were thickly covered with reeds, and 400 yards upstream it broadened out to form a large marsh studded with several pools. Downstream, north of the confluence of the river and the donga, was a long pool, or *seekoeigat*, deeper than the Boers could sound with a whipstock.[6] The river was high (it had rained again on 12 December and on the following day), but it was possible to cross it at an easily defensible *drift* between the *seekoeigat* and the marsh. About 650 yards downstream, south beyond the confluence of the river and the donga, and much more difficult to command from the laager, was another, frequently-used *drift*. Across the Ncome, a level plain, interspersed by reed-choked shallow pools, stretched east-south-east as far as a low rocky ridge, known as the Shogane, some 2,000 yards away.

Sarel Celliers later insisted that the ideal positioning of the laager was entirely thanks to 'God's mercy'.[7] And certainly, because of the donga and the river, the laager could be attacked only on two sides, from the north and west, and that allowed the defenders to concentrate their forces in those two sectors. Normally, as at the battles of Vegkop and Veglaer, branches from thorn trees would have closed the gaps between and under the wagons. However, since Pretorius knew that he would be advancing though treeless, open grassland, with his habitual foresight he had had hurdles—portable panels of stakes and withes used for enclosing livestock some three yards long and one-and-a-half yards high—prepared to replace the thorn bushes. The *kommando* referred to them as *veghekke*, or 'fighting gates', and supplemented them ox-skins to stretch over the spokes of the wagon-wheels. The laager had its main entrance, from which a mounted sortie could be made, facing north across the plain. It is possible that there were several other, narrower ones too. Since he anticipated a dawn attack, Pretorius had lanterns burning thick dim candles suspended from whipstocks placed at the front and rear of each wagon, rather as they had been at Veglaer, so that their light would make it easier to load muskets and illuminate (albeit very faintly) any enemy approaching close.

The *kommando* defending the laager was made up of Pretorius in command, his deputy, Karel Landman who had brought in the Port Natal Contingent, six *kommandants* (including Hans Dons de Lange and Koos Potgieter), 464 Boers and three Port Natal settlers. Alexander Biggar commanded about 60 black levies from Port Natal. As trained hunters, they too were armed with muskets (including elephant guns) and doubtless played their part in defending the laager, even if (as was typical) they were largely excluded from the narrative. Besides these combatants, the laager was crammed with animals. After the heavy stock losses at Vegkop and Veglaer they could hardly be left outside the laager to be driven off by the amaZulu. But the great number of animals, probably about 650 draught-oxen and some 750 horses—as was the norm, most of the mounted *burgers* would have had two horses each on *kommando*—constituted a threat in itself. If unattended, they would have likely stampeded during the fighting and dangerously dislocate the defence. This is where the other inhabitants of the laager came into play, men who, along

---

6   A *seekoeigat* (literally a hippopotamus hole) is a deep pool in a river.
7   *Annals* 1, p.245: Journal of the Late Charl Celliers.

with the Port Natal contingent, have been left all but invisible in the story. It seems that the 130 or so black wagon drivers and leaders tied their teams of oxen forehead to forehead, pegged them to the ground with *rieme* and talked soothingly to them throughout the battle. Likewise, the approximately 100 *agterryers* who had ridden with the *kommando* held their master's terrified horses in clusters of four until they were required for a sortie or for the pursuit. They doubtless also assisted in bringing up ammunition, with loading muskets, and a few probably joined the firing line. Thus, although this is all too often not noted, there were about 300 blacks in the laager alongside the 475 whites.

The defenders all knew what station they had to take up in the coming battle. There was a gap of about two yards between each of the wagons drawn up into the laager, and about eight men were to be positioned kneeling or standing in every one of these openings, firing in ordered rotation to keep up a constant and uninterrupted volume of fire. Pretorius had supplied them with *lopers* to meet the amaZulu approaching to within 40 yards or so with a lethal burst of buckshot, just as had the defenders had at Vegkop and Veglaer. There had been one small muzzle-loading cannon at Veglaer; it seems Pretorius certainly had two cannons, and some sources suggest a third as well. The ship's gun he had brought with him from the Cape had a range of several thousand yards with solid shot, and it seems it was positioned facing the river. The range of the other cannon(s) was only about 300 yards. They fired grapeshot (roundshot packed into canvas bags like large *lopers*) or, instead of roundshot, small projectiles such as stones and metal pot legs. One cannon was certainly positioned at the north-western side of the laager, and the other (if it indeed was present) was placed at the vulnerable entrance to the laager. All the cannons were mounted on wheeled carriages and could be swiftly repositioned if necessary.

Once they had finished forming their laager during the late afternoon of 15 December, and the patrols had all been called in by a cannon shot, the members of the *kommando* attended evening service as usual and renewed their Vow. The lanterns were then lit against a surprise night attack, the *veghekke* placed in position, the entrances closed and the guards posted. The interminable night was misty and very dark for it was the last phase of the waning crescent moon. Zulu advance-parties heard singing coming from the laager across the river as the defenders raised their voices in outlandish, doleful harmony, calling in unison on God, in the words of the 38th Psalm, not to forsake them in the face of their enemies. To add to the eeriness of the moment, it is said that the amaZulu surveyed the distant circle of flickering, swaying lights on the wagons with dread and foreboding, convinced that they were being called upon to attack an unearthly army of evil spirits.

Well before dawn on the morning of Sunday, 16 December, Ndlela and Nzobo roused their army from their bivouac south-east of the laager and sent it forward to the attack. It was not as if they did not know what had befallen the *impi* that had tried in vain to capture the Gatslaer, and they had every reason to doubt the outcome of a direct assault on Potolozi's laager. Yet what alternative was there? Their orders were to repel the Boer *kommando's* advance, and it was obvious that Potolozi was not going to allow it to be ambushed and caught in the open like the *Vlugkommando*. All Ndlela and Nzobo could hope for was that courage, perseverance and superiority of numbers—somewhere about 20:1—would even yet win the day if they succeeded in surrounding the laager and attacking it from all sides at once. In anticipation of victory, the

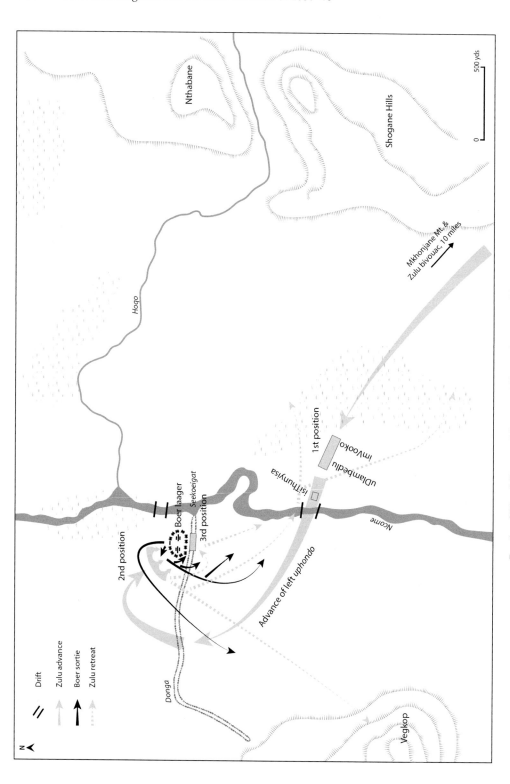

imVoko and iziNyosi *amabutho* were assigned to carry off the captured wagons and draught-oxen 'and to use the waggons' irons to make hoes with.'[8]

To the defenders of the laager, there would appear throughout the day of battle to be some disorder among the *amabutho* as they deployed. Doubtless Ndlela and Nzobo would have found it difficult to maintain even a modicum of control over the army as it moved into the attack. For one thing, it was larger than usual. Much had to be left to the initiative of *izinduna* further down the chain of command who necessarily made snap decisions of their own to respond to challenges in their part of the battlefield. Moreover, the *amabutho* were always in reckless competition with each other to achieve glory, and younger *amabutho* were in any case less amenable to discipline than older, more experienced ones. Consequently, once their army was committed to battle, Ndlela and Nzobo knew it was unrealistic to suppose it would adhere strictly to any plan they had devised. What was critical, though, was how far it would diverge from it, and so jeopardise the entire enterprise.

The Zulu left *uphondo* led the attack. In the forefront were the isiThunyisa, a small unit of men mounted on horses and carrying the firearms they had been trained in using for hunting, or had looted from the battlefields of eThaleni and the Thukela. The officials at the Cape learned that there were about 200 of them,[9] but it seems that 'their ill-aimed shots produced no visible effect.'[10] The left *uphondo* advanced far more rapidly than the *isifuba* and the right *uphondo* leaving them far to its rear. This disjuncture might have been deliberate, for it was usual for one horn of a Zulu army, normally made of young *amabutho* who were fleet of foot, to be rapidly thrown out to surround the enemy so as to cut off any prospect of their retreat while the rest of the army moved up and engaged. And certainly, at the Ncome the left horn was made up of some younger *amabutho*, the unmarried uDlambedlu and elements of the large, composite *ibutho*, the imVoko (or imVokwe), most notably the recently formed imHaye. However, it is more probable that the over-eager and headstrong left *uphondo* surged ahead of the rest of army, disregarding and disrupting Ndlela's and Nzobo's plans for a more co-ordinated attack.

It was still before the break of day when the 3,000 or so young warriors of the left horn stealthily crossed the river at the *drift* about 650 yards south of the laager and, keeping well out of range of effective musket-fire, circled around it to the west. In the laager, where the men had been awakened two hours before daybreak, the experienced Port Natal contingent detected the sound of thousands of stealthily shuffling feet and gave warning of an imminent attack. Yet it did not immediately materialise. For when the Zulu left *uphondo* reached the open plain to the north-west of the laager, it quietly sat down some 175 yards away, neatly formed in a semi-circle about 100 yards deep, each *ibutho* ranged behind its *izinduna*, there to await the dawn.

When at about 6:30 a.m. the morning mist began to rise, the defenders inside the laager gained their first clear sight of the menacing Zulu presence. Understandably, fear washed over them. But before they could give way to it, the *amabutho* of the left horn suddenly sprang to their feet at some word of command. They rattled the hafts of their spears on their raised shields, whistled, shouted their war-cry and stormed the laager at a run. There was to be no probing and fencing out of range as at Veglaer. Clearly, Ndlela and Nzobo had instructed their *izinduna* to

---

8   *JSA* 5, p.72: Ngidi, 9 November 1904.
9   *RN* 4, p.141, no. 95: Cape of Good Hope Government Gazette, no. 1728, 1 February 1839.
10 Delegorgue, *Travels, Volume Two*, p.71.

make a direct assault on the laager. Casualties would inevitably be very heavy, but no alternative presented itself if they were to break through the ring of wagons.

The Zulu assault on the Boer laager at the battle of Blood River or Ncome. Anonymous engraving. (Campbell Collections, Durban, with permission)

Fortunately for the *Wenkommando*, that fatal day of the Sabbath broke 'clear and bright' without a wind – 'as if ordained for us' by God's favour, recorded Bantjes.[11] There was no rain in the air so that the defenders' powder remained dry, and the bright sunshine helped them find their marks accurately.[12] At short range, sometimes at no more than 10 paces, the *lopers* fired from their *voorlaiers*, augmented by the grapeshot from the cannons, did terrible execution among the amaZulu, gouging holes in their ranks that became ever more tightly packed as they converged on the laager. Because there was no wind, the north-western side of the laager was enveloped in dense white smoke from the exploding gunpower that rose up in the air 'straight as a plumb-line.' Apart from this phenomenon, nothing remained in Daniel Bezuidenhout's memory of this stage of the battle but 'shouting and tumult and lamentation, and a sea of black faces.'[13]

---

11 *Annals* 1, p.448: Bantje's Journal of the Expedition.
12 The Boers would have preferred not to have been forced to fight on the Sabbath, thus profaning a day when (according to their beliefs) blood should not have been spilt.
13 *Annals* I, p.375: Bezuidenhout's narrative.

Disregarding their appalling casualties, the gallant *amabutho* again and again tried to push home their assault, their *izinduna* encouraging them with the exhortation: 'Tshaka is among you; here is a small greenish snake!'[14] The defenders were compelled to fire so rapidly that they found they did not have the time to ram their lead bullets home down the barrels of the muskets and simply dropped them in slicked with saliva. At length, once the *amabutho* had realised that they could find no weak gap in the unremitting barrage of terrible fire, brave as they were, they would no longer obey the commanders' order to charge yet once more. Instead, they fell back out of range and, as had been the fruitless case at Veglaer, began manoeuvring to find a less well-defended sector of the laager. Many began to lose their nerve when they failed to do so and the deadly fire from the laager would not let up. As Ngidi, who fought as a member of the imVoko later expressed it, 'We Zulus die lying facing the enemy—all of us—but at the Ncome we turned our backs. This was caused by the Boers and their guns.'[15] Large numbers retired and took shelter in the deep *donga* south of the laager where they huddled too close together to be able to hurl their spear, while others, caught in the open, lay under their shields in the vain hope they would protect them. When Pretorius, with the experience of much *kommando* warfare behind him, saw the amaZulu bunched up in the *donga* and so obviously demoralised, he understood that was the moment to order out a mounted sally to disperse them.

Ngidi, who was 'running off with the others' escaped being shot by being caught up in the press of bodies.[16] Even so, until his dying day he bore the 'marks of ricochets or bits of bullets on the inner sides of his two thighs in front.'[17] He remembered that as the mounted Boers charged out at them, Nongqobo kaSenzangakhona of the iziNyosi, a member of the royal house and Dingane's half-brother, was shot through the side at the base of the stomach. Ngidi credited him, as he lay dying, with apostrophising his comrades with the elevated sentiments appropriate for true warrior: 'Take my greetings to my brother, and say my farewells to him. Why do you cry, Zulu people? It is well that we should die, we who are in the forefront. Do you think this is famine, famine which carries off common people?' Once he expired, he was borne off by some young warriors and buried in a donga.[18]

As Pretorius had anticipated, the *amabutho* were not disposed after their severe battering to stand up against a mounted charge. They broke and ran, hotly pursued by the mounted *burgers*. Some fled south-eastwards, back to the *drift* across the Ncome, while others broke off in the opposite direction and made for a saddle-shaped hill lying to the south-west of the laager (and later named Vegkop by the Boers) that offered the illusion of sanctuary. The Boers finally called off their pursuit at about 8:00 a.m. when Pretorius noticed that the rest of the Zulu army was beginning to advance. Hundreds of Zulu dead and pitifully groaning wounded lay scattered on the ground between the laager and the *drift*, and piled up in the donga.

Despite their crushing success against the Zulu left horn, the defenders of the laager were allowed scant respite before the right horn and chest joined the fray. The right *uphondo* was made up of the umKhulutshane and isiGulutsahne (that incorporated the recently formed iHlaba),

---

14 *SA* 5, p.72: Ngidi, 9 November 1904. The amaZulu believed that the *amadlozi* of their dead monarchs appeared in the form of a snake.
15 *JSA* 5, p.77: Ngidi, 18 October 1905.
16 *JSA* 5, p.71: Ngidi, 9 November 1904.
17 *JSA* 5, p.94: Ngidi, 30 October 1905.
18 *JSA* 5, p.72: Ngidi, 9 November 1904.

198 The Zulu Kingdom and the Boer Invasion of 1837-40

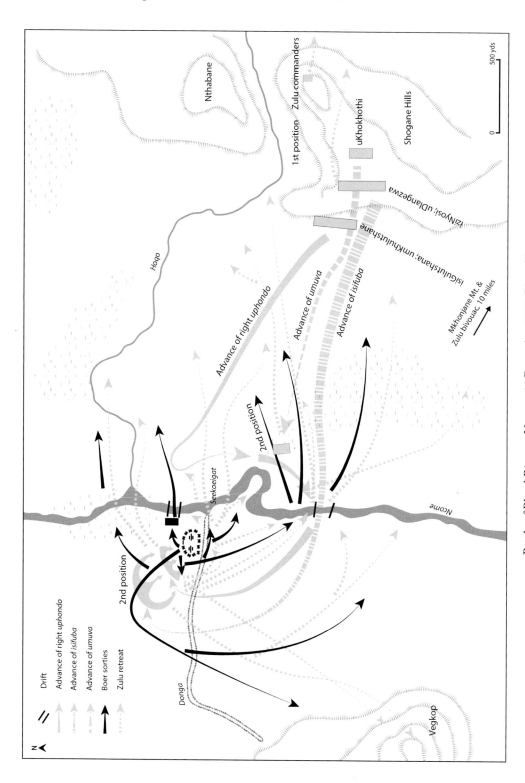

Battle of Blood River or Ncome, 16 December 1838: Phase Two

all of them part of the composite imVoko. As was customary, it streamed forward somewhat in advance of the *isifuba*, but not so out of touch with it as the left *uphondo* had been. The chest comprised two experienced, mature *amabutho*, the uDlangezwa and the iziNyosi. The uKhokhothi, a recently formed *ibutho* carrying only *amawisa*—knobbed sticks absolutely useless against gunfire, as one of its members wryly reflected—was kept back east of the Ncome in the traditional role of the *umuva*,[19] to be thrown in only if the attack was a success when they would take part in the pursuit and round up captured livestock. (All of the *amabutho* mentioned here had been formed in Dingane's reign, but the older ones *buthwa'd* by King Shaka are nowhere specifically mentioned as having taken part in the battle. But since Zulu mobilisation for this campaign had been so comprehensive, it is more than likely that elements of these older *amabutho* would have been present, either as part of the *isifuba* or *umuva*.)

Proceeding in the wake of the right *uphondo*, the *isifuba* and *umuva* had reached the Shogane, the low range of hills about a bit over a mile south-east of the laager east of the Ncome. There, while the right horn began its advance towards the laager, they formed up on the lower slopes. Ndlela, Nzobo, and their senior commanders took up position on a conical hill at the northern extremity of the range from where, as was the typical practice of Zulu generals, they could direct operations—or attempt to do so—through runners sent out to their subordinate officers. The right horn, meanwhile, continued its advance straight across the plain towards the laager and the *drift* between the *seekoeigat* and the marsh to its north. Until it approached close to the Ncome, it was protected by dead ground from fire directed from the laager. Realising that the Boer firing was being ineffective, Pretorius dispatched a party of horsemen (the second sortie of the day) to line the west bank of the river opposite the approaching Zulu right *uphondo*. From there they opened up a withering fire supported by the cannons and wrought havoc with the Zulu right horn. Meanwhile, well-directed fire from the ship's cannon found the Zulu commanders on their hilltop and a lucky shot compelled them to scatter for cover after sustaining several casualties.

Prevented from attacking the laager from the north-east by the Boer musketeers at the northern *drift*, the discomforted but still eager right *uphondo* veered directly south to cross the Ncome by the lower *drift*, the same one the now scattered left *uphondo* had forded before dawn. The *isifuba* now moved forward in stately fashion to follow in the wake of the right horn across the *drift* and joined it on the right bank. Bantjes could not refrain from admitting that 'their approach, although frightful on account of the great numbers, yet presented a beautiful appearance.'[20] Pretorius's wisdom in his siting of the laager was proved again. The Zulu right *uphondo*, with the *isifuba* in support, had no option but to follow the precedent of the defeated left horn in also attacking the laager only on its western and northern sides and not from every direction simultaneously. The point of contact was a constricted sector of the laager only about 200 yards long where overwhelming Zulu numbers did not count because most of the warriors were piled up uselessly behind those in the front ranks who were taking the brunt of the shot the Boers were pouring into them.

This was the crucial stage of the battle. The warriors of the *uphondo* made repeated and determined onslaughts, but were mown down by concentrated musket and cannon fire, just as

---

19 *JSA* 1, p.313: Lunguza, 14 March 1909.
20 *Annals* 1, p.448: Bantje's Journal of the Expedition.

those of the left *uphondo* had been earlier. After being thrown back again and again, they began to falter and their pressure on the laager slackened. Behind them, the older *amabutho* of the *isifuba* began to taunt their younger rivals as cowards, and attempted to push through their hesitating ranks to come to grips with the *amaBunu* themselves. Fighting even broke out between some elements of the discomforted right *uphondo* and the impatient and contemptuous men of the *isifuba*. This undisciplined and self-destructive behaviour only increased the confusion in the Zulu ranks. It also packed them tighter as the *isifuba* mingled with the right *uphondo*, making the seething mass of warriors an even better target for the *Wenkommando*. Sensing that they were on the verge of victory, the *Trekkers* did their best to goad the amaZulu into coming on again into zone of deadly fire they were laying down. Pushed from behind and not daring to move forward, any remaining discipline in the Zulu ranks collapsed and all cohesion evaporated. The assault by the Zulu right *uphondo* and the *isifuba* broke down, and at about 11:00 a.m. some units began to withdraw in confusion and dismay.

This was the critical moment for which Pretorius had been waiting. However, for a sortie to be its most effective perfect timing was essential: too soon, and the amaZulu might rally to repel it; too late and they would have a chance to retire in good order and regroup. As it happened, Pretorius got it completely right and brought on a complete rout as occurs only when the enemy have abandoned the offensive, no longer listen to their officers, and can think only of saving their lives. Potolozi sallied out with a mounted force of about 160 men, leaving the rest of the *kommando* to hold the laager. The horsemen, firing as they came on, immediately broke into small groups of five or six and were among the amaZulu (as they recalled) like 'a swarm of bees',[21] breaking their army in two. Some warriors were driven towards the river where, to avoid their relentless pursuers, they hid among the rushes of the marshy margins, or plunged into the waters of the *seekoeigat*. There, like veritable hippopotamuses, they remained submerged except for their noses. Their inexorable pursuers soon discovered this subterfuge. Carefully searching the pool, they made a sport of picking off their helpless prey. Soon the waters of the river flowing sluggishly through the *seekoeigat* were stained with the blood from the hundreds who perished there. Henceforth, the victorious *Trekkers* would know the fatal stream as Bloedrivier, or Blood River.[22]

As with some of the left horn earlier, other Zulu fugitives made for Vegkop, and others for the *drift* downstream. According to Lunguza, a member of the uKhokhothi *ibutho* who survived the battle, fugitives tried to hide themselves 'in antbear holes, under antheaps, stuffing their heads in even though otherwise exposed in dongas, whilst others hid themselves under the piles of corpses to be found in every direction and even under the heaps of bodies.'[23] But the Boers fired at even apparently dead bodies (just as they had at Vegkop) to make doubly sure. As the veteran fighter Sarel Celliers expressed it in his bucolic simile, the Zulu dead 'lay on the ground like pumpkins on a rich soil that had borne a large crop.'[24] The *kommando* was relentless in its pursuit of the scattering amaZulu, and continued it east across the river until, after nearly three hours,

---

21 Fuze, *Black People*, p.77.
22 For a modern Zulu historian's rejection (based on no discernible evidence) of the possibility of a Boer mounted pursuit, or of the river turning red with blood, see Maphalala, 'War of Ncome', in DACST, *Blood River / Ncome*, pp. 61–3.
23 *JSA* 1, p.312: Lunguza, 14 March 1909.
24 *Annals* 1, p.246: Journal of the Late Charl Celliers.

the horses were too exhausted to go any further. Hundreds more warriors died on the 'plain of bones' as the amaZulu called it afterwards. In late January 1840 when the French traveller, Adulphe Delegorgue traversed it, he discovered 'a large number of whitened bones and Cafre skulls lying scattered in the long grass.'[25]

According to the official Boer body-count, the Zulu dead numbered more than 3,000, not including those who limped away but later died of their wounds.[26] This tally is undoubtedly an over-estimation, for even in a better-attested similar battle, like that of Gingindlovu on 2 April 1879 during the Anglo-Zulu War, when the amaZulu were repulsed when they attacked the British laager and were likewise routed in a mounted pursuit, their losses amounted to no more than 10 percent of their army.[27] However, something of the scale and social consequences of even a reduced number of a 1,000-plus Zulu casualties can be gauged from Lunguza's recollection that over 30 elders of the Thembu chiefdom of which he was a member perished in the battle.[28] Tununu who, as Dingane's *inceku* would have known many of them personally, likewise deplored the 'large numbers of persons of rank' who perished at the Ncome. Revealingly, he admitted that these were 'the fellows with the big bellies',[29] comfortable, fat men of status who could not run fast enough to escape the rampaging Boers. Two half-brothers of Dingane's (one of whose accredited final words were quoted above) were among the dead, and Zulu tradition has it that they preferred death at the hands of the Boers rather than risk being executed by the king on their return. Both were sons of Senzangakhona's wife, Langazana, a figure of considerable influence in the kingdom who would live on to 1882 and so survive its overthrow by the British in 1879.[30]

In comparison, the *Wenkommando's* casualties were minimal. Not one person was killed and only three were wounded, one of whom was Pretorius himself who was stabbed through the left hand during the pursuit in a deadly tussle he did not neglect to describe in heroic detail.[31] The pursuit was called off at about midday with the horses exhausted and the ammunition all shot away. The Zulu army had been destroyed before the sun even reached its zenith that day. As a Zulu man would express it during the Afrikaners' celebrations of the centenary of Blood River, 'The sun went down for us as Zulus that day while the shadows on the mountains were still high on the slopes.'[32]

Once all the horsemen had all returned to the laager by the early afternoon, they cleaned their muskets, replenished their ammunition, and attended a thanksgiving service to praise God for their great and astonishing victory against overwhelming odds and a determined enemy. That done, Pretorius, who remained in the laager nursing his wound, sent out another mounted patrol to follow up the defeated Zulu *impi*. But the great army had broken up and scattered as the dispirited surviving *amabutho* dispersed home to be ritually cleansed after the

---

25 Delegorgue, *Travels, Volume One*, p.109.
26 For a Zulu individual's recollections of those of his immediate circle who were killed at the Ncome, or who subsequently died of their wounds, see *JSA 2*, p.81: Magidi, 8 February 1904.
27 Laband and Thompson, *Anglo-Zulu War*, pp. 86–9.
28 *JSA 1*, p.313: Lunguza, 14 March 1909.
29 *JSA 6*, p.268: Tununu, 1 June 1903.
30 Gibson, *Story of the Zulus*, p.71.
31 See *Annals* I, p.454: Pretorius's Despatches, 22 December 1838.
32 Schoeman, P.J., 'Wat die Zoeloes Vertel', *Die Huisgenoot* (Gedenkuitgawe, Desember 1838), p.135, quoted in Grobler, 'Retief Massacre', p.128.

fighting—although they did not have the blood of a single killed enemy on their hands—and to recuperate. So great had been the slaughter, remembered Tununu, 'that there was no mourning in Zululand. No one went to mourn with others.'[33] For the moment, there was no organised force left in the Zulu kingdom to oppose the continued advance of the *Wenkommnado* towards emGungundlovu.

---

33 *JSA* 6, p.268: Tununu, 1 June 1903.

24

They Are Surrounded, Men of the King

Dingane's defeat at the Ncome and the dispersal of his demoralised army temporarily crippled the king's ability to carry on the war. His *amabutho* failed to offer any resistance to the *Wenkommando* that reached the near environs of emGungundlovu by forced marches on 20 December. Pretorius and his men could be forgiven for believing that their victory was complete. Yet, Zulu resistance was far from over.

On the night of the battle the Zulu commanders ordered Ngidi and others of Dingane's *izinceku* to go as fast as they could to emGungundlovu to warn Dingane that his army had suffered a terrible defeat. Msiyana kaMhlana, the *induna* of the imVoko, instructed them to advise Dingane to leave at once for the large emVokweni *ikhanda* just on the southern side of the *drift* across the White Mfolozi. From there, he would be able to make his escape north if pursued. It was after dark when the *izinceku* arrived at emGungundlovu, probably on 18 December, and it was forbidden for any man save the king to enter the *isigodlo* by night. But Velenjeni kaMamfongo, who was in command of the detachments of several *amabutho* that had remained behind to guard the *ikhanda* and the king's person, took stock of the critical situation and hurried them straight to the king in his sleeping hut. They told him that 'the Boers were chasing us' and Dingane, thoroughly alarmed, needed no further persuasion to leave that very night for emVokweni. He was accompanied by all the *izikhulu* who had remained with him at emGungundlovu and not gone on campaign, and was escorted by all the warriors stationed there.[1]

When Dingane was informed on 19 December that the rapidly approaching *Wenkommando* was already at the Mhlathuze River, he ordered Velenjeni to put emGungundlovu and two neighbouring *amakhanda* to the torch in order to deny them to the *Trekkers*.[2] He then abandoned emVokweni, crossed the White Mfolozi, and dismally watched the distant conflagration in the emaKhosini from the hills on the north-eastern rim of the Mahlabathini plain. While there, he gathered together the women of his *isigodlo* along with much of the royal cattle, thus preserving his portable wealth. At the same time, he energetically set about mustering his scattered *amabutho* to defend him against further Boers aggression.

---

1 *JSA* 5, p.76: Ngidi, 18 October, 1905.
2 *JSA* 5, p.92: Ngidi, 29 October, 1905. The three *amakhanda* closest to emGungundlovu were emBelebeleni, eziNyosini and esiKlebheni.

Meanwhile, when on 20 December the men of the *Wenkommando* rode with grim satisfaction into emGungundlovu, the semi-burned huts were still smouldering. Much of its contents, and that of the two neighbouring *amakhanda* that the amaZulu had also set ablaze, had survived the flames. With so much left to loot, on 24 December the victors held an auction at emGungundlovu of elephant tusks, beads, and other valuables they came across while poling among the charred embers. Pretorius himself bought a handsome silver goblet, once Dingane's property.[3]

The day after they had first entered emGungundlovu, 21 December, the members of the *Wenkommando* encamped outside the *ikhanda* at kwaMatiwane, the place of execution. There they discovered the scattered bones and crushed skulls of Retief and his party lying exposed on its rocky slopes. *Izikhwili*, the short fighting-sticks the amaZulu had wielded on the terrible day of the killing, lay strewn about. Grief and rage were intermingled as the Boers identified various fathers, brothers, and comrades by means of fragments of cloth, such as Retief's glossy waistcoat, still adhering to the poor bones, and by small personal belongings such as silver shirt studs, knives, tinderboxes, snuffboxes and the like. In Retief's portmanteau (as we have seen) they found the treaty ceding Natal to the *Voortrekkers*, a document Dingane had not even tried to retrieve since he clearly set no store by it whatsoever. Pretorius's men collected all the bones they could find, enough to have filled a wagon, many of them unidentified, and buried them at the base of kwaMatiwane in a mass grave about eight feet long. And who was to tell if they belonged to the *amaBunu* or to their *agterryers* who died alongside them? Thus, masters and servants lay haphazardly intermingled in death.[4]

Besides destroying emGungundlovu and decently interring Retief's party—as well as those who had been killed at the battle of eThaleni nearby—another of the objectives of the *Wenkommando's* punitive expedition was to recover as many as they could of the precious livestock the amaZulu had driven off in the battles prior to Blood River. Their attempt to do so almost lured Pretorius's men to disaster, just when they believed nothing more was to be feared from the defeated amaZulu.

On Christmas day, the Boers seized yet another supposed Zulu spy close by their camp at emGungundlovu. His name was Bhongoza kaMefu of the Ngongoma people and he had his home near the Mzinyathi River. As a member of the uFasimba *ibutho* he was about 40 years old and had put on the *isicoco*. No commoner in the Zulu kingdom attained such fame as he, or remained as firmly ensconced in the people's memory.[5] For Bhongoza was a decoy, and played his part to perfection.

---

3   For the Boers at emGungundlovu and the burial of Retief and his comrades, see *RN 4*, p.203, no. 119, annex. 1, enc. 2: J.S. Maritz et al. in the name of the Volksraad to Charters, 9 January 1839; *Annals* 1, pp.234–5: Narrative of Willem Jurgen Pretorius; pp. 247–8: Journal of the Late Charl Celliers; p.375: Bezuidenhout's narrative; pp.450–1: J.G. Bantjes, Journal of the Expedition against Dingaan; pp. 454–6: Pretorius's Despatches, 22 December 1838.
4   Some amaZulu later insisted that they had earlier buried the bodies of Retief and his Boer companions in a *donga* 200 yards north-east of kwaMatiwane, leaving the *agterryers* lying in the open. It was the latter's remains, they claimed, that Pretorius interred. However, in 1956 an archaeological investigation failed to find any bones in the *donga*, so there the matter rests. See Dlamini, *Two Kings*, pp.14, 111 n. 8.
5   For Bhongoza, see *JSA* 3, p.129: Mini ka Ndhlovu, 6 April 1910; *JSA* 4, p.117: Ndabambi, 23 March 1909; *JSA* 5, p.8: Nduna, 27 April 1910; *JSA* 6, p.128: Socwatsha, 19 August 1921; p.256: Tununu, 29 May 1905; Fuze, *Black People*, p.78; Bryant, *Olden Times*, p.493.

While the *Wenkommando* was still laagered close by the burnt-out emGungundlovu, Bhongoza had approached Dingane with a plan to lure the *amaBunu* into the thornbush country around the White Mfolozi and to ambush them there. Nzobo agreed that this was indeed the ideal place 'to strike at them and destroy them.'[6] Dingane thereupon adopted the stratagem as his own, crowing, 'Now see my clever plan.'[7] Before Bhongoza left on his dangerous mission, the *izinyanga* doctored him so that the Boers would be 'soft' and be taken in by him. It would seem, though, that Bhongoza had had some prior contact with the whites, most probably from being part of a diplomatic Zulu mission to Port Natal, and knew how to comport himself with them.

When roughly interrogated, Bhongoza blurted out in apparent terror the plausible fabrication he and Dingane had concocted in order to dupe the Boers. Dingane's army, he asserted, was utterly destroyed and posed no further threat. Moreover, the king and his household had fled north to the Gaza kingdom, and he had left his precious cattle behind in the valley of the White Mfolozi River in the hope that the Boers would be content with capturing them and would consequently give up their pursuit. Some of Pretorius's men disbelieved this likely tale, and Bhongoza was in imminent danger of being shot out of hand, like so many 'spies' before him. But the majority were hoodwinked, and in return for his life Bhongoza agreed to show them where all those desirable cattle were secreted.

On Boxing Day, 26 December, in stormy weather, the Boers moved their laagered camp eastwards, close to a spring on the Mthonjaneni heights, a plateau that commanded a breathtaking view of the valley of the White Mfolozi below and the Mahlabathini plain beyond.[8] The next day, 27 December, Bhongoza was put on a spare horse and secured by a rope halter around his neck. He set off towards the edge of the heights, guiding a column of just under 300 mounted *amaBunu* under Karel Landman—soon after setting out Pretorius had returned to the laager to nurse his painful wounded hand—followed by the 60 or so Port Natal levies on foot under the command of Alexander Biggar. The *kommando* took a cannon along with them, but before long sent it back because it was impractical to move it over the increasingly broken ground. As they neared the edge, a small body of amaZulu appeared and immediately fell back on being fired at, thus confirming Bhongoza's earlier assurance that that the Boers could expect little resistance. Looking down over the side of Mthonjaneni, the *kommando* saw forms moving far below that they mistook for black, white, and red cattle wandering about unguarded. In fact, they were *amabutho* with their oxhide shields on their backs moving among the rocks and bushes trying to give the impression of being livestock. The Boers took the bait. The entire *kommando* dismounted and, leading their horses by the reins, began the descent in a long column, following Bhongoza down a steep path along the narrow crest of a spur of the mountain. They finally approached the floor of the valley close to where the uPhathe stream

6 *JSA* 6, p.128: Socwatsha, 29 August 1921.
7 *JSA* 5, p.8: Nduna, 27 April 1910.
8 For the battle of the White Mfolozi, or oPathe, see *RN 4*, p.160, no. 101, annex. 2: Charters to Napier, 5 January 1839; *Smit's Diary*, pp.156–7: 3 January 1839: letter from Retief to the President of the Council, 31 December 1838; *Annals* 1, pp.235–6: Narrative of Willem Jurgen Pretorius; pp.248–9: Journal of the Late Charl Celliers; pp.450–1: J.G. Bantjes, Journal of the Expedition against Dingaan; pp.456–7: Pretorius's Despatches, 9 January, 1839; p.492: Charters to Napier, 5 January 1839; *JSA* 5, pp.91–2: Ngidi: 29 October 1905; *JSA* 6, pp.128–9: Socwatsha, 29 August 1921; pp.268–9: Tununu, 1 June 1903; Gibson, *Story of the Zulus*, pp.72–6; Fuze, *Black People*, pp.78–9; Nathan, *Voortrekkers*, pp.263–5: Smail, *Land of the Zulu Kings*, p.71; Leśniewski, *Zulu–Boer War*, pp.236–44.

flows into the White Mfolozi through a narrow *kloof*, or gorge. Stunted mimosa trees and aloes dotted the rocky slopes, unnervingly resembling human sentinels.

It was only once they had followed Bhongoza into the *kloof* that the members of the *kommando* finally began to suspect the peril into which they had been lured. Bhongoza, making the excuse that he needed to defecate, suddenly threw off his halter and made off. To the consternation of the Boers, he melted into the thickets of thorn trees where, unbeknown to them, he joined the amaZulu concealed in ambush. Just then, from a sharp, rocky, bush-covered hill to the right of the *kommando*, a Zulu lookout called Xwana (although some amaZulu remember the person being an unnamed married woman) who had been alertly waiting to give the pre-arranged signal, suddenly cried out in the high-pitched tones the amaZulu employ to allow their voices to carry clearly over great distances: 'They are surrounded, men of the king!'[9]

Dingane had succeeded against the odds in reassembling a large portion of the *impi* scattered at the Ncome, and concentrating it with forces that had been held in reserve at emGungundlovu or who had not been called up for that campaign. Their numbers are unknown, but were certainly sufficient to take on with confidence a *kommando* that was not much smaller than the *Vlugkommando* had been. In classic ambush mode, an *uphondo* of the *impi* had been hidden either side of the path the Boers were stumbling down in order to attack them from both sides and from behind, and then to close in around them. When Xwana called out the signal, the trap was sprung, and the *amabutho* sprung up from among the rocks where they had been lurking, well prepared with several spears apiece. The *amabutho*, especially the younger ones, attacked with reckless determination, but they were nevertheless unable to get close to the Boers for, unavoidably, 'they now knew about guns and were afraid of them and had been driven off at the Ncome … and emaGebeni.'[10]

Even so, the *kommando* was in a perilous situation. With his men all still on foot and hemmed in on every side by the enemy, Karl Landman called on them to stand back-to-back and fight it out. Fortunately for them, the indomitable Hans Dans de Lange had other ideas, and though not in command, he saved the day for them. He persuaded Landman that they must fight their way out of the trap since they had insufficient ammunition for a prolonged stand. The *kommando* could hardly clamber back up the steep mountainside to the laager above, so the only alternative was to carry on downhill to the level ground below where the horsemen could remount, form up and manoeuvre. That was not going to be at all easy, because at first the way was strewn with jagged rocks, overgrown with thorn trees and aloes, and intersected by many deep dongas.

Beset on all sides by the amaZulu, but still keeping them at a distance with their musket fire, the straggling column finally reached more level ground. Under De Lange's inspired leadership, the Boers mounted their horses and charged. Firing from horseback, and without sustaining any losses, they broke right through the Zulu cordon followed by Biggar's Port Natal levies who were hard put to keep up (or so we must suppose for, predictably, they largely disappear from the narrative related by the Boers.) But in what direction should the *kommando* go? It was impracticable to follow the southern bank of the White Mfolozi because of the dense riverine bush. The river was swollen with the summer rains, but where the *kommando* found itself there was a large island in the middle of the stream. Following De Lange, the *kommando*

9 *JSA* 6, pp.269: Tununu, 1 June 1903.
10 *JSA* 6, pp.128–9: Socwatsha, 29 August 1921.

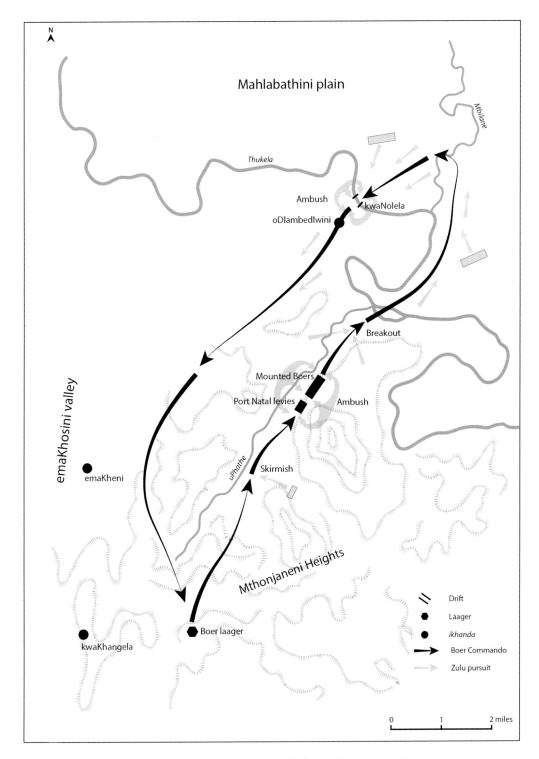

Battle of the White Mfolozi or oPathe, 27 December 1838

successfully forded the river there and crossed onto the open ground of the Mahlabathini plain beyond. Watching the affray through a telescope from the Mthonjaneni heights, Bantjes saw the amaZulu surround them 'as so many ants.'[11] The *amabutho*, including the isiThunyisa—the 130 or so amaZulu who carried firearms—tried to shepherd the *kommando* north across the plain, away from their camp. Some of the Boers feared they were heading into another trap. Under the leadership of Stephanus Lombard some 50 of them broke away from the *kommando* and headed south-east along the White Mfolozi. Their subsequent movements are unclear, but they manged to return unscathed to the laager early the next day. Once Lombard and his men had ridden away, the main body of horsemen wheeled to their left in the opposite direction and fell back across the plain. The horsemen adopted their customary tactics of alternately firing and retiring and were followed at some distance on foot by the Port Natal contingent who were also employing their muskets against the amaZulu in pursuit. They were making for the kwaNolela *drift* where they intended to cross the White Mfolozi and then head back to their laager on the height. By this stage the *kommando* was in imminent danger of running out of ammunition, and were desperate to break free of the amaZulu before they did so. Nearing the *drift*, the horsemen halted to allow the Port Natal levies who had been toiling in their wake to catch up. Drawing together on the track to the *drift*, they then attempted to cross while still under attack from the amaZulu behind them. This last hurdle was to prove the worst they had to face that disastrous day.

A miniature of Alexander Biggar from Port Natal who fought at the battle of Blood River and was killed at the battle of the White Mfolozi. (Campbell Collections, Durban, with permission)

The oDlambedlwini *ikhanda* was situated on the southern side of the White Mfolozi, facing the *drift*. It was the *ikhanda* of the young uDlambedlu *ibutho* that had been tracking the movements of the *kommando* in the plain from the opposite bank of the river. The men of the uDlambedlu were determined to prevent the fugitives from crossing the river and escaping. They deployed in the narrow bed of the river at the *drift* and among the crags on either side. When the horsemen tried to cross, they swarmed them and stabbed at their horses. Five of the mounted *amaBunu* were killed in the well-laid ambush, but the remainder managed to break through and gain the southern bank of the river. The Port Natal levies were not so fortunate. On foot and

11 *Annals*, 1, p.452: J.G. Bantjes, Journal of the Expedition against Dingaan.

exhausted, the uDlambedlu succeeded in cutting them off. Alexander Biggar might have escaped, but he refused to abandon his men and died gallantly fighting alongside them. Few if any escaped with their lives.

As for the horsemen who had made it through the ambush at the fatal crossing-place, they were not yet out of danger. Fighting continued among the huts in oDlambedlwini itself. The Boer horsemen again broke free and made for the sanctuary of their laager on the Mthonjaneni heights, keeping for most of the way to fairly level ground with the emaKhosini valley on their right. They were mounted, but their horses were exhausted and the uDlambedlu and other younger, fit warriors kept up the chase for several miles, constantly harrying them and forcing them to turn and fire at intervals. At long last the *amabutho* gave up their chase in the overwhelming heat of a summer's day when they became aware that Pretorius had despatched a body of mounted men to support the fugitives, and the shattered horsemen were allowed to regain their camp.

It has been estimated that the Boers had covered some 35 miles since first setting out five hours before. Their losses were far heavier than those in any other engagement since the disastrous battle of the Thukela. Their later claiming—with wild exaggeration—that in return they had killed 1,000 amaZulu, could not disguise that they had been as thoroughly routed as had the *Vlugkommando* at eThaleni. The field of battle was littered with so many abandoned muskets that Dingane was able to beef up the isiThunyisa, the firearm-carriers, to form them into a new *ibutho* in its own right.[12] And although the Boer campaign against Dingane continued until early 1840, this debacle, and not their great victory at Blood River, was the last time they encountered the amaZulu in a full-scale battle. Yet, the lustre of that triumph has served to dim, if not entirely to obscure, the Boer rout at the White Mfolozi and it has earned scant place in Afrikaner historiography. The amaZulu, by contrast, long celebrated the battle of oPathe (as they called it) along with Bhongoza its hero, and there is far more reference to it in recorded Zulu oral testimony than to the battle of emaGebeni, or even to Ncome itself.

Despite their ignominious rout, and the destruction of the entire Port Natal contingent, the *Wenkommando* remained remarkably resilient. Pretorius stayed put on Mthonjaneni sending out patrols with the intention of provoking the amaZulu into attacking his laager with predictably disastrous consequence for them. But the amaZulu knew better by now than to attempt such a thing, and declined to take up the challenge. With the Boers' over-worked horses too out of condition to attempt many more raids, and with the amaZulu now taking better measures to keep their herds and flocks out of easy reach, Pretorius decided on 31 December to withdraw. On the way back his men burned three more great *amakhanda* in the emaKhosini valley as a symbolic indication of the *Trekkers'* dominance. The *Wenkommando* went deliberately slowly in the hope that the shadowing Zulu forces would find the courage to attack and so give the Boers their opportunity to secure a final, decisive victory. But the amaZulu let the *kommando* go unmolested, content that their enemies were retiring and that the ultimate outcome of the war still hung undecided in the balance.

The Boers continued to be on the lookout for cattle, however, one of the major objectives of the punitive expedition. A strong patrol that Pretorius had sent out on 31 December rejoined the *Wenkommando* on 4 January 1839 at the Mzinyathi River. It brought in a herd of between

---

12 *JSA* 5, p.39: Ngidi, 14 August 1904.

3,600 and 5,000 captured cattle (accounts differ regarding the number) and reported it had engaged the 100 or so amaZulu guarding them, and had killed most of them. This was not nearly as many cattle as Pretorius had hoped to capture, but for the moment he had to be content since no more could be expected of his exhausted men or their horses. Nevertheless, it remained his intention to send out another *kommando* when they were sufficiently recovered in order to 'scour the country' and drive off more Zulu livestock. But, for now, the campaign was over. To great rejoicing, the *Wenkommando* finally arrived back at the Sooilaer on the Little Thukela on 6 January 1839. There the booty was divided up, and the members of the *kommando* dispersed to their own encampments.[13]

Where did that leave the two warring sides? The amaZulu were temporarily too chastened by their crushing defeat at the Ncome to risk following up their success at oPathe by launching a counter-offensive. Yet, the Zulu army was still essentially intact, and given the right circumstances, Dingane might yet rally his forces and resume the war. For their part, the Boers understood when they withdrew from Mthojaneni that they had failed to break Dingane's power once and for all. Nor had they conquered his entire kingdom. Their punitive expedition had been just that, a punitive expedition with limited objectives. Yet, the consequences of the campaign were more far-reaching than this might suggest. Besides slaking the *Trekker* desire for vengeance, the exploits of the *Wenkommando* had delivered a stunning military blow against the amaZulu at Blood River that their subsequent victory at the battle of the White Mfolozi could not undo. Moreover, the destruction of emGungundlovu and other *amakhanda* in the emaKhosini valley, the very seat of Dingane's power, had dealt the Zulu king's prestige a further shattering blow. Crucially, therefore, the *Wenkommando's* campaign had reversed the dynamic of the war. Ever since Retief's death, it had been the *Trekkers* who had been on the defensive; now it was the amaZulu. Dingane could no longer expect to expel the Boer invaders of his kingdom. Instead, he would have somehow to accommodate their unwelcome and dangerous presence. At the same time, he would have to shore up his own tarnished authority among his shaken and dismayed subjects, a warrior people accustomed since Shaka's time to victory and conquest, not defeat and occupation.

---

13   *Annals*, 1, p.452: J.G. Bantjes, Journal of the Expedition against Dingaan; p.457: Pretorius's Despatches, 9 January, 1839; *Smit's Diary*, pp.157–8: 3 January 1839: letter from Retief to the President of the Council, 31 December 1838; pp.159–60: 4 January 1839: letter from Retief to the Council, 4 January 1839; p.160: 6 January 1839.

25

Building Two Countries

Once the *Wenkommando* had withdrawn across the Thukela, Dingane did not return to the emaKhosini to rebuild emGungundlovu. Instead, he lingered for a while in the Mahlabathini plain where (as in the past) his *umndlunkulu* continued to supply him with the sweet water drawn from the spring on the Mthonjaneni heights close by where the *amaBunu* had recently laagered. In due course, Dingane removed his royal establishment north-east to the valley of the Hluhluwe River. There he began building a second, smaller emGungundlovu in the country of the Mdletshe chiefdom. But malaria was endemic in this low-lying country of dense valley bushveld. Soon finding the new emGungundlovu to be disease-ridden, Dingane removed once again. He chose the site for the third emGungundlovu further inland, on higher, healthier ground, on the south bank of the Vuna River, just before the stream flows into the Black Mfolozi River, some eight miles from the present town of Nongoma. From this region, which had once been the heartland of the Ndwandwe chiefdom, King Shaka's most powerful and tenacious rival, Dingane set about reconsolidating his shaken royal authority and building up his army again.[1]

The *Trekkers*, meanwhile, were still living in unsanitary conditions in their crowded, stockaded camps, suffering from a measles epidemic and running short of supplies of every sort. They were eager to begin fanning out to take occupation of the lands they claimed by right of conquest where, in those places where good pasture and perennial water were to be had, they intended to commence cultivation: in short, to settle down after the hardships of years of a migratory and dangerous existence. Their many trials on trek had not changed them, though, and the British military at Port Natal noted their continual 'petty quarrels and animosities' and the perpetual disagreements in their *Volksraad*. Nevertheless, the British were in no doubt that all these differences would be instantly laid aside 'for defence or to revenge aggression,' and that the Emigrants fully intended to 'make their footing good' in the conquered land.[2]

---

1   *JSA* 1, pp.20–1: Baleni, 10 May 1914; *JSA* 5, p.52: Ngidi, 5 November 1904; *JSA* 6, p. 291: Tununu, 11 June 1903; Gibson, *Story of the Zulus*, pp.76–7. The third emGungundlovu was also known as kwaDenge after the district in which it was built.
2   *RN 4*, p.223, no. 128, annex. 1: Capt. Henry Jervis to Napier, 27 March 1839; pp. 304–5, no. 197, annex. 4: Jervis to Napier, 28 July. In early June 1839 Kobus Potgieter's camp on the Bushmans River burned down and exploding gunpowder stores prevented anything from being saved. Nine men and children were burned to death.

To that end, the *Trekkers* were busy establishing a *dorp* (village) in the centre of the region they occupied—the Republiek Natalia—to serve as the administrative seat of their *Volksraad*. Piet Retief, when he and his small party visited Port Natal in November 1837, had chosen the site for the future township on the banks of the Msunduze River, a place originally occupied by the *umuzi* of Machibise, the daughter of Mlifa.[3] On 23 October 1838 the *Volksraad* had named the newly planned 'first village settlement' Pieter Maritz Burg in memory of Retief and Maritz.[4] After Blood River and the burning of emGungundlovu, to indicate where power now lay, the Boers deliberately transferred the name of Dingane's capital to Pietermaritzburg, frequently referring to it as emGungundlovu.[5]

In its layout (as with other *Voortrekker* villages), Pietermaritzburg followed the grid pattern typical of every *dorp* founded by the Dutch in the Cape, and had eight long streets and five cross streets down which water could be led in furrows. With the exception of the large, central market block, all the blocks delineated by the street pattern were divided into 10 *erwe*, or plots, over 100 in all. The owner of each *erf* was obliged to fence it in and cultivate it, and to build the house close and parallel to the street.[6] It would be some time, though, before the *dorp* took on the aspect of a permanent settlement. In the last months of 1839 Delegorgue would describe Pietermaritzburg as still 'only a stockaded camp, simply a collection of crude shanties made of wood and reeds, and plastered with cow-dung ... wretched shelters [that] swarmed with bugs and remarkably vigorous rats.'[7]

On 2 January 1839, Major Charters learned of Pretorius's victory at Blood River. In accordance with the purpose of his occupation of Port Natal, he wrote to the *Volksraad* rebuking the Boers for their 'great slaughter' of the Zulus 'and the unwarranted invasion of their country.' He went on to warn them of the 'marked displeasure of the British Government' should they contemplate another *kommando* against Dingane.[8] Despite this stern rebuke and the consequent potential for conflict between the Boers and Charters' troops, affairs between the two parties continued to be conducted amicably. There were now only five English settlers at wrecked Port Natal. Half a mile westward around the bay from the forlorn settlement was Congella, originally a cluster of three Boer laagers, where *erwe* were being sold by November 1839. Nevertheless, Congella was still no more than a miserable little settlement surrounded by a palisade of tree trunks. At this stage, the best-built structures to be found anywhere in the vicinity of the bay were those erected by the British soldiers at Fort Victoria. During the course of 1839, the fort came to comprise a stockade of mangrove trees that enclosed barracks, officers' huts, a magazine, a hospital, and sheds and marquees for commissariat stores. The stockade was commanded in turn by an earthwork redoubt and gun emplacement: altogether,

---

3   *JSA* 5, p.144: Nombashini ka Ndhlela, 25 October 1907; pp.249–50: Qalizwe ka Dhlozi, 11 May 1908.
4   *Smit's Diary*, p.143: 23 October 1838. Until 1843 Mauritz, the older form of Maritz, was usually preferred in official documents.
5   *JSA* 5, p.333: Sijewana ka Mjanyelwa, 17 November 1899; Adrian Koopman, 'The Names and Naming of Durban', *Natalia*, 34 (December 2004), p.82.
6   Robert Haswell, 'The Voortrekker Dorps of Natal', *Natalia*, 10 (December 1980), pp.23–4, 26–8; Robert Haswell, 'Pieter Mauritz Burg: The Genesis of a Voortrekker *Hoofdplaats*' in Laband and Haswell (eds), *Pietermaritzburg*, pp. 24–7.
7   Delegorgue, *Travels, Volume One*, p.96.
8   *RN* 4, p.167, no. 110, annex. 2, enc. 7: Charters to Maritz and Meyer, 5 January 1839.

too strong a fortified camp for the Boers to contemplate attacking it should relations with the British break down.[9] But they did not.

The Point at Port Natal, showing Fort Victoria, constructed in 1839 by the British garrison. Anonymous engraving, *c*.1839. (Author's Collection)

Satisfied that Fort Victoria was thoroughly established, on 7 February 1839 Major Charters left overland for the Cape and turned over his command to the prudent and experienced Captain Henry Jervis. Although the Boers staunchly denied he held any authority over them, they nevertheless welcomed his good offices. And Jervis read his strict instructions to hold Port Natal as a temporary military base to prevent further bloodshed in the region to encompass facilitating negotiations for a lasting treaty between the Emigrants Farmers and King Dingane.[10]

The young Theophilus Shepstone—the son of an 1820 settler in the Cape turned Wesleyan missionary, who was a fluent linguist and who had accompanied Charters to Port Natal as his secretary—had already elicited important intelligence from Zulu sources concerning the chances of securing peace. He had learned that after Blood River Dingane had attempted to negotiate a truce with the Boers, but that they had first insisted on impossibly steep terms,

---

9 Haswell, 'Voortrekker Dorps', p.28, Laband, *Historical Dictionary*, pp. 97–8; Cubbin, 'Port Natal', pp.182–4.
10 *RN 4*, p.159, no. 101, annex. 1: Charters to Napier, 5 January 1839; p.157, no. 101: Napier to Glenelg, 4 February 1839.

and had then refused to negotiated further for fear of treachery.[11] And certainly, Dingane was anxious to reopen negotiations. His *izinduna* were informing him that his *amabutho* were 'tired,' and were insisting that, in order 'to put the matter right' with the *amaBunu*, that he should pay them tribute and return the cattle he had captured from them.[12]

For their part, the Boers, itching (as we have seen) to settle down in peace, were now more prepared to make a settlement than they had been in the heat of the *Wenkommando* campaign, even if many among them were pressing for a fresh campaign to compel Dingane to capitulate on their terms. Jervis intervened and took it on himself to contact Dingane though the good offices of Henry Ogle, an old hand personally known to the Zulu king, who was one of the few settlers still hanging on at the Port. Dingane responded by despatching a trusted *inceku* called Gambusha to parlay with Jervis. Gambusha arrived in the British camp on 23 February 1839. Speaking for Dingane, and Zulu emissaries were under strict instructions to confine themselves rigidly to the message entrusted to them by the king,[13] he revealed that the Zulu king considered himself 'on the brink of ruin' and was willing to accept any terms the British might propose on behalf of the Boers. Gambusha further made it clear that Dingane looked to the British to act as actual allies by ensuring that no future Boer aggression would be permitted against him, and by assisting him to send the Boers 'out of the country.' This was more than Jervis was empowered or inclined to undertake, and he insisted on confining his role to that of honest broker.

And that was the role Jervis carried out when, on 23 March, 1839—just short of a month since Gambusha had returned to Dingane with the Captain's response—the *inceku* arrived back at Fort Victoria with two *amakhosi*, Gikwana and Gungwana. These two dignitaries were empowered with Dingane's full authority to negotiate on his behalf. In earnest of the seriousness of their mission, the two chiefs brough with them about 300 horses the amaZulu had captured during the fighting in 1838. Jervis at once set up a meeting between the Zulu envoys and Andries Pretorius, grandiloquently styled the 'Chief Commandant of the Right Worshipful the Representative Assembly of the South African Society at Natal'. Peace between the two parties was duly concluded on 26 March 1839. The terms of the treaty stipulated that Dingane would restore all the arms, cattle, sheep, and remaining horses taken from the Boers, and would allow them to live unmolested south of the Thukela River. In return, the Boers would assist the amaZulu if they were attacked unjustly by another party. Loaded with presents of beads and snuff, the Zulu delegation returned to the new emGungundlovu to report back to Dingane.[14] From Governor Napier's perspective, Jervis's praiseworthy intervention, by preventing 'the further effusion of blood,' had justified the military occupation of Port Natal, and it was now s possible to consider the withdrawal of the troops since their objective had been achieved.[15]

The Boers, however, were left sceptical of Dingane's good faith in fulfilling the terms of the treaty. Yet, it seemed that he intended to do so. In the second week of April, the indefatigable Gambusha reappeared at Fort Victoria to report that the cattle and firearms had been collected,

---

11 *RN 4*, pp.168–9, no. 101, annex. 2, enc. 9: Theophilus Shepstone to Charters, 7 January 1839.
12 *JSA* 6, p.128: Socwatsha, 29 August 1921.
13 O.F. Raum, 'Aspects of Zulu Diplomacy in the 19th Century', *Afrika und Übersee*, 66: 1 (1983), pp.35–6. Gambusha was typical of many envoys who survived succession conflicts, and went on to serve Mpande in the 1840s and 1850s.
14 *RN 4*, pp.224–5, no. 128, annex. 1: Jervis to Napier, 27 March 1839.
15 *RN 4*, p.220, no. 128: Napier to Glenelg, 15 April 1839.

Andries Pretorius negotiating with King Dingane's emissaries near Port Natal on 26 March 1839. Sketch by Lt J.A. Harding, 72nd Highlanders. (MuseumAfrica, Johannesburg, with permission)

and that Dingane wished to hand them over to the British in the presence of the Boers. To this, the Boers would not agree and stood upon their dignity. In terms of the treaty they had concluded with Dingane, they were now sovereign south of the Thukela, and Pretorius took umbrage that Gambusha had entered Boer territory without carrying a white flag of truce as instructed. Moreover, he informed Gambusha that the cattle must be handed over directly to him in his camp, and not through the British.[16] To that end, Pretorius proceeded to open direct negotiations with Dingane, leaving Jervis out of the picture. Accordingly, on 24 May 1839, a small mission led by William Cowie, a Scot with an Afrikaner wife whom the *Trekkers* had appointed *veldkornet* of Port Natal in May 1838,[17] set off to visit Dingane. He carried Pretorius's instructions to urge the Zulu king to yield up all the items required by the treaty.[18] On their way, the commissioners were encouraged to find the amaZulu everywhere rejoicing that the war

16 *RN 4*, p.301, no. 197, annex. 2: Jervis to Napier, 14 April 1839.
17 Tabler, *Pioneers*, p.26.
18 *RN 4*, p.306, no. 197, annex. 4, enc. 1: Instructions for the mission to Dingaan by Andries Pretorius, 23 May 1839.

was over. When they met Dingane on 27 May, they found him 'covered with a large red mantle, with a spy-glass in his hand' and surrounded by his chief councillors. The talks went smoothly, and Dingane assured Cowie that he was determined that the war should end, and that he would comply with the terms of the treaty.

On 7 June 1839, two *izinduna* (whose names were not recorded) came trembling in fear of their lives into Pretorius's camp near the Thukela River. They were standing in for Ndlela and Nzobo who should have been the ones to represent Dingane in this, the formal confirmation of the treaty. But the pair of chief *izinduna* were afraid to approach the Boers who (they were informed) held them responsible for advocating Retief's execution. So it was their stand-ins who delivered over 1,300 head of cattle, about 400 sheep, 52 muskets and 43 saddles. The Chief Commandant, after haranguing the *izinduna* about the 'cruel' way the amaZulu had waged war and murdered women and children, asked them if Dingane would be willing to offer ivory tusks in part payment for the rest of the cattle he was obliged to surrender? On being assured that he was, and that the amaZulu were already hunting elephant for that purpose, Pretorius fixed the number of cattle still required for full 'indemnification' at 19,300. Gambusha arrived back from Dingane on 16 July to assure Captain Jervis that the king was willing to confirm the agreement reached on 7 June, and indeed, 2,000 lbs of ivory were duly delivered. But by the end of the year most of the cattle still had not been finally made over.[19]

With the payment of ivory, Dingane was seen in Zulu eyes to *ukuthela*, to submit formally to the *amaBunu* by tendering them tribute. Yet, as the Boers had always suspected would be the case, 'he did so only with his mouth,'[20] and was buying time to rebuilt his forces and to plan how best to secure his future. It was obvious that he could not trust the land-hungry Boers to be sated by their recent gains, even if for the moment they were sowing their crops for the next season and were settling in. The time would surely come when they would cast their acquisitive eyes on the truncated Zulu kingdom north of the Thukela. Nor could the British presence at the bay be counted on to restrain them indefinitely. Consequently, Dingane set about securing his future position by 'building two countries.' That entailed carving out a new kingdom in the lands north of the Phongolo River at the expense of the neighbouring Swazi kingdom to augment the diminished Zulu domain. Dingane calculated that if he succeeded in doing so, he would be able to defy the Boers indefinitely, even if, at some later stage, they conquered the Zulu territory between the Thukela and Phongolo.[21] Nor was there anything novel or unrealistic in such a scheme, for had not Mzilikazi relocated his kingdom several times on the highveld, as had other migratory rulers such as Soshangane kaZikode and Zwangendaba kaZiguda who, respectively, had established their Gaza and Jele kingdoms in the lands north of Delagoa Bay?

Ironically, the Boers unintentionally aided Dingane in furthering his plan to establish a second kingdom. During the final stage of the peace negotiations, Pretorius had imposed one further condition on Dingane when he insisted that the Zulu king require his unmarried *amabutho* to *ukuthunga*, that is, to sew on the headring, marry women from the female *amabutho* he designated, and settled down to raise a family. In this way, the Boers calculated, the aggressive younger *amabutho* would be domesticated, and Dingane's military potential tamed. However,

---

19 *RN 4*, pp.307–10, no. 197, annex. 4, enc. 2: W. Cowie to Jervis, 12 June 1839; p.303, no. 197, annex 4: Jervis to Napier, 28 July 1839; *JSA 6*, p.268: Tununu, 1 June 1903.
20 *JSA 4*, p.276: Ndukwana, 15 September 1900.
21 *JSA 4*, pp.273, 276: Ndukwana, 15 September 1900.

Dingane seized on this stipulation as the ideal means of physically occupying the great tracts of the Swazi kingdom he planned to conquer, for who would make for better colonists than the large number of freshly-made *abanumzane* (married headmen of their own *imizi*) to whom he would allocate the land?[22]

There was yet a further aspect to Dingane's planned Swazi campaign. It was intended as an *ihlambo*, or final purification ceremony that marked the end of a period of mourning, in this case one occasioned by defeat and humiliation at the hands of the *amaBunu*. An *ihlambo* culminated in a 'washing of the spears' against an enemy people so that the *umnyama* (or evil influence) associated with the cause of mourning was cast into the foe's country, just as Shaka's *ihlambo impi*, launched against the amaMpondo in May 1828, had marked the end of the hysterical mourning for his mother Nandi.[23]

Dingane's Swaziland campaign during the winter of 1839 was consequently no mere sideshow, and was far more than an extensive raid to procure cattle to make up for losses to the Boers. Rather, it was a full-scale attempt at conquest and occupation involving the full mobilisation of his remaining military resources. As his first step in the campaign, Dingane mobilised four *amabutho*—the umBelebele, the uNomdayana, the umKhulutshane and the imVoko—under the command of Klwana kaNgqengelele of the Buthelezi chiefly house, one of the most powerful *amakhosi* in the northern part of Zululand. Klwana set off with his *impi* in mid-1839 to clear the bush and establish a new *ikhanda* called emBelebeleni on the Nguthumeni Ridge, north of the Phongolo River and near of the sources of the Ngwavuma River in south-western Swaziland (or Eswatini, as it is now known). Planting an *ikhanda* there was an unmistakable assertion of Zulu possession, one that 'opened the way' for Dingane to conquer the country.

At the time of the Zulu invasion, Sobhuza I was the Swazi king, or *ingwenyama*. A canny survivor, he appreciated that the *Trekkers* were the new power in the region and would be a useful ally against the amaZulu, his kingdom's traditional enemy. Soon after the battle of Blood River he had sent an embassy to seal an alliance with the victorious Boers, one (it seems) that was precautionary and did not include any undertaking to provide mutual military assistance.[24] Consequently, when Klwana's *impi* began building emBelebeleni, a provocative action that Sobhuza realised heralded a major Zulu offensive and not simply a raid, the *ingwenyama* understood that he would have to resist it unaided. He also saw that it would not be enough for his people to adopt the usual Swazi strategy of retiring to their mountain strongholds, there to defy the raiders until they retired. This time, he ordered a full military mobilisation with the objective of meeting the invaders in the field and driving them out. Sobhuza appears to have died during the course of the Zulu invasion, and to have been succeeded by the 13-year-old Mswati II with Lojiba Simelane, the Queen Mother, wielding actual power. But news of Sobhuza's death was kept secret for some time so as not to lower the morale of the Swazi forces facing the amaZulu during the winter of 1839. Under the charismatic leadership of Mngayi Fakudze, they met the amaZulu in a pitched battle in the valley of the Lubuye River near the modern town of Hlatikulu in south-western Swaziland.[25]

22 *JSA* 4, pp.273–4, 276: Ndukwana, 15 September 1900; *JSA* 5, p.91: Ngidi, 29 October 1905; *JSA* 6, p.268: Tununu, 1 June 1903.
23 *JSA* 2, p.92: Magidigidi, 9 May 1905; Laband, *Assassination*, pp. 108–9.
24 *Annals*, 1, p.375: Bezuidenhout's narrative.
25 Bonner, *Swazi State*, p.41, 43–4.

The Zulu and Swazi armies that faced each other at Lubuye were very similar in their style of warfare since many Swazi military practices were borrowed from their formidable Zulu neighbours. Royal power was based on the authority of the *ingwenyama* over the *emabutfo*, or regiments, drawn from the same age-grade of young men across the entire kingdom without regard to regional loyalties and local chiefs. Like the Zulu *amabutho*, the Swazi *emabutfo* were quartered in royal barracks, great horseshoes of thatched huts, established across the kingdom as nodes of royal authority, and the *emajaha*, or warriors, went to war both to prove their prowess against external foes and to exact tribute for the king.[26]

Swazi military ritual was very similar to that of the amaZulu and was intended to imbue the *emajaha* with strength and courage, to preserve them from mortal wounds and to put confusing darkness before the eyes of their foes so that they could not effectively fight back or escape. On campaign, warriors were armed with a variety of traditional weapons, but made no use of firearms. For disconcerting the enemy at a distance, they had a sheaf of throwing spears, each with a shaft four feet long or more and with a thin, tapered blade. But heroic, hand-to-hand fighting is what a *lijaha* sought (as did a Zulu warrior with his similar military culture), and for this he had two possible types of short-hafted stabbing spear, one with a heavy, broad blade and another with a long, narrow one. Unlike the amaZulu, but in common with Sesotho-speaking people like the neighbouring Bapedi to the west or the Basotho further to the south, for close-in work *emajaha* also favoured a battle-axe that came either with straight points or flanged tips. Just as effective was the wooden knobkerrie with notches cut in its heavy head to give skull-shattering blows greater purchase. All *emajaha* carried an oval oxhide war-shield, rounder and smaller than the Zulu version.

Like the Zulu *amabutho* at this date, the *emajaha* wore their finery into battle—a practice the amaZulu increasingly discontinue in later years when they stripped off most of their regalia on campaign. The *emajaha* wore white cow tails bound around their ankles, arms and necks; a mantle of wild animal skins over their shoulders; and their heads and faces almost concealed beneath a headdress of black ostrich plumes and the streaming black feathers of the long-tailed widow bird (*sakabula*). Around their necks they wore amulets and a hollow bone which they sounded when going into battle. On approaching the enemy, they knocked their knees against their lowered shields, making a daunting sound likened to the roar of the surf upon the beach.

Swazi battle formation mirrored that of the amaZulu with the young, reckless *emabutfo* forming the swiftly encircling horns, while the stolid veteran *emabutfo* anchored them at the centre. While always applauding and celebrating those who performed heroic deeds, the amaSwazi had little patience with pointless loss of life in war. Cautious commanders would normally deploy their *emabutfo* with a careful eye to the terrain, and would always keep some units in reserve as reinforcements or for pursuit. If circumstances were against risking a pitched battle, commanders saw no shame in retiring to the fortified mountain caves that had always stood the amaSwazi in such good stead. As with the amaZulu, the ritual contamination caused by the shedding of blood required purification ceremonies after combat.

The battle of Lubuye (oBuya in isiZulu) is justly famed in Swazi tradition. The amaSwazi made the mistake of dividing their forces. The larger contingent attacked down the surrounding heights and the smaller one deployed in the valley. The main body of the amaZulu worsted the

---

26 For a full account of the Swazi military system, see Laband, *Zulu Warriors*, pp. 46–52.

latter in desperate fighting during which the great warrior Dambuza Lukhele distinguished himself in his heroic fight to the death. Fortunately for the amaSwazi, their main force under Mngayi Fakudze himself came to the rescue and eventually fought the amaZulu to a standstill, forcing them to retire with heavy casualties. Dingane was compelled to call up elements of the uDlambedlu, iziNyosi, inDabenkulu and other *amabutho* and hurry them north to retrieve the foundering Swazi campaign. Nevertheless, persistent, tough Swazi resistance eventually compelled him to withdraw from emBelebeleni, and with that his attempt to create 'two countries' dwindled away in complete failure.[27]

The consequences for Dingane's reputation and royal authority were dire. The humiliating drubbing of his *amabutho* by the despised amaSwazi came hard on the heels of their thorough defeat by the Boers. For Dingane, these military disasters were compounded by the territorial concessions the victorious Boers had wrung out of him, along with compelling him to be seen to *ukuthela* to them with the payment of ivory and the restitution of livestock and firearms. Now, with the final dashing of any hope of establishing a second, reserve kingdom on Swazi soil that was out of the hostile range of the Boers, Dingane had to accept that he had no alternative but to maintain his reduced kingdom against all comers where he stood, or die in the attempt.

---

27 For the Swazi campaign, see *Annals* 1, pp.536–7: Minutes of the Volksraad, 15 October 1839: Panda's interrogation; *JSA* 2, pp.91–2: Magidigidi, 9 May 1905; *JSA* 3, p.149: Mkando, 11 July 1902; *JSA* 4, pp.276–7, 345: Ndukwana, 16 September 1900; 23 December 1901; *JSA* 5, pp.91–2: Ngidi, 29 October 1905; Bryant, *Olden Times*, p.324; Leśniewski, *Zulu–Boer War*, pp. 275–8.

26

You Who Crossed All the Rivers on the Way to Restoring Yourself

In February 1839, Lord Glenelg resigned as Secretary of State for War and Colonies, and was replaced by the Marquis of Normanby who had been serving since 1835 as the Lord Lieutenant of Ireland. When in April 1839 Normanby finally turned his attention to the situation in Natal, he expressed himself deeply concerned with 'the calamities to which the natives of Southern Africa have been exposed by the unprovoked and unjustifiable irruption into their country of large bodies of armed men' from the Cape. He consequently was reluctant to deviate from Glenelg's policy of maintaining a temporary garrison at Port Natal to dissuade the *Trekkers* from further warlike acts. That said, he did not believe that Jervis's little force at Fort Victoria was achieving its objective with much success, and intimated that he would like to see Port Natal 'abandoned' as soon as was practicable in terms of its mission.[1]

When Napier received Normanby's letter nearly five months later (even for those days, the despatch had been an inordinately long time in arriving), the Governor needed no persuading. He admitted that the British troops at the Port had failed to cut the Boers off from securing 'warlike stores,' and were too few in number to prevent them from employing them, should they wish, against 'the native tribes.' Nevertheless, Napier believed that Jervis's success in brokering a peace treaty between the Boers and Dingane meant that hostilities between them had ceased, and did 'not appear likely to be resumed.' He therefore declared it his intention to 'relinquish the post' at Port Natal at 'the earliest opportunity', even if that made for an unresolved and anomalous situation in which the Emigrants Farmers regarded themselves as independent, while he was directed to consider them still British subjects.[2] Indeed, however brave a face Normanby and Napier might put on it, Glenelg's policy aimed at discouraging and containing the *Trekkers* in Natal had signally failed.

Yet another of those mass migrations of peoples that had so destabilised southern Africa over the past few decades very soon tested the Republiek Natalia's ability to act as a sovereign power. In September 1839, Mpande kaSenzangakhona, Dingane's half-brother and the dominant magnate in the south-east of the Zulu kingdom, fled across the Thukela with some

---

1 *RN 4*, pp.239–40, no. 141: Marquis of Normanby to Napier, 30 April 1839.
2 *RN 4*, pp. 295–6, no. 197: Napier to Normanby, 30 September 1839.

17,000 adherents and 25,000 cattle to seek the protection of the Boers.³ As Mpande's *izibongo* expressed it:

> He who crossed afterwards
> Of the house of Shaka;
> The swallow that got lost in the sky,
> He who appears in the feather head-dress
> Between the English and the Boers.⁴

Mpande's defection came as a major new threat to Dingane's already badly shaken power and authority, one he could not afford to countenance, even if it brought with it the danger of renewed conflict with the Boers. *Amabutho* loyal to Dingane, with frantic orders to bring Mpande and his people back, hotly pursued the fugitives over the Thukela border into the territory of the Republiek Natalia. The chase continued as far south as the Mvoti River, some 50 miles from Port Natal. There Dingane's *impi* turned back for fear of a direct armed confrontation with the Boers. But if immediate fighting was avoided, the consequences of Mpande's flight could not be. Tununu later lamented that had Mpande 'not crossed over,' Dingane would have remained king and continued to pay tribute to the Boers.'⁵ But Mpande's exodus had initiated a dynastic conflict within the Zulu royal house that, when combined with unsated Boer territorial ambitions, would bring civil war and ruin to the already diminished Zulu kingdom. So fraught with dire repercussions was Mpande's defection, that it has always been known to the Zulu people as 'the breaking of the rope that held the nation together.'⁶

Mpande had good reasons for his flight. Although in the latter days of his subsequent reign he was all too easily dismissed as an obese, indolent, and ineffectual king, he was in fact a shrewd and determined survivor. Unlike his two half-brothers Shaka and Dingane he was neither assassinated nor driven off his throne and killed. When he died in 1872 it was of old age, and he was still king.

Mpande was born to Senzangakhona and Songiya, the Zulu *inkosi's* ninth wife, between 1795 and 1798.⁷ In order to foster good relations between the amaZulu and the Cele chiefdom to the south, Mpande was sent as a boy to be reared at kwaGqikazi, the *umuzi* of Dibandlela, the Cele *inkosi*, on the northern side of the Mdloti River not far north of what would later be Port Natal. In 1819 he was enrolled in the newly-formed umGumanqa *ibutho* stationed at the kwaKhangela *ikhanda* in the rich grazing country of the Qwabe chiefdom, a few miles southeast of the present town of Eshowe. As a member of the umGumanqa, Mpande took part in several campaigns and his half-brother King Shaka rewarded him with at least two wives.

---

3   For the circumstances of Mpande's flight, see Philip A. Kennedy, 'Mpande and the Zulu Kingship', *Journal of Natal and Zulu History*, IV (1981), pp.29–30; and Peter Colenbrander, 'The Zulu Kingdom, 1828–1879', in Duminy and Guest (eds), *Natal and Zululand*, pp.95–6.
4   Fuze, *Black People*, p.80.
5   *JSA* 6, p.268: Tununu, 1 June 1903.
6   *JSA* 4, p.67: Mtshapi, 3 April 1904; *JSA* 5, p.8: Nduna, 27 April 1910; Fuze, *Black People*, p.79.
7   For a detailed account of Mpande's early career, see Kennedy, 'Mpande', pp.24–8; Colenbrander, 'Zulu Kingdom', pp. 94–5.

Dingane and his fellow assassins did not bring Mpande into their conspiracy against Shaka in 1828, and he was in great danger once they had assassination the king and Dingane had seized the throne. Yet, as we have seen, Mpande was one of the very few of Dingane's male siblings—and potential rivals—whom the new king permitted to live. For his escape from execution, Mpande was subsequently hailed in his *izibongo* as 'The brass rod which remained from the other sticks,'[8] although why Dingane spared the *umntwana* is not entirely clear.

One likely reason is that he was not considered eligible to succeed Shaka because he was 'of the *umsizi* hut.'[9] During the annual *umkhosi* (first fruits festival) when a chief or king was ritually strengthened to ensure a good harvest, when he and his people were bound together anew, and when mystical confusion sent out among their enemies, he underwent various rituals. In one of these, Mpande's father Senzangakhona would have been smeared with *imisizi* (powdered, charred ritual medicines) to purify him and strengthen him against mystical evil influences, or *umnyama*. While being thus 'doctored', he would have remained alone in the especially prepared *umsizi* hut, but at night he would have been attended by a selected wife or concubine with whom he 'wiped the hoe'. It seems that Songiya was his sexual partner on such an occasion. Any child born of this intercourse, such as Mpande was purported to be, was accepted as a member of the royal house, but only as one of inferior rank.[10] Thus, as a low-ranking *umntwana* he could never be in contention for the crown.[11]

Nevertheless, Mpande must still have presented a potential threat to Dingane. Possibly, another reason besides his inferior rank why Dingane spared him was the common perception that he was something of a harmless simpleton, an *isithuthakazana*,[12] a reputation which Mpande fostered out of self-preservation. Then again, there is the repeated suggestion that Mpande owed his survival to the patronage and protection of Ndlela, Dingane's powerful *induna*. Perhaps Ndlela's support stemmed from political affiliation and the bonds of lineage, for Ndlela's Ntuli chiefdom stretched along the northern bank of the Thukela and abutted the territory between the Mlalazi and Thukela Rivers in south-eastern Zululand dominated by Mpande. There was an additional reason for his supporting Mpande that reveals Ndlela as a statesman. Mpande had already fathered many sons, and Ndlela seems to have persuaded Dingane that since neither he nor Shaka before him had married or sired acknowledged heirs, only Mpande's legitimate offspring could guarantee the continuity of the royal line.

Even so, Mpande knew that Dingane would always remain deeply suspicious of him as his heir presumptive. As a consequence, he went out of his way to deflect Dingane's distrust by letting it be widely known that he entertained no aspirations to be king. He always adopted a humble demeanour in the royal presence and never presumed on his royal blood. Yet there was no getting away from the fact that Mpande was an *umntwana* and very close to the throne. And while he maintained a very low profile in Dingane's presence, at his own great emLambongwenya *ikhanda* at the Matigulu River in the south-east of the kingdom where he was assiduously

---

8   C.L.S Nyembezi, 'The Historical Background to the Izibongo of the Zulu Military Age, Part II', *African Studies* 7: 4 (June 1948), p.162.
9   *JSA* 4, p.214: Ndhlovu, 11 January 1903.
10 *JSA* 6, p.49: Socwatsha, 24 April 1905.
11 Laband, *Zulu Kings*, p.140.
12 *JSA* 4, p.346: Ndukwana, 27 December 1901.

building up a powerful personal following, Mpande kept royal state, maintained a large *isigodlo*, and distributed largesse to his adherents on a princely scale.

In later life, the self-indulgent Mpande became so fat that he could hardly walk, and had to be wheeled about in a small cart.[13] Even in his prime he was noticeably stout with pendulous breasts and had the typically heavy thighs of Senzangakhona's sons. His most obvious foible was his extreme fondness for ostentatious and expensive dress with a profusion of ornaments— but that was seen as an essentially royal whim, as was his love of dancing and interest in breeding cattle.[14] Yet what most struck those about him were his noble but easy bearing and his obvious intelligence. His speech was always fluent and measured, even when angered. Delegorgue, who observed him closely, admired his shining, stout body, jutting brows, high, square forehead, generous mouth and firm, square chin. What the French adventurer noticed above all were Mpande's brilliant eyes, large and well-shaped—eyes that he never permitted to betray his thoughts.[15]

Mpande knew only too well that Dingane only reluctantly suffered him to live and at a word could have him put to death. To guard against this, Mpande set about building up alliances with the Zulu elite. Ndlela was already his patron, and he fostered strong personal and political bonds with the other powerful *amakhosi* in the region of the Thukela River. Fully aware that Senzangakhona's widows continued to exercise huge political influence and presided over many of the kingdom's great *amakhanda*, and that Mnkabayi, Shaka's aunt, had twice played king-maker, he assiduously polished his confidential relations with these formidable matrons. In addition, he forged new and critical contacts with some of the *amakhosi* in northern Zululand, especially Maphitha kaSojiyisa of the Mandlakazi branch of the royal house.

Maphitha ruled the former territory of the Ndwandwe chiefdom in the capacity of the king's viceroy, even exercising some his prerogatives such as placing *izinduna* on the land. He also had charge over the tributary chiefdoms to the north-east, those around and beyond the Lubombo Mountains. Such people never assembled at emGungundlovu but at Maphitha's great place, when he took it on himself to decide what matters of importance he would transmit to the king. Quasi-independence such as his, and that of other northern *amakhosi*, made them, and Maphitha in particular, allies of significant weight. Still, it is unclear if Mpande were secretly working with them against Dingane.[16]

Whatever suspicions Dingane may have harboured about his half-brother's loyalty, he permitted him to live in peace until the catastrophic Swazi campaign of 1839. Then, after the defeat at Lubuye, he summoned Mpande to furnish some of the reinforcements required to help retrieve the military situation. Furthermore, he ordered him to prepare to move north with all his followers to colonise the lands the king still hoped—despite his setbacks—to conquer north of the Phongolo. Mpande knew that such a migration would scatter his adherents and deprive him of his well-established power base in the south-east. Consequently, he stalled and temporised, ceased paying Dingane his customary visits of respect, and with the transparent excuse that he was ill, stayed home at emLambongwenya. Dingane, already chronically suspicious of Mpande's intentions, became convinced that his behaviour indicated his half-brother was intending to

---

13   *JSA* 4, p.74: Mtshapi, 8 April 1918; Gibson, *Story of the Zulus*, p. 111.
14   *JSA* 1, pp. 46–7: Baleni, 17 May 1914; Webb and Wright (eds), *Zulu King Speaks*, p.15.
15   Delegorgue, *Travels, Volume One*, pp. 85, 87–8.
16   *JSA* 4, pp.314, 321: Ndukwana, 21, 31 October 1900; *JSA* 6, p.44: Socwatsha, 29 June 1904.

rebel and seize his throne. If he were to nip the plot in the bud, he needed to lure the elusive Mpande to emGungundlovu and there to execute him. Cunningly, he sent the supposedly ailing Mpande a princely gift of 100 heifers, knowing that according to Zulu etiquette the *umntwana* must come in person to thank and praise the king for his munificence. Fortunately for Mpande, the two *izinduna* who drove the cattle to emLambongwenya, Ncagwana kaZivalele and Mathunjana kaSibhaxa, were in the service of Ndlela, Mpande's patron, who did not wish to see him killed. Ndlela privately ordered Mathunjana to give Mpande 'a scratch with his fingernail' warning him of Dingane's evil intentions. In later years, Mpande would hold Mathunjana in high favour, and present him with many cattle for saving his life. [17]

Apprised of the danger in which he stood, Mpande urgently consulted with his *izinduna* and with his mother, Siguyana. In terror of Dingane's wrath, they all urged him to flee for his life. Mpande accepted their counsel and sent out messengers all across southern Zululand between the Mhlathuze and Thukela Rivers to persuade the people to seek sanctuary with him among the Boers. Not all of them were Mpande's adherents. Some were the people that Dingane—in order to stop the flow of refugees to Port Natal—had ordered in the mid-1830s to evacuate the coastal areas south of the Thukela, and who now simply wished to grasp the opportunity to return to their ancestral homes. Certainly, neither they nor the other people of southern Zululand had any wish to be resettled in distant Swaziland. Many others simply wished to escape Dingane's increasingly arbitrary and discredited rule, and hoped to be allowed to live in peace, undisturbed by further destructive conflicts with the Boers. Moreover, they all recognised that as Mpande's adherents or allies they were guilty by association of his supposed treason, and that if they stayed in southern Zululand they risked being 'eaten up' by the vengeful king. It was for a combination of compelling reasons, therefore, that they abandoned their *imizi*, and with their families and livestock followed their *umntwana* across the Thukela into the Republiek Natalia.[18] As they went, they hailed him as 'You who crossed all the rivers on the way to restoring yourself.'[19]

During the initial turmoil and panic of flight, Mpande had little opportunity to think of anything but saving his and his people's lives from Dingane's retribution. But once across the Thukela and encamped far down the coast with his following near the Thongati River only 25 miles from Port Natal,[20] the canny *umntwana* had time to reflect on his situation. And it was one that, far from being disastrous, proffered him the alluring possibility of returning to the Zulu kingdom as its king. To achieve that ambition required him to initiate civil war. That in turn necessitated the forging of a political and military alliance with the Boers against Dingane, something that would require the subtle and patient diplomacy at which Mpande was long adept.

When the *umntwana* opened up preliminary communication with the Boers, he was careful to profess his peaceful intentions and to reassure them that he posed no threat. The

---

17 *JSA* 1, p.197: Jantshi, 4 February, 1903; *JSA* 2, pp.200–1: Mangati, 1 July 1918; *JSA* 4, p.67: Mtshapi, 3 April 1918; *JSA* 6, pp.71–2: Socwatsha, 19 August 1909; Fuze, *Black People*, p.80. It seems that Ncagwana was double-crossed. Mthunjana manged to throw the blame for warning Mpande onto him, and Dingane had him executed.
18 *Annals* 1, p.537: Minutes of the Volksraad, 15 October 1839: Panda's interrogation. For the personal experiences of individuals who found it expedient to desert Dingane for Mpande, see *JSA* 5, pp.75, 92: Ngidi, 17, 29 October 1905; and pp.254, 256: Tununu, 28, 29 May 1903
19 *JSA* 4, p.140: Mtshayankomo, 22 January 1922: his father Magolwana's *izibongo* of Mpande.
20 For an account of Dingane in Natal, see Delegorgue, *Travels, Volume One*, pp. 92–5.

next step required him to consult the members of the *Volksraad* in person, so he proceeded to Pietermaritzburg on foot with his belongings carried on a wagon.[21] Walking with him were the men of high lineage who had accompanied him in his flight, notably Nongazala kaNondlela, the *inkosi* who had been his principal commander at the battle of the Thukela.[22] When Mpande was received by the *Volksraad* on 15 October 1839, he modestly requested only that he be permitted to settle his adherents on the territory between the Mvoti River and the Mhlali River to its south, the region where he had spent his childhood years among the Cele people. Moreover, he solemnly promised that he would do so peaceably as a subject of the Republiek Natalia.[23]

Despite Mpande's pacific demeanour and emollient words, many members of the *Volksraad* remained deeply suspicious of his intentions. They knew little of him except that he had rebelled against Dingane, and there were those who feared that he was perpetrating a ruse, and had led a hostile army into their territory under false pretences. Such fears were most pronounced among the inhabitants of Congella who were in closest reach of Mpande's host. They advocated attacking him and hurling his people back across the Thukela—but of course keeping their cattle. Temperate counsel eventually prevailed, however. Despite the terrible precedent of Retief's fate at emGungundlovu, the *Volksraad* resolved to send a deputation to Mpande to negotiate further. Meanwhile, at Fort Victoria, Jervis entertained his distinct reservations about the direction in which relations between Mpande and the Boers were trending because he did not wish to see the peace between Dingane and the Boers, one he had striven so hard to foster, jeopardised. But there was nothing he could do.

On 21 October a Boer deputation of 28 men, dressed as for hunting, set out under the elderly but resolute F. Roos for Mpande's hastily erected abode which had been constructed following the pattern of a royal *ikhanda*.[24] Mpande received the wary *amaBunu* with royal panache, entertaining them with great exhibitions of dancing by his *amabutho* and with extravagant feasting. And, despite Boer apprehensions, this was to be no reprise of Retief's execution. On 27 October 1839, sitting in a long tent the Boers erected for the occasion, they struck a formal alliance with Mpande. Firstly, they recognised him as 'Reigning Prince of the Emigrant Zulus.' The two parties then agreed upon a joint attack on Dingane with the objective of overthrowing him as king and placing Mpande on the Zulu throne in his stead. In return for the Boers' military assistance, Mpande undertook to pay them the balance of the cattle still owed them by Dingane, and to cede them the Bay of St Lucia, a potential harbour north up the Zululand coast. Furthermore, Mpande promised not to take any military action against Zululand's neighbours without the prior consent of the *Volksraad*.

There matters rested for the next few months. Committed to the prospect of civil war in Zululand, Mpande kept in close touch with the *Volksraad*. But the Boers felt they could not safely implement their treaty with him while the British troops were still at Fort Victoria and Jervis remained true to his instructions to prevent any further bloodshed between the Boers and Dingane. Dingane, meanwhile, had received word of Mpande's defection with the utmost

---

21 *JSA* 1, p.109: Dinya, 2 April 1905; Webb and Wright (eds), *Zulu King Speaks*, p.13.
22 For a rollcall of the influential individuals who accompanied Mpande across the Thukela, see Kennedy, 'Mpande', p.29.
23 *Annals* 1, pp.538–40: Minutes of the Volksraad, 15 October 1839: Panda's interrogation.
24 For the Boer deputation to Mpande, see *Annals* 1, pp. 540–44: Report of the Landdrost of Tugela, October 1839.

consternation.[25] He bitterly reproached Ndlela for advising him against killing Mpande while he had the chance, inveighing against his half-brother as a 'swollen, scrofulous thing' and berating Ndlela for harbouring that 'venomous snake' against him.[26] There was little Dingane could do, though, except pin some hope on Jervis's mediation, and he could try to discredit Mpande in the eyes of his Boer allies. To that end, he sent an envoy to the *Volksraad* who warned its members that Mpande that was 'not a man: he has turned away his face: he is a woman. He was useless to Dingaan his master, and he will be of no use to you. Do not trust him, for his face may turn again.'[27] But the Boers declined to be persuaded of Mpande's purported duplicity.

In December 1839 Jervis reported that the country remained 'far from settled,' and that since a clash involving Mpande, Dingane and the Boers was ever more likely, the British garrison should remain to prevent it.[28] But Napier stubbornly stuck to the conclusion he had reached in September before Mpande's flight changed the situation and threatened Zulu civil war. He continued to insist that further hostilities were unlikely and that the garrison's continued presence was both unnecessary and futile. With signally inopportune timing, in late November —month after Mpande and the Boers had agreed to attack Dingane together—he set in motion the arrangements necessary for the withdrawal of the garrison from Port Natal. There was nothing Jervis could do. On Christmas Eve 1839, the *Mazeppa* with its shallow draught took the British troops and stores over the bar to deeper water where the brig *Vectis* with its two square-rigged masts lay waiting take them on board. Once embarked, Jervis and his men sailed away, leaving Fort Victoria dismantled behind them. On shore, the jubilant Boers fired a derisive salute. They then hoisted for the first time the new flag of the Republiek Natalia, described as being equally divided into red above and blue below, the two colours overlaid by a white triangle having as its base the entire outer edge of the flag and as its apex a point in the middle of the edge lying against the flagpole.[29]

With the British garrison safely over the horizon, and unwelcome British interference in the affairs of Republiek Natalia consequently at an end, the Boers resolved without further delay to activate their treaty with Mpande and mount their agreed-upon joint campaign against Dingane.

25 *JSA* 1, p.197: Jantshi, 14 February 1903.
26 *JSA* 4, p.191: Ndabazezwe ka Mfuleni, 24 June 1921.
27 Delegorgue, *Travels, Volume One*, p.95.
28 *Annals* 1, p.601: Jervis to Napier, 8 December 1839.
29 Delegorgue, *Travels, Volume One*, pp.98–9; Brookes and Webb, *History of Natal*, p.35; Cubbin, 'Port Natal', pp.194–5.

27

He Has Ruined My Army

On 4 January 1840, before they resumed their war against Dingane, the legalistically-minded members of the *Volksraad* formally repudiated their treaty with the Zulu king on the grounds that he had failed to comply with its terms and had not delivered up all the cattle stipulated. As an indication of their displeasure, they now increased the number they demanded in token of his submission from the 19,300 agreed upon in June 1839 to a staggering 40,000.[1] Having thus justified their intended aggression against the Zulu kingdom to their own satisfaction, the Boers opened their campaign on 14 January 1840. The strategic plan was that Mpande's army under the command of Nongalaza kaNondela would act in concert with the Boer *kommando* under Chief Commandant Andries Pretorius (who was growing more ineffably conceited by the day and, to the sly amusement of Delegorgue—who accompanied the *kommando*—was now counting himself alongside Napoleon as one of history's great conquerors).[2] Both forces were to converge by different routes on the new emGungundlovu north of the Black Mfolozi. Nongalaza's army was to advance by way of the lower Thukela and the coastal route, and Pretorius's *kommando* was to follow the route the *Wenkommando* had taken in 1838 across the Mzinyathi and Ncome Rivers. Mpande did not accompany his army but marched with the Boers who effectively held him hostage against Nongalaza's full and loyal cooperation in their joint operations.

When Dingane learned that Mpande's army and Pretorius's *kommando* were both advancing against him, and that the *amaBunu* had promised to reward anyone who delivered him up to them with 50 cattle, his heart nearly failed him. He doubted whether his forces could hold their own against both invading armies, but with the recent failure of the Swazi campaign there was no escape north to a second kingdom. So, with no viable alternative, Dingane stood fast and did what he could. He first attempted to halt the invasion by diplomatic means. Calculating that the Boers' *kommando* with its horses and firearms presented the greater threat, he attempted to assuage them first. This was no time to entrust such a mission to emissaries of secondary importance. He therefore chose Nzobo, his powerful and ferocious *induna* who, along with

---

1   For the campaign of 1840 up to the battle of the amaQongqo Hills, see *Annals* 1, pp.576–83: Journal of the Commando under Chief Commandant Pretorius against Dingaan, 4 January–30 January 1840, P.H. Zietsman, Secretary of War, 24 February 1840; Delegorgue, *Travels, Volume One*, pp.101–10; Gibson, *Story of the Zulus*, pp.85–6; Leśniewski, *Zulu–Boer War*, pp.305–11.
2   Delegorgue, *Travels, Volume One*, p 108.

Ndlela, was his chief advisor, to speak for him.[3] Yet Dingane's choice of emissary was one calculated to infuriate the Boers. He should have taken into account his knowledge that the Boers associated Nzobo directly with the killing of Retief and his party and regarded him as a criminal deserving of the direst punishment. So, when Nzobo as the chief envoy, typically supported by an *induna* of lesser rank called Khambezana, appeared in Pretorius's camp with instructions to make what terms they could, the Boers refused to accept their credentials as ambassadors and observe the customary, inviolate status they should have enjoyed as ambassadors. Instead, they immediately threw them into chains. (They did not scruple, of course, to keep the herd of 200 cattle the two emissaries had brought with them as a gift, a gesture inextricably bound up with Zulu diplomatic exchanges, but far more munificent than usual in keeping with the importance of their mission.)

His diplomatic initiative still-born and the advance of the combined forces against him unchecked, Dingane became increasingly alarmed. It was not long before he feared that he was vulnerable to attack in his latest emGungundlovu on the Vuna River, and that the terrain thereabout was not suitable for a defensive battle. He therefore put the *ikhanda* to the torch like the first of that name in the emaKhosini valley, and shifted 30 miles north to take up position on Magudu Mountain, a flat-topped eminence that stands conspicuously in the rolling plain about eight miles south of the Phongolo River. Dingane had meanwhile been mobilising those *amabutho* that remained loyal to him, and placed them under Ndlela's command with Silwana kaNdlovu as his deputy. Ndlela, experienced veteran that he was of many a battle, took up a defensive position a few miles south-west of Magudu just south across the Mkhuze River. There he disposed his *amabutho* with their backs to the eMpisini hill and facing the amaQongqo hills, a modest group of hillocks with rounded peaks that stand out in the gently undulating countryside, and waited for what might befall.

Pretorius's *kommando* consisted of 308 armed Boers, nearly 500 Khoisan and black *agterryers*, drivers and attendants, 50 wagons, and some 600 horses and 700 draught-oxen. Most of the Boers regarded the affair as nothing more than a glorified hunting expedition, and Delegorgue observed many of the younger men embraced it as a time for merry-making and heavy drinking away from their staid families.[4] All were far more anxious to make their fortunes in captured cattle than to face Dingane in yet another battle. So blatant were these mercenary considerations, and so considerable the booty in livestock that it eventually did amass, that this rather chaotic expedition came to be derisively known as the *Beeskommando*, the Cattle Commando.

On Sunday 27 January 1840, after advancing laboriously over swollen streams and ground made soggy by the heavy summer rains, the *Beeskommando* reached the Sundays River. There two messengers sent by Nongalaza informed Pretorius that his much faster-moving *impi*, unencumbered by wagons (and in less of a lax party mood), had already arrived in the vicinity of the amaQongqo hills, and that it was preparing to engage Dingane's army in battle. The *Beeskommando* was still some 125 miles away. Determined to be part of the action, and anxious that Mpande's forces might suffer a reverse and dislocate their joint strategy if they fought alone, Pretorius sent back orders with Nongalaza's messengers that he was not to risk a battle until his *kommando* had come up to reinforce him. Putting on more speed, on 29 January the

---

3 *JSA* 6, p.72 Socwatsha, 29 August 1909; Raum, 'Zulu Diplomacy', pp.34, 36, 39.
4 Delegorgue, *Travels, Volume One*, p.104.

Beeskommando traversed the site of the battle of Blood River. A large number of whitened Zulu bones and many skulls lay scattered in the long grass. What the Boers did not know as they contemplated the site of their great victory just over 13 months before, was that at that very moment Nongalaza's *amabutho* were engaging Ndlela's in a great battle. Ironically, the final, decisive battle in the Boers' war against Dingane was being fought without their being present, and between men armed as they would have been before the coming of the white men and their muskets, clashing hand-to-hand with spear and shield.

The two *izimpi* that fought for the crown in this, the first of the three Zulu civil wars,[5] were equally matched in size and probably numbered no more than about 5,000 men each.[6] They were armed alike with their traditional weapons and were dressed in the same fashion. To differentiate themselves from Dingane's warriors, and to identify themselves as his, Mpande's *amabutho* wore an insignia consisting of two thongs of white cowhide suspended from the neck and hanging over the back and chest.[7] Ndlela's *impi* was made up of all the great *amabutho* of Dingane's reign, notably the uDlambedlu, the iziNyosi, the umKhulutshane which was incorporated into the imVoko, and the uKhokhothi that had remained in reserve at the battle of Ncome. Nongalaza's army was a more *ad hoc* collection of units. It consisted of the imiHaye which was incorporated into the imVoko, but most of whose members had defected to Mpande's cause, the iziMpohlo which was made up of remnants of older *amabutho* from Shaka's day, the uZwangendaba, and a motley collection of elements known after the *amakhanda* where they had been stationed: the umLambongwenya, uDukuza and isiKlebhe.

Less renowned and less cohesive than Ndlela's *amabutho* Nongalaza's might have been, but their morale was higher. They were acting in concert with the fearsome *amaBunu*, while it was doubtless dispiriting for Ndlela's men to know that even if they defeated Mpande's army they would still have to confront Pretorius's *kommando*. Surely, though, it was rash of Nongalaza to stake his master's cause on the outcome of a battle that promised to be infinitely more uncertain than it would have been if the Boers had been fighting alongside him and deployed all their firepower? Certainly: but it could also have been that he was acting on Mpande's instructions. For Mpande, with his canny eye on the future, would have wagered that if his general could but defeat Dingane without Boer help, he would afterwards be less beholden to them, and that he would secure legitimacy in the eyes of the Zulu people by overthrowing Dingane unaided.

The scouts sent out from Ndlela's position facing the amaQongqo hills and from Nongalaza's approaching *impi* spotted each other at dawn on Wednesday, 29 January. It was not until the middle of the day, though, that the two armies were drawn up in battle array opposite each other. Nongalaza's forces were greatly heartened by the presence with their army of Mahlungwana kaTshoba, the most renowned *isangoma* in the service of the Zulu kings. Mahlungwana had

---

5 Historians usually identify three Zulu civil war: the first (1840); the second (1856); and the third and worst (1883–1884). See Laband, *Historical Dictionary*, pp.314–17.
6 For the battle of the amaQongqo Hills, see *JSA* 2, p.90: Magidigidi, 8 May 1905; *JSA* 4, p.70: Mtshapi, 4 April 1918; *JSA* 6, pp.69–70: Socwatsha, 28 August 1909; pp. 257–8, 291: Tununu, 30 May, 11 June 1903; *Annals* 1, pp. 585, 587: Commando against Dingaan, 1 February 1840; Delagorgue, *Travels, Volume One*, pp.109, 115; Gibson, *Story of the Zulus*, p.86; Fuze, *Black People*, p.82. The following account of the battle differs in many tactical particulars from Leśniewski, *Zulu–Boer War*, pp. 311–16 who also argues that it took place on 30 January rather than the day before, and that it was fought on the plain south of the amaQongqo hills, rather than to their north.
7 Delegorgue, *Travels, Volume One*, p.114.

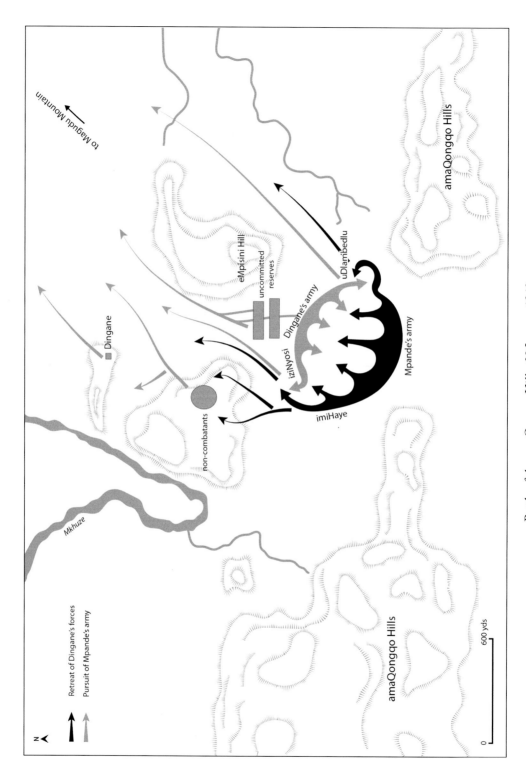

Battle of the amaQongqo Hills, 29 January 1840

pointedly abandoned Dingane's cause and defected to Mpande's, and was there to doctor his army with his superior supernatural skills before battle was joined. He burnt a patch of grass in front of Nongalaza's men and treated it with *intelezi* and other *imithi* to ensure that Dingane's *amabutho* would be defeated they moment they set foot on the supernaturally charged ground.

If Nongalaza's men were charged with confidence, there was discord in the top echelons of Ndlela's army. Dingane was confident that the contemptable Mpande would be 'no match whatever for him,'[8] and considered it beneath to his dignity to fight in person with his *impi*. He therefore was content to leave the conduct of the battle to Ndlela while he observed it from a safe distance. But before he withdrew, and while his army was drawn up in an *umkhumbi* being ritually prepared for combat, he and his general conferred over the tactics he was to adopt. It was soon clear the two men were at odds. The king wanted Ndlela to break with tradition and to mount an all-out attack with his entire army, urging him to advance in columns and to deploy in a solid front with all his men engaging the enemy, leaving no units in reserve to hang back and watch on. That was not how the cautious Ndlela preferred to fight a battle. Most likely, he would not have dared openly disagree with his royal master, but he was determined nevertheless to fight as he considered best. His intention was to engage the enemy in a more flexible, piecemeal fashion, committing his forces where and if required, and holding back a large division in reserve.

While the two armies manoeuvred opposite each other and readied for combat, the tension mounted unbearably. Tununu, Dingane's *inceku* who had deserted him for Mpande and was with his army, later drew a candid picture of the pre-battel nerves that afflicted even men of high rank: 'The *izinduna* themselves were agitated and they defecated and urinated, for an assegai would not be forgiving; even though they were *izinduna* they would not escape.'[9]

Battle was finally joined in the early afternoon and continued until darkness fell, a night with a waning moon and poor visibility. It was fought with great ferocity. As Nsuze ruefully commented, there was 'no sparing in civil war.' The custom was that brothers fighting on opposite sides did their best to kill each other. 'For if your brother calls for mercy and you grant it,' he declared, 'you will not live long: misfortune will overcome you and you will become rubbish.'[10]

Ndlela did indeed hold back a large section of his army while sending in only the iziNyosi to attack on the right and the uDlambedlu on the left. In the heavy fighting the imiHaye of Nongalaza's left *uphondo* drove back the iziNyosi, while the uDlambedlu prevailed over the less cohesive collection of *izigaba* of *amabutho* on the opposite flank. As a consequence of the uneven fortunes of the combatants on either wing, the outcome of the battle long remained in the balance. At one time Ndlela's men believed the victory would be theirs, but Nongalaza's men rallied and forced them back. As the shadows lengthened, Ndlela's army began to take ever heavier casualties. Increasing numbers of his discomforted warriors, believing the day to be lost, began to go over to Nongalaza's side. Their defection conclusively turned the tide of battle. According to tradition, the hero among Ndlela's men was Nozitshada kaMagoboza of the Nzuza people, the *induna* of the uDlambedlu who wore coverings of oxtails presented by the king all over his body. His 'shield became soft with the blood of men' and he stabbed and stabbed until his fighting arm became so tired and swollen that he had to transfer his spear to

---

8   *JSA* 6, p.69: Socwatsha, 27 August 1909.
9   *JSA* 6, p.257: Tununu, 30 May 1903.
10 *JSA* 5, p.167: Nsuze, 17 May 1912.

his left hand. At last, overwhelmed by numbers, he sank dying to the ground and cried out: 'Wo! I am exhausted. Come close: stab me. I do not want to be ruled by Mpande.'[11]

The fighting only started to die away as darkness fell. Tununu recalled that he and his companions 'fought the uDlambedlu when the sun had set, but they were no longer in order,' and that they stabbed them in the back as they began to run.[12] But, defeated as they certainly were, and in no condition to continue the fight, Ndlela's *amabutho* were not so badly worsted that they were routed, and they managed to withdraw in reasonable order. Nongalaza's men were in no fit state to pursue them with any vigour. For if Ndlela's losses had been considerable (their actual number is unknown), then Nongalaza had also sustained significant casualties. The Boers later observed 1,200 men in his camp with stab wounds, some 25 percent of his total force, and he was reported to have lost 1,000 men.[13]

Even so, enough of Nongalaza's warriors remained with sufficient vigour and intent to scour the field of battle once their enemies had made off, flushing out and killing all the wounded they left behind. They then fanned further out and caught up with members of Dingane's household who had been watching the battle (as was the practice) and did not escape in time when it was lost. Their pursuers killed them out of hand, and one of these unfortunates was no less a person than Bhibhi, Ndlela's sister, a celebrated beauty who had been Senzangakhona's eighth and favourite wife.[14] She tried to take refuge in the dense bush at the bottom of a small stream near a little sharp-pointed hill called uVe, but Nongalaza's men killed her without any regard for her exalted status. When he later learned of her death Mpande was aghast, for she was one of those experienced *amakhosikazi* with whom he was hoping to establish his rule. Indeed, at the beginning of the campaign he had specifically commanded: 'Let her not be killed. I shall need her to rule.'[15]

Although left as the victors in possession of the field of battle, Nongalaza's *amabutho* feared that Dingane's *impi*, although mauled, might well resume the battle the next day. They correctly suspected that not all Dingane's forces had been committed to the battle, and that they could still overwhelm them with superior numbers. They consequently spent an uneasy night in dread of being attacked, and some of the *izinduna* even made plans to divest themselves of their finery of feathers and skins should they need to flee. But Dingane was not willing to resume the battle for fear that the Boer *kommando* was approaching. While he waited to ascertain its whereabouts and gauge just how disastrous his situation was, he took temporary sanctuary back on Magudu Mountain in one of the *imizi* belonging to the Buthelezi people of Klwana, one of the powerful northern *amakhosi*. With him were the remnants of his household, a number of his councillors and an *isigaba* of the young uKhokhothi *ibutho* that had served as his bodyguard while the battle was being fought.[16]

There Ndlela found him. During the closing stages of the battle, the defeated general had tried to take refuge in the bush. More fortunate than his sister Bhibhi, when he was rooted out,

---

11 *JSA* 5, pp.222–3: Pindulmini ka Matshekana, 13 July 1917. See also *JSA* 3, p.123: Mgundeni ka Matshekana, 11 July 1918; *JSA* 6, p.43: Socwatsha, 24 January 1904.
12 *JSA* 6, pp.257–8: Tununu, 30 May 1903.
13 *Annals* I, p.626: anonymous letter dated 8 April 1840 in Lord John Russell to Napier, 6 January 1841.
14 Laband, *Assassination*, pp.22, 27–8.
15 *JSA* 2, pp.204, 206: Mangati, 14 June 1920.
16 *JSA* 6, p.291: Tununu, 11 June May 1903.

he was only wounded on the outside of his right thigh by a spear-thrust and not killed, and managed to make his way back to his infuriated and frightened king.[17] He received no kind welcome, for Dingane required a scapegoat on whom to heap the blame for his unexpected defeat. He been raging against his unsuccessful general: 'Woh! Where is Ndhlela? He too must die. It was he who used to say that Mpande was less than nothing, I see that it is he who has ruined my army as well.'[18] And, it is fair to say, perhaps Dingane was not being entirely unreasonable in his accusations, for it is not inconceivable that Ndlela was indeed playing a double game, he who had long been Mpande's protector. Certainly, Ndlela would not have been the only *isikhulu* in that uncertain time of civil war to be hedging his bets. What is certain, is that Dingane believed Ndlela guilty of disobeying his orders and treacherously favouring Mpande by holding back his *impi*, vehemently complaining that 'he hid it; it did not fight.'[19]

It is no surprise, then, that when Dingane's chief *induna* crawled wounded into his presence, the king greeted him with the damning accusation: 'So, Ndlela, you have destroyed my impi? ... You have killed my impi and left it there. So you favour Mpande? So you want to destroy me?[20] He thereupon ordered Ndlela's immediate execution for 'spoiling' his *impi*. Some of the young men of the uKhokhothi cast a volley of spears at him as he sat humbly on the ground, wounding him further. Then Sofoca kaMbelekwana put an ox-hide noose around his neck (the form of execution for men of status), pulled it tight and beat it with a stick until Ndlela was dead.[21] Dingane declared that the body of this man who, since the beginning of his reign, had been second only to him in the Zulu kingdom, was unworthy of burial. So, his corpse was cast aside like carrion for the wild animals to feed upon.

Mpande would not forget the many services Ndlela had rendered him, not least saving his life on several occasions—and perhaps ensuring that his army won the battle of the amaQongqo hills. Once he became king, he honoured Ndlela's sons, Godide and Mavumengwana, lavishing cattle on them, and raising them to become the most prominent *izikhulu* in the south of his kingdom.[22]

---

17 *JSA* 3, p.128: Mini, 6 April 1910.
18 *JSA* 3, p.123: Mgundeni, 11 July 1918.
19 *JSA* 6, pp.131: Socwatsha, 30 August 1921.
20 *JSA* 6, pp.131: Socwatsha, 30 August 1921.
21 *JSA* 6, pp.13, 69, 72, 131: Socwatsha, 31 December 1901, 28 August 1909, 30 August 1921; p.274: Tununu, 2 June 1903.
22 *JSA* 2, p.201: Mangati, 1 July 1918.

28

The Wild Beasts Have Killed One Another

The *Beeskommando* was just south of the White Mfolozi River, still nearly 60 miles short of the amaQongqo hills, when on the evening of 30 January Nongalaza's messengers brought word that he had triumphed in battle and that Dingane was in flight. With their war against Dingane won, even if they had taken no part in the final battle, the Boers set about cleaning the slate and imposing their final settlement on Zululand.[1]

Their intention was to execute both Dingane and Ndlela if they could be captured, but at present they did not know their whereabouts, or even if they still lived. But Nzobo was in their hands, naked, in chains and exposed to the freezing rain. The Boers decided this was the moment to proceed against him, and Nzobo was doubly unfortunate that Mpande was in the Boer camp, for the *umntwana* loathed him for repeatedly trying to persuade Dingane to kill him.[2] Legalistic as ever, the Boers convened a court martial on 31 January to try Nzobo along with Khambenzana, his unfortunate fellow envoy. Sentence was a foregone conclusion, for judges and counsel for the prosecution were one and the same, and Mpande and several of his *izinduna* were called to give evidence, all of them hostile witnesses. All accused Nzobo of advising Dingane in his various bloody acts against his own brothers, his subjects and Retief and his companions. Mpande was reduced to tears when he gave his testimony, assuring the judges that all the terrible things that had befallen the Boers 'stemmed from this fellow, who, when he spoke, was never contradicted by the king.'[3]

The impassive Nzobo comported himself with the utmost dignity. His honourable response to the accusations hurled against him was not to deny them, but to state with simple dignity that he had always attempted to act in his master Dingane's best interests. (And we might consider that if the execution of Retief had been a miscalculation, even if adopted for cogent reasons, his advice to eliminate Mpande had been proven right.) All that Nzobo requested of the court was that Khambezana be shown mercy. But the court was not swayed, and sentenced both men to immediate execution by firing squad. Pretorius tried to talk to Nzobo of the redemptive powers of Christ, just as Erasmus Smit had ministered to the young warrior executed after the battle of

---

1   For continuing operations by the *Beeskommando*, see *Annals* 1, pp.582–99: Commando against Dingaan, 30 January–24 February 1840; Delegorgue, *Travels, Volume One*, pp.110–27: 30 January –25 February 1840.
2   *JSA* 6, p.10: Socwatsha, 29 December 1901.
3   *JSA* 1, p.172: Hoye ka Soxalase, 21 September 1921.

Veglaer. But Dingane's great *induna* silenced the Chief Commandant with his determined and dignified reply. He had only one master, he declared, and it had been his duty to remain faithful to him. If there was indeed some other master in heaven, then he 'could not fail to be grateful to him for having performed his duty.'[4]

Nzobo and Khambezana were led, still tied together, to the place of execution. Both fell at the first volley but Nzobo was only wounded. With physical bravery matching the moral courage he had already exhibited, he struggled to his feet and steadfastly faced his executioners again. He died at their next volley. The amaZulu could not credit that Nzobo had been simply shot, and believed the Boers must have inflicted a much more terrible death on their implacable enemy. The widespread tale had it that he had been tied by the feet, face downwards, from the brake of a wagon and dragged to his death. Alternatively, it was said that he had been lashed to the spokes of the wheel of a moving wagon, and kept there until he died.[5]

On 3 February, 220 Boers of the *Beeskommando* set out under Pretorius from their camp at the White Mfolozi to join Nongalaza's men in pursuit of Dingane. Delegorgue was unimpressed by the 'strange sight' they made 'setting off in the greatest confusion, riding up the hills in disorderly fashion, their long guns slung clumsily over one shoulder.'[6] The heavy summer rain and mist slowed down the pursuing Boers who engaged several pockets of Dingane's supporters in a few minor skirmishes. Unbeknown to them, the Boers had now entered the tsetse fly zone, and their horses began to succumb to the ravages of Equine trypanosomiasis. With their horses mysteriously dying, the terrain unsuitable for wagons and the campaign becoming an increasingly frustrating and pointless operation, the Boers were soon looking for an excuse to call it off. On 5 February the *kommando* made contact with Nongalaza who informed them that Dingane had already crossed over the Phongolo with only a few followers, and that most of his *amabutho*, disgusted by his craven flight, were dispersing.

The Zulu used to say that 'a king who left his home and went to the mountains was finished'.[7] That certainly was holding true for Dingane. Significantly, the Boers learned on 7 February that the greatest *izikhulu* of the north, Klwana of the Buthelezi people and Maphitha, the Mandlakazi *inkosi*, were both signifying their desire to make peace with Mpande. Dingane had tried to keep them by him, but their decision to break away signified that his last supporters were melting away This intelligence was confirmed when the *kommando* began encountering numerous parties of the king's dispersed former adherents straggling south for home. Everything confirmed that the authority of fugitive Zulu king, whether still alive or dead, was shattered beyond repair, and that there was no point in continuing to pursue him through increasingly inhospitable country. Accordingly, and with considerable relief, on 8 February the Boers turned back when they reached the banks of the Phongolo which were thickly covered in impenetrable bush, and resigned the pursuit of Dingane to Nongalaza. While Mpande's general pushed north in search of the fugitive king, the Boers returned the way they had come. They drove away with them the 10,000 cattle they had captured, along with 1,000 or more 'apprentices', young

---

4 Delegorgue, *Travels, Volume One*, p.114.
5 *JSA* 2, p.202: Mangati, 1 July 1918; *JSA* 6, pp.10, 72, 129: Socwatsha, 29 December 1901, 29 August 1909, 29 August 1921; Gibson, *Story of the Zulus*, p.88.
6 Delegorgue, *Travels, Volume One*, pp. 116–17: 2 February 1840.
7 *JSA* 3, p.123: Mgundeni, 11 July 1918.

Zulu boys and girls they had abducted with force from their parents and who were destined for domestic service in the households of their wives.[8]

It would seem that Dingane only finally decided to retire across the Phongolo River with the remaining intact units of his army, those of his counsellors and other officers who had remained loyal (or feared capture and retribution), the surviving women of his household and all the cattle he could salvage, when he was informed on 3 February that the Boers had set out in pursuit of him. He did not contemplate for a moment making a stand against them, reportedly declaring, 'Never again will I face up to guns'.[9] Deliberately giving out misleading information about his intended destination to throw his pursuers off his track,[10] he led his remaining followers northeast into the dense, malaria-ridden bushveld, making for the western slopes of the Lubombo Mountains. His dwindling following followed reluctantly, fearing they would die of *imbo*, malarial fever compounded by dysentery.[11]

Nongalaza's forces pursued Dingane for about 30 miles and captured his mother, Mphikase. She was too old and exhausted to keep up any longer with the women of the *isigodlo*, and her son, determined to break free from his pursuers, pitilessly abandoned her to her fate. But Nongalaza did not long keep up the gruelling chase. Confident that the fugitive king had been forced sufficiently far away from the Zulu kingdom to pose no future threat to Mpande, he called a halt and withdrew. As for Dingane, who was still on the run, he must have realised that his authority as king had all but dissipated. Even so, while he still had some of his *izinduna* and the remnants of his *amabutho* and *isigodlo* about him, he could still convince himself that all was not entirely lost, and that—against all odds—he might yet follow in the steps of a Soshangane or Mzilikazi and carve out a new kingdom elsewhere.

Dingane called a halt to his flight at Hlathikhulu hill below the Lubombo Mountains. On its rugged, forested slopes he ordered the erection of a makeshift, but classic, royal residence with an *isigodlo* section and called it eSankoleni, or 'The Secluded Spot'. This, the last and most diminutive of Dingane's *amakhanda*, was built in the territory of Silevana, the regent for Sambane kaNhlolaluvalo, the heir to the chiefdom of the abakwaNyawo that lay along the western slopes of the Lubombo Mountains south of the Ngwavuma River which flows into the Phongolo. Silevana was a tributary of King Mswati II, the new Swazi king. The amaSwazi were understandably Dingane's inveterate foes and wished him only harm;[12] and it was in any case Swazi policy to forge good relations with the Boers who required that, as a sign of their good faith, that they assist in apprehending the fugitive Zulu king.[13] Thus Dingane's arrival in Silevana's domain put the regent in a difficult bind. He had no wish to antagonise his Swazi overlord, but the number of armed men Dingane still had about him left him no choice but to welcome his uninvited guest, even if that meant turning a blind eye to the activities of his *amabutho* who were soon helping themselves to his people's food supplies at the point of the spear. It consequently did not take Silevana long to decide that he must find some means of ridding himself of Dingane's unwelcome presence.

---

8   Cubbin, 'Port Natal', p.197.
9   *JSA* 6, p.131: Socwatsha, 30 August 1921.
10 *JSA* 6, pp.13, 131: Socwatsha, 31 December 1901; 30 August 1921.
11 *JSA* 6, p.14: Socwatsha, 1 January 1902.
12 *JSA* 6, p.228: Tikuba ka Magongo, 27 November 1898.
13 Bonner, *Swazi State*, p.45.

For their part, the Zulu notables still with Dingane at eSankoleni were becoming increasingly disaffected with their lot. In Socwatsha's words:

> The great men when alone said to each other: 'Where are we going? We are being killed by fever ... We are leaving the country of our people, the country of the Zulu.' They said, 'Let us kill him [Dingane], and go back to our own country.' But some asked, 'which people ... will kill him?' They said, 'Let the *amankengane* [an *inkengane* is a poor, destitute common fellow, a term contemptuously applied to any member of a foreign tribe] be decoyed into doing it. Let them kill him for us, while we go back. For Mpande is a son of Senzangakhona; he will rule us.' They said, 'Wo! Let amaSwazi be fetched.'[14]

The plotters' opportunity arose when Dingane despatched some members of his remaining *amabutho*, including his loyal bodyguard of the uKhokhothi, back across the Phongolo to retrieve as many as possible of the valuable props of royalty he had abandoned during his rapid withdrawal after the battle.[15] Dingane retained only the iziToyatoyi at eSankoleni, an untested *ibutho* of young lads—not unlike the iziNyosi whom Shaka had kept by him at the last—to act as his guards. The disloyal *izinduna* then persuaded the remaining *amabutho* that they had learned that a hostile *impi* was approaching with the intent of 'eating up' Dingane's cattle, and that they should disperse to guard the various cattle posts that had been established some distance away from eSankoleni. Once the *amabutho* had set off, leaving Dingane all but defenceless, they sent word to Silevana. He in turn alerted a roaming Swazi patrol under Sonyezane Dlamini of the situation, and they agreed to work together to liquidate Dingane.[16]

A picked force of Swazi *emajaha* and Nyawo warriors surrounded eSankoleni in the early hours of the morning, and it was said that some of the inhabitants had a sudden, strong whiff of birds, nor realizing they were smelling the feathered headdresses of a war party. Some of the *impi* crept into the *isigodlo* section where Dingane slept. He had always kept a number of large dun, red or black dogs by him acquired during Shaka's campaigns in the Mpondo country, and the fat and notoriously sluggish Makwedlana, much favoured by the king and fed on only beef and milk, gave the alarm before being run through. Dingane strode resolutely out of his *indlu*, *iklwa* in hand. A cast spear struck him, and he is said to have snarled, 'Fellow (*umfokazana*, a term of contempt meaning common person, menial), are you stabbing me with an assegai?'[17] Wounded as he was, Dingane managed to escape into the bush, valiantly protected by a few attendants including Makhanda whose job it was to sew on his *isicoco*. His assailants caught and killed a number of the women of Dingane's *isigodlo* including his sister, Nozilwane. The survivors (as we shall see) managed to make it back across the Phongolo into Zululand.

The Nyawo and Swazi war party melted away before the surprised iziToyatoyi could rally to their king's defence, shouting as they retired: 'Your people called us to come and kill him

---

14 *JSA* 6: pp.131–2: Socwatsha, 30 August 1921.
15 *JSA* 6, p.14: Socwatsha, 1 January 1902; p.291: Tununu, 11 June May 1903.
16 *JSA* 6, pp.13, 44, 132: Socwatsha, 31 December 1901, 29 June 1904, 29 August 1921 Bryant, *Olden Times*, pp.325–6; Bonner, *Swazi State*, p.44.
17 *JSA* 5, p.53: Ngidi, 5 November 1904.

Col H.C. Lugg photographed at King Dingane's grave in 1947. With him are Ndoda Nyawo, the son of Sambane kaNhlolaluvalo, the Nyawo *inkosi* in whose territory the king was killed, and his grandson, Zibunu Nyawo. (Campbell Collections, Durban, with permission)

because he has tired you out.'[18] The iziToyatoyi finally found Dingane as dawn was breaking, sitting rather than lying in the dense bush. And here accounts begin seriously to diverge. The lurid tale, concocted for the Boers' vengeful delectation, that their mortal enemy was tortured to death by being pricked from head to toe with sharp spears, bitten by dogs, blinded and starved, was a complete fabrication.[19] Ngidi attributed Dingane's death to his humiliation and remorse at having to wander the hills a fugitive, and to being stabbed by common people.[20] Others held that Silevana himself, and no commoner, had cast the spear that passed through Dingane's thigh and pierced his lower intestines. The iziToyatoyi were said to have carried Dingane back to eSankoleni where they inspected his deep wound and saw it was fatal. Rather than prolong his agony, they enlarged the wound with a spear so that he quickly died. The Zulu historian, Magema Fuze, moralistically reflected that they 'did well' to do so, 'so that he too should feel the spear as he made his great brother Shaka feel it.'[21] Socwatsha held that Dingane suffered only from a single wound in the upper arm. On being brought back to eSankoleni he sent an *induna* to fetch a narcotic potion to allay his pain. Dingane always carried an assortment of antidotes

18 *JSA* 6, p.13: Socwatsha, 31 December 1901.
19 *Annals* 1, pp. 375–6: Bezuidenhout's Narrative.
20 *JSA* 5, p.53: Ngidi, 5 November 1904.
21 Fuze, *Black People*, p.85.

and poisons with him, and whether by design or by mistake (who can tell?) he was administered a deadly draught. The moment he drank it, insisted Socwatsha, 'his colour changed to a darker hue, a perspiration came over him and in a short time he expired.'[22] But by whatever means Dingane suffered his painful and ignominious death, he must surely have reflected that Shaka's *idlozi* was finally exacting its revenge. Truly, as Dingane's *izibongo* lamented of the three half-brothers, 'The wild beasts of Jama have killed one another.'[23]

Dingane's remaining faithful attendants buried their king at eSankoleni. Perhaps he was laid alone in his grave like a commoner, but some maintained that the royal funeral customs were adhered to, and that a small retinue of attendants were killed to accompanied him into the next life and that black cattle were sacrificed at the funeral.[24] The site of the grave was known to the members of the Nyawo ruling house who courteously placed ritual stones on top of it.[25] Fearful that the Zulu royal house might exact revenge for their part in killing Dingane, for more than a century they kept the site a closely guarded secret, known only to a few.[26] Finally, on 18 June 1983 King Goodwill Zwelithini unveiled a monument erected by the KwaZulu Monuments Council close to the supposed location of Dingane's grave. The site is remote and difficult to reach and, like so many other out-of-the-way monuments in Zululand, King Dingane's memorial is not well protected and is at risk of falling into decay or being vandalised.

22 *JSA* 6, pp.44–5, 132: Socwatsha, 29 June 1904, 29 August 1921.
23 Rycroft and Ncobo (eds), *Praises of Dingana*, p.87.
24 *JSA* 6, p.132: Socwatsha, 29 August 1921.
25 Voortrekker sources state that the amaSwazi, in order to indicate their desire to cooperate with the Boers and to cement their alliance with them, brought them the purported scalp of Dingane adorned with ornaments Mpande confirmed were the king's. See Bonner, *Swazi State*, p.45. Whether this grisly trophy was indeed Dingane's scalp is highly debateable and does not accord with Zulu testimony concerning his burial.
26 In 1947 H.C. Lugg succeeded in locating the grave and photographing it. The stones were still there but the site was thickly covered in trees and bush. See Lugg, *Historic Natal*, pp.162–8.

29

Return to Mpande and Pay Homage to Him

With Dingane's flight and death, Mpande was left with several daunting goals. One was that of imposing his authority over the rump of the Zulu kingdom. Just how difficult this was going to prove was indicated by the high-handed and provocative behaviour of Maphitha, the great *isikhulu* in northern Zululand. When Mnkabayi, Dingane's redoubtable aunt who had stuck resolutely by the *umntwana* she had raised to be king, rallied the surviving women of his *isigodlo* and led them and a great number of cattle back across the Phongolo to find sanctuary with Maphitha, the Mandlakazi *inkosi* insolently detained half the women for his own *isigodlo* and seized all the cattle they had with them, thus depriving Mpande of considerable wealth.[1]

For the moment, though, Mpande allowed Maphitha's insubordination to slide because the most immediate problem was what to do with Dingane's erstwhile followers who had stuck by him to the end, and who were now disconsolately drifting back to offer their submission. With his last, laboured breaths, Dingane is believed to have whispered to those about him: 'I am now dead. Go and return to Mpande and pay homage to him. But there is one thing that is painful to me, and that is our people will always be maligned at Songiya's [Mpande's mother] as evil-doers.'[2] And indeed, many of Mpande's councillors believed that such people should be summarily 'cleared out of Zululand'. They were reflecting the popular sentiment among those on the winning side of the civil war who were derisively referring to the losers as *'umdidi kaNdlela'*, or 'Ndlela's rectum',[3] and were patting themselves on the back as the *'igeja* of Mpande,' the reversible plough of the Europeans that had ploughed them under.[4] Mpande ordered such talk to cease,[5] for he was determined to heal the bitter rifts of civil war and to live up to his name that meant (so Fuze believed) 'that he was the root *[impande]* of the Zulu nation'.[6]

Mpande's greatest challenge, however, was how to accommodate his rapacious 'allies', the Boers. On the morning of 10 February 1840, he and his chief councillors apprehensively obeyed

---

1 *JSA* 6, pp.14, 44: Socwatsha, 1 January 1902, 29 June 1904.
2 Fuze, *Black People*, p.83.
3 Ndlela's widows never again ate the lower intestines of a beast (considered a delicacy), because people would insult them and say, 'this is Ndlela's rectum who did not join Mpande cross over the river.' See *JSA* 4, pp.107–8: Mtshayankomo, 10 January 1921; p. 298: Ndukwana, 14 October 1900.
4 *JSA* 5, p.346: Singcofela, 3 April 1910.
5 *JSA* 4, p.68: Mtshapi, 3 April 1918.
6 Fuze, *Black People*, p.89.

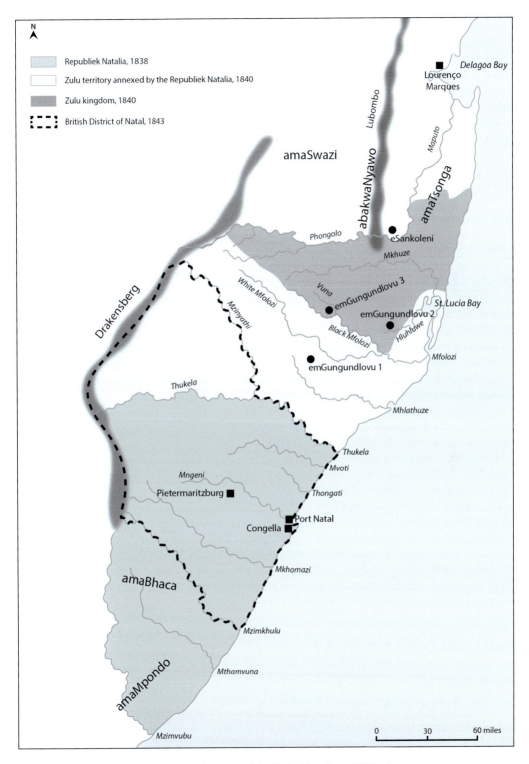

The Dismemberment of the Zulu Kingdom, 1838–43

the summons to appear before Chief Commandant Pretorius in the intimidating encampment of the *Beeskommando* on the southern bank of the Black Mfolozi.[7] They would have feared that the Boers were not intending to honour the terms of the treaty they had struck with Mpande on 27 October 1839, whereby they undertook to recognise him as king once Dingane had been overthrown. Initially, they must have been relieved when Pretorius, speaking in the name of the *Volksraad* of the Republiek Natalia, did indeed proclaim Mpande 'king or chief of the Zulus'. But it would quickly have dawned on them that the way in which the proclamation was couched constituted an unexpected affront. Rather than hailing Mpande as king by right of his royal lineage, it instead indicated that he was the new Zulu monarch thanks entirely to the favour of the Boers who 'were instruments in the hands of God' in putting 'an end to the indescribable cruelties and murders committed by Dingaan'. Mpande diplomatically indicated he 'was filled with excessive joy from head to heels.' But he must have been inwardly seething, not merely because Nongalaza's unaided victory over Dingane at the amaQongqo hills had been conveniently ignored, but because the Boer proclamation effectively reduced him to the status of the vassal of his 'great ally', the Republiek Natalia.

Nor was Pretorius yet done. On the morning of 14 February, he raised the flag of the Republiek Natalia. He then caused a proclamation to be read informing the dumbfounded Mpande that the Boers, to compensate themselves against the 122,600 *rixdollars* (or about £9,500) they arbitrarily claimed to have incurred as expenses in their 'unprovoked war' against Dingane,[8] were now going to annex a further vast swathe of Zulu territory between the Drakensberg Mountains and the sea. It comprised all the lands between the Thukela River to the south and the Black Mfolozi River to the north, including St Lucia Bay—in other words, about two-fifths of the kingdom Mpande had thought was to be his.[9] Following the announcement, the Boers fired a salute of 21 guns in self-congratulation and gave a general cheer. This time, Mpande could not manage to disguise his chagrin. He abruptly informed Pretorius that he could not stand the 'violent roaring' of the guns, and stooping every time one was fired, led his dismayed *izinduna* and *amakhosi* back to their own camp.

Delegorgue, who witnessed the contemptuously one-side ceremony, reflected critically on the conceit of the Boers who unjustly and foolishly annexed an already populated and enormous stretch of country they had no means of occupying or controlling.[10] The Boers entertained no such qualms. They engraved the date of their proclamation on two large stones, one of which they set up on the banks of the Black Mfolozi, and the other they buried nearby for safekeeping. Its business done, the *Beeskommando* withdrew south of the Thukela with an enormous booty of 31,000 head of cattle, not quite the 40,000 they had demanded of Dingane, but many enough. Each Boer in the *Beeskommando* received at least 20 head as his share of the booty. To placate their hard-done-by 'ally', Mpande, who was hardly pleased to see the cattle-wealth of his new

---

7 For Boer negotiations with Mpande, see *Annals* 1, pp. 591–6: Commando against Dingaan, 9–14 February 1840.
8 The *rixdollar* was a unit of currency introduced in the Cape by the VOC. It was still in circulation in the Colony during early 1840s when it was valued at 1s 6d to the pound sterling.
9 *Annals* 1, p.595: Commando against Dingaan, 14 February 1840: Proclamation by A.W.J. Pretorius.
10 Delegorgue, *Travels, Volume One*, pp.120–1: 14 February 1840.

kingdom being driven away, the Boers gave him a further 15,000 head to distribute among those *amakhosi* who had supported him in the civil war.[11]

Yet, despite appearances to the contrary, the Boers did not leave Mpande king as they supposed by their favour and under their sufferance—as undermined as might be imagined. Nor did they prove to be the great obstacle to the secure establishment of his rule they initially promised to be. For one thing, as Delegorgue predicted, the Boers simply did not have the manpower or capacity to make good their annexation of the territory between the Thukela and Black Mfolozi. So Mpande found he could continue to govern that region as if it were still his, and not the Boers', and was able to reside—as had the Zulu kings before him—in the valley of the White Mfolozi. Critically, the Zulu people continued to accept the institution of the Zulu monarchy as established by Shaka, and recognised Mpande's right to the throne through his indubitably royal lineage. He therefore received all the respect and deference due to the monarch and continued to perform all the royal functions previously exercised by Shaka and Dingane. He enrolled the *amabutho* and gave them permission to *ukuthunga*, or marry, kept up the various *amakhanda* (still often under the command of women of the royal house), maintained an extravagant royal *isigodlo*, and was regularly confirmed in his ritual powers at the national ceremonies. As had his two predecessors, he presided over his royal council, administered justice, and sent out his *amabutho* to levy fines, punish wrong-doers, collect tribute, and raid his neighbours.[12] Mpande also possessed personal skills that ensured he kept his throne. He was remembered by later generations as being naturally good and kind, not possessing the 'wicked heart' of either Shaka and Dingane whom Fuze described as 'wild beasts' by comparison.[13]

And crucially, considering that the Zulu kingdom was now abutted by an aggressive settler state possessing superior military technology, Mpande was a consummate diplomat. His dexterity had been honed over long, fraught years, during which he had soothed Dingane's suspicion and enmity, and he was able to coexist peaceably with the Boers despite their arrant breach of faith in depriving him of so much of his kingdom's territory. Even so, Mpande must be considered fortunate that (thanks to no initiative on his part) his rapacious and unreliable neighbours, the Boers of the Republiek Natalia, were very soon replaced by a colonial power with which he could establish stable relations.

Once the Boers had set up Mpande as their virtual vassal and had commenced to consolidate their rule in Republiek Natalia, it did not take long before the British government became genuinely concerned about their expansionist activities that menaced neighbouring black polities to their south, and consequently threatened the stability of the Cape's eastern frontier. Coupled to these strategic anxieties was growing humanitarian dismay at the Boers' harsh and destabilising racial policies in their republic. Consequently, Lord John Russell, who had succeeded Lord Normanby in September 1839 as Secretary for War and Colonies, took action. He wrote to Governor Napier on 14 June 1840 instructing him to resume the military occupation of Port Natal that had been given up only six months before. The object, wrote Russell, was to

---

11 *Annals* 1, p.376: Bezuidenhout's Narrative; p.596: Commando against Dingaan, 14 February 1840; Delegorgue, *Travels, Volume One*, p.127.
12 Laband, *Zulu Kings*, pp.156–7.
13 Fuze, *Black People*, pp. 93, 146.

'establish the influence of the British name in a country which is being devastated by the reckless proceedings of the Queen's subjects',[14] that is, the Emigrant Boers.

Russell did not expect Napier to act before he found it expedient to do so and had sufficient troops available for the mission. It was therefore only on 4 May 1842 that British troops raised the Union Flag over Port Natal.[15] The Boers resisted and defeated the British in a skirmish at Congella on 23 May, forcing them to take refuge in their fort. But reinforcements under Colonel Josias Cloete were shipped in and relieved the fort on 25 June. The Boers fell back on Pietermaritzburg and on 5 July 1842 the *Volksraad* submitted to the Queen. Then followed a curious period of shared rule between the British and Boer authorities while the British government pondered what to do with the territory it seemed to have acquired. On 12 May 1843 it was reluctantly annexed to the Crown as the District of Port Natal, but it was not until 31 May 1844 that the Republiek Natalia was finally extinguished and Natal annexed as a separate District of the Cape Colony. Its southern boundary was redefined as the Mzimkhulu River, and the territory to the south between it and the Mzimvubu River, which had formed part of the Republiek Natalia, was excluded. Only on 15 July 1856 would Natal finally be created a separate British colony.

The Boers of the former Republiek Natalia could not readily accept living under British rule —after all, they had trekked away from the Cape in the first place to escape it.[16] By 1848 most had trekked back over the Drakensberg to the highveld, there to join the communities of Emigrant Farmers that were gradually establishing a number of little republics.[17] By the Sand River Convention of 17 January 1852, the British recognised the full independence of the Boers statelets north of the Vaal River, and by September 1853 they had united to establish the Zuid-Afrikaansche Republiek (also known as the Transvaal Republic). By the Bloemfontein Convention of 23 February 1854, the British also recognised the independence of the Oranje Vrijstaat, the Boer republic between the Orange and Vaal rivers. So even if the Republiek Natalia had come to naught, the *Trekkers* settled on the highveld had achieved their objective and were fully independent of British rule.[18]

In Zululand, Mpande trod cautiously and with great skill during the nebulous period of the British takeover of Natal. He quickly divined that by cultivating the British he could undo the Boers' titular control over the southern two-fifths of his kingdom. His efforts bore fruit on 5 October 1843, when, in his esiKlebheni *ikhanda* in the emaKhosini valley, Mpande assented to a document written in English that Henry Cloete, Her Majesty's Commissioner in Natal, ordered to be painstakingly translated for him word for word. By its terms, Mpande recognised British sovereignty in the District of Port Natal. In return, the British recognised him as 'King of the Zulu Nation'. This was vital, for unlike the Boers who had 'proclaimed' him king at

---

14 *Annals* 1, p.605: Lord John Russell to Napier, 18 June 1840.
15 For the transition of Natal from Boer republic to British colony, see Charles Ballard, 'Traders, Trekkers and Colonists', in Duminy and Guest (eds), *Natal and Zululand*, pp. 122–128; Brookes and Webb, *History of Natal*, pp.35–75.
16 Between 1849 and 1852 nearly 5,000 British immigrants flowed into Natal, giving settler society there its distinctive British cast.
17 A few Boers living between the Thukela and Mzinyathi Rivers set up their Klip River Republic in January 1847. This territory was part of British Natal, and the authorities brought the 'Klip River Insurrection' to an end in January 1848.
18 See Giliomee, *Afrikaners*, pp.166–75.

their discretion, the British 'recognised' him as the monarch of a sovereign kingdom. The Boer annexation of Zululand between the Black Mfolozi and Thukela rivers was annulled, and a new boundary line between the Zulu kingdom and Natal was drawn from the sea north-west along the Thukela and Mzinyathi Rivers to the Drakensberg. By this arrangement the British hung onto nearly half of the territory the Boers had annexed in 1840, and Mpande abandoned any claims to the territory south-west of the Mzinyathi and south of the Thukela formerly ruled by Shaka and Dingane. In recompense, he secured the continued independence of the historic core of the much-reduced Zulu kingdom.[19]

Despite his kingdom being wedged uncomfortably between British Natal to the south and the Boer Zuid-Afrikaansche Republiek to the north-west, Mpande succeeded in maintaining its integrity by fostering close ties with the British. While he was careful never to acknowledge that the British held any authority over him, he nevertheless (as Cetshwayo, his son who succeed him in 1872, expressed it) treated them 'like relations', keeping them as frankly informed as he would members of the royal house and his *izikhulu* of everything that went on in his kingdom.[20] Once Cetshwayo succeeded Mpande as king, he sedulously attempted to maintain his father's good relations with the British. It was due to no fault of his that they turned against him. He was the victim of their confederation policy that aimed at uniting all the white-ruled states of southern Africa—both British colonies and Boer republics—under the Crown. As the corollary of this policy, the British were committed to eliminating any potential military threats against the new political order by the few remaining independent African kingdoms in the subcontinent. The Zulu kingdom was consequently shattered beyond repair in the ensuing Anglo-Zulu War of 1879. Its territory was then wracked by devastating civil war, and by 1887 its British and Boer neighbours had divided up and annexed all the fragments.[21]

The Boer republics finally lost their hard-won independence in the Anglo-Boer (South African) War of 1899–1902, and on 31 May 1910 became part of the Union of South Africa, a self-governing dominion of the British Empire. But that was not the end of the story. On 31 May 1961, after a close-fought referendum confined to those of white descent, South Africa became an independent republic. The achievement of their republic was a triumph for resurgent Afrikaner nationalists over their 'English' rivals. They proceeded to govern the county in the spirit of the *Voortrekkers* and implemented the fully segregationist policy of apartheid. Only with the first free and universal elections of 1994 did their political organ, the National Party, relinquish its hold on power in today's officially non-racial democracy.[22]

And if not one descendent of the *Voortrekkers* any longer holds a position of political authority in the top echelons of the ruling African National Congress (ANC) government, there is still a Zulu king. King Goodwill Zwelithini (r. 1968–2021) emerged from the long eclipse of the Zulu monarchy under colonial and apartheid rule, and his status was recognised by the South

---

19 See *Annals* II, pp.299–300: Articles of a Treaty between King Panda and Commissioner Henry Cloete, 5 October 1843. Mpande made his own mark to the treaty, and Cloete signed. The treaty did not specify Zululand's northwestern and northern boundaries.
20 Webb and Wright (eds), *Zulu King Speaks*, pp.79–80, 93–4.
21 For a recent history of Zululand from the accession of Mpande to 2021, see Laband, *Zulu Kings*, pp.140–356.
22 For an authoritative and well-illustrated history of South Africa from the 1840s until recent times, see Giliomee and Mbenga, *South Africa*, pp. 145–437.

African Constitution of 1996 and by the Traditional Leadership and Governance Framework Act of 2003. He was paid an extremely generous state stipend, but was essentially no more than a ceremonial figure embodying Zulu traditions and customs, and wielded only indirect political influence. On his death, Misuzulu Sinqgobile kaZwelithini, his son by his Great Wife, was appointed as the next Zulu king on 7 May 2021. He has yet to be crowned, however, because his accession is facing a legal challenge in the Pietermaritzburg High Court brought by a rival faction of the royal house. In January 2022 judgment was reserved, and it could be months, if not years, before the matter is resolved.[23]

Both Dingane and Mpande would have viewed the current Zulu king's emasculated royal prerogatives with incredulity. Indeed, it was the very different royal powers at Dingane's command and his exercise of them that have made him the pivotal figure in the war of 1837–1840. Egged on by his advisers, it was his decision to kill Retief and his party and to send out his *izimpi* to annihilate the *Trekkers* in their encampments, thus setting the war in motion. His centrality was recognised in 1910 when the government of the new Union of South Africa proclaimed 16 December a public holiday, and named it 'Dingaan's Day', not to honour the Zulu king, but rather to serve as a reminder of his supposed perfidy and wickedness.[24]

For many years, Dingane was regarded in this entirely negative light. Magema Fuze, the first Zulu historian, violently characterised him in 1921 as a sheer 'torment', a king who, while masquerading in an outwardly human form, actually possessed 'the heart of a dog' and was 'truly like a poisonous snake'.[25] In penning this damning judgement, the mission-trained Fuze was associating himself with what Felix Okoye, writing in 1969, termed the 'undying hatred' of white historians who based their hostile representation of the Zulu king on the impressions and judgments of contemporary Port Natal settlers, missionaries, and *Trekkers*.[26] Yet, only a few decades later, in the middle years of the 20th century, isiZulu-speaking academics like Bhambatha W. Vilakazi and Sibusiso Nyembezi were assiduously working with Zulu oral traditions and *izibongo* to modify the stubbornly-held image of Dingane as a treacherous and bloodthirsty tyrant. They did not minimise his failings as a man or as a ruler, but they also placed him in his proper historical context as an African king who strove as best he could to preserve his kingdom and his people from invading white settlers. In doing so, they believed that Dingane proved that Africans were capable of defending their own independence, and that his defiance was a proud signpost on the road to liberation.[27]

No serious historian, whether black or white, would today fail to contextualise Dingane in his time and place, or neglect to consult the Zulu oral sources alongside the written record. But that does not mean that Dingane has ceased to be a controversial figure. If no longer the unredeemed monster of *Trekker* myth, Dingane has become a figure of contention in Zulu ranks. Conservatives and Zulu nationalists, who revere Shaka as the heroic founder of the Zulu

---

23   For the current status of the Zulu monarch in South Africa, see Laband, *Zulu Kings*, pp.5–7, 356–65. For Misuzulu's contested succession, see Cyril Madlala, 'Of Kings and Courts', *Daily Maverick*, September 2021; and Julia Madibogo, 'Zulu King Goes Rogue', *City Press*, October 2021. For the legal tussle in the High Court, see Chris Makhaye, 'Battle Royale', *Daily Maverick*, 12 and 13 January 2022.
24   Since 1995, the public holiday on 16 December has been called the Day of Reconciliation.
25   Fuze, *Black People*, pp.83–4.
26   Okoye, 'Dingane', p.221.
27   Ndlovu, 'Representations of King Dingane', pp. 97–110.

kingdom, still tend to denounce Dingane for bringing down ruin upon it through his disastrous handling of the *Trekker* invasion. Radicals, on the other hand, represented today by the ruling ANC, have continued to hale Dingane as a valiant freedom fighter, worthy of their pantheon of heroes.[28]

In this historian's view, when Dingane is divested of the ideological trappings that have been thrust upon him, he presents something of a tragic figure. Defeat, flight, and ignominious death were not his inevitable fate. For, if the Emigrant Farmers had not decided to make his kingdom their new home when they trekked away from the Cape, would he have been compelled to resist them by every means he could, and then been violently driven from a throne on which he had seemed so firmly seated? Would Shaka, if he had survived assassination in 1828, have been any more successful a decade later in staving off the battle-hardened *Trekkers* with their firearms, horses and wagons? After all, the interlopers presented an entirely unprecedented military challenge, while the structure of the Zulu kingdom and the Zulu way of war continued unchanged from Shaka's reign to Dingane's. Nor is it beyond reasonable possibility that, even after his crushing defeat at Boer hands and his failure to carve out a 'second kingdom' in Swaziland, Dingane and the Republiek Natalia might have managed to co-exist relatively peaceably, just as the Zulu kingdom and Port Natal had managed to rub along since 1824.

In the end, it was dynastic conflict within the Zulu royal house and ensuing civil war that brought Dingane down to final ruin. The Boers took every advantage of this situation, but their attempt to establish the Republiek Natal on the ruins of the Zulu kingdom were thwarted. All their hardships and heartbreak, all the desperate battles they had fought against Dingane's *izimpi* were brought to naught, not by the amaZulu who had valiantly resisted their unprovoked invasion of their kingdom, but by the British who had stood on the sidelines and tried to broker peace between the warring sides. As we have seen, within a couple of years, the British had annexed all of Dingane's kingdom south of the Thukela and Mzinyathi Rivers as the Colony of Natal, and the disgruntled Boers had trekked away to the highveld to escape the reimposition of British rule they had attempted to escape when they first abandoned the Cape Colony over a decade before. It is thus one of history's many ironies that the ultimate winners in the war of 1837–1840 were not the *Trekkers* who had defeated Dingane, but the British who intervened once it was over to prevent the Boers from enjoying the untrammelled, destabilising fruits of victory and territorial conquest.

---

28 Sithole, 'Meanings of the Battle of Ncome', pp.326–8. These conflicting imaginings of Dingane played out during the civil war between conservatives and radicals that beset KwaZulu-Natal between 1985 and 1993, a terrible period during which some 20,000 people were killed and another 200,000 were rendered homeless.

Glossary

Afrikaans –English

agterryer (pl. **agterryers**) attendant on horseback; servant or auxiliary of colour on commando
boer (pl. **boere**) farmer; Dutch-speaking settler (Boer)
Boerperd (pl. **Boerperde**) Cape pony
burger (pl. **burgers**) burgher, citizen
Burgerraad (pl. **Burgerrade**) Burgher Council
disselboom (pl. **disselbome**) wagon shaft
dorp (pl. **dorpe**) village
drift (pl. **driwwe**) ford
droster (pl. **drosters**) runaway, deserter; raider
erf (pl. **erwe**) plot of ground
gat (pl. **gate**) pit
herneutermes (pl. **herneutermesse**) hunter's knife, Bowie knife
goewerneur (pl. **goewerneurs**) governor
inspan to yoke oxen
kaalveld naked veld; the open, flat highveld
kakerbeenwa (pl. **kakerbeenwaens**) 'jawbone' wagon
kappie (pl. **kappies**) sun-bonnet, hood
kaptein (pl. **kapteins**) chief, headman
kloof (pl. **klowe**) gorge
kommandant (pl. **kommandants**) commandant
kommando (pl. **kommandos**) commando
kommissietrek (pl. **kommissietrekke**) expedition of exploration, scouting party
koppie (pl. **koppies**) hillock
laer (pl. **laers**) laager
landdros (pl. **landdroste**) magistrate
lafaard (pl. **lafaards**) coward
loper (pl. **lopers**) bag of buckshot
maatskappy (pl. **mattaskappye**) community
meester (pl. **meesters**) teacher
Nagmaal (sing. only) Holy Communion
ossewa (pl. **ossewaens**) ox-wagon
poort (pl. **poorte**) narrow mountain pass; defile
predikant (pl. **predikante**) minister

riem (pl. **rieme**) raw-hid thong
roer (pl. **roers**) gun
seekoei (pl. **seekoeie**) hippopotamus
skof (pl. **skofte**) distance covered in one day's trek by ox-wagon
smous (pl. **smouse**) pedlar
snaphaan (pl. **snaphane**) flintlock musket
trek (pl. **trekke**) to pull, to migrate; emigration
trekboer (pl. **trekboere**) migrant farmer/settler
trekker (pl. **trekkers**) emigrant
trektou (pl. **trektoue**) drag-rope for wagon
trippel slow canter
veldkornet (pl. **veldkornette**) field cornet
verenigde maatskappy (pl. **verenigde maatskappye**) united community
volk (pl. **volkere**) nation, people
volksraad (pl. **volksrade**) parliament
voorlaier (pl. **voorlaiers**) muzzle-loader
voorloper (pl. **voorlopers**) leader of a span of oxen
voortrekker (pl. **voortrekkers**) pioneer

siSwati–English

In accordance with modern practice, words in siSwati and isiZulu are entered under the stem (here capitalised) and not under the prefix

liButfo (pl. **emaButfo**) age-grade regiment
liJaha (pl. **emaJaha**) warrior
iNgwenyama (pl. **tiNgwenyama**) king

isiZulu–English

isAngoma (pl. **izAngoma**) diviner inspired by ancestral spirits
isiBamu (pl. **iziBamu**) gun
iBandla (pl. **amaBandla**) assembly of notables
isiBaya (pl. **iziBaya**) enclosure for livestock
imBongi (pl. **izimBongi**) praise-singer
iziBongo (pl. only) praises
iBunu (pl. **amaBunu**) Boer
iButho (pl. **amaButho**) age-grade regiment of men or women; warrior
ukuButhwa to enrol young men into an *ibutho*
isiCoco (p. **iziCoco**) headring
uDibi (pl. **izinDibi**) baggage boy
umDidi (pl. **imiDidi**) rectum
iDlozi (pl. **amaDlozi**) ancestral spirit
inDlu (pl. **izinDlu**) hut
inDuku (pl. **izinDuku**) heavy stick for fighting or walking

inDuna (pl. **izinDuna**) appointed officer of state, headman, councillor
umFokozana (pl. **abaFokozana**) destitute, insignificant stranger
isiFuba (pl. **iziFuba**) chest, or central part of an army
isiGaba (pl. **iziGaba**) section of an *ibutho*; its assigned quarters in an *ikhanda*
iGebe (pl. **amaGebe**) game-pit
iGeja (pl. **amaGeja**) plough
ukuGiya to perform a war-dance
isiGodlo (pl. **iziGodlo**) king's private enclosure at upper end of *ikhanda*; women of the king's establishment
isiGqiki (pl. **iziGqiki**) wooden head-rest; section of an *ikhanda* next to the *isigodlo*
isiGqila (pl. **iziGqila**) maid-servant, concubine
inGxotha (pl. **izinGxotha**) brass armlet conferred by king as mark of distinction
umHanga (pl. **imiHanga**) ferocious animal or person; tanned white man
iHawu (pl. **amaHawu**) small shield for dancing or travelling
isiHlambelo (pl. **iziHlambelo**) washing enclosure
iHlambo (pl. **amaHlambo**) ritual cleansing ceremony
isiHlangu (pl. **iziHlangu**) large war-shield
uHlangothi (pl. **izinHlangothi**) wing of huts at *ikhanda*
iHubo (pl. **amaHubo**) anthem
isiJula (pl. **iziJula**) throwing-spear
iKhanda (pl. **amakhanda**) royal military homestead where *amabutho* were stationed
umKhandlu (pl. **imiKhandlu**) council
ukuKhetha to perform a slow, rhythmical dance
ukuKleza to drink milk directly form the udder; to serve as a cadet
ukuKhonza to pay allegiance to king or chief
umKhosi (pl. **imiKhosi**) annual 'first-fruits' ceremony
isiKhwili (pl. **iziKhwili**) short, thick, knobless fighting-stick
iKhubalo (pl. **amaKhubalo**) medicine to ward off evil or disease
isiKhulu (pl. **iziKhulu**) great one of the realm, nobleman
umKhumbi (pl. **imiKhumbi**) assembly of men
iKlwa (pl. **amaKlwa**) stabbing-spear (assegai)
inKosana (pl. **amaKhosana**) king's heir by chief wife
inKosi (pl. **amaKhosi**) chief, king
inKosikazi (pl. **amaKhosikazi**) woman of status, principal wife of king
iLawu (pl. **amaLawu**) hut set aside for unmarried men
iLobolo (sing. only) goods or cattle handed over by man's family to formalise marriage transaction
iMbo (sing. only) malaria fever
uMnyama (sing. only) spiritual force of darkness or evil influence
iMpande (pl. **iziMpande**) root
iMpi (pl. **iziMpi**) military force; battle; campaign
iNceku (pl. **iziNceku**) king's confidential household attendant and advisor of the king
ukuNcinda to suck from the fingertips
umNdlunkulu (sing. only) maids-of-honour; girls of royal establishment
iNkatha (pl. **iziNkatha**) sacred grass coil, symbol of the nation

iNkengane (pl. **amaNkengane**) derogatory term applied to a foreign person, a destitute, common individual
iNtelezi (pl. only) ritual medicines to counteract evil influence or sorcery
umNtwana (pl. **abaNtwana**) prince of the royal house
umNumzane (pl. **abaNumzane**) married headman of a homestead
iNyanga (pl. **iziNyanga**) traditional healer, herbalist
umPhakathi (pl. **imiPhakathi**) general assembly of commoners
ukuPhalaza to vomit
ukuPhehla to stir ritual medicine to a foam
uPhondo (pl. **izimPondo**) horn; flank of the army
iQadasi (pl. **amaQadasi**) able-bodied person; Boer
ukuQomana to ritually challenge
isiQu (pl. **iziQu**) badge of bravery
umQulu (pl. **imiQulu**) rolled-up mat; throne
amaSi (pl. only)) sour curdled milk
inSila (pl. **izinSila**) body dirt
ukuSisa to pasture livestock in the care of a subordinate
umSizi (pl. **imiSizi**) powdered, charred ritual medicines
ukuThefula Zulu dialect spoken by the abakwaQwabe and other people of eastern seaboard
umThakathi (pl. **abaThakathi**) witch or wizard
ukuThela to submit; pay tribute
ukuThetha to go through the ceremony of giving praise to the ancestors
umuThi (pl. **imiThi**) occult medicine
ukuThunga to sew on the headring; receive royal permission to marry
isiThunyisa (pl. **iziThunyisa**) gun-holder
isiThuthakazana (pl. **iziThuthakazana**) little fool
uTshwala (sing. only) sorghum beer
umuVa (pl. **imiVa**) loins of a beast; reserve of an army
iViyo (pl. **amaViyo**) company of an *ibutho*
ukuVeza to bring forward, exhibit
iWisa (pl. **amaWisa**) knobbed stick (knobkerrie)
umuZi (pl. **imiZi**) homestead of huts under a headman
ukuZila to observe ritual abstinence

Bibliography

Recorded Zulu Oral Testimony

Cope, Trevor, *Izibongo: Zulu Praise Poems* (Oxford: Oxford University Press, 1968)

Dlamini, Paulina, edited by H. Filter and S. Bourquin, *Servant of Two Kings* (Durban: Killie Campbell Africana Library; Pietermaritzburg: University of Natal Press, 1986)

Rycrof, D.K., and Ngcobo, A.B. (eds.) *The Praises of Dingana (Izibongo zikaDingana)* (Pietermaritzburg: University of Natal Press; Durban: Killie Campbell Africana Library, 1988)

Webb, C. de B., and Wright, J.B. (eds), *The James Stuart Archive of Recorded Oral Evidence Relating to the History of the Zulu and Neighbouring Peoples*, 6 volumes (Pietermaritzburg: University of Natal Press; Durban: Killie Campbell Africana Library, 1976, 1979, 1982, 1986, 2001, 2014)

— *A Zulu King Speaks: Statements Made by Cetshwayo kaMpande on the History and Customs of His People* (Pietermaritzburg: University of Natal Press; Durban: Killie Campbell Africana Library, 1978)

Published Collections of Official Documents; Diaries; Letters, Newspaper Reports; Memoirs

Bird, John, *The Annals of Natal 1495 to 1845*, 2 volumes (facsimile reprint, Cape Town: C. Struik, 1965)

Chase, John Centlivres, *The Natal Papers: A Reprint of All Notices and Public Documents Connected with That Territory Including a Description of the Country and a History of Events from 1498 to 1843 in Two Parts* (facsimile reprint, Cape Town: C. Struik, 1968)

Cory, Sir George E. (ed.), *The Diary of the Rev. Francis Owen* (Cape Town: Van Riebeeck Society, 1926)

Delegorgue, Adulphe, edited by Fleur Webb, Stephanie J. Alexander and Colin de B. Webb, *Travels in Southern Africa, Volume One* (Durban: Killie Campbell Africana Library; Pietermaritzburg: University of Natal Press, 1990)

— edited by Fleur Webb, Stephanie J. Alexander and Colin de B. Webb, *Travels in Southern Africa, Volume Two* (Durban: Killie Campbell Africana Library; Pietermaritzburg: University of Natal Press, 1997)

Gardiner, Captain Allen Francis, *Narrative of a Journey to the Zooloo Country in South Africa, Undertaken in 1835* (facsimile reprint, Cape Town: C. Struik, 1966)

Grobler, Jackie (ed.), *Louis Tregardt se Dagboek 1836–1838* (Pretoria: Litera Publikasies, 2013)

Isaacs, Nathaniel, edited by Louis Herman and Percival R. Kirby, *Travels and Adventures in Eastern Africa Descriptive of the Zoolus, Their Manners, Customs with a Sketch of Natal* (Cape Town: C. Struik, 1970)

Kirby, Percival R. (ed.), *Andrew Smith and Natal. Documents Relating to the Early History of That Province* (Cape Town: The Van Riebeeck Society, 1955)

Kotzé, D.J. (ed.), *Letters of the American Missionaries 1835–1838* (Cape Town: Van Riebeeck Society, 1950)

Leverton, Dr B.J.T (ed.), *Records of Natal, Volume One 1823–August 1828* (Pretoria: The Government Printer, 1984)

— *Records of Natal, Volume Two September 1828–July 1835* (Pretoria: The Government Printer, 1989)

— *Records of Natal, Volume Three August 1835–June 1838* (Pretoria: The Government Printer, 1990)

— *Records of Natal, Volume Four July 1838–September 1839* (Pretoria: The Government Printer, 1992)

Maclean, Charles Rawdon. Stephen Gray (ed.), *The Natal Papers of 'John Ross'* (Pietermaritzburg: University of Natal Press; Durban: Killie Campbell Africana Library, 1992)

Schoon, the Rev. H.F., and Mears, W.G.A. (tr.), *The Diary of Erasmus Smit* (Cape Town: C. Struik, 1972)

Stuart, James, and Malcolm, D. McK (eds), *The Diary of Henry Francis Fynn* (Pietermaritzburg: Shuter & Shooter, 1969)

Webb, C. de B. (ed.), 'Captain Allen Gardiner: A Memoir by His Wife' *Natalia*, 4 (December 1974), pp.28–41

Books

Angas, George French, *The Kaffirs Illustrated in a Series Drawings* (London: G. Barclay for J. Hogarth, 1849)

Anon., *Pictorial History of South Africa* (London: Odhams Press, c.1937)

Ballard, Charles, *The House of Shaka: The Zulu Monarchy Illustrated* (Durban: Emoyeni Books, 1988)

Becker, Peter, *Rule of Fear. The Life and Times of Dingane, King of the Zulu* (London: Longmans, 1964)

Bonner, Philip, *Kings, Commoners and Concessionaires: The Evolution and Dissolution of the Nineteenth-Century Swazi State* (Johannesburg: Ravan, 1983)

Brookes, Edgar H., and Webb, Colin de B., *A History of Natal* (Pietermaritzburg: University of Natal Press, 1965)

Bryant, the Rev. A.T., *Olden Times in Zululand and Natal Containing Earlier Political History of the Eastern-Nguni Clans* (London: Longman Green, 1929)

— *The Zulu People as They Were before the White Man Came* (Pietermaritzburg: Shuter & Shooter, 1949)

D'Assonville, Victor E., *Blood River* (Weltevreden Park: Marnix: 2000)

Eldredge, Elizabeth A., *The Creation of the Zulu Kingdom, 1815–1828: War, Shaka and the Consolidation of Power* (Cambridge: Cambridge University Press, 2014)

— *Kingdoms and Chiefdoms in Southeastern Africa* (Rochester, NY: University of Rochester Press, 2015)

Etemad, Bouda, *Possessing the World: Taking the Measurement of Colonialism from the 18th to the 20th Century* (New York and Oxford: Berghan Books, 2007)

Etherington, Norman, *The Great Treks: The Transformation of Southern Africa, 1815–1854* (Harlow, England: Longman, 2001)

Fuze, Magema M., edited by H.C. Lugg and A.T. Cope, *The Black People and Whence They Came: A Zulu View* (Pietermaritzburg: University of Natal Press; Durban: Killie Campbell Africana Library, 1979)

Gibson, James Young, *The Story of the Zulus*, (new edition, London: Longman Green, 1911)

Giliomee, Hermann, *The Afrikaners: Biography of a People* (Cape Town: Tafelberg; Charlottesville: University of Virginia Press, 2003)

Giliomee, Hermann, and Mbenga, Bernard, *New History of South Africa* (Cape Town: Tafelberg, 2007)

Gordon-Brown, A., *Pictorial Africana* (Cape Town: A.A. Balkema, 1975)

Guy, Jeff, *The Destruction of the Zulu Kingdom: The Civil War in Zululand, 1879–1884* (London: Longman, 1979)

Hammond-Tooke, David, *The Roots of Black South Africa* (Johannesburg: Jonathan Ball Publishers, 1993)

Hattersley, Alan F., *An Illustrated Social History of South Africa* (Cape Town: A.A. Balkema, 1973)

Holden, the Rev. William C., *History of the Colony of Natal, South Africa* (London: Alexander Heylin, 1855)

Holmes, Richard (ed.), *The Oxford Companion to Military History* (Oxford: Oxford University Press, 2001)

Iliffe, John, *Africans. The History of a Continent* (Cambridge: Cambridge University Press, 2000)

— *Honour in African History* (Cambridge: Cambridge University Press, 2005)

Knight, Ian, *The Anatomy of the Zulu Army from Shaka to Cetshwayo 1818–1879* (London: Greenhill Books, 1995)

— *Warrior Chiefs of Southern Africa* (Poole: Firebird Books, 1994)

Krige, Eileen Jensen, *The Social System of the Zulus* (2nd edition, Pietermaritzburg: Shuter & Shooter, 1974)

Laband, John, *The Assassination of King Shaka* (Johannesburg and Cape Town: Jonathan Ball, 2017)

— *Bringers of War: The Portuguese in Africa during the Age of Gunpowder and Sail from the Fifteenth to the Eighteen Century* (London: Frontline Books, 2013)

— *The Eight Zulu Kings from Shaka to Goodwill Zwelithini* (Johannesburg and Cape Town: Jonathan Ball, 2018)

— *Historical Dictionary of the Zulu Wars* (Lanham, Maryland: The Scarecrow Press, 2009)

— *The Land Wars: The Dispossession of the Khoisan and AmaXhosa in the Cape Colony* (Cape Town: Penguin, 2020)

— *The Rise and Fall of the Zulu Nation* (London: Arms & Armour, 1997)

— *The Transvaal Rebellion: The First Boer War 1880–1881* (London: Pearson Longman, 2005)

— *Zulu Warriors: The Battle for the South African Frontier* (New Haven and London: Yale University Press, 2014)

Laband, John, and Thompson, Paul, *The Illustrated Guide to the Anglo-Zulu War* (Pietermaritzburg: University of Natal Press, 2000)

Labuschange, Pieter, *Ghostriders of the Anglo-Boer War (1899–1902): The Role and Contribution of Agterryers* (Pretoria: University of South Africa Press, 1999)
Landau, Paul S., *Popular Politics in the History of South Africa* (Cambridge: Cambridge University Press, 2010)
Leśniewski, Michał, *The Zulu–Boer War 1837–1840* (Leiden; Boston: Brill, 2021)
Lugg, H.C., *Historic Natal and Zululand* (Pietermaritzburg: Shuter & Shooter, 1949)
Mackeurtan, Graham, *The Cradle Days of Natal (1497–1845)* (London: Longmans Green, 1930)
Mann, Robert James, *The Zulus and Boers of South Africa. A Fragment of Recent History* (London: Edward Stanford, 1879)
Maylam, Paul, *A History of the African People of South Africa: From the Early Iron Age to the 1970s* (London: Croom Helm, 1989)
Mossop, E.E, *Old Cape Highways* (Cape Town: Maskew Miller, 1927)
Muller, C.F.J., *A Pictorial History of the Great Trek* (Cape Town: Tafelberg, 1978)
Naidoo, Jay, *Tracking Down Historical Myths: Eight South African Cases* (Johannesburg: Ad. Donker, 1989)
Natal Provincial Museum Service, *uMgungundlovu* (Melmoth: uMgungundlovu Museum, n.d.)
Nathan, Manfred, *The Voortrekkers of South Africa* (South Africa: Central News Agency, 1937)
Penn, Nigel, *The Forgotten Frontier: Colonists and Khoisan on the Cape's Northern Frontier in the 18th Century* (Athens: Ohio University Press; Cape Town: Double Story Books, 2006)
Poland, Marguerite, Hammond-Tooke, David, and Voight, Leigh, *The Abundant Herds. A Celebration of the Nguni Cattle of the Zulu People* (Vlaeberg, South Africa: Fernwood Press, 2003)
Rankin, Elizabeth, and Schneider, Rolf Michael, *From Memory to Marble: The Historical Frieze of the Voortrekker Monument. Part I: The Frieze* (Berlin and Boston: Walter de Gruyter, 2019)
— *From Memory to Marble: The Historical Frieze of the Voortrekker Monument. Part II: The Scenes* (Berlin and Boston: Walter de Gruyter, 2020)
Rasmussen, R. Kent, *Migrant Kingdom: Mzilikazi's Ndebele in South Africa* (London: Rex Collings; Cape Town: David Philip, 1978)
Roberts, B., *The Zulu Kings* (London: Sphere Books, 1974)
Rogers, Col. H.C.B., *Weapons of the British Soldier* (London: Sphere Books, 1968)
Samuelson, R.C.A., *Long, Long Ago* (Durban: Knox, 1929)
Saunders, Christopher (ed.), *Reader's Digest Illustrated History of South Africa: The Real Story* (3rd edition, Cape Town: The Reader's Digest Association South Africa, 1994)
Shamase, M.Z., *Zulu Potentates from Earliest to Zwelithini kaBhekuzulu* (Durban: S.M. Publications, 1996)
Shillington, Kevin, *Luka Jantjie: Resistance Hero of the South African Frontier* (London: Aldgate Press, 2011)
Smail, J.L., *From the Land of the Zulu Kings* (Durban: A.J. Pope, 1979)
Stapleton, Timothy J., *A Military History of South Africa from the Dutch-Khoi Wars to the End of Apartheid* (Santa Barbara: Praeger, 2010)
Storey, William Kelleher, *Guns, Race, and Power in Colonial South Africa* (Cambridge: Cambridge University Press, 2008)
Summers, R., and Pagden, C.W., *The Warriors* (Cape Town: Books of Africa, 1970)

Swart, Sandra, *Riding High: Horses, Humans and History in South Africa* (Johannesburg: Wits University Press, 2010)

Tabler, Edward C., *Pioneers of Natal and South-Eastern Africa 1552–1878* (Cape Town and Rotterdam: A.A. Balkema, 1977)

Taylor, Stephen, *Shaka's Children: A History of the Zulu People* (London: HarperCollins, 1994)

Walker, Eric A., *The Great Trek* (London: Adam and Charles Black, 1938)

— *A History of Southern Africa* (London: Longmans, 1968)

Articles and Chapters

Ballard, Charles, 'Natal 1824–44: The Frontier Interregnum', *Journal of Natal and Zulu History*, IV (1982), pp.49–64

— 'Traders, Trekkers and Colonists', in Andrew Duminy and Bill Guest (eds), *Natal and Zululand from Earliest Times to 1910: A New History* (Pietermaritzburg: University of Natal Press and Shuter & Shooter, 1989), pp.116–45

Berning, Gillian, '*Indaba Yamakhos' Ayibanjelwa Mlando* / The Matter of Kings in Not Kept', in Marilee Wood (coordinator), *Zulu Treasures: Of Kings and Commoners. A Celebration of the Material Culture of the Zulu People*, (Ulundi: KwaZulu Cultural Museum; Durban: The Local History Museums, 1996), pp.43–72

Chadwick, George, 'The Battle of Blood River', *Military History Society Battlefield Tour Notes* (May 1878), <samilitaryhistory.org/misc/bldrvr.html>, accessed 1 November 2020

Cobbing, Julian, 'The Evolution of Ndebele Amabutho, *Journal of African History*, 15: 4 (1974), pp.607–31

— 'The Ndebele State', in J.B. Peires (ed.), *Before and After Shaka: Papers in Nguni History* (Grahamstown: Rhodes University, Institute of Social and Economic Research, 1981), pp.160–77

Colenbrander, Peter, 'The Zulu Kingdom, 1828–1879', in Andrew Duminy and Bill Guest (eds), *Natal and Zululand from Earliest Times to 1910: A New History* (Pietermaritzburg: University of Natal Press and Shuter & Shooter, 1989), pp.83–115

Cooper, Barbara M., 'Oral Sources and the Challenge of African History', in John Edward Philips (ed.), *Writing African History* (Rochester, NY: University of Rochester Press, 2006), pp.191–215

De Wet, H.C., 'Die Grafte van Piet en Dirkie Uys', *Historia*, 8: 3 (September 1963), pp.166–174

— 'Waar het Piet Uys and sy Seun Dirkie Geval?', *Historia*, 4: 2 (June 1959), pp.75–88

Dlamini, Nsizwa, 'Monuments of Division: Apartheid and Post-apartheid Struggles over Zulu Nationalist Heritage Sites', in Benedict Carton, John Laband and Jabulani Sithole (eds), *Zulu Identities: Being Zulu, Past and Present* (Pietermaritzburg: University of KwaZulu-Natal Press, 2008), pp.383–94

Eldredge, Elizabeth A., 'Sources of Conflict in Southern Africa c. 1800–1830', in Carolyn Hamilton (ed.), *The Mfecane Aftermath. Reconstructive Debates in Southern African History* (Johannesburg: Witwatersrand Press; Pietermaritzburg: University of Natal Press, 1995), pp.122–61

Etherington, Norman, 'Christianity and African Society in Nineteenth-Century Natal', in Andrew Duminy and Bill Guest (eds), *Natal and Zululand from Earliest Times to 1910: A New History* (Pietermaritzburg: University of Natal Press and Shuter & Shooter, 1989), pp.275–301

Grobler, Jackie, 'Afrikaner- en Zoeloeperspektiewe op die Slag van Bloedrivier, 16 Desember 1838', *Tydskrif vir Geesteswetenskappe,* 50: 3 (September 2010); pp.363–82
— 'The Retief Massacre of 6 February 1838 Revisited', *Historia: Journal of the Historical Association of South Africa,* 56: 2 (November 2011), pp.113–32
Hanretta, Shaun, 'Women, Marginality and the Zulu State: Women's Institutions and Power in the Early Nineteenth Century', *Journal of African History,* 39 (1998), pp.389–415
Haswell, Robert, 'Pieter Mauritz Burg: The Genesis of a Voortrekker *Hoofdplaats*' in John Laband and Robert Haswell (eds), *Pietermaritzburg 1838–1988: A New Portrait of an African City* (Pietermaritzburg: University of Natal Press and Shuter & Shooter, 1988), pp.24–7
— 'The Voortrekker Dorps of Natal', *Natalia,* 10 (December 1980), pp.23–33.
Hattersley, Alan F., 'Slavery at the Cape, 1652–1838', in Eric A. Walker (ed.), *The Cambridge History of the British Empire, Volume VIII, South Africa, Rhodesia and the High Commission Territories* (Cambridge: Cambridge University Press, 1963), pp.266–78
Henige, David, 'Oral Tradition as a Means of Reconstructing the Past', in John Edward Philips (ed.), *Writing African History,* (Rochester, NY: University of Rochester Press, 2006), pp.169–90
Kennedy, Philip A., 'Mpande and the Zulu Kingship', *Journal of Natal and Zulu History,* IV (1981), pp.21–38
Koopman, Adrian, 'The Names and Naming of Durban', *Natalia,* 34 (December 2004), pp.70–87
Laband, John, '"Bloodstained Grandeur": Colonial and Imperial Stereotypes of Zulu Warriors and Zulu Warfare', in Benedict Carton, John Laband and Jabulani Sithole (eds) Jabulani, *Zulu Identities: Being Zulu, Past and Present* (Pietermaritzburg: University of KwaZulu-Natal Press, 2008), pp.168–76
— '"Fighting Stick of Thunder": Firearms and the Zulu Kingdom: The Cultural Ambiguities of Transferring Weapons Technology', *War & Society,* 33: 4 (October 2014), pp.229–43
— 'Mfecane (1815–1840)', in Gordon Martel (ed.), *The Encyclopedia of War* (Oxford: Wiley-Blackwell, 2011), <http://onlinelibrary.wiley.com/doi/10.1002/9781444338232.wbeow400/abstract>,accessed 7 August 2020)
— 'The Military Significance of the Battle of Blood River', in Department of Arts, Culture, Science and Technology, *Seminar on the Re-interpretation of the Battle of Blood River/Ncome* (Kwa-Dlangezwa: University of Zululand, seminar held on 31 October 1998), pp.24–8
— 'The Rise and Fall of the Zulu Kingdom', in Benedict Carton, John Laband and Jabulani Sithole (eds) Jabulani, *Zulu Identities: Being Zulu, Past and Present* (Pietermaritzburg: University of KwaZulu-Natal Press, 2008), pp.87–96
— 'Zulu Civilians during the Rise and Fall of the Zulu Kingdom', in John Laband (ed.), *Daily Lives of Civilians in Wartime Africa form Slavery Days to Rwandan Genocide* (Westport and London: Greenwood Press, 2007), pp.51–84
Labuschange, J. Andre, 'The Church of the Vow', in John Laband and Robert Haswell (eds), *Pietermaritzburg 1838–1988: A New Portrait of an African City* (Pietermaritzburg: University of Natal Press and Shuter & Shooter, 1988), p.28
Labuschagne, Pieter, 'A Spatial Analysis of the Ncome/Blood River Monument/Museum Complex as Hermeneutic Objects of Reconciliation and Nation Building', *South African Journal of African History,* 28: 3 (2013), pp.104–16

Leśniewski, Michał, 'Deconstructing the Myth of the Deaths of Piet and Dirk Uys: A Reconstruction of the Battle of eThaleni, 10 April 1838', *Journal of African Military History*, 2 (2018), pp.1–23.

Liesegang, Gerhard, 'Dingane's Attack on Lourenço Marques in 1833', *Journal of African History*, 10: 4 (1969), pp.565–79

Lye, William F., 'The Ndebele Kingdom South of the Limpopo River', *Journal of African History*, 10: 1 (1969), pp.87–104

Maphalala, J.S.M., 'The Re-interpretation of the War of Ncome, 16 December 1838', in Department of Arts, Culture, Science and Technology, *Seminar on the Re-interpretation of the Battle of Blood River/Ncome* (Kwa-Dlangezwa: University of Zululand, seminar held on 31 October 1998), pp.54–63

Ndlovu, Sifiso Mxolisi, '"He Did What Any Other Person in His Position Would Have Done to Fight the Force of Invasion and Disruption": Africans, the Land and Contending Images of King Dingane ("The Patriot") in the Twentieth Century, 1916–1950s', *South African Historical Journal*, 38 (May 1998), pp. 99–143

— 'A Reassessment of Women's Power in the Zulu Kingdom', in Benedict Carton, John Laband and Jabulani Sithole (eds) Jabulani, *Zulu Identities: Being Zulu, Past and Present* (Pietermaritzburg: University of KwaZulu-Natal Press, 2008), pp.111–21

— 'Zulu Nationalist Representations of King Dingane', in Benedict Carton, John Laband and Jabulani Sithole (eds) Jabulani, *Zulu Identities: Being Zulu, Past and Present* (Pietermaritzburg: University of KwaZulu-Natal Press, 2008), pp.97–110

Ntuli, Deuteronomy Bhekinkosi, '"Praises Will Remain"', in Marilee Wood (coordinator), *Zulu Treasures: Of Kings and Commoners. A Celebration of the Material Culture of the Zulu People* (Ulundi: KwaZulu Cultural Museum; Durban: The Local History Museums, 1996), pp.27–34

Nyembezi, C.L.S., 'The Historical Background to the Izibongo of the Zulu Military Age, Part I', *African Studies* 7: 2-3 (June 1948), pp.110–25

— 'The Historical Background to the Izibongo of the Zulu Military Age, Part II', *African Studies* 7: 4 (June 1948), pp.157–174

O'Connor, Damian, 'Dragoons and Commandos: The Development of Mounted Infantry in Southern Africa 1654–1899', *RUSI Journal*, 153: 1 (February 2008), pp.90–4

Okoye, Felix N.C., 'Dingane: A Reappraisal', *Journal of African History*, 10: 2 (1969), pp.221–35

Parkington, John E., and Cronin, Mike, 'The Size and Layout of Mgungundlovu 1829–1838', *South African Archaeological Society Goodwin Series*, No. 3. Iron Age Studies in South Africa (1979): pp.133–48

Poland, Marguerite, 'Zulu Cattle: Colour Patterns and Imagery in the Names of Zulu Cattle', in Marilee Wood (coordinator), *Zulu Treasures: Of Kings and Commoners. A Celebration of the Material Culture of the Zulu People* (Ulundi: KwaZulu Cultural Museum; Durban: The Local History Museums, 1996, pp.35–42

Pols, Ivor, 'The Voortrekker Museum', in John Laband and Robert Haswell (eds), *Pietermaritzburg 1838–1988: A New Portrait of an African City* (Pietermaritzburg: University of Natal Press and Shuter & Shooter, 1988), pp.163–4

Porter, Andrew, 'Religion, Missionary Enthusiasm, and Empire', in Andrew Porter and Alaine Low (eds), *The Oxford History of the British Empire*, vol. III, *The Nineteenth Century*, (Oxford: Oxford University Press, 2001), pp.222–46

Raum, O.F., 'Aspects of Zulu Diplomacy in the 19th Century', *Afrika und Übersee*, 66: 1 (1983), pp.25–42

'Report of the Panel of Historians (Professors J.S. Maphalala, J. Laband, C.Λ. Hamilton and Dr. J.E.H. Grobler)', in Department of Arts, Culture Science and Technology, *The Re-Interpretation of the Battle of Blood River / Ncome:* (Kwa-Dlangezwa: University of Zululand, seminar, 31 October 1998), pp.63–8

Retief, Johannes J., 'The Voortrekkers and the Ndebele. Part One: Attacks on the Vaal River and Liebenbergskoppie, 21 and 23 August 1836', *Military History Journal*, 16: 1 (December 2015), <samilitaryhistory.org/vol166jr.html>, accessed 30 July 2020

— 'The Voortrekkers and the Ndebele. Part Two: The Battle of Vegkop, 20 October 1836', *Military History Journal*, 17: 1 (June 2016), <samilitaryhistory.org/vol171jr.html>, accessed 20 July 2020

Roodt, Frans, 'Zulu Metalworking', in Marilee Wood (coordinator), *Zulu Treasures: Of Kings and Commoners. A Celebration of the Material Culture of the Zulu People* (Ulundi: KwaZulu Cultural Museum; Durban: The Local History Museums, 1996), pp.93–105

Ross, Robert, 'The !Kora Wars on the Orange River, 1830–1888', *Journal of African History*, 16: 4 (1975): pp.556–76

Schönfeldt-Aultman, Scott, M., 'Monument(al) Meaning-Making: The Ncome Monument & Its Representation of Zulu Identify', *Journal of African Cultural Studies* 18: 2 (December 2006), pp.215–34

Sithole, Jabulani, 'Changing Images of the Battle of Blood River/iNcome', in Department of Arts, Culture Science and Technology, *The Re-Interpretation of the Battle of Blood River/ Ncome:* (Kwa-Dlangezwa: University of Zululand, seminar, 31 October 1998), pp.29–42

— 'Changing Meanings of the Battle of Ncome and Images of King Dingane in Twentieth-Century South Africa', in Benedict Carton, John Laband and Jabulani Sithole (eds) Jabulani, *Zulu Identities: Being Zulu, Past and Present* (Pietermaritzburg: University of KwaZulu-Natal Press, 2008), pp.322–30

Stapleton, Timothy J. 'Firearms Technology', in Timothy J. Stapleton (ed.), *Encyclopedia of African Colonial Conflicts*, vol. 1 (Santa Barbara and Denver: ABC-CLIO, 2017), pp.287–92

— 'South Africa', in Ian F.W Beckett (ed.), *Citizen Soldiers and the British Empire, 1837–1902* (London: Pickering and Chatto, 2012), pp.139–54

Thompson, Leonard, 'Co-operation and Conflict: The High Veld', in Monica Wilson and Leonard Thompson (eds), *The Oxford History of South Africa, Volume 1: South Africa to 1870* (Oxford: Oxford University Press, 1969), pp.391–446

— 'Co-operation and Conflict: The Zulu Kingdom and Natal', in Monica Wilson and Leonard Thompson (eds), *The Oxford History of South Africa, Volume 1: South Africa to 1870* (Oxford: Oxford University Press, 1969), pp.334–90

Tylden, George, 'The Development of the Commando System in South Africa, 1715 to 1922', *Africana Notes and News*, 13 (March 1958–December 1959), pp.303–13

— 'The Wagon Laager', *Society for Army Historical Research*, 41: 168 (1963), pp.200–5

Uys, Ian S., 'The Battle of Italeni', *Military History Journal*, 4: 5 (June 1979), <samilitaryhistory.org/vol045iu.html>, accessed 18 May 2020

— 'A Boer Family', *Military History Journal*, 3: 6 (December 1976), <www.boereafrikana.com/Mense/Groot_Trek_Leiers/Piet_Uys/Piet_Uys.htm>, accessed 18 May 2020

— 'Her Majesty's Loyal and Devoted Trekker Leader: Petrus Lafras Uys', *Natalia*, 18 (December 1988), pp.30–40

Van Jaarsveld, Floris A., "n Afrikanerperspektief op die Groot Trek: Simbool en Ritueel', *Historia: Journal of the Historical Association of South Africa*, 31: 2 (November 1988): pp.11–26

Van Zyl, M.C., 'Die Slag van Vegkop', *Historia: Journal of the Historical Association of South Africa*, 3: 21 (October 1986): pp.63–70

Venter, C., 'Die Voortrekkers en die Ingeboekte Slawe Wat die Groot Trek Meergemaak Het', *Historia: Journal of the Historical Association of South Africa*, 36: 1 May (1991): pp.14–29

Wright, John, 'Turbulent Times: Political Transformations in the North and East, 1760s–1830s', in Carolyn Hamilton, Bernard K. Mbenga and Robert Ross (eds), *The Cambridge History of South Africa, Volume I: From Early Times to 1885* (Cambridge: Cambridge University Press, 2012), pp.211–52

Wright, John, and Hamilton, Carolyn, 'Ethnicity and Political Change before 1840', in Robert Morrell (ed.), *Political Economy and Identities in KwaZulu-Natal: Historical and Social Perspectives* (Durban: Indicator Press, 1966), pp.15–32

— 'Traditions and Transformations: The Phongolo-Mzimkhulu Region the Late Eighteenth and Early Nineteenth Centuries', in Andrew Duminy and Bill Guest (eds), *Natal and Zululand from Earliest Times to 1910: A New History* (Pietermaritzburg: University of Natal Press and Shuter & Shooter, 1989), pp.49–82

Unpublished Theses and Workshop Papers

Cubbin, Anthony Edward, 'Origins of the British Settlement at Port Natal, May 1824–June 1842' (unpublished Ph.D. thesis, University of the Orange Free State, 1983)

— 'Retief's Negotiations with Dingana: An Assessment' (University of Natal, Pietermaritzburg: Natal History Workshop, 23–24 October 1990), 14pp.

— 'A Study in Objectivity: The Death of Piet Retief' (unpublished MA dissertation, University of the Orange Free State, 1980)

Dictionaries

Doke, C.M., and Vilakazi, B.W. (compilers), *Zulu–English Dictionary*, (2nd edition, Johannesburg: Witwatersrand University Press, 1972)

Kritzinger, M.S.B., Steyn, H.A., Schoonees, P.C., and Cronjé, U.J., *Groot Woordeboek: Afrikaans–Engels/English–Afrikaan* (9th edition, Pretoria: J.L. van Schaik, 1965)

Index

72nd (Dule of Albany's Own Highlanders) Regiment of Foot 175, 188, 212, 214, 215, 220, 225, 226

Albany settlers 15–16, 105
Algoa Bay 13, 14
agterryers 59–60, 98, 137, 144, 150, 151, 152, 159, 164, 193, 204, 228
Army of Natal 160–1, 162

Bahurutshe 85, 109
Barends, Barend 74, 84, 86, 90, 109
Barolong 78, 80, 84, 85, 90, 91, 101, 103, 110
Basotho 76, 77, 80, 82, 218
Bataung 84, 90, 91
Batlhaping 73, 74–6, 82, 85, 90, 109
Batlokwa 77, 80, 84, 90, 91, 97, 103, 139, 143
Battle of Blood River Reinterpretation Committee xi
Beeskommando 227, 228–9, 232, 234, 235, 242
umBelebele *ibutho* 217
emBelebeleni *ikhanda*
 1st 130, 203
 2nd 217, 219
Bergenaars 74, 84
Bezuidenhout, Daniel 157, 158, 159
Bhalule *impi*, 1828 37–8, 39–40, 41
Bhibhi kaNkobe 36, 125, 135, 232
Bhongoza kaMefu 204–6, 209
Biggar, Alexander 118, 160, 172, 178, 188, 192, 205, 206, 208, 209
Biggar, Robert 172, 173, 175, 176, 177, 188
Bloem, Jan 84, 85, 86, 90, 109
Blood River, battle of, 1838 viii, xii, 168, 178, 189–202, 209, 210, 212, 229. *See also* Ncome, battle of
Blood River battlefield monuments x–xii
Bloukrans, battle of, 1838 155–9, 170, 185
Boerperd 51–2

Cane, John 32, 33, 35, 37, 41–2, 113, 118, 119, 137, 141, 160–1, 172, 173, 175, 176, 177
cannons 45, 62, 178, 182, 184, 186, 193, 196, 199, 205
Cape Colony viii, 13, 14–15, 16, 30, 64, 93, 188, 244, 247
Cape Town 35, 42, 50, 58, 63, 64, 67, 68, 86, 105, 124, 180
Cape Frontier Wars 14
 Second 58
 Fourth 15, 51, 91
 Fifth 15, 31, 49, 91
 Sixth 49, 61, 64, 65, 86, 105, 118
Celliers, Charl (Sarel) 88, 90, 91, 97, 98–9, 100, 102, 103–4, 110, 158, 159, 190, 192, 200
Cetshwayo kaMpande 36, 40, 122, 245
Charters, Maj. Samuel 187–8, 212, 213
Cloete, Henry 244, 245
Cloete, Col. Josias 244
Cole, Sir Lowry 35, 42, 43
Comet 178, 179
Congella 212, 215, 225, 244
Cowie, William 215–16

Delagoa Bay 16, 30, 37, 45, 66, 88, 91–2, 107, 124, 132, 216
De Lange, Johan Hendrik ('Hans Dons') 157–8, 162, 181, 182, 184, 185, 191, 192, 296, 208
Delegorgue, Adulphe 68, 201, 212, 223, 227, 228, 235, 242, 243
Difaqane 16, 73, 27, 77, 80. *See also Mfecane*
Dingane kaSenzangakhona viii, 21, 22, 23, 37–42, 44–6, 49, 81, 82, 100, 108–9, 111, 112–19, 120, 121, 123–36, 137–54, 159, 160, 161, 162, 164, 166, 170, 171, 172,178, 180, 181, 187, 191, 203, 205, 206, 209, 210, 211, 213–17, 219, 220, 221, 222, 223, 224, 225,231, 232–3, 234, 235–9, 240, 242, 243, 246–7
uDlambedlu *ibutho* 109, 135, 195, 197, 208, 209, 219, 229, 231, 232

261

oDlambedlwini *ikhanda* 130, 208, 209
uDlangezwa *ibutho* 199 201
Dlokweni, battle of, 1838, 174, 176, 177. *See also* Thukela, battle of
Doppers 69–70, 91, 102
Drakensberg passes 109, 111, 142, 155
drosters 73–4, 75, 76, 77, 78, 79, 84, 85, 86, 87, 90, 93, 103, 110, 139, 161
kwaDukuza *ikhanda* 38, 39, 41, 120, 122, 151
D'Urban, Maj Genl Sir Benjamin 46–7, 48, 64, 66, 67, 85, 86, 107, 108, 115, 116, 142, 187

Elizabeth and Susan 13, 14, 33, 35

Farewell, Lt Francis George 30–1, 32, 33, 35, 39, 43
firearms *See* muskets
Fort Victoria 187, 212–13, 214, 220, 225, 226
Fuze, Magema 238, 240, 243, 246
Fynn, Henry Francis 30, 31, 32, 33, 34, 35, 43, 120

eGabeni 87, 103, 109
 battle of, 1837 110, 119, 137, 143, 164, 166, 170
Gambusha 214–15, 216
Gardiner, Capt Allen 14–17, 118, 122, 137, 139, 143, 147, 161, 173, 178
Gatslaer 181–5, 186, 193
Gaza kingdom 37, 39, 40, 88, 205, 211
emaGebeni, battle of, 1838 181–6, 206, 209. *See also* Veglaer, battle of
Glenelg, Baron 47, 64, 66, 86, 115, 117, 187, 220
isiGodlo 83, 118, 124–8, 129, 130, 131, 134, 146, 148, 149, 152, 178, 203, 223, 236, 237, 243
Goodwill Zwelithini kaBhekuzulu xi, 239, 245
Grahamstown 15, 15, 35, 41, 43, 58, 67, 105, 157, 172, 175
Grand Army of Natal 172–7, 178, 185
Great Trek 61–6, 70–1
Griquas 73, 74, 75, 76, 77, 78, 79, 84, 85, 90, 103, 109
isiGulutshane *ibutho* 166, 197–201
umGumanqa *ibutho* 221
emGumanqeni *ikhanda* 131
emGungundlovu *ikhanda*
 1st 19, 22, 43, 109, 113, 114, 118, 119, 120–30, 133, 135, 137, 140, 141, 144, 145–6, 148, 150, 151, 153, 155, 162, 164, 166, 172, 178, 181, 188, 191, 202, 203–4, 206, 210, 211, 212, 223, 225
 2nd 211
 3rd 211, 214, 224, 227, 228

Halstead, Thomas 32, 119, 142, 152–3, 160
Hartenaars 74, 84
imiHaye *ibutho* 178, 195, 197, 229, 231
herneuetermes 55, 152
Hintsa kaKhawuta 31, 88
iHlaba *ibutho* 24, 151–2, 197–201
emaHlabaneni *ikhanda* 23

Isaacs, Nathaniel 32, 35, 39, 120, 136, 138

Jervis, Capt Henry 213, 214, 215, 216, 220, 225, 226

Kaliphi 93, 95, 96, 97, 99, 101, 103
Khambezana 228, 234, 235
kwaKhangela *ikhanda* 114, 124, 130, 140, 175, 221
Khoikhoin 14, 59
Khoisan 15, 32, 33, 56, 63, 64–5, 69, 73, 88, 93, 94, 95, 113, 118, 138, 155, 159, 160, 173, 177, 181, 182, 228
uKhokhothi *ibutho* 21, 199–201, 229, 232, 233, 237
umKhulutshane *ibutho* 109, 131, 135, 166, 175, 197–201, 217, 229
King, James 13, 32, 34, 35
esiKlebheni *ikhanda* 130, 203, 244
Klwana kaNgqengelele 217, 232, 235
Kok, Adam II 74, 75, 90, 107
Kok, Cornelis 84, 109
kommando system 50–1, 56, 58–60
kommissietrekke 48, 49, 58, 92, 93, 95, 108, 157
Kopjeskraal, battle of, 1836 94
Korana 73–4, 77, 78, 84, 85, 103, 109
Kuruman mission 76, 82, 93, 103

laager system 58–9
emLambongwenya *ikhanda* 175, 222, 223, 224–5
Landman, Karel 148, 168, 178, 180, 186, 187, 188, 189, 192, 205, 206
Leśniewski, Michał vii, 163, 164, 166, 181, 229
Liebensbergkoppie, battle of, 1836 94–5
London Missionary Society 74, 76, 104
Lourenço Marques 30, 31, 45, 178, 179
Lubuye, battle of, 1839 217–19, 223
Lugg, Col H.C. 238, 239
Lunguza kaMpukane 21, 138, 200, 201

Maclean, Charles 32
Mahlungwana kaTshoba 229, 231
Makwedlana 128, 131, 237
MaNthatisi 77, 143
Maphitha kaSojiyisa 223, 235, 240
Maritz, Gerrit 90, 101, 102, 104, 106, 107, 108,

111, 141,142, 143, 157, 158–9, 163, 181, 185, 186, 212
Maritz, J. Stephanus 186, 188
Mathunjana kaSibhaxa 224
Matiwane kaMasumpa 34, 135
kwaMatiwane 119, 135, 147, 148, 150, 152, 153, 155, 204
Mbholompo, battle of, 1828 34, 35, 135
Mbopha kaSitayi 38, 41
Mfecane 16, 34 *see also Difaqane*
Mhlangana kaSenzangakhona 37–8, 39, 41
Mnkabayi kaJama 23, 36–7, 38, 39, 40, 149, 223, 240
Modderlaer 170, 181
Moffat, Revd Robert 75, 76, 81, 82, 86, 93
Moroka II 91, 141, 107, 110
Mosega 85, 87, 93, 95, 96, 110
  battle of, 1837 103–4, 170, 199
Moshweshwe I 76–7, 78, 86, 107
Mpande kaSenzangakhona 40, 122, 126, 127, 135, 154, 172, 175, 177, 214, 220–6, 227, 229, 231, 232, 233, 234, 235, 236, 237, 239, 240, 242–3, 244–5, 246
Mphikase kaMyiyeya 38, 40, 236
amaMpondo 14, 29, 30, 48,
Mswati II 217, 236
abakwaMthethwa 16, 17
Mthonjaneni heights 130, 205, 208, 209, 211
muskets viii, 33, 34, 45–6, 50, 51, 52–6, 62, 73, 74, 76, 77, 84, 90, 92, 98, 99, 100, 112, 113, 116, 143, 146, 150, 152, 157, 158, 166, 168, 170, 173, 175, 176, 177, 182, 186, 192, 193, 195, 199, 201, 206, 208, 209, 216, 229
Mzilikazi kaMashobana 80–2, 83, 84, 85, 86–7, 90, 93, 96, 97–8, 99, 100, 103, 104, 107–8, 109, 110–11, 119, 139, 140, 142, 143, 145, 150, 163, 171, 216, 236

Napier, Maj Gen Sir George 187, 214, 220, 226, 243, 244
Natal, Colony of 244, 247
Natalia, Republiek 147, 180, 212, 220, 221, 224, 225, 226, 242, 243, 244, 247
Ncome, battle of, 1838 viii, xi, xii, 188, 198–202, 203, 206, 209, 210, 229. *See also* Blood River, battle of
Ncome battlefield monument x–xii
Ndebele-Boer wars
  1836 92–101
  1837 103–4, 110
Ndebele-*droster* wars, 1828, 1831, 1834, 1837 84, 85, 87, 90, 109–10
Ndebele kingdom 80–2, 83–4, 85, 87, 110-11
Ndebele military system 82–3, 86–7

Ndlela kaSompisi 84, 109, 113, 115, 125, 129, 132, 135–6, 147, 148, 149, 151, 181, 184, 185, 186, 191, 193, 195, 199, 216, 222, 223, 224, 226, 228, 229, 231, 232–3, 234
Ndlovu, Sifiso 159, 153
umNdlunkulu 118, 124–6, 127, 131, 135, 178, 211, 236, 240
Ndondakusuka, battle of, 1838 177. *See* Dolokweni, battle of, and Thukela, battle of
abakwaNdwandwe 16–17, 33, 37, 80–1, 82, 211, 223
Ngidi kaMcikaziswa 23, 24, 28, 151, 197, 203, 238
amaNgwane 34, 135
Nieuw Holland, Vrye Provincie van 106, 140, 141, 180
kwaNkatha 134, 135
kwaNobamba *ikhanda* 22, 116
uNomdayana *ibutho* 217
Nongalaza kaNondela 175, 225, 227, 228, 229, 231, 232, 234, 235, 236, 242
Normanby, Marquis of 220, 243
Nozitshada kaMagoboza 231–2
Ntunjambili raid, 1838 160–1, 172, 173
abakwaNyawo 236, 237–8, 239
iziNyosi *ibutho* 109, 135, 195, 197–201, 199, 219, 229, 231, 237
eziNoyisini *ikhanda* 130
Nzobo kaSobadli 113, 114, 115, 129, 132, 133, 135, 136, 147, 148, 150, 151, 166, 170, 172, 191, 193, 195–6, 199, 216, 227–8, 234–5

Ogle, Henry 32, 33, 35, 161, 172, 214
Oorlams 73–4
ossewa 56–8
Owen, Revd Francis 118–19, 134, 137, 139, 141, 143, 146–7, 148–9, 151, 153, 160, 162

oPathe, battle of, 1838 209, 210. *See also* White Mfolozi, battle of
Philippolis 74, 75, 76, 90
Pietermaritzburg 161, 190, 212, 225, 244
Port Elizabeth 14, 15, 30, 34, 35, 38, 178, 179
Port Natal viii, 13, 30–1, 32, 34, 42, 43–4, 46, 48–9, 58, 66, 108, 111, 114, 115, 116–17, 124, 137, 139, 144, 147, 178–80, 187, 188, 211–13, 214, 220, 221, 224, 226, 243–4, 247
Port Natal, 1st British occupation of, 1838–1839 187, 213, 220, 226
Port Natal, 2nd British occupation of, 1842–1843 243–4
Port Natal, British District of, 1843–1856 244
Port Natal hunter-traders 31–3, 35, 38, 41–2, 43–5, 47–8, 53, 108, 111, 112–15, 116, 117–18,

119, 140–1, 142, 143, 145, 148–9, 152–3, 160–2, 177–80, 181, 188, 189, 191, 192–3, 195, 205, 206, 208, 209, 246
Port Nata, Zulu sack of, 1838 178–9
Potgieter, (Andries) Hendrik 88, 90, 91, 93, 94, 95, 96, 97, 98, 99, 100, 101,102 –3, 104, 106, 107, 108, 109, 110, 111, 119, 137, 141, 160, 163–4, 166–8, 170, 171
Potgieter, Koos 167, 168, 177, 181, 182, 192, 211
Pretorius, Andries 186, 187, 188, 189, 190, 192, 193, 197, 199, 200, 201, 203, 204, 205, 209, 210, 212, 214, 216, 228, 234, 235, 242
Pretorius, Willem Jurgen 91, 92, 100

amaQongqo hills, battle of, 1840 228–34, 242

Retief, Pieter 71, 100, 104–6, 107, 108, 109, 111, 112, 117, 118, 119, 120, 123, 124, 129, 130, 131, 135, 137, 138, 139–40, 141–2, 143–4, 145, 146, 147, 148, 150, 151, 152, 153, 155, 157, 158, 159, 163, 168, 180, 204, 212, 216, 225, 228, 234, 246
  kommando against Sekonyela, 1837–1838 142–3, 149
  emGungundlovu *kommando*, 1838 143–53
Russell, Lord John 243–4

San 14, 15
eSankoleni *ikhanda* 236, 237–9
Senzangakhona kaJama 22, 26, 188, 221, 222
Sekonyela 77, 78, 86, 91, 103, 107, 139, 142, 143, 145, 146, 147, 149, 159
Shaka kaSenzangakhona 13, 17, 30, 31–2, 33, 34–5, 36–42, 76, 80–1, 126, 132, 135, 136, 137, 138, 147, 175, 197, 199, 210, 211, 217, 221, 222, 237, 238, 239, 243, 245, 246–7
Silevana 236, 237, 238
slaves 14, 16, 45, 59, 62, 63, 65, 70, 73, 88, 175
Smit, Erasmus 104, 105, 106, 108, 141, 143, 144, 147, 157, 159, 170, 179, 180, 181, 184, 185, 186, 234
Smith, Dr Andrew 43–4, 45–8, 58, 78, 85–6, 87, 120, 126, 127, 129, 130, 132, 134
Sobhuza I 217
Sokwatsha kaPapu 27, 237, 238, 239
Songiya 221, 222, 240
Sooilaer 181, 185, 186, 187, 188, 210
Soshangane kaZikode 37, 80, 88, 216, 236
Sothobe kaMpangalala 13, 33–4, 41
St Lucia Bay 225, 242
Stuart, James, 21, 122
Stubbs, John, 160, 172, 177
amaSwazi 14, 28, 66, 236–8, 239
Swazi military system 218

Thaba Nchu 78, 85, 91, 96, 101, 102, 103, 104
eThaleni, battle of, 1838 161, 164–71, 172, 173, 175, 177, 178, 186, 190, 195, 204, 209
Thukela, battle of, 1838 173–8, 188, 209, 225.
  See also Dlokweni, battle of
isiThunyisa *ibutho* 195, 208, 209
iziToyatoyi *ibutho* 237–8
treaties
  Cape–Griqua, 1834 74
  Cape–Ndebele, 1835 86
  Retief–Griqua, 1837 107
  Gardiner–Dingane, 1835 114–15, 137
  Gardiner–Dingane, 1837 116–17, 139
  Retief–Dingane, 1838 147–8, 204
  Pretorius–Dingane, 1839 214–16, 220, 205, 227
  Natalia–Mpande, 1839 225, 226, 242
  Pretorius–Mpande, 1840 240–2
  Cloete–Mpande, 1843 244–5
Tregardt, Louis 88, 92, 93
trekboere 63, 64, 68
Tununu kaNonjiya 112–13, 138, 145, 151, 191, 201, 202, 221, 231, 232

Uys, Dirkie 168, 170–1
Uys, Jakobus 166, 168, 178
Uys, Petrus Lafras 49–50, 51, 58, 61, 67, 106–7, 108 –9, 110, 111, 119, 137, 142, 160, 163–4, 166–8, 170–1

Van Rensburg, Janse 88, 92, 93
Vegkop, battle of, 1836 96–101, 102, 104, 105, 109, 150, 158, 184, 185, 190, 192, 193
Veglaer, battle of, 1838 181–6, 190, 192, 193, 195, 197, 194–5. *See also* emaGebeni, battle of
Vlugkommando 163–71, 173, 185, 190, 191, 193, 206, 209
imVoko (imVokwe) *ibutho* 109, 166, 177, 195, 197, 199, 203, 217, 229
emVokweni *ikhanda* 203
Volksraad of Republiek Natalia 180, 188, 211, 212, 225, 226, 227, 242, 244
Voortrekkers viii, x –xi, 21, 63, 66–70, 79, 153, 204, 245
  governance 104, 106, 107, 108–9, 180
Voortrekker Monument ix–x
Vow of the Covenant 190

Waterboer, Andries 74, 76, 107
Wenkommando, 187, 188–202, 204–10
White Mfolozi, battle of, 1838 205–9, 210. *See also* oPathee, battel of
Wood, William 151

amaXhosa 14, 15, 16, 30, 31, 49, 61, 64, 65, 74, 86, 88, 90

Zulu kaNogandaya 173, 174, 175
Zulu embassies to the Cape 13–14, 33–34, 35, 41–2
Zulu kingship 131–6
Zulu civil war, 1st, 1840 227–33, 235–6
Zulu military system 17–29, 129–30
Zulu-Mpondo campaign 1824 128, 147, 237
Zulu-Mpondo campaign 1828 34, 35, 37, 128, 147, 217, 237
Zulu-Ndebele campaign 1826 33
Zulu-Ndebele campaign 1832 84
Zulu-Ndebele campaign 1837 109, 150
Zulu-Ndwandwe campaign, 1826 80–1
Zulu-Portuguese campaign 1833 45
Zulu-Swazi campaign, 1836 113, 119, 159, 166
Zulu-Swazi campaign 1839 216, 217–19, 223, 224, 227, 247